U0857150

The International Development of China

英汉对照

实业计划

孙中山 著

外语教学与研究出版社
FOREIGN LANGUAGE TEACHING AND RESEARCH PRESS
北京 BEIJING

图书在版编目(CIP)数据

实业计划：英汉对照／孙中山著. — 北京：外语教学与研究出版社，2011.11

ISBN 978-7-5135-1540-5

Ⅰ. ①实… Ⅱ. ①孙… Ⅲ. ①经济规划—中国—民国—英、汉 Ⅳ. ①F129.6 ②D693.0

中国版本图书馆 CIP 数据核字（2011）第 247386 号

审图号：GS（2011）709 号

出 版 人：蔡剑峰
系列策划：吴 浩
责任编辑：易 璐
执行编辑：张昊媛
装帧设计：视觉共振设计工作室
出版发行：外语教学与研究出版社
社 址：北京市西三环北路 19 号（100089）
网 址：http://www.fltrp.com
印 刷：中国农业出版社印刷厂
开 本：650×980 1/16
印 张：22
版 次：2011 年 12 月第 1 版 2011 年 12 月第 1 次印刷
书 号：ISBN 978-7-5135-1540-5
定 价：45.00 元

* * *

购书咨询：(010)88819929 电子邮箱：club@fltrp.com
如有印刷、装订质量问题，请与出版社联系
联系电话：(010)61207896 电子邮箱：zhijian@fltrp.com

物料号：215400001

“博雅双语名家名作”出版说明

1840年鸦片战争以降，在深重的民族危机面前，中华民族精英“放眼看世界”，向世界寻求古老中国走向现代、走向世界的灵丹妙药，涌现出一大批中国主题的经典著述。我们今天阅读这些中文著述的时候，仍然深为字里行间所蕴藏的缜密的考据、深刻的学理、世界的视野和济世的情怀所感动，但往往会忽略：这些著述最初是用英文写就，我们耳熟能详的中文文本是原初英文文本的译本，这些英文作品在海外学术界和文化界同样享有崇高的声誉。

比如，林语堂的 *My Country and My People*（《吾国与吾民》）以幽默风趣的笔调和睿智流畅的语言，将中国人的道德精神、生活情趣和中国社会文化的方方面面娓娓道来，在美国引起巨大反响——林语堂也以其中国主题系列作品赢得世界文坛的尊重，并获得诺贝尔文学奖的提名。再比如，梁思成在抗战的烽火中写就的英文版《图像中国建筑史》文稿（*A Pictorial History of Chinese Architecture*），经其挚友费慰梅女士（Wilma C. Fairbank）等人多年的奔走和努力，于1984年由麻省理工学院出版社（MIT Press）出版，并获得美国出版联合会颁发的“专业暨学术书籍金奖”。又比如，1939年，费孝通在伦敦政治经济学院的博士论文以 *Peasant Life in China—A Field Study of Country Life in the Yangtze Valley* 为名在英国劳特利奇书局（Routledge）出版，后以《江村经济》作为中译本书名——《江村经济》使得靠桑蚕为生的“开弦弓村”获得了世界性的声誉，成为国际社会学界研究中国农村的首选之地。

此外，一些中国主题的经典人文社科作品经海外汉学家和中国学者的如椽译笔，在英语世界也深受读者喜爱。比如，艾恺（Guy S. Alitto）将他1980年用中文访问梁漱溟的《这个世界会好吗——梁漱溟晚年口述》一书译成英文（*Has Man a Future? —Dialogues with the Last Confucian*），备受海内外读者关注；此类作品还有徐中约英译的梁启超著作《清代学术概论》(*Intellectual Trends in the Ch'ing Period*)、狄百瑞（W. T. de Bary）英译的黄宗羲著作《明夷待访录》(*Waiting for the Dawn: A Plan for the Prince*)，等等。

有鉴于此，外研社人文社科出版分社推出“博雅双语名家名作”系列。

博雅，乃是该系列的出版立意。博雅教育（Liberal Education）早在古希腊时代就得以提倡，旨在培养具有广博知识和优雅气质的人，提高人文素质，培养健康人格，中国儒家六艺“礼、乐、射、御、书、数”亦有此功用。

双语，乃是该系列的出版形式。英汉双语对照的形式，既同时满足了英语学习者和汉语学习者通过阅读中国主题博雅读物提高英语和汉语能力的需求，又以中英双语思维、构架和写作的形式予后世学人以启迪——维特根斯坦有云：“语言的边界，乃是世界的边界”，诚哉斯言。

名家，乃是该系列的作者群体。涵盖文学、史学、哲学、政治学、经济学、考古学、人类学、建筑学等领域，皆海内外名家一时之选。

名作，乃是该系列的入选标准。系列中的各部作品都是经过时间的积淀、市场的检验和读者的鉴别而呈现的经典，正如卡尔维诺对“经典”的定义：经典并非你正在读的书，而是你正在重读的书。

胡适在《新思潮的意义》(1919年12月1日，《新青年》第7卷第1号)一文中提出了“研究问题、输入学理、整理国故、再造文明”的范式。秉着“记载人类文明、沟通世界文化”的出版理念，我们推出“博雅双语名家名作”系列，既希望能够在中国人创作的和以中国为主题的博雅英文文献领域“整理国故”，亦希望在和平发展、改革开放的新时代为“再造文明”、为“向世界说明中国”略尽绵薄之力。

外语教学与研究出版社
人文社科出版分社

编者说明

孙中山于 1918 年 11 月开始用英文写作《实业计划》。1919 年 8 月起，《实业计划》的中译稿在《建设》杂志连载。1920 年，上海商务印书馆出版英文本。1921 年 10 月，上海民智书局出版中文本。《实业计划》后作为“物质建设”与《孙文学说》（“心理建设”）、《民权初步》（“社会建设”）一起合编为《建国方略》。

此英汉对照版的英文部分以美国 G. P. Putnam's Sons 旗下 The Knickerbocker Press 1929 年第二版为底本，附有孙科 1928 年 10 月为第二版所作的序言；中文部分依据华夏出版社 2002 年版《建国方略》，以民智书局本作为底本。

本书作于民国初年，彼时也是中国国内政局不稳、社会经济亟待发展的时期，作品无可避免地带有其所处时代的背景与印记。举例来说，当时对一些地名、译名、朝代称谓、民族关系、世界政治的表述等与当前的通行用法不尽一致，亦有部分词语已不再使用，因而不为读者所熟悉——对于此类情况，均作注说明于书后，供读者参阅。除部分编者注外，承蒙张小莉、申学锋为中译文部分词语作注，王希教授、李典蓉博士对编辑工作给予了热心指导，特此一并感谢。

This work is

affectionately dedicated

to

Sir James and Lady Cantlie

My revered teacher and devoted friends

to whom I once owed my life

PREFACE TO SECOND EDITION

During the eve of the Manchu Régime[1], the first spark of industrialization took place in China in the forms of various state and quasi-state enterprises; railways and steamship lines, iron and steel works and coal mines, arsenals and docks all began to bedeck the Empire but they were soon found toiling under a corrupt and decadent political system. Then came the 1911 Revolution with its almost immediate reverses in the hands of Yuan Shi-kai and his military satellites. It has taken the Kuomintang fully seventeen years to wipe out these reactionaries and establish its undisputed political authority over the whole country. Although much to the sacrifice of our economic progress, we have, in these long years of bitter struggles, achieved a great political revolution; and a new, healthy political order is necessary for proper economic development.

How would Nationalist China carry out her program of economic reconstruction and development? This is necessarily a question of world interest.

In 1921 my father, the late Dr. Sun Yat-sen, wrote this "International Development of China." It was then his desire that international capital should come to China to develop railroads and highways, river conservancy and irrigation, new ports and modern cities, basic industries and public utilities.

The nature of the whole plan, in the words of my father, is a "rough sketch—from a layman's thought with very limited materials at his disposal; alterations and changes will have to be made after scientific investigations and detailed survey." It shows the stupendous requirements to modernize China. It will be the acme of economic rationalization when fully carried out. In its policies of reconstruction and economic development, the Nationalist Government will essentially follow this plan as its supreme guidance.

Naturally, working schedules will have to be carefully mapped out in order of the importance and urgency of these different projects. As means of communication are a prime mover to drag a country out of its economic stagnation, construction of sufficient trunk lines of railways with highways serving as their feeders should engage our serious attention at present. In my father's plan, seven great systems of railways are to traverse the whole of China. As North China is comparatively better served with railways at present than South China, special preference should be given to regions in the latter, especially to those places where even proper means of water transportation are lacking. In this respect, some trunk lines of the Southwestern System, which is to cover Kwangsi, Kweichow, Yunnan, southeastern Szechuen, southwestern Hunan and the western half of Kwangtung, should be constructed to tap the rich mineral resources in these regions and to provide rapid means of transport in place of the present tedious travel requiring weeks to reach these inner provinces. Turning back to the north, the Northwestern System is all important to open up Mongolia and Sinkiang and to release the population pressure in China Proper by colonization of these grazing lands and irrigable tracts. As to the existing railways, the completion of the unfinished section of the Canton-Hankow Line and the extension of the Lunghai Line to Lanchow should merit special attention.

Then the improvement of the present telegraph system and the extensive introduction of long-distance telephones and wireless service should contribute much in promoting greater efficiency and stronger unity of the national life. Some of the projects have the great advantage of being immediately very profitable.

Concerning other parts of my father's plan, that which will directly help agriculture and promote industry should form the complement to the communication program and should be as equally urgent. River conservancy and land irrigation to add more acreage to agriculture, better mobilization of coal resources and proper harnessing of water power to provide cheap motive power for industry; these are the agencies through which national production will be stimulated and increased. Past studies have shown the Hwaiho regulation and Sikiang regulation to be immensely profitable. Possibilities of the North River of Kwangtung for hydroelectric development have also been carefully studied and found to be very attractive. Incidentally, increased national production means greater purchasing power, and that in turn means bigger international trade.

Enough have been mentioned to indicate the vast opportunities of profitable investment. To show our readiness to accept foreign capital upon equitable and businesslike terms, we can do no better than to refer again to the words of my father. He tells us that "the Chinese people will welcome the development of our country's resources provided that it can be kept out of Mandarin corruption and ensure the mutual benefit of China and the countries cooperating with us." He further says that "international cooperation of this kind cannot but help to strengthen the Brotherhood of Man." For the realization of the worthy objects of such financing, all necessary safeguards will be granted to the lenders, who should provide us with "organizers, administrators and experts." In other words, we welcome sound business arrangements.

Looking over the activities of the international capital market in recent years, we find it has been principally absorbed in the herculean task of the reconstruction of post-war Europe. Capital did not merely flow passively to openings already safe and lucrative, but, on account of preponderant interests involved, it actually went to put things to order. Now Europe has fully revived, and in some quarters there is even an alarm against American financial imperialism. But New York and London will keep on busy finding outlets for the immense accumulation of wealth in America and England. Hand in hand with financiers, there are also producers of industrial equipments who constantly seek wider and greater markets. As to the China market, what is mostly needed at present is information. Always more ***Information,*** better collected and more widely distributed.

Finally, let us consider the economic development of China as a world problem. Commenting on the purpose of his book, my father tells us that it is his desire "to contribute my (his) humble part in the realization of the world peace—for the good of the world in general and the Chinese people in particular." The mere thought of the size of China and her population will prompt one to the correct appreciation of the question. I have no doubt that far-sighted and well-meaning statesmen will actively help in solving it.

SUN FO.

NANKING, Oct. 6, 1928.

自　序

欧战甫完之夕，作者始从事于研究国际共同发展中国实业，而成此六种计划。盖欲利用战时宏大规模之机器，及完全组织之人工，以助长中国实业之发达，而成我国民一突飞之进步；且以助各国战后工人问题之解决。无如各国人民久苦战争，朝闻和议，夕则懈志，立欲复战前原状，不独战地兵员陆续解散，而后路工厂亦同时休息。大势所趋，无可如何。故虽有三数之明达政治家，欲赞成吾之计划，亦无从保留其战时之工业，以为中国效劳也。我固失一速进之良机，而彼则竟陷于经济之恐慌，至今未已。其所受痛苦，较之战时尤甚。将来各国欲恢复其战前经济之原状，尤非发展中国之富源，以补救各国之穷困不可也。然则中国富源之发展，已成为今日世界人类之至大问题，不独为中国之利害而已也。惟发展之权，操之在我则存，操之在人则亡，此后中国存亡之关键，则在此实业发展之一事也。吾欲操此发展之权，则非有此知识不可。吾国人欲有此知识，则当读此书，尤当熟读此书。从此触类旁通，举一反三，以推求众理。庶几操纵在我，不致因噎废食，方能泛应曲当[2]，驰骤于今日世界经济之场，以化彼族竞争之性，而达我大同之治也。

此书为实业计划之大方针，为国家经济之大政策而已。至其实施之细密计划，必当再经一度专门名家之调查，科学实验之审定，乃可从事。故所举之计划，当有种种之变更改良，读者幸毋以此书为一成不易之论，庶乎可。

此书原稿为英文，其篇首及第二、第三计划及第四之大部分为朱执信所译，其第一计划为廖仲恺所译，其第四之一部分及第六计划及结论为林云陔[3] 所译，其第五计划为马君武所译。特此志之。

民国十年十月十日　孙文序于粤京[4]

PREFACE

As soon as Armistice was declared in the recent World War, I began to take up the study of the International Development of China, and to form programs accordingly. I was prompted to do so by the desire to contribute my humble part in the realization of world peace. China, a country possessing a territory of 4,289,000 square miles, a population of 400,000,000 people, and the richest mineral and agricultural resources in the world, is now a prey of militaristic and capitalistic powers—a greater bone of contention than the Balkan Peninsula. Unless the Chinese question can be settled peacefully, another world war greater and more terrible than the one just past will be inevitable. In order to solve the Chinese question, I suggest that the vast resources of China be developed internationally under a socialistic scheme, for the good of the world in general and the Chinese people in particular. It is my hope that as a result of this, the present spheres of influence can be abolished; the international commercial war can be done away with; the internecine capitalistic competition can be got rid of, and last, but not least, the class struggle between capital and labor can be avoided. Thus the root of war will be forever exterminated so far as China is concerned.

Each part of the different programs in this International Scheme, is but a rough sketch or a general policy produced from a layman's thought with very limited materials at his disposal. So alterations and changes will have to be made after scientific investigation and detailed survey. For instance, in regard to the projected Great Northern Port, which is to be situated between the mouths of the Tsingho and the Lwanho, the writer thought that the entrance of the harbor should be at the eastern side of the port but from actual survey by technical engineers, it is found that the entrance of the harbor should be at the western side of the port instead. So I crave great indulgence on the part of experts and specialists.

I wish to thank Dr. Monlin Chiang[5], Mr. David Yui[6], Dr. Y. Y. Tsu[7], Mr. T. Z. Koo[8], and Dr. John Y. Lee[9], who have given me great assistance in reading over the manuscripts with me.

SUN YAT-SEN.

CANTON, April 25, 1921.

THE INTERNATIONAL DEVELOPMENT OF CHINA—A PROJECT TO ASSIST THE READJUSTMENT OF POST-BELLUM INDUSTRIES

It is estimated that during the last year of the World War the daily expenses of the various fighting nations amounted to two hundred and forty millions of dollars gold. It is accepted by even the most conservative, that only one half of this sum was spent on munitions and other direct war supplies, that is, one hundred and twenty millions of dollars gold. Let us consider these war supplies from a commercial point of view. The battlefield is the market for these new industries, the consumers of which are the soldiers. Various industries had to be enlisted and many new ones created for the supplies. In order to increase the production of these war commodities day by day, people of the warring countries and even those of the neutral states had to be content with the barest necessities of life and had to give up all former comforts and luxuries.

Now the war is ended and the sole market of these war supplies has closed, let us hope, forever, for the good of humanity. So, from now on we are concerned with the problem as to how a readjustment may be brought about. What must be considered first is the reconstruction of the various countries, and next the supply of comforts and luxuries that will have to be resumed. We remember that one hundred and twenty million dollars were spent every day on direct war supplies. Let us then suppose that the two items mentioned will take up one half of this sum, that is, sixty millions of dollars a day which will still leave us a balance of sixty million dollars a day. Besides, the many millions of soldiers who were once consumers will from now on become producers again. Furthermore, the unification and nationalization of all the industries, which I might call the Second Industrial Revolution, will be more far-reaching than that of the first one in which Manual Labor was displaced by Machinery. This second industrial revolution will increase the productive power of man many times more than the first one. Consequently, this unification and nationalization of industries on account of the World War will further complicate the readjustment of the post-war industries. Just imagine sixty million dollars a day or twenty-one billions and nine hundred millions of dollars a year of new trade created by the war suddenly have to stop when peace is concluded! Where in this world can Europe and America look for a market to consume this enormous saving from the war?

国际共同发展中国实业计划书——补助世界战后整顿实业之方法

世界大战最后之一年中，各国战费每日须美金二万四千万元。此中以极俭计，必有一半费于药弹及其他直接供给战争之品，此已当美金一万二千万元矣。如以商业眼光观察此种战争用品，则此新工业乃以战场为其销场，以兵士为其消费者，改变种种现存之他种实业，以为此供给，而又新建以益之。各交战国民，乃至各中立国民，日夕缩减其生活所需至于极度，而储其向日所费诸繁华及安适者，以增加生产此种战争货品之力。

今者战事告终，诚可为人道庆。顾此战争用品之销场同时闭锁，吾人当图善后之策。故首当谋各交战国之再造，次则恢复其繁华与安适。此两项事业，若以日费六千万元计之，只占此战争市场所生余剩之半额，而所余者每日仍有六千万元，尚无所用之地。且此千数百万军人，向从事于消费者，今又一转而事生产，则其结果必致生产过多。不特此也，各国自推行工业统一与国有后，其生产力大增，与前此易手工用机器之工业革命相较，其影响更深。吾人欲命以第二工业革命之名，似甚正确。若以其增加生产力而言，此次革命之结果，实较前增加数倍。然则以世界战争而成此工业统一与国有之现象者，于战后之整理，必多纠纷。今夫一日六千万，则一年二百一十九万万也，贸易如是其巨也，以战争而起者，乃忽以和平而止。试问欧美于此世界中，将向何处觅销场，以消纳战争时储节所赢之如许物产乎？

If the billions of dollars worth of war industries can find no place in the post-bellum readjustment, then they will be a pure economic waste. The result will not only disturb the economic condition of the producing countries, but will also be a great loss to the world at large.

All the commercial nations are looking to China as the only "dumping ground" for their over-production. The pre-war condition of trade was unfavorable to China. The balance of imports over exports was something over one hundred million dollars gold annually. The market of China under this condition could not expand much for soon after there will be no more money or commodities left for exchanging goods with foreign countries. Fortunately, the natural resources of China are great and their proper development would create an unlimited market for the whole world and would utilize the greater part, if not all of the billions of dollars worth of war industries soon to be turned into peace industries.

China is the land that still employs manual labor for production and has not yet entered the first stage of industrial evolution, while in Europe and America the second stage is already reached. So China has to begin the two stages of industrial evolution at once by adopting the machinery as well as the nationalization of production. In this case China will require machinery for her vast agriculture, machinery for her rich mines, machinery for the building of her innumerable factories, machinery for her extensive transportation systems and machinery for all her public utilities. Let us see how this new demand for machinery will help in the readjustment of war industries. The workshops that turn out cannon can easily be made to turn out steam rollers for the construction of roads in China. The workshops that turn out tanks can be made to turn out trucks for the transportation of the raw materials that are lying everywhere in China. And all sorts of warring machinery can be converted into peaceful tools for the general development of China's latent wealth. The Chinese people will welcome the development of our country's resources provided that it can be kept out of Mandarin corruption and ensure the mutual benefit of China and of the countries coöperating with us.

It might be feared by some people in Europe and America that the development of China by war machinery, war organization and technical experts might create unfavorable competition to foreign industries. I, therefore, propose a scheme to develop a new market in China big enough both for her own products and for products from foreign countries. The scheme will be along the following lines:

I. The Development of a Communications System.

(a) 100,000 miles of Railways.

如当整理战后工业之际，无处可容此一年二百一十九万万之贸易，则其工业必停，而投于是之资本乃等于虚掷，其结果不惟有损此诸生产国之经济状况，即于世界所失亦已多矣。

凡商业国，无不觅中国市场，以为消纳各国余货之地。然战前贸易状态，太不利于中国，输入超过输出，年逾美金一万万。循此以往，中国市场不久将不复能销容大宗外货，以其金钱、货物俱已枯竭，无复可持与外国市易也。所幸中国天然财源极富，如能有相当开发，则可成为世界中无尽藏之市场；即使不能全消费此一年二百十九万万之战争生产剩余，亦必能消费其大半无疑。

中国今尚用手工为生产，未入工业革命之第一步，比之欧美已临第二革命者有殊。故于中国两种革命必须同时并举，既废手工采机器，又统一而国有之。于斯际中国正需机器，以营其巨大之农业，以出其丰富之矿产，以建其无数之工厂，以扩张其运输，以发展其公用事业。然而消纳机器之市场，又正战后贸易之要者也。造巨炮之机器厂，可以改制蒸汽辘压，以治中国之道路；制装甲自动车之厂，可制货车以输送中国各地之生货；凡诸战争机器，一一可变成平和器具，以开发中国潜在地中之富。此种开辟利源之办法，如不令官吏从中舞弊，则中外利益均沾，中国人民必欢迎之。

欧美人或有未之深思者，恐以战争时之机器、战争时之组织与熟练之技工开辟中国利源，将更引起外国工业之竞争。故予今陈一策，可使中国开一新市场，既以销其自产之货，又能销外国所产，两不相妨。其策如下：

甲　交通之开发。

子　铁路一十万英里。

(b) 1,000,000 miles of Macadam Roads.

(c) Improvement of Existing Canals.

(1) Hangchow-Tientsin Canals.

(2) Sikiang-Yangtze Canals.

(d) Construction of New Canals.

(1) Liaoho-Sunghwakiang Canal.

(2) Others to be projected.

(e) River Conservancy.

(1) To regulate the Embankments and Channel of the Yangtze River from Hankow to the Sea thus facilitating Ocean-going Ships to reach that port at all seasons.

(2) To regulate the Hoangho Embankments and Channel to prevent floods.

(3) To regulate the Sikiang.

(4) To regulate the Hwaiho.

(5) To regulate various other rivers.

(f) The Construction of more Telegraph Lines and Telephone and Wireless Systems all over the Country.

II. The Development of Commercial Harbors.

(a) Three largest Ocean Ports with future capacity equalling New York Harbor to be constructed in North, Central and South China.

(b) Various small Commercial and Fishing Harbors to be constructed along the Coast.

(c) Commercial Docks to be constructed along all navigable rivers.

III. Modern Cities with public utilities to be constructed in all Railway Centers, Termini and alongside Harbors.

IV. Water Power Development.

V. Iron and Steel Works and Cement Works on the largest scale in order to supply the above needs.

VI. Mineral Development.

VII. Agricultural Development.

VIII. Irrigational Work on the largest scale in Mongolia and Sinkiang.

IX. Reforestation in Central and North China.

X. Colonization[10] in Manchuria[11], Mongolia, Sinkiang, Kokonor[12], and Tibet.

丑　碎石路一百万英里。

寅　修浚现有运河：

（一）杭州、天津间运河。

（二）西江、扬子江间运河。

卯　新开运河：

（一）辽河、松花江间运河。

（二）其他运河。

辰　治河：

（一）扬子江筑堤浚水路，起汉口，迄于海，以便航洋船直达该港，无间冬、夏。

（二）黄河筑堤，浚水路，以免洪水。

（三）导西江。

（四）导淮。

（五）导其他河流。

巳　增设电报线路、电话及无线电等，使遍布于全国。

乙　商港之开辟。

子　于中国中部、北部、南部各建一大洋港口，如纽约港者。

丑　沿海岸建种种之商业港及渔业港。

寅　于通航河流沿岸建商场船埠。

丙　铁路中心及终点并商港地设新式市街，各具公用设备。

丁　水力之发展。

戊　设冶铁、制钢并造士敏土[13]之大工厂，以供上列各项之需。

己　矿业之发展。

庚　农业之发展。

辛　蒙古、新疆之灌溉。

壬　于中国北部及中部建造森林。

癸　移民于东三省、蒙古、新疆、青海、西藏。

If the above program could be carried out gradually, China will not only be the "Dumping Ground" for foreign goods but actually will be the "Economic Ocean" capable of absorbing all the surplus capital as quickly as the Industrial Nations can possibly produce by the coming Industrial Revolution of Nationalized Productive Machinery. Then there will be no more competition and commercial struggles in China as well as in the world.

The recent World War has proved to Mankind that war is ruinous to both the Conqueror and the Conquered, and worse for the Aggressor. What is true in military warfare is more so in trade warfare. Since President Wilson has proposed a League of Nations to end military war in the future, I desire to propose to end the trade war by coöperation and mutual help in the Development of China. This will root out probably the greatest cause of future wars.

The world has been greatly benefited by the development of America as an industrial and a commercial Nation. So a developed China with her four hundred millions of population, will be another New World in the economic sense. The nations which will take part in this development will reap immense advantages. Furthermore, international coöperation of this kind cannot but help to strengthen the Brotherhood of Man. Ultimately, I am sure, this will culminate to be the keystone in the arch of the League of Nations.

In order to carry out this project successfully I suggest that three necessary steps must be taken: First, that the various Governments of the Capital-supplying Powers must agree to joint action and a unified policy to form an International Organization with their war work organizers, administrators and experts of various lines to formulate plans and to standardize materials in order to prevent waste and to facilitate work. Second, the confidence of the Chinese people must be secured in order to gain their coöperation and enthusiastic support. If the above two steps are accomplished, then the third step is to open formal negotiation for the final contract of the project with the Chinese Government. For which I suggest that it be on the same basis as the contract I once concluded with the Pauling Company of London, for the construction of the Canton-Chungking Railway, since it was the fairest to both parties and the one most welcomed by the Chinese people, of all contracts that were ever made between China and the foreign countries.

如使上述规划果能逐渐举行，则中国不特可为各国余货消纳之地，实可为吸收经济之大洋海，凡诸工业国其资本有余者，中国能尽数吸收之。不论在中国抑在全世界，所谓竞争、所谓商战者，可永不复见矣。

近时世界战争，已证明人类之于战争不论或胜或负，均受其殃，而始祸者受害弥重。此理于以武力战者固真，于以贸易争者尤确也。威尔逊总统[14]今既以国际同盟防止将来之武力战争，吾更欲以国际共助中国之发展，以免将来之贸易战争。则将来战争之最大原因，庶可从根本绝去矣。

自美国工商发达以来，世界已大受其益。此四万万人之中国一旦发达工商，以经济的眼光视之，何啻新辟一世界？而参与此开发之役者，亦必获超越寻常之利益，可无疑也。且此种国际协助，可使人类博爱之情益加巩固，而国际同盟亦得借此以巩固其基础，此又予所确信者也。

欲使此计划举行顺利，余以为必分三步以进：第一，投资之各政府，务须共同行动，统一政策，组成一国际团，用其战争时任组织、管理等人材及种种熟练之技师，令其设计有统系，用物有准度，以免浪费，以便作工。第二，必须设法得中国人民之信仰，使其热心匡助此举。如使上述两层，已经办到，则第三步，即为中国政府开正式会议，以议此计划之最后契约。而此种契约，吾以为应取法于曩者吾与伦敦波令公司所立建筑广州重庆铁路合同，以其为于两方最得宜，而于向来中国与外国所结契约中为人民所最欢迎者也。

And last but not least, a warning must be given that mistakes such as the notorious Sheng Shun Hwai's nationalized Railway Scheme in 1911 must not be committed again. In those days foreign bankers entirely disregarded the will of the Chinese people, and thought that they could do everything with the Chinese Government alone. But to their regret, they found that the contracts which they had concluded with the Government, by heavy bribery, were only to be blocked by the people later on. Had the foreign bankers gone in the right way of first securing the confidence of the Chinese people, and then approaching the Government for a contract, many things might have been accomplished without a hitch. Therefore, in this International Project we must pay more attention to the people's will than ever before.

If my proposition is acceptable to the Capital-supplying Powers, I will furnish further details.

吾人更有不能不预为戒告者，即往日盛宣怀[15]铁路国有之覆辙，不可复蹈也。当时外国银行家不顾中国之民意，以为但与中国政府商妥，即无事不可为；及后乃始悔其以贿成之契约，终受阻于人民也。假使外国银行先遵正当之途，得中国人民之信仰，然后与政府订契约，则事易行，岂复有留滞之忧？然则于此国际计划，吾人不可不重视民意也。

如资本团以吾说为然，吾更当继此有所详说。

PROGRAM I

The industrial development of China should be carried out along two lines: (1) by private enterprise and (2) by national undertaking. All matters that can be and are better carried out by private enterprise should be left to private hands which should be encouraged and fully protected by liberal laws. And in order to facilitate the industrial development by private enterprise in China, the hitherto suicidal internal taxes must be abolished, the cumbersome currency must be reformed, the various kinds of official obstacles must be removed, and transportation facilities must be provided. All matters that cannot be taken up by private concerns and those that possess monopolistic character should be taken up as national undertakings. It is for this latter line of development that we are here endeavoring to deal with. In this national undertaking, foreign capital have to be invited, foreign experts and organizers have to be enlisted, and gigantic methods have to be adopted. The property thus created will be state owned and will be managed for the benefit of the whole nation. During the construction and the operation of each of these national undertakings, before its capital and interest are fully repaid, it will be managed and supervised by foreign experts under Chinese employment. As one of their obligations, these foreign experts have to undertake the training of Chinese assistants to take their places in the future. When the capital and interest of each undertaking are paid off, the Chinese Government will have the option to employ either foreigners or Chinese to manage the concern as it thinks fit.

Before entering into the details of this International development scheme, four principles have to be considered:

(1) The most remunerative field must be selected in order to attract foreign capital.

(2) The most urgent needs of the nation must be met.

(3) The lines of least resistance must be followed.

(4) The most suitable positions must be chosen.

In conformity with the above principles, I formulate PROGRAM I as follows:

I. The construction of a great Northern Port on the Gulf of Pechihli.

II. The building of a system of railways from the Great Northern Port to the Northwestern extremity of China.

III. The Colonization of Mongolia and Sinkiang (Chinese Turkestan[16]).

壹 第一计划

中国实业之开发，应分两路进行。（一）个人企业，（二）国家经营是也。凡夫事物之可以委诸个人，或其较国家经营为适宜者，应任个人为之，由国家奖励，而以法律保护之。今欲利便个人企业之发达于中国，则从来所行之自杀的税制应即废止，紊乱之货币立需改良，而各种官吏的障碍必当排去；尤须辅之以利便交通。至其不能委诸个人及有独占性质者，应由国家经营之。今兹所论，后者之事属焉。此类国家经营之事业，必待外资之吸集、外人之熟练而有组织才具者之雇佣、宏大计划之建设，然后能举。以其财产属之国有，而为全国人民利益计以经理之。关于事业之建设运用，其在母财、子利[17]尚未完付期前，应由中华民国国家所雇专门练达之外人任经营监督之责；而其条件，必以教授训练中国之佐役，俾能将来继承其乏，为受雇于中国之外人必尽义务之一。及乎本利清偿而后，中华民国政府对于所雇外人当可随意用舍矣。

于详议国家经营事业开发计划之先，有四原则必当留意：

一、必选最有利之途以吸外资。

二、必应国民之所最需要。

三、必期抵抗之至少。

四、必择地位之适宜。

今据上列之原则，举其计划如下：

一、筑北方大港于直隶湾[18]。

二、建铁路统系，起北方大港，迄中国西北极端。

三、殖民蒙古、新疆。

IV. The construction of canals to connect the inland waterway systems of North and Central China with the Great Northern Port.

V. The development of the Iron and Coal fields in Shansi and the construction of an Iron and Steel Works.

These five projects will be worked out as one program, for each of them will assist and accelerate the development of the others. The Great Northern Port will serve as a base of operation of this International Development Scheme, as well as a connecting link of transportation and communication between China and the outer world. The other four projects will be centered around it.

● Part I The Great Northern Port

I propose that a great deep water and ice free port be constructed on the Gulf of Pechihli. The need of such a port in that part of China has been keenly felt for a long time. Several projects have been proposed such as the deepening of the Taku Bar, the construction of a harbor in the Chiho estuary, the Chinwangtao Harbor which has actually been carried out on a small scale and the Hulutao Harbor which is on the point of being constructed. But the site of my projected port is in none of these places for the first two are too far from the deep water line and too near to fresh water which freezes in winter. So it is impossible to make them into deep water and ice free ports, while the last two are too far away from the center of population and are unprofitable as commercial ports. The locality of my projected port is just at midway between Taku and Chinwangtao and at a point between the mouths of the Tsingho and Lwanho, on the cape of the coast line between Taku and Chinwangtao. This is one of the points nearest to deep water in this Gulf. With the fresh water of the Tsingho and Lwanho diverted away, it can be made a deep water and ice free port without much difficulty. Its distance to Tientsin is about seventy or eighty miles less than that of Chinwangtao to Tientsin. Moreover, this port can be connected with the inland waterway systems of North and Central China by canal, whereas in the case of Chinwangtao and Hulutao this could not be done. So this port is far superior as a commercial harbor than Hulutao or Chinwangtao which at present is the only ice free port in the Gulf of Pechihli.

From a commercial standpoint this port will be a paying proposition from the very beginning of its construction, owing to the fact that it is situated at the center of the greatest salt industry in China. The cheapest salt is produced here by sun evaporation only. If modern

四、开浚运河，以联络中国北部、中部通渠及北方大港。

五、开发山西煤铁矿源，设立制铁、炼钢工厂。

上列五部，为一计划，盖彼此互相关联，举其一有以利其余也。北方大港之筑，用为国际发展实业计划之策源地。中国与世界交通运输之关键，亦系夫此。此为中枢，其余四事旁属焉。

• 第一部　北方大港

兹拟建筑不封冻之深水大港于直隶湾中。中国该部必需此港，国人宿昔[19]感之，无时或忘。向者屡经设计浚渫[20]大沽口沙，又议筑港于岐河口。秦皇岛港已见小规模的实行，而葫芦岛港亦经筹商兴筑。今余所策，皆在上举诸地以外。盖前两者距深水线过远而淡水过近，隆冬即行结冰，不堪作深水不冻商港用；后两者与户口集中地辽隔，用为商港，不能见利。兹所计划之港，为大沽口、秦皇岛两地之中途，青河、滦河两口之间，沿大沽口、秦皇岛间海岸岬角上。该地为直隶湾中最近深水之一点，若将青河、滦河两淡水远引他去，免就近结冰，使为深水不冻大港，绝非至难之事。此处与天津相去，方诸天津、秦皇岛间少差七、八十咪[21]。且此港能借运河以与北部、中部内地水路相连，而秦皇、葫芦两岛则否。以商港论，现时直隶湾中唯一不冻之港，惟有秦皇岛耳。而此港则远胜秦皇、葫芦两岛矣。

由营业上观察，此港筑成，立可获利，以地居中国最大产盐区域之中央故也。在此地所产至廉价之盐，只以日曝法产出；倘能

methods could be added, also utilizing the cheap coal near by, the production could increase many times more and the cost could thus be made cheaper. Then it can supply the whole of China with much cheaper salt. By this industry alone it is quite sufficient to support a moderate sized harbor which must be the first step of this great project. Besides, there is in the immediate neighborhood the greatest coal mine that has yet been developed in China, the Kailan Mining Company. The output of its colliery is about four million tons a year. At present the company uses its own harbor, Chinwangtao, for shipping its exports. But our projected port is much nearer to its colliery than Chinwangtao. It can be connected with the mine by canal thus providing it with a much cheaper carriage than by rail to Chinwangtao. Furthermore, our projected port will in future consume much of the Kailan coal. Thus eventually the Company must use our port as a shipping stage for its exports. Tientsin, the largest commercial center in North China, has no deep harbor and is ice bound several months a year in winter, and so has to use our projected port entirely as an outlet for its world trade. This is the local need only but for this alone it is quite sufficient to make our projected port a paying proposition.

But my idea is to develop this port as large as New York in a reasonable limit of time. Now, let us survey the hinterland to see whether the possibility justifies my ideal or not. To the southwest are the provinces of Chihli and Shansi, and the Hoangho valley with a population of nearly a hundred millions. To the northwest are the undeveloped Jehol district and the vast Mongolian Prairie with their virgin soil waiting for development, Chihli with its dense population and Shansi with its rich mineral resources have to depend upon this port as their only outlet to the sea. And if the future Dolon Nor and Urga Railway is completed with connection to the Siberian line then Central Siberia will also have to use this as its nearest seaport. Thus its contributing or rather distributing area will be larger than that of

New York. Finally, this port will become the true terminus of the future Eurasian Railway System, which will connect the two continents. The land which we select to be the site of our projected port is now almost worth next to nothing. Let us say two or three hundred square miles be taken up as national property absolutely for our future city building. If within forty years we could develop a city as large as Philadelphia, not to say New York, the land value alone will be sufficient to pay off the capital invested in its development.

加以近代制盐新法，且可利用附近廉价之煤，则其产额必将大增，而产费必将大减，如此中华全国所用之盐价可更廉。今以本计划遂行之始，仅能成中等商港计之，只此一项实业，已足支持此港而有余。此外直接附近地域，尚有中国现时已开最大之煤矿（开滦矿务公司），计其产额，年约四百万吨。该公司现用自有之港（秦皇岛），借为输出之路。顾吾人所计划之港，距其矿场较近，倘能以运河与矿区相联，则其运费，方诸陆运至秦皇岛者廉省多矣。不特此也，兹港将来必畅销开滦产煤，则该公司势必仰资此港为其运输出口之所。今天津一处在北方为最大商业之中枢，既无深水海港可言，每岁冬期，封冻数月，亦必全赖此港以为世界贸易之通路。此虽局部需要，然仅以此计，已足为此港之利矣。

顾吾人之理想，将欲于有限时期中发达此港，使与纽约等大。试观此港所襟带[22]控负之地，即足证明吾人之理想能否实现矣。此地西南为直隶、山西两省与夫黄河流域，人口之众约一万万。西北为热河特别区域及蒙古游牧之原，土旷人稀，急待开发。夫以直隶生齿[23]之繁，山西矿源之富，必赖此港为其唯一输出之途。倘将来多伦诺尔、库伦间铁路完成，以与西伯利亚铁路联络，则中央西伯利亚一带皆视此为最近之海港。由是言之，其供给分配区域，当较纽约为大。穷其究竟，必成将来欧亚路线之确实终点，而两大陆于以连为一气。今余所计划之地，现时毫无价值可言。假令于此选地二三百方咪置诸国有，以为建筑将来都市之用，而四十年后，发达程度即令不如纽约，仅等于美国费府[24]，吾敢信地值所涨，已足偿所投建筑资金矣。

The need of such a port in this part of China goes without saying. For the provinces of Chihli, Shansi, Western Shantung, Northern Honan, a part of Fengtien and the greater part of Shensi and Kansu with a population of about 100 million are lacking of a seaport of this kind. Mongolia and Sinkiang as well as the rich coal and iron fields of Shansi will also have to depend on the Chihli coast as their only outlet to the sea. And the millions of congested population of the coast and the Yangtze Valley need an entrance to the virgin soil of the Mongolian Prairie and the Tienshan Valley. The port will be the shortest doorway and the cheapest passage to these regions.

The locality of our projected port is nearest to deep water line, and far away from any large river which might carry silt to fill up the approach of the harbor like those of the Hoangho entrance and the Yangtze estuary which cause great trouble to conservancy work. So it has no great natural obstacle to be overcome. Moreover, it is situated in an arid plain with few people living on it, so it has no artificial hindrance to be overcome. We can do whatever we please in the process of construction.

As regards the planning and estimation of the work of the harbor construction and city building, I must leave them to experts who have to make extensive surveys and soundings before detailed plan and proper estimation could be made. Whereas for rough reference see Map I, and figures 1 and 2.*

* As soon as this first program reached the American Legation in Peking, the former Minister, Dr. Paul S. Reinsch, immediately sent an expert to survey the site which the writer indicated, and found that it is really the best site on the Chihli Coast for a world harbor, excepting that the entrance of the port should be at the west side instead of the east side as the writer proposed. Detailed plans have been made as figures 1 and 2.

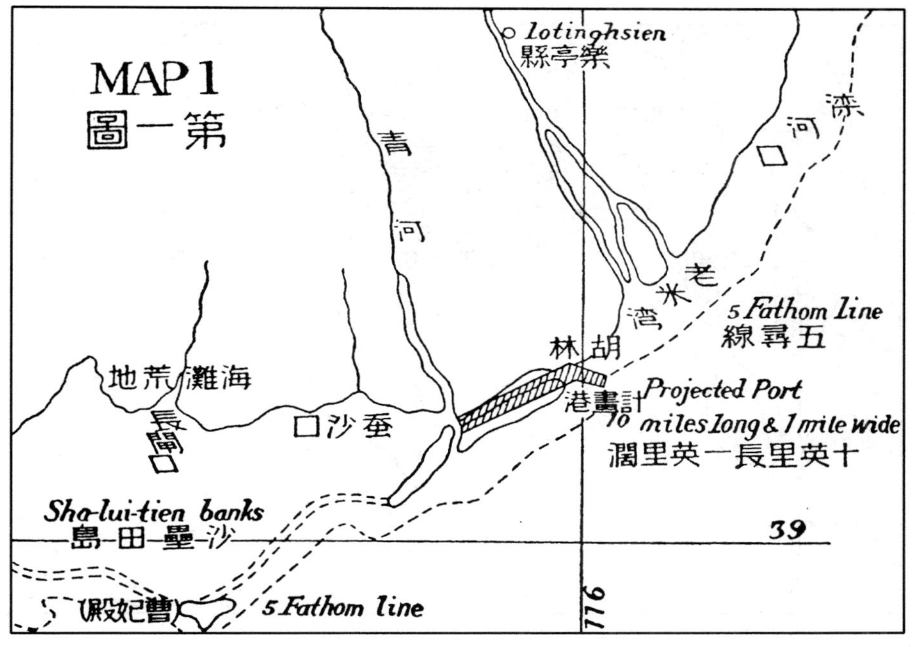

中国该部地方，必需如是海港，自不待论。盖直隶、山西、山东西部、河南北部、奉天[25]之一半、陕甘两省之泰半，约一万万之人口，皆未尝有此种海港。蒙古、新疆与夫煤铁至富之山西，亦将全恃直隶海岸，为其出海通衢。若乎沿海、沿江各地稠聚人民，必需移实蒙古、天山一带从事垦殖者，此港实为最近门户，且以由此行旅为最廉矣。

兹港所在，距深水至近，去大河至远，而无河流滞淤，填积港口，有如黄河口、扬子江口时需浚渫之患。自然之障碍，于焉可免。又为干燥平原，民居极鲜，人为障碍丝毫不存，建筑工事，尽堪如我所欲。至于海港、都市两者之工程预算，当有待于专门技士之测勘，而后详细计划可定。（参观第一图，并观详图一、二）

详图之说明：自第一计划寄到北京公使馆之后，美使芮恩诗[26]博士即派专门技师，往作者所指定之北方大港地点实行测量，果发见此地确为直隶沿海最适宜于建筑一世界港之地。惟其不同之点，只有港口当位于西边耳。因作者当时无精确之图也。读者一观此两详细图，便可一目了然矣。

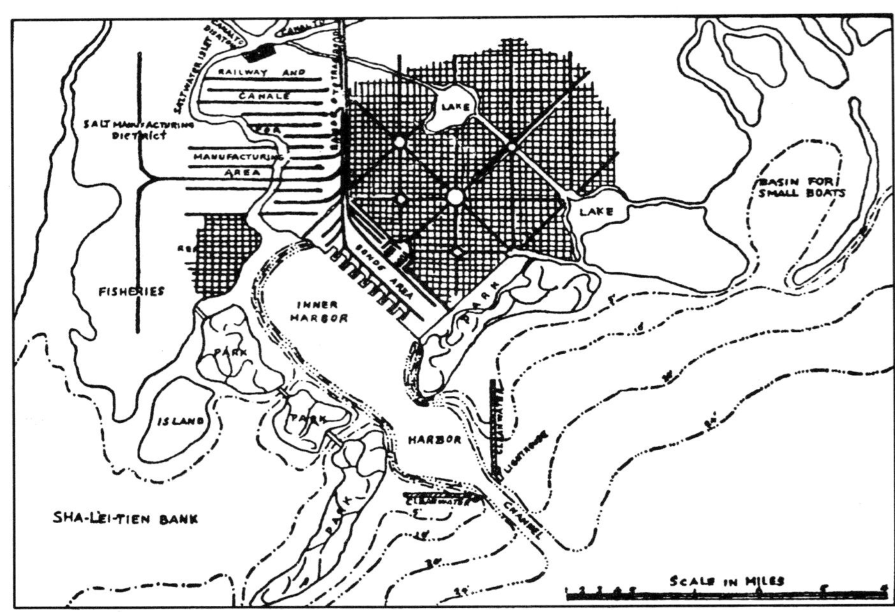

详图一、二

Figures 1 and 2

● Part II The Northwestern Railway System

Our projected Railway will start at the Great Northern Port and follow the Lwan Valley to the prairie city of Dolon Nor, a distance of three hundred miles. This railway should be built in double tracks at the commencement. As our projected Port is a starting point to the sea, so Dolon Nor is a gate to the vast prairie which our projected Railway System is going to tap. It is from Dolon Nor our Northwestern Railway System is going to radiate. First, a line N. N. E. will run parallel to the Khingan Range to Khailar, and thence to Moho, the gold district on the right bank of the Amur River. This line is about eight hundred miles in length. Second, a line N. N. W. to Kurelun, and thence to the frontier to join the Siberian line near Chita. This line has a distance of about six hundred miles. Third, a trunk line northwest, west, and southwest, skirting off the northern edge of the desert proper, to Urumochi at the western end of China, a distance of about one thousand six hundred miles all on level land. Fourth, a line from Urumochi westward to Ili, a distance of about four hundred miles. Fifth, a line from Urumochi southeast across the Tienshan gap into the Darim basin, then turning southwest running

• 第二部　西北铁路系统

吾人所计划之铁路，由北方大港起，经滦河谷地，以达多伦诺尔，凡三百咪。经始之初，即筑双轨，以海港为出发点，以多伦诺尔为门户，以吸收广漠平原之物产，而由多伦诺尔进展于西北。第一线，向北偏东北走，与兴安岭山脉平行，经海拉尔，以赴漠河。漠河者，产金区域，而黑龙江右岸地也。计其延长，约八百咪。第二线，向北偏西北走，经克鲁伦，以达中俄边境，以与赤塔城附近之西伯利亚铁路相接，长约六百咪。第三线，以一干线向西北，转正西，又转西南，沿沙漠北境，以至国境西端之迪化城[27]，长约一千六百咪。地皆平坦，无崇山峻岭。第四线，由迪化迤西以达伊犁，约四百咪。第五线，由迪化东南，超出天山山峡，以入戈壁边境，转而西南走，经

along the fertile zone between the southern watershed of the Tienshan and the northern edge of the Darim Desert, to Kashgar, and thence turning southeast to another fertile zone between the eastern watershed of the Pamir, the northern watershed of the Kuenlum Mountain and the southern edge of the Darim Desert, to the city of Iden or Keria, a distance of about one thousand two hundred miles all on level land. Sixth, a branch from the Dolon Nor Urumochi Trunk Line, which I shall call Junction A, to Urga and thence to the frontier city Kiakata, a distance of about three hundred and fifty miles. Seventh, a branch from Junction B to Uliassutai and beyond N. N. W. up to the frontier, a distance of about six hundred miles. And eighth, a branch from Junction C northwest to the frontier, a distance of about four hundred and fifty miles. See Map II.

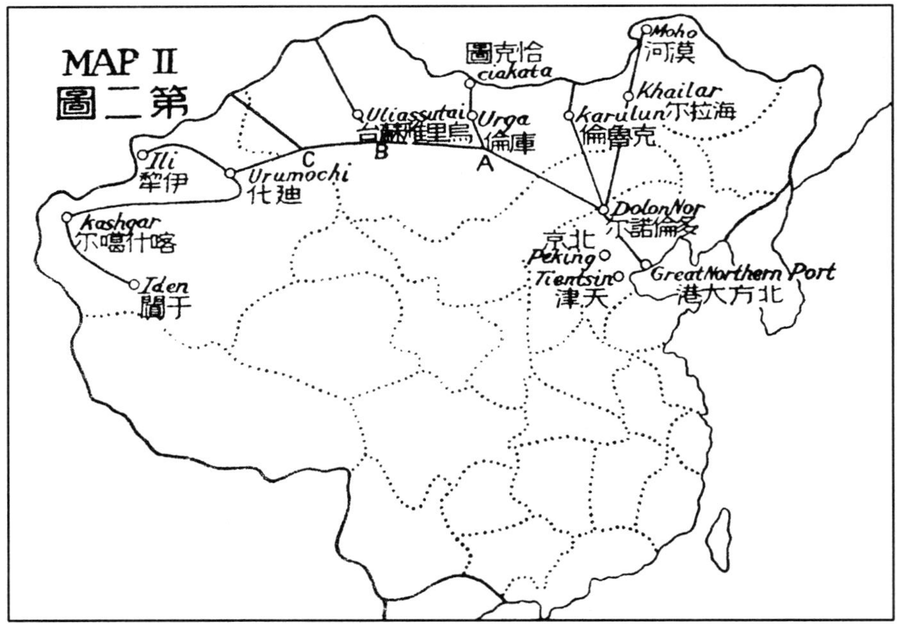

Regarded from the principle of "following the line of least resistance" our projected railways in this program is the most ideal one. For most of the seven thousand miles of lines under this project are on perfectly level land. For instance, the Trunk Line from Dolon Nor to Kashgar and beyond, about a distance of three thousand miles right along is on the most fertile plain and encounters no natural obstacles, neither high mountains nor great rivers.

Regarded from the principle of "the most suitable position," our projected railways will command the most dominating position of world importance. It will form a part of the trunk line of the Eurasian system which will connect the two populous centers, Europe and China, together. It will be the shortest line from the Pacific Coast to Europe. Its branch from Ili will connect with the future Indo-European line, and through Bagdad, Damascus and Cairo, will link up also with the future African system. Then there will be a through route from our projected

天山以南沼地与戈壁沙漠北偏之间一带腴沃之地，以至喀什噶尔；由是更转而东南走，经帕米尔高原以东，昆仑以北，与沙漠南边之间一带沃土，以至于阗，即克里雅河岸。延长约一千二百咪，地亦平坦。第六线，于多伦诺尔、迪化间干线，开一支线，由甲接合点出发，经库伦，以至恰克图，约长三百五十咪。第七线，由干线乙接合点出发，经乌里雅苏台，倾北偏西北走，以至边境，约六百咪。第八线，由干线丙接合点出发，西北走，达边境，约四百咪。（参观第二图）

兹所计划之铁路，证以"抵抗至少"之原则，实为最与理想相符合者。盖以七千余咪之路线为吾人计划所定者，皆在坦途。例如多伦诺尔至喀什噶尔之间，且由斯更进之路线，延袤三千余咪，所经均肥沃之平野，并无高山大河自然之梗阻横贯其中也。

以"地位适宜"之原则言之，则此种铁路，实居支配世界的重要位置。盖将为欧亚铁路系统之主干，而中、欧两陆人口之中心，因以联结。由太平洋岸前往欧洲者，以经此路线为最近；而由伊犁发出之支线，将与未来之印度、欧洲线路（即行经伯达[28]，以通达马斯加斯[29]及海楼[30]府者）联络，成一连锁。将来由吾人

port to Capetown. There is no existing railway commanding such a world important position as this.

Regarded from the principle of the "most urgent need of the Nation," this railway system becomes the first in importance, for the territories traversed by it are larger than the eighteen provinces of China Proper. Owing to the lack of means of transportation and communication at present these rich territories are left undeveloped and millions of laborers in the congested provinces along the Coast and in the Yangtze Valley are without work. What a great waste of natural and human energies. If there is a railway connecting these vast territories, the waste labor of the congested provinces can go and develop these rich soils for the good not only of China but also of the whole commercial world. So a system of railways to the northwestern part of the country is the most urgent need both politically and economically for China to-day.

I have intentionally left out the first principle—"the most remunerative field must be selected"—not because I want to neglect it but because I mean to call more attention to it and treat it more fully. It is commonly known to financiers and railway men that a railway in a densely populated country from end to end is the best paying proposition, and a railway in a thinly settled country from end to end is the least paying one. And a railway in an almost unpopulated country like our projected lines will take a long time to make it a paying business. That is why the United States Government had to grant large tracts of public lands to railway corporations to induce them to build the Transcontinental lines to the Pacific Coast, half a century ago. Whenever I talked with foreign railway men and financiers about the construction of railways to Mongolia and Sinkiang, they generally got very shy of the proposition. Undoubtedly they thought that it is for political and military reasons only that such a line as the Siberian Railway was built, which traversed through a thinly populated land. But they could not grasp the fact which might be entirely new to them, that a railway between a densely populated country and a sparsely settled country will pay far better than one that runs from end to end in a densely populated land. The reason is that in economic conditions the two ends of a well populated country are not so different as that between a thickly populated country and a newly opened country. At the two ends of a well populated country, in many respects, the local people are self-supplying, excepting a few special articles which they depend upon the other end of the road to supply. So the demand and supply between the two places are not very great, thus the trade between the two ends of the

所计划之港，可以直达好望角城。综观现在铁路，于世界位置上无较此重要者矣。

以“国民需要”之原则言之，此为第一需要之铁路。盖所经地方，较诸本部十八行省[31]尤为广阔。现以交通动输机关缺乏之故，丰富地域，委为荒壤，而沿海沿江烟户稠密省分，麕聚[32]之贫民无所操作，其弃自然之惠泽而耗人力于无为者，果何如乎？倘有铁路与此等地方相通，则稠密省区无业之游民，可资以开发此等富足之地。此不仅有利于中国，且有以利世界商业于无穷也。故中国西北部之铁路系统，由政治上、经济上言之，皆于中国今日为必要而刻不容缓者也。

吾人所以置“必选有利之途”之第一原则而未涉及者，非遗弃之也，盖将详为论列，使读者三致意焉耳。今夫铁路之设，间于人口繁盛之区者其利大，间于民居疏散之地者其利微，此为普通资本家、铁路家所恒信；今以线路横亘于荒僻无人之境，如吾人所计划者，必将久延岁月，而后有利可图。北美合众国政府于五十年前，所以给与无垠之土地于铁路公司，诱其建筑横跨大陆干路，以达太平洋岸者，职是之故。余每与外国铁路家、资本家言兴筑蒙古、新疆铁路，彼辈恒有不愿。彼将以为兹路之设，所过皆人迹稀罕，只基于政治上、军事上理由，有如西伯利亚铁路之例，而不知铁路之所布置，由人口至多以达人口至少之地者，其利较两端皆人口至多之地为大。兹之事实，盖为彼辈所未曾闻。请详言其理。夫铁路两端人口至多之所，彼此经济情况大相仿佛，不如一方人口至多、他方人口至少者，彼此相差之远。在两端皆人口至多者，舍特种物产此方仰赖彼方之供给而外，两处居民大都生活于自足经济情况之中，

railway could not be very lucrative. While the difference of the economic condition between a well populated country and an unpopulated country is very great. The workers of the new land have to depend upon the supplies of the thickly populated country almost in everything excepting foodstuffs and raw materials which they have in abundance and for disposal of which they have to depend upon the demand of the well populated district. Thus the trade between the two ends of the line will be extraordinarily great. Furthermore, a railway in a thickly populated place will not affect much the masses which consist of the majority of the population. It is only the few well-to-do and the merchants and tradesmen that make use of it. While with a railway between a thickly populated country and a sparsely settled or unsettled country, as soon as it is opened to traffic for each mile, the masses of the congested country will use it and rush into the new land in a wholesale manner. Thus the railway will be employed to its utmost capacity in passenger traffic from the beginning. The comparison between the Peking-Hankow Railway and the Peking-Mukden[33] Railway in China is a convincing proof.

The Peking-Hankow Railway is a line of over eight hundred miles running from the capital of the country to the commercial center in the heart of China right along in an extraordinarily densely settled country from end to end. While the Peking-Mukden line is barely six hundred miles in length running from a thickly populated country to thinly populated Manchuria. The former is a well paying line but the latter pays far better. The net profit of the shorter Peking-Mukden line is sometimes three to four millions more yearly than that of the longer Peking-Hankow line.

Therefore, it is logically clear that a railway in a thickly populated country is much better than one that is in a thinly populated country in remuneration. But a railway between a very thickly populated and a very thinly populated or unpopulated country is the best paying proposition. This is a law in Railway Economics which hitherto had not been discovered by railway men and financiers.

According to this new railway economic law, our projected railway will be the best remunerative project of its kind. For at the one end, we have our projected port which acts as a connecting link with the thickly populated coast of China and the Yangtze Valley and also the two existing lines, the Kingham and the Tsinpu, as feeders to the projected port and the Dolon Nor line. And at the other end, we have a vast and rich territory, larger than China Proper, to be developed. There is no such vast fertile field so near to a center of a population of four hundred millions to be found in any other part of the world.

而彼此之需要供给不大，贸迁交易，不能得巨利。至于一方人口多而他方人口少者，彼此经济情况，大相径庭。新开土地从事劳动之人民，除富有粮食及原料品，以待人口多处之所需求而外，一切货物，皆赖他方之繁盛区域供给，以故两方贸易必臻鼎盛。不特此也，筑于两端皆人口至多之铁路，对于人民之多数无大影响，所受益者惟少数富户及商人而已；其在一方人口多而他方人口少者，每筑铁路一咪开始输运，人口多处之众必随之而合群移住于新地，是则此路建筑之始，将充其量以载行客。京奉、京汉两路比较，其明证也。

京汉路线之延长八百有余咪，由北京直达中国商业聚中之腹地，铁路两端之所包括，皆户集人稠之所；京奉路线长仅六百咪耳，然由人口多处之京、津，开赴人口少处之满洲。前者虽有收益，则不若后者所得之大。以较短之京奉线，方诸较长之京汉线，每年纯利所赢，其超过之数有至三四百万者矣。

故自理则上言之，从利益之点观察，人口众多之处之铁路，远胜于人口稀少者之铁路。然由人口众多之处筑至人口稀少之处之铁路，其利尤大。此为铁路经济上之原则，而铁路家、资本家所未尝发明者也。

据此铁路经济上之新原则，而断吾人所计划之铁路，斯为有利中之最有利者。盖一方联接吾人所计划之港，以通吾国沿海沿江户口至多省分；又以现存之京汉、津浦两路，为此港暨多伦诺尔路线之给养，他方联接大逾中国本部之饶富未开之地。世界他处，欲求似此广漠腴沃之地，而邻近于四万万人口之中心者，真不可得矣。

● Part III The Colonization of Mongolia and Sinkiang

The Colonization of Mongolia and Sinkiang is a complement of the Railway scheme. Each is dependent upon the other for its prosperity. The colonization scheme, besides benefiting the railway, is in itself a greatly profitable undertaking. The results of the United States, Canada, Australia, and Argentina are ample proofs of this. In the case of our project, it is simply a matter of applying waste Chinese labor and foreign machinery to a fertile land for production for which its remuneration is sure. The present Colonization of Manchuria, notwithstanding its topsy turvy way which caused great waste of land and human energy, has been wonderfully prosperous. If we would adopt scientific methods in our colonization project we could certainly obtain better results than all the others. Therefore, I propose that the whole movement be directed in a systematic way by state organization with the help of foreign experts and war organizers, for the good of the colonists particularly and the nation generally.

The land should be bought up by the state in order to prevent the speculators from creating the dog-in-the-manger system, to the detriment of the public. The land should be prepared and divided into farmsteads, then leased to colonists on perpetual term. The initial capital, seeds, implements and houses should be furnished by the state at cost price on cash or on the instalment plan. For these services, big organizations should be formed and war work measures should be adopted in order to transport, to feed, to clothe and to house every colonist on credit in his first year.

As soon as a sufficient number of colonists is settled in a district, franchise should be given for self-government and the colonists should be trained to manage their own local affairs with perfect democratic spirit.

If within ten years we can transport, let us say, ten millions of the people, from the congested provinces of China, to the Northwestern territory to develop its natural resources, the benefit to the commercial world at large will be enormous. No matter how big a capital that shall have been invested in the project it could be repaid within a very short time. So in regard to its bearing to "the principle of remuneration" there is no question about it.

Regarded from "the principle of the need of the Nation" colonization is the most urgent need of the first magnitude. At present China has more than a million soldiers to be disbanded. Besides, the dense population will

- **第三部　蒙古、新疆之殖民**

殖民蒙古、新疆，实为铁路计划之补助，盖彼此互相依倚，以为发达者也。顾殖民政策，除有益于铁路以外，其本身又为最有利之事业。例如北美合众国、加拿大、澳洲及阿尔然丁[34]等国所行之结果，其成绩至为昭彰。至若吾人之所计划，不过取中国废弃之人力，与夫外国之机械，施于沃壤，以图利益昭著之生产。即以满洲现时殖民言之，虽于杂乱无章之中，虚耗人工地力，不知凡几，然且奇盛；假能以科学上方法行吾人之殖民政策，则其收效，将无伦比。以此之故，予议于国家机关之下，佐以外国练达之士及有军事上组织才者，用系统的方法指导其事，以特惠移民，而普利全国。

土地应由国家买收，以防专占投机之家置土地于无用，而遗毒害于社会。国家所得土地，应均为农庄，长期贷诸移民。而经始之资本、种子、器具、屋宇应由国家供给，依实在所费本钱，现款取偿，或分年摊还。而兴办此事，必当组织数大机关，行战时工场制度，以为移民运输居处衣食之备。第一年不取现值，以信用贷借法行之。

一区之移民为数已足时，应授以自治特权。每一移民，应施以训练，俾能以民主政治的精神，经营其个人局部之事业。

假定十年之内，移民之数为一千万，由人满之省徙于西北，垦发自然之富源，其普遍于商业世界之利，当极浩大。靡论所投资本庞大若何，计必能于短时期中，子偿其母[35]。故以"有利"之原则论，别无疑问也。

以"国民需要"之原则衡之，则移民实为今日急需中之至大者。夫中国现时应裁之兵，数过百万；生齿之众，需地以养。殖民政策于

need elbow room to move in. This Colonization project is the best thing for both purposes. The soldiers have to be disbanded at great expense and hundreds of millions of dollars may be needed for disbandment alone, in paying them off with a few months' pay. If nothing more could be done for these soldiers' welfare, they will either be left to starve or to rob for a living. Then the consequences will be unimaginable. This calamity must be prevented and prevented effectively. The best way for this is the colonization scheme. I hope that the friendly foreign financiers, who have the welfare of China at heart, when requested to float a reorganization loan for the Chinese Government in the future, will persist on the point—that the money furnished must first be used to carry out the colonization scheme for the disbanded soldiers. Otherwise, their money will only work disasters to China.

For the million or more of the soldiers to be disbanded, the district between our projected port and Dolon Nor is quite enough to accommodate them. This district is quite rich in mineral resources and is very sparsely settled. If a railway is to start at once from the projected port to Dolon Nor these soldiers could be utilized as a pioneer party for the work of the port, of the railway, of the developing of the adjacent land beyond the Great Wall, and of preparing Dolon Nor as a jumping ground for further colonization development of the great northern plain.

● Part IV The Construction of Canals to Connect the Inland Waterway Systems of North and Central China with the Great Northern Port

This scheme will include the regulation of the Hoangho and its branches, the Weiho in Shensi, and the Fenho in Shansi and connecting canals. The Hoangho should be deepened at its mouth in order to give a good drawing to clear its bed of silt and carry the same to the sea. For this purpose, jetties should be built far out to the deep sea, as those at the mouths of the Mississippi in America. Its embankments should be parallel in order to make the width of the channel equal right along, so as to give equal velocity to the current which will prevent the deposit of silt at the bottom. By dams and locks, it could be made navigable right up to Lanchow, in the province of Kansu, and at the same time water power could be developed. The Weiho and the Fenho can also be treated in the same manner so as to make them navigable to a great extent in the provinces of Shensi and Shansi. Thus the provinces of Kansu, Shensi, and Shansi can be connected by waterway with our projected port on the Gulf of Pechihli, so that cheap carriage can be provided for the rich mineral and other products from these three hitherto secluded provinces.

斯两者，固最善之解决方法也。兵之裁也，必须给以数月恩饷，综计解散经费，必达一万万元之巨。此等散兵无以安之，非流为饿莩[36]，则化为盗贼，穷其结果，宁可忍言。此弊不可不防，尤不可使防之无效。移民实荒，此其至善者矣。予深望友好之外国资本家，以中国福利为怀者，对于将来中国政府请求贷款以资建设，必将坚持此旨，使所借款项第一先用于裁兵之途；其不然者，则所供金钱，反以致祸于中国矣。

对于被裁百余万之兵，只以北方大港与多伦诺尔间辽阔之地区，已足以安置之。此地矿源富而户口少，倘有铁路由该港出发以达多伦诺尔，则此等散兵可供利用，以为筑港、建路及开发长城以外沿线地方之先驱者。而多伦诺尔将为发展极北殖民政策之基矣。

• 第四部　开浚运河以联络中国北部、中部通渠及北方大港

此计划包含整理黄河及其支流、陕西之渭河、山西之汾河暨相连诸运河。黄河出口，应事浚渫，以畅其流，俾能驱淤积以出洋海。以此目的故，当筑长堤，远出深海，如美国密西悉比河[37]口然。堤之两岸，须成平行线，以保河辐之划一，而均河流之速度，且防积淤于河底。加以堰闸之功用，此河可供航运，以达甘肃之兰州。同时，水力工业亦可发展。渭河、汾河亦可以同一方法处理之，使于山、陕两省中，为可航之河道。诚能如是，则甘肃与山、陕两省，当能循水道与所计划直隶湾中之商港联络，而前此偏僻三省之矿材物产，均得廉价之运输矣。

The expenses of regulating the Hoangho may be very great. As a paying project, it may not be very attractive but as a flood preventive measure, it is the most important task to the whole nation. This river has been known as "China's Sorrow" for thousands of years. By its occasional overflow and bursting of its embankments, millions of lives and billions of money have been destroyed. It is a constant source of anxiety in the minds of all China's statesmen from time immemorial. A permanent safeguard must be effected, once for all, despite the expenses that will be incurred. The whole nation must bear the burden of its expenses. To deepen its mouth, to regulate its embankments and to build extra dykes are only half of the work to prevent flood. The entire reforestation of its watershed to prevent the washing off of loess is another half of the work in the prevention of flood.

The Grand Canal, the former Great Waterway of China between the North and the South for centuries, and now being reconstructed in certain sections, should be wholly reconstructed from end to end, in order to restore the inland waterway traffic from the Yangtze Valley to the North. The reconstruction of this canal will be a great remunerative concern for it runs right along from Tientsin to Hangchow in an extremely rich and populous country.

Another new canal should be constructed from our projected port to Tientsin to link up all the inland waterway systems to the new port. This new canal should be built extra wide and deep, let us say, similar to the present size of the Peiho, for the use of the coasting and shallow-draft vessels which the Peiho now accommodates for other than the winter seasons. The banks of this canal should be prepared for factory sites so as to enable it to pay not only by its traffic but also from the land on both sides of its banks.

As for planning and estimating these river and canal works, the assistance of technical experts must be solicited.

● Part V The Development of the Iron and Coal Fields in Chihli and Shansi, and the Construction of Iron and Steel Works

Since we have in hand in this program the work of the construction of the Great Northern Port, the work of the building of a system of railways from the Great Northern Port to the North Western Extremity of China, the work of the Colonization of Mongolia and Sinkiang, and the work of the construction of canals and improvement of rivers to connect with the Great Northern Port, the demand for materials will be very great. As the iron and coal resources of every industrial country are decreasing rapidly

修理黄河费用或极浩大，以获利计，亦难动人。顾防止水灾，斯为全国至重大之一事。黄河之水，实中国数千年愁苦之所寄。水决堤溃，数百万生灵、数十万万财货为之破弃净尽。旷古以来，中国政治家靡不引为深患者。以故一劳永逸之策，不可不立，用费虽巨，亦何所惜，此全国人民应有之担负也。浚渫河口，整理堤防，建筑石坝，仅防灾工事之半而已；他半工事，则植林于全河流域倾斜之地，以防河流之漂卸土壤是也。

千百年来，为中国南北交通枢纽之古大运河，其一部分现在改筑中者，应由首至尾全体整理，使北方、长江间之内地航运得以复通。此河之改筑整理，实为大利所在。盖由天津至杭州，运河所经皆富庶之区也。

另应筑一新运河，由吾人所计划之港，直达天津，以为内地诸河及新港之连锁。此河必深而且广，约与白河相类，俾供国内沿岸及浅水航船之用，如今日冬期以外之所利赖于白河者也。河之两岸，应备地以建工厂，则生利者不止运输一事，而土地价格之所得，亦其一端也。

至于建筑之计划预算，斯则专门家之责，兹付阙如。

• 第五部　开发直隶、山西煤铁矿源，设立制铁炼钢工厂

本计划所举诸业，如筑北方大港，建铁路统系由北方大港以达中国西北极端，殖民蒙古、新疆，与夫开浚运河、改良水道以联络北方大港，之四者所需物料当极浩大。夫煤铁矿源，在各实业国中累岁锐减，

every year, and as all of them are contemplating the conservation of their natural resources for the use of future generations, if all the materials for the great development of China were to be drawn from them, the draining of the natural resources of those countries will be detrimental for their future generations. Besides, the present need of the post-bellum reconstruction of Europe has already absorbed all the iron and coal that the industrial world could supply. Therefore, new resources must be opened up to meet the extraordinary demand of the development of China.

The unlimited iron and coal fields of Shansi and Chihli should be developed on a large scale. Let us say a capital of from five hundred to a thousand million dollars Mex. should be invested in this project. For as soon as the general development of China is started we would have created a vast market for iron and steel which the present industrial world will be unable to supply. Think of our railway construction, city building, harbor works, and various kinds of machineries and implements that will be needed! In fact, the development of China means the creation of a new need of various kinds of goods, for which, we must undertake to create the supply also, by utilizing the raw materials near by. Thus a great iron and steel works is an urgent necessity as well as a greatly profitable project.

In this FIRST PROGRAM, we have followed the four principles set forth at the outset pretty closely. As needs create new needs and profits promote more profits, so our first program will be the forerunner of the other great developments, which we will deal with shortly.

而各国亟思所以保存天惠，以遗子孙。如使为开发中国故，凡夫物料所需，取给各国，则将竭彼自为之富源，贻彼后代患。且以欧洲战后，各国再造所费，于实业界能供给之煤铁，行将吸收以尽。故开发新富源，以应中国之特别需求者，势则然也。

直隶、山西无尽藏之煤铁，应以大规模采取之。今假以五万万或十万万元资本，投诸此事业。当中国一般的开发计划进行之始，钢铁销场立即扩大，殊非现时实业界所能供给。试思铁路、都市、商港等之建筑，与夫各种机械器具之应用，所需果当何若。质而言之，则中国开发，即所以起各种物品之新需要，而同时不得不就附近原料，谋相当之供给。故制铁、炼钢工厂者，实国家之急需，亦厚利之实业也。

此第一计划，皆依据前此所述之四原则而成。果如世论所云，“一需要即以发生更新之需要，一利益即以增进较多之利益”，则此第一计划，可视为其他更大发展中国计划之先导，后当继续论之。

PROGRAM II

As the Great Northern Port is the center of our first program, so the Great Eastern Port will be the center of our second program. I shall formulate this program as follows:

I. The Great Eastern Port.
II. The Regulating of the Yangtze Channel and Embankments.
III. The Construction of River Ports.
IV. The Improvement of the Existing Waterways and Canals in Connection with the Yangtze.
V. The Establishment of Large Cement Works.

● Part I The Great Eastern Port

Although Shanghai is already the largest port in all China, as it stands it will not meet the future needs and demands of a world harbor. Therefore there is a movement at present among the foreign merchants in China to construct a world port in Shanghai. Several plans have been proposed such as to improve the existing arrangement, to build a wet dock by closing the Whangpoo, to construct a closed harbor on the right bank of the Yangtze outside of Whangpoo, and to excavate a new basin just east of Shanghai with a shipping canal to Hangchow Bay. It is estimated that a cost of over one hundred million dollars Mex. must be spent before Shanghai can be made a first-class port.

According to the four principles I set forth in Program I, Shanghai as a world port for Eastern China is not in an ideal position. The best position for a port of that kind is at a point just south of Chapu on the Hangchow Bay. This locality is far superior to Shanghai as an eastern port for China from the standpoint of our four principles as set forth in our first program. Henceforth, in our course of discussion, we shall call this the "Projected Port" so as to distinguish it from Shanghai, the existing port of Eastern China.

The Projected Port

The "Projected Port" will be on the Bay which lies between the Chapu and the Kanpu promontories, a distance of about fifteen miles. A new sea wall should be built from one promontory to the other and a gap should be left at the Chapu end, a few hundred feet from the

贰 第二计划

东方大港之为第二计划中心，犹之北方大港之为第一计划中心也。故第二计划，亦定为五部，即：

一、东方大港。

二、整治扬子江水路及河岸。

三、建设内河商埠。

四、改良扬子江之现存水路及运河。

五、创建大士敏土厂。

• 第一部 东方大港

上海现在虽已成为全中国最大之商港，而苟长此不变，则无以适合于将来为世界商港之需用与要求。故今日在华外国商人有一运动，欲于上海建一世界商港。现经有种种计划提出，即如将现在之布置更加改良，堵塞黄浦江口及上游以建一泊船坞，于黄浦口外扬子江右岸建一锁口商港，于上海东方凿一船池，并浚一运河到杭州湾；而预算欲使上海成为一头等商港，必须费去洋银一万万元以上然后可。

据第一计划中吾所举之四原则，则上海之为中国东方世界商港也，实不可谓居于理想的位置。而此种商港最良之位置，当在杭州湾中乍浦正南之地。依上述四原则以为观察，论其为东方商港，则此地位远胜上海。是以吾等于下文将呼之为计划港，以别于现在中国东方已成之商港即上海也。

甲 计划港

计划港当位于乍浦岬与澉浦岬之间，此两点相距约十五英里。应自此岬至彼岬建一海堤，而于乍浦一端离山数百英尺之处，开一缺口，

hill as an entrance to the harbor. The sea wall should be divided into five sections of three miles each. For the present, one section of three miles in length and one and a half miles in width should be built and a harbor of three or more square miles so formed would be sufficient. With the growth of commerce one section after another could be added to meet the needs. The front sea wall should be built of stone or concrete, while the transverse wall between the sea wall and the land side should be built of sand and bush mattress as a temporary structure to be removed in case of the extension of the harbor. Once a harbor is formed there need be no trouble regarding the future conservancy work, for there is no silt-carrying water in the vicinity by which the harbor and its approaches may be silted up afterwards. The entrance of our harbor is in the deepest part of the Hangchow Bay, and from the entrance to the open sea there is an average depth of six to seven fathoms[38] at low water. The largest ocean liner could therefore come into port at any hour. Thus as a first-class seaport in Central China our Projected Port is superior to Shanghai. See Map III.

以为港之正门。此种海堤可分为五段，每段各长三英里。因现在先筑一段，长三英里，阔一英里半，已得三四方英里之港面，足供用矣。至于商务长进，则可以逐段加筑，以应其需用。前面海堤，应以石块或士敏土坚结筑之。其横于海堤与陆地间之堤，则可用沙及柴席垒成，作为暂时建造，以备扩张港面时之移动。此港一经作成，永无须为将来浚渫之计。盖此港近旁，并无挟泥之水日后能填满此港面及其通路者也。在杭州湾中，此港正门为最深之部分，由此正门出至公海，平均低潮水深三十六英尺至四十二英尺，故最大之航洋船，可以随时进出口。故以此计划港作为中国中部一等海港，远胜上海也。（参观第三图）

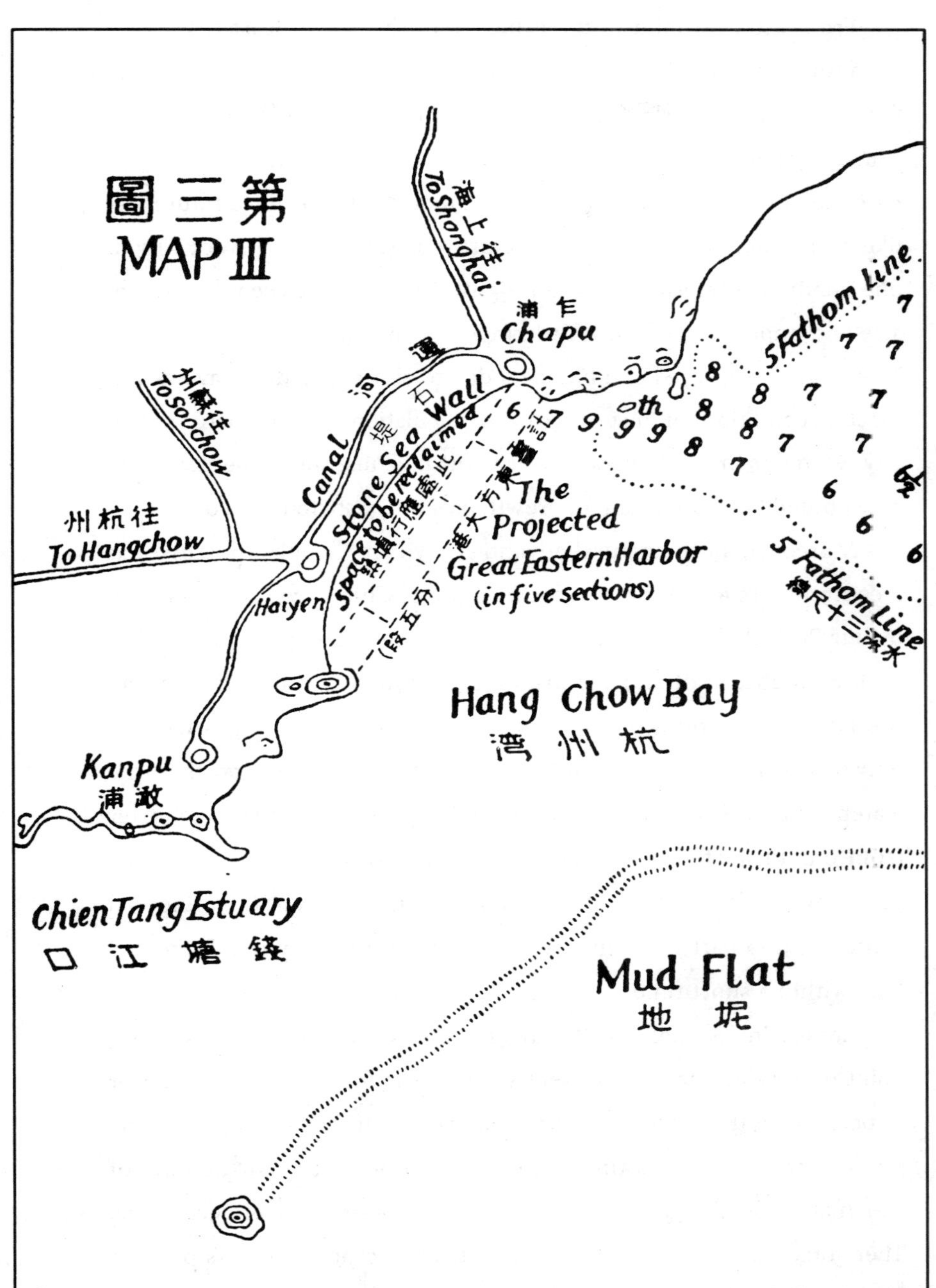
第三圖
MAP III
往上海
To Shanghai
乍浦
Chapu
往蘇州
To Soochow
往杭州
To Hangchow
運河
Canal
石堤
Stone Sea Wall
此處應行填築
Space to be reclaimed
東方大港計畫
(分五段)
The Projected
Great Eastern Harbor
(in five sections)
Haiyen
Kanpu
澉浦
5 Fathom Line
5 Fathom Line
水深三十尺線
Hang Chow Bay
杭州灣
Chien Tang Estuary
錢塘江口
Mud Flat
泥地

From the viewpoint of the principle of the line of least resistance, our Projected Port will be on new land which will offer absolute freedom for city planning and industrial development. All public utilities and transportation plants can be constructed according to the most up-to-date methods. This point alone is an important factor for a future city like ours which in time is bound to grow as large as New York City. If one hundred years ago human foresight could have foreseen the present size and population of New York, much of the labor and money spent could have been saved and blunders due to shortsightedness avoided in meeting conditions of the ever growing population and commerce of that city. With this in view a great Eastern Port in China should be started on new ground to insure room for growth proportionate to its needs.

Moreover, all the natural advantages which Shanghai possesses as a central mart and Yangtze Port in Eastern China are also possessed by our Projected Port. Furthermore, our Projected Port in comparison with Shanghai is of shorter distance, by rail communication, to all the large cities south of the Yangtze. And if the existing waterway between this part of the country and Wuhu were improved then the water communication with the upper Yangtze would also be shorter from our Projected Port than from Shanghai. And all the artificial advantages possessed by Shanghai as a large city and a commercial center in this part of China can be easily attained by our Projected Port within a short time.

Comparing Shanghai with our Projected Port from a remunerative point of view in our development scheme, the former is much inferior in position to the latter, for valuable lands have to be bought and costly plants and existing arrangements have to be scrapped the cost of which alone is enough to construct a fine harbor on our projected site. Therefore, it is highly advisable to construct another first-class port for Eastern China like the one I here propose, leaving Shanghai to be an inland mart and manufacturing center as Manchester is in relation to

Liverpool, Osaka to Kobe, and Tokyo to Yokohama.

Our Projected Port will be a highly remunerative proposition for the cost of construction will be many times cheaper than Shanghai and the work simpler. The land between Chapu and Kanpu and farther on will not cost more than fifty to one hundred dollars a mow. The State should take up a few hundred square miles of land in this neighborhood for the scheme of our future city development. Let us say two hundred square

以“抵抗最少”之原则言，吾之计划，乃在未开辟地规划城市、发展实业皆有绝对自由，一切公共营造及交通计划均可以最新利之方法建设之。即此一层，已为我等之商港将来必须发展至大如纽约者之最重要之要素矣。如使人之远见，在百年前能预察纽约今日人口之多与其周围之广，则此空费之无数金钱劳力与无远见之失误皆可避去，而恰就此市不绝长进之人口及商务，求其适合矣。吾人既知其如此，则中国东方大港务须经始于未开辟之地，以保其每有需用，随时可以推广也。

且上海所有天然利益，如其为中国东部长江商港，为其中央市场，我之计划港亦复有之。更加以由铁路以与大江以南各大都市相交通，此港较之上海为近。抑且如将该地近旁与芜湖之间水路加以改良，则此港与长江上游水上交通，亦比上海为近。而上海所有一切人为的繁荣，所以成为一大商埠，为中国此方面商务之中心者，不待多年，此港已能追及之矣。

由吾发展计划之观察点，以比较上海与此计划港，则上海较此港遥劣[39]。因其须购高价之土地，须毁除费用甚多之基址与现存之布置，即此一层所费，已足作成一良好港面，于我所计划之地矣。是以照我所提，别建一头等港供中国东部之用，而留上海作为内地市场与制造中心，如英国孟遮斯打[40]之于利物浦、日本大阪之于神户、东京之于横滨，最为得策也。

以其建造将较上海廉数倍，工作亦简单数倍，故此计划港将为可获厚利之规划。乍浦、澉浦间及其附近，土地之价每亩当不过五十元至一百元，国家当划取数百英方里[41]之地于其邻近，以供吾等将来市街发展之计划所用。假如划定为二百英方里，每亩价值百元，

miles of land at the price of one hundred dollars a mow be taken up. As six mows make an acre and six hundred and forty acres a square mile, two hundred square miles would cost 76,000,000 dollars Mex. An enormous sum for a project indeed! But the land could be fixed at the present price and the State could buy only that part of land which will immediately be taken up and used. The other part of the land would remain as State land unpaid for and left to the original owners' use without the right to sell. Thus the State only takes up as much land as it could use in the development scheme at a fixed price which remains permanent. The payment then would be gradual. The State could pay for the land from its unearned increment afterwards. So that only the first allotment of land has to be paid for from the capital fund; the rest will be paid for by its own future value. After the first section of the harbor is completed and the port developed, the price of land then would be bound to rise rapidly, and within ten years the land value within the city limits would rise to various grades from a thousand to a hundred thousand dollars per mow. Thus the land itself would be a source of profit. Besides there would also be the profit from the scheme itself, i.e., the harbor and the city. Because of its commanding position, the harbor has every possibility of becoming a city equal to New York. It would probably be the only deep-water seaport for the Yangtze Valley and beyond, an area peopled by two hundred million inhabitants, twice the population of the whole United States. The rate of growth of such a city would be in proportion to the rate of progress of the working out of the development scheme. If war work methods, that is, gigantic planning and efficient organization, were applied to the construction of the harbor and city, then an Oriental New York City would spring up in a very short time.

Shanghai as the Great Eastern Port

If only to provide a deep-water harbor for the future commerce in this part of China is our object then there is no question about the choice between Shanghai and our Projected Port. From every point of view Shanghai is doomed. However, in our scheme of development of China, Shanghai has certain claims for our consideration which may prove its salvation as an important city. The curse of Shanghai as a world port for future commerce is the silt of the Yangtze which fills up all its approaches rapidly every year. This silt, according to the estimation of Mr. Von Heidenstam, Engineer-in-chief of the Whangpoo Conservancy Board, is a hundred million tons a year and is sufficient to cover an

每六亩当一英亩，而六百四十英亩当一英方里，故二百英方里地价当费七千六百万元。以一计划论，此诚为巨额。但政府可以先将地价照现时之额限定，而仅买取所须用之地，其余之地，则作为国有地未给价者留于原主手中，任其使用，但不许转卖耳。如此，国家但于发展计划中需用若干地，即随时取若干地，而其取之，则有永远不变之定价，而其支付地价可以徐徐，国家将来即能以其所增之利益，还付地价。如此，惟第一次所用地区之价须以资本金支付之，其余则可以其本身将来价值付之而已足。至港面第一段完成以后，此港发达，斯时地价急速腾贵，十年之内，在其市街界内地价将起自千元一亩至十万元一亩之高价，故土地自体已发生利益矣，而又益之以计划本来之港面及市街之利益。因其所挟卓越之地位，此港实有种种与纽约媲美之可能。而在扬子江流域，控有倍于美国之二万万人口之一地区，想当以此为唯一之深水海港也。此种都市长进之率，将与实行此发展计划全部之率为正比例。如使用战时工作之伟大规模、完密组织之方法，以助长此港面与市街之建造，则此时将有东方纽约崛起于极短时间之中。于是无须更虑其过度扩展与资本之误投，因有无限之富源与至大之人口，正待此港而用之也。

乙　以上海为东方大港

如使我之计划，唯欲以一深水港面，供中国此部分将来商务之用，则必取前之计划港，而舍上海无疑。任从何点观察，上海皆为僵死之港，然而在我之中国发展计划，上海有特殊地位。由此审度之，于上海仍可求得一种救济法也。扬子江之沙泥，每年填塞上海通路，迅速异常，此实阻上海为将来商务之世界港之噩神也。据黄浦江浚渫局技师长方希典斯坦君所推算，此种沙泥每年计有一万万吨，此数

area of forty square miles ten feet deep. So before Shanghai can be considered ever likely to become a world port this silt problem must first be solved. Fortunately, in our program, we have the regulation of the Yangtze Channels and Embankments, which will coöperate in solving the problem of Shanghai. Thus with this scheme in mind we might just as well consider that the silt question of Shanghai has been solved and let us go ahead, while leaving the regulation of the Yangtze Estuary to the next part, to deal with the improvement of the Shanghai Harbor.

There are many plans proposed by experts for improving the Shanghai Harbor as stated before, and some of them will necessitate the scrapping of all the work which has been done by the Whangpoo Conservancy Board for the last twelve years, at the cost of eleven million taels. Here I wish to present a layman's plan for the consideration of specialists and the public.

My project for the construction of a world harbor in Shanghai is to leave the existing arrangement intact from the mouth of the Whangpoo to the junction of Kao Chiao Creek above Gough Island. Thus all the work hitherto done by the Whangpoo Conservancy Board for the last twelve years will be saved. The plan is to cut a new canal from the junction of Kao Chiao Creek right into Pootung to prolong that part of the channel which has been completed by the Conservancy Work, and to enlarge the curve along the right side of the Whangpoo River and join it again, at the second turn above Lunghwa Railway Junction, so as to make the river from that point to a point opposite Yangtzepoo Point almost in a straight line and thence a gentle curve to Woosung. This new canal would encircle nearly thirty square miles of land which would form the civic center and the New Bund of our future Shanghai. Of course the present crooked Whangpoo right in front of Shanghai would have to be filled up to form boulevards and business lots. It goes without saying that the reclaimed lots from the Whangpoo would become State property and the land between this and the new river and beyond should be taken up by the State and put at the disposal of the International Development Organization. Thus it may be possible for Shanghai to compete with our Projected Port economically in its construction and therefore to attract foreign capital, to the improvement of Shanghai as a future world port. See Map IV.

Below Yangtzepoo Point I propose to build a wet dock. This dock should be laid between the left bank of the present Whangpoo, from Yangtzepoo Point to the turn above Gough Island and the left bank of the

足以铺积满四十英方里之地面，至十英尺之厚。必首先解决此沙泥问题，然后可视上海为能永成为一世界商港者也。幸而在吾计划中，本有整治扬子江水道及河岸一部，将有助于上海通路之解决。故常以此计划置诸心中，即可将沙泥问题作为已解决者，而将整治长江入海口一事让之次部。现在先商上海港面改良一事。

现有诸专门家提出种种计划，以图上海港面改良，如前所述。其中有欲将十二年来黄浦江浚渫局用一千一百万两所作之工程，尽行毁弃者。是以吾欲献一常人之规划，以供专门家及一般公众之研究。

我之设世界港于上海之计划，即仍留存现在自黄浦江口起至江心沙上游高桥河合流点止已成之布置，如此则浚渫局十二年来所作之工程均不虚耗。于是依我计划，当更延长浚渫局所已开成之水道，又扩张黄浦江右岸之湾曲部，由高桥河合流点开一新河，直贯浦东，在龙华铁路接轨处上流第二转湾复与黄浦江正流会。如此，则由此点直到斜对杨树浦之一点，江流直几如绳，由此更以缓曲线达于吴淞。此新河将约三十英方里之地圈入，作为市宅中心，且作成一新黄浦滩；而现在上海前面缭绕潆洄之黄浦江，则填塞之以作广马路及商店地也。此所填塞之地，当然为国家所有，固不待言；且由此线以迄新开河中间之地，暨其附近，亦均当由国家收用，而授诸国际开发之机关所支配。如此，然后上海可以追及前述之计划港，其建造能为经济的，可以引致外国资本也。关于改良上海以为将来世界商港（参观第四图），在杨树浦下游，吾主张建一泊船坞。此坞应就现在黄浦江左岸自杨树浦角起，至江心沙上流转湾处止，跨旧黄浦江面及新开地，而邻于

new river. The space of the dock should be about six square miles. A lock entrance is to be constructed at the point above Gough Island. The wet dock should be forty feet deep and the new river can also be made the same depth by flushing with the water, not as proposed by experts, from a lock canal between the Yangtze and the Taihu, at Kiangyin, but from our improved waterway between this part of the country and Wuhu so that a much stronger current could be obtained.

As we see that the present Whangpoo has to be reclaimed from the second turn above Lunghwa Railway Junction to Yangtzepoo Point for city planning, then the question of how to dispose of the Soochow Creek must be answered. I propose that this stream should be led alongside the right bank of the future defunct river and straight on to the upper end of the wet dock, thence joining the new canal. At the point of contact of the Creek and the wet dock a lock entrance may be provided in order to facilitate water traffic from Soochow as well as the inland water system directly with the wet dock.

新开河之左岸以建之。坞之面积应有约六英方里，并应于江心沙上游之处建一水闸以通船坞，而坞当凿至四十英尺深。新开河之深，亦当以河流之冲刷，而使之至四十英尺。惟此冲刷之水，非如专门家所提议于江阴设一长江、太湖间之闭锁运河而引致之，乃由我计划所定之改良此部分地方与芜湖间之水道而引致之，如此乃能得较猛之水力也。

我辈既已见及现在之黄浦江，须由龙华接轨处上面第二转湾起，填至杨树浦角，以供市街规划，则如何处分苏州河之问题，又须解决。吾意当导此小河，沿黄浦江故道右岸，直注泊船坞之上端，然后合于新开之河；于此小河与泊船坞之间，当设一水闸，所以便于由苏州及内地之水运系统直接与船坞联络也。

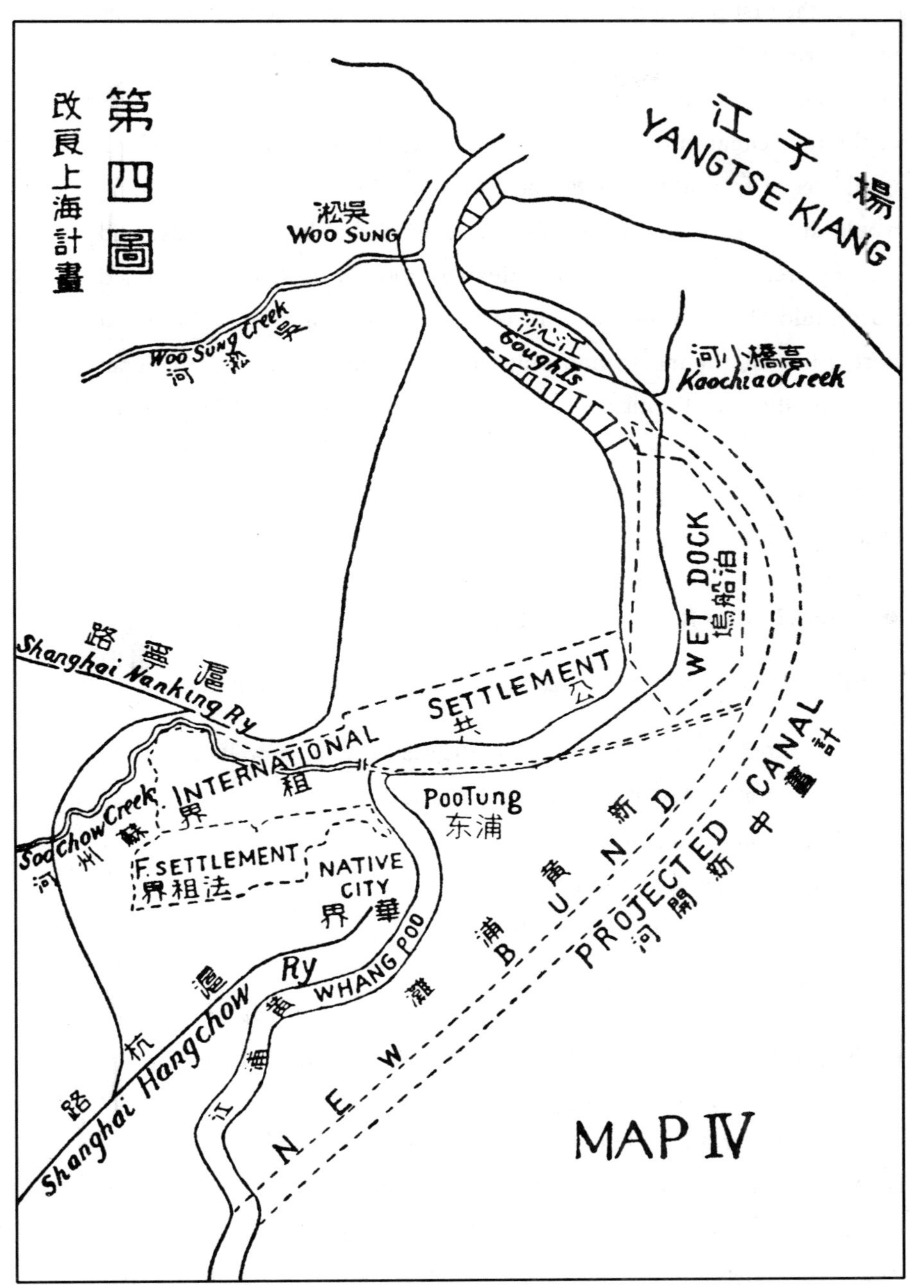

第四圖
改良上海計畫
YANGTSE KIANG
揚子江
吳淞
WOO SUNG
Woo Sung Creek
吳淞河
Kaochiao Creek
高橋小河
WET DOCK
泊船塢
Shanghai Nanking Ry
滬寧路
INTERNATIONAL SETTLEMENT
公共租界
Soochow Creek
蘇州河
PooTung
浦东
F. SETTLEMENT
法租界
NATIVE CITY
華界
WHANG POO
黃浦江
Shanghai Hangchow Ry
滬杭路
NEW BUND
新黃浦灘
PROJECTED CANAL
計畫中新開河
MAP IV

As the first principle in our program was remuneration, all our plans must strictly follow this principle. To create Pootung Point, therefore, as a civic center and to build a new Bund farther on along the left bank of the new canal in order to increase the value of the new land which would result from this scheme must be kept in mind. Only by so doing would the construction of Shanghai as a deep harbor be worthwhile. And only by creating some new and valuable property in this fore-doomed port could Shanghai be saved from the competition of our Projected Port. After all, the most important factor for the salvation of Shanghai is the solution of the silt question of the Yangtze Estuaries. Now let us see what effect and bearing the regulating of the Yangtze Channel and Embankments have upon the question, and this we are going to deal with in the next part.

● Part II The Regulating of the Yangtze River

The regulating of the Yangtze River may be divided as follows:

a. From the deep-water line of the sea to Whangpoo Junction.
b. From Whangpoo Junction to Kiangyin.
c. From Kiangyin to Wuhu.
d. From Wuhu to Tungliu.
e. From Tungliu to Wusueh.
f. From Wusueh to Hankow.

a. Regulating of the Estuary from Deep-water Line Up to the Junction of Whangpoo

It is a natural law that the obstruction to navigation in all rivers is begun at their mouths, therefore the improvement of any river for navigation must start from the estuary. The Yangtze River is no exception to this rule, therefore to regulate the Yangtze, we must begin by dealing with its estuaries.

The Yangtze has three estuaries, namely: The North Branch lying between the left bank and the Island of Tsungming, the North Channel lying between the Tsungming Island and the Tungsha Banks and the South Channel lying between the Tungsha Banks and the right bank. Henceforth for the sake of convenience I shall call them the North, Middle, and South Channels.

在我计划，以获利为第一原则，故凡所规划皆当严守之。故创造市宅中心于浦东，又沿新开河左岸建一新黄浦滩，以增加其由此计划圈入上海之新地之价值，皆须特为注意者也。盖惟如此办去，而后上海始值得建为深水海港。亦惟为此垂死之港，新造出有价值之土地，然后上海可以与计划港争胜也。究竟救济上海之最重要要素，为解决扬子江口沙泥问题，故整治扬子江水道及河岸一事于此沙泥问题有何影响、有何意义，吾人将于次部论之。

• 第二部　整治扬子江

整治扬子江一部，当分六节：

甲　由海上深水线起，至黄浦江合流点。
乙　由黄浦江合流点起，至江阴。
丙　由江阴至芜湖。
丁　由芜湖至东流。
戊　由东流至武穴。
己　由武穴至汉口。

甲　整治扬子江口自海上深水线至黄浦江合流点

凡河流航行之阻塞，必自河口始，此自然原则也。故凡改良河道以利航行，必由其河口发端，扬子江亦不能居于例外也。故吾人欲治扬子江，当先察扬子江口。

扬子江入海有三口：最北为北支流，在左岸与崇明岛间；中间为中水道，在崇明岛与铜沙坦之间；最南为南水道，在铜沙坦与右岸之间。故为便利计，以后当分别称之为北水道、中水道、南水道。

The silting up of a river's mouth is due to the loss of velocity in its current when the water gets into the wide opening at its junction with the sea and causes the silt to deposit there. The remedy is to maintain the velocity of the current by narrowing the mouth of the river so that it equals that of the upper part. In this way the silt is suspended in the water moving on into the deep sea. The narrowing process may be accomplished by walls or training jetties. And thus the silt may be carried by the water into the deepest part of the open sea and before it settles down upon the bottom a returning tide will carry it from the approach into the shallow parts on both sides of the river's mouth. The mouth of a river can be kept clear from deposit of silt by the action and reaction of the ebb and flow tide. The conservancy of an estuary of any river is accomplished by utilizing these natural forces.

In order to regulate the estuary of the Yangtze we have to study the three channels which form its mouth and to find out which of these channels is to be selected as the regulated entrance into the sea. In Mr. Von Heidenstam's proposal for the improvement of the approach of Shanghai Harbor, he recommends two alternatives, viz., either to block up the North and Middle Channels and to leave the South Channel only for the mouth of the Yangtze, or to train the South Channel only and leave the other two alone. For the present, he thinks, perhaps for the sake of economy, the latter scheme would be enough. But the training of the South Channel alone as the approach to Shanghai would leave it in a state of perpetual anxiety as has been apprehended by Mr. Von Heidenstam and other experts, for the main volume of the water of the Yangtze may be diverted into either of the other two channels and leave the Southern one to be silted up at any time. Therefore to make the approach of Shanghai once for all safe and permanent, it is necessary to block up two of the three channels, leaving only one as an approach to the port. This is also the only feasible way of regulating the estuary of the Yangtze.

In our scheme of regulating the Yangtze Estuary I should recommend using the North Channel only and to block the other two. Because the North Channel is the shortest way to the deep-sea line and by using it as the only mouth of the Yangtze, we have on both sides of it more shallow banks to be reclaimed by its silt. Thus the expenditure would be less and the results greater. But this would leave Shanghai in the lurch. Therefore in a coöperative scheme like this I would apply the theory of killing two birds with one stone by using the Middle Channel, since it would suit both of our purposes. The reason for this is because the regulating of the Yangtze Estuary and the securing of a Shanghai approach have different purposes, hence we must consider them differently.

凡河口所以被沙泥填塞者，以河水将入海汇流，河口宽阔，湍流减其速力，而沙泥因之沉淀也。救之者，收窄其河口，令与上流无异，以保其湍流之速力；由此道，则沙泥被水裹挟，直抵深海。收窄之工程，当筑海堤以成之，或用一连之石坝。如是，其沙泥为水所混，直至深海广阔之处，未及沉淀，复遇回潮冲击，还填入河口两旁附近浅水之洼地，以潮长、潮退之动力与反动力，遂使河口常无淤积。凡疏浚一河之河口，皆以利用此天然力助成之。

欲治扬子江口，吾辈须将构成其口之三水道一一研究，又择出其一道以为入海之口。在方希典斯坦君所提议改良上海港面通路策，列有二案：其一，闭塞北、中两水道，独留南水道，以为扬子江口；其二，独修浚南水道，而置余两水道不理。现在彼意以为用第二案已足，此或因经济上目的而然。顾惟修浚南水道，则上海通路将常见不绝提心吊胆之情形，仍如方希典斯坦君暨其他专门家现所忧虑者；因扬子江水流之大部，随时可以改灌入他两水道，而令南水道淤塞也。故为使上海通路永久安全、一劳永逸计，必须于三水道之中，闭塞其二，独留一股，以为上海通路。此又整治扬子江口唯一可得实行之路也。

在我整治扬子江口之计划，本应选用北水道，而闭塞中南二水道。因北水道为入深海最短之线，又用之以为唯一之扬子江口，则其两旁有更多之沙坦洼地，正待沙泥填堵也。故其费用为较少，而收效为较多。但此本不为上海作计故然耳。如其统筹全局，必须以一箭双雕之法行之，而采中水道以为河口，则于治河与筑港两得其便。盖专谋治扬子江口与单谋上海之通路者，各有所志，其考察自有不同也。

In my project of regulating the Yangtze Estuary I have two aims, namely, to secure a deep channel to the open sea and to save as much silt as possible for the purpose of reclamation of land. The Middle Channel provides three ready receptacles for the deposit of the silt for the formation of new land: the Haimen, the Tsungming, and the Tungsha Banks. Besides these banks there are many hundreds of square miles of shallow bottom which in the course of ten or twenty years will also form land. As remuneration is our first principle we must consider it in every step of our progress. The reclamation of about a thousand square miles of land even in forty not to say twenty years would be ample profit. At the lowest estimate the reclaimed land would be worth twenty dollars per mow. If after ten years five hundred square miles would be ready for cultivation purposes then we would gain a profit of 38,000,000 dollars. Whereas to make an approach by the South Channel the receptacle ground will be on one side only, that is, the Tungsha Banks, while on the right of the approach is the deep Hangchow Bay which would take hundreds of years to fill up, and in the meanwhile half of the silt would be wasted. To Shanghai as a seaport the silt is a curse but to the shallow banks the silt would be a blessing.

Since it is a profitable undertaking to reclaim the above mentioned banks and the neighboring shallows, we can quite well afford to build a double stone wall from the shore end of the Yangtze right out into the deep sea far beyond Shaweishan Island which is a distance of about forty miles. A stone wall from one fathom to five fathoms in height at low-water level would likely not exceed an average cost of two hundred thousand dollars a mile as cheap stone can easily be obtained from the granite islands nearby, in the Chusan Archipelago. A wall of forty miles on each side that is eighty miles in all will cost sixteen million dollars or thereabouts. And considering that 200 or 300 square miles of Haimen, Tsungming, and the Tungsha banks could be converted into arable land within a short time, the expense of building the wall is well justified.

Furthermore, the construction of this wall means that there will be a safe and permanent approach for a world port in Shanghai as well as a deep outlet for the Yangtze. See Map V.

The regulating wall on the right side should be built from the junction of the Whangpoo by prolongation of its right jetty describing a gentle curve into the depths of the South Channel and turning toward the opposite side and cutting through the Blockhouse Island into the Middle Channel, then running eastward right into the five-fathom line southeast of Shaweishan Island. The left wall would be a continuation from that

在我治扬子江口之计划，所取者有两端：其一，则求深水道以达海洋；其二，则多收其沙泥，以填海为田，惟力所及。中水道具有三堆积场，以受沙泥而成新陆地，即海门坦、崇明坦、铜沙坦是也。此外尚有渟水[42]洼地千数百英方里，循现在之势以往，不过十年至二十年便成陆地。以我之第一原则为获利故，每一举足，不可忘之。即令二十年不能成地，姑倍之为四十年，而所填筑者有约一千英方里之多，其于利益，已不菲矣。以至贱计之，填积之地值二十元一亩，如使十年之后，五百英方里之地可备耕作之用，其所得之利已为三千八百四十万元。如使由南水道以通上海，则接受沙泥之地面只在一偏，即惟有铜沙坦在其左方，而右方则为深水之杭州湾，非数百年不能填满，在此数百年间沙泥之半数归于无用矣。夫以上海为海港，故沙泥为之噩神；至于低地，正欢迎沙泥，而以福星视之也。

此种企业，既有填筑上述海坦洼地为田之利，我等自可建一双石堤，自长江入海之处起，直达深海，至离岸四十英里之沙尾山为止。以舟山列岛附近有花冈石岛，廉价之石，不难运致。故筑一石堤，高六英尺至三十英尺，使刚与低潮面平，其平均所需，当不过每一英里费二十万元；石堤每边长四十英里，统共八十英里，其所费约在一千六百万元左右。而在海门坦、崇明坦暨铜沙坦有二三百英方里地，转瞬之间，可变为农田计之，则建此石堤，已非不值矣。况其建此石堤，实足以为上海世界港得一永久通路，又为扬子江得一深水出路也耶！（参观第五图）

右边之石堤，应从黄浦江合流点起，延长其右边石坝，画一缓曲线，到南水道深处，然后转向对岸，横截鸭窝沙，以至中水道，又折向东方，直筑至沙尾山东南水深三十英尺处。左边之堤，

of Tsungming at Tsungpaosha Island parallel with the right wall by a distance of about two miles. This wall should curve to a point at or near Drinkwater Point at Tsungming Island, then project into the five-fathom line at the open sea passing by just at the south side of the Shaweishan Island. A glance at the map here attached would be sufficient to show how the future outlet of the Yangtze as well as the future approach of Shanghai should be. The two regulating submerged walls on both sides would be as high as low-water level so as to give a free passage of the water over the top at flood tide. This will serve the purpose of carrying back the silt from the sea when the tide comes in, thus to reclaim the shallow spaces inclosed behind the walls on both sides of the river more quickly than otherwise. The new channel formed by these two parallel walls would likely be deeper than the present South Channel outside the Whangpoo, which is forty to fifty feet deep because the velocity of the current will be greater than the present one, due to the concentration of three channels into one. Furthermore, the depth would be more uniform and stable than at present. Although the regulating walls end at the five-fathom line, the momentum of the current would continue beyond that point, and so would cut into the deep water outside. This would serve the double purpose of draining the Yangtze Estuary as well as keeping open the approach to Shanghai.

由崇宝沙起，直至崇明角，与右堤平行，两堤中间相距约两英里。此堤当在崇明之饮水角附近，稍作曲线，然后直达深海三十英尺深之线，恰在沙尾山南端经过。试一览附图，当知将来上海通路当何如，扬子江出路当何如矣。此一双水底石堤，断不容高过低潮面，以使潮涨时水流自由通过堤面，如此则潮涨时可将沙泥夹带回两堤之旁，于是填塞两堤旁所括之低地，更迅速矣。现在南水道在黄浦江外面，已有四五十英尺之深，而新水道以两平行石堤夹成，料必比南水道更深，因其聚三水道入于一流，其水流速力必较现在者为多也，而河身之深亦将较现在为确定，且一律。在石堤，虽止于水深三十英尺处，而水流不于是遽停，必过此一点更突入较深之外海而后止。则上海通路常开，与扬子江口无阻之两目的，可得同时俱达矣。

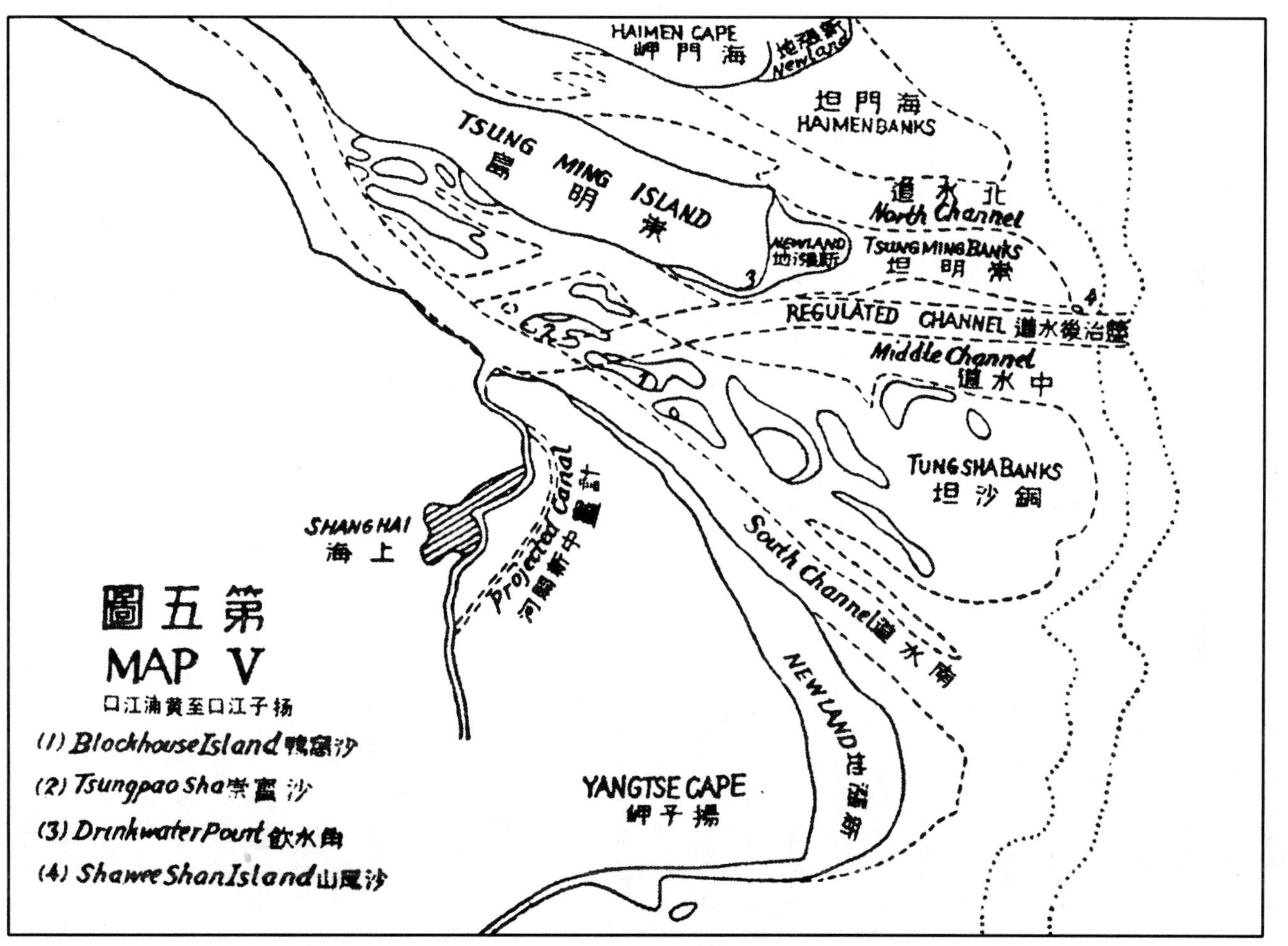

圖五第
MAP V
口江浦黃至口江子扬
(1) Blockhouse Island 鴨窩沙
(2) Tsungpao Sha 崇寶沙
(3) Drinkwater Point 飲水角
(4) Shawe Shan Island 山尾沙
HAIMEN CAPE
岬門海
New Land
坦門海
HAIMEN BANKS
TSUNG MING ISLAND
島明崇
道水北
North Channel
NEW LAND
TSUNG MING BANKS
坦明崇
REGULATED CHANNEL
Middle Channel
道水中
TUNG SHA BANKS
坦沙銅
South Channel
道水南
NEW LAND
YANGTSE CAPE
岬子揚
SHANGHAI
海上
Projected Canal

b. From Whangpoo Junction to Kiangyin

This part of the channel of the Yangtze River is most irregular and changeable. The widest part is over ten miles while the Kiangyin Narrow is only but three-quarters of a mile. The depth of the channel at the open part is from five to ten fathoms while that of Kiangyin Narrow is twenty fathoms. Judging by the depth of the water at this point a width of one and a half miles must be provided for the channel in order to slow down the current and to give a uniform velocity right along the river. So the two-mile-wide channel at Whangpoo Junction has to be tabulated into one mile and a half at Kiangyin. See Map VI.

The north or left embankment commencing at Tsungpao Sha continues with the sea wall and makes a convex curve up to Tsungming Island at a point about six miles northwest from Tsungming city. Then it follows along the shore of Tsungming right up to Mason Point and transversing across the north channel parallel to the north shore at a distance of three or four miles right up to Kinshan Point, thence it cuts across the deep channel which was

乙 由黄浦江合流点起至江阴

扬子江水道中，此一部分为最不规则，又最转变无常者。其江流广处，在十英里以上；至其狭处，才得四分英里之三，即江阴窄路是也。在此广阔之处，河深不过三十英尺至六十英尺；至于江阴窄路，实有一百二十英尺之深。由江阴窄路之水深以判断之，必须有一英里半阔之河身，以缓和此地方湍流之速力，令全河流速始终如一。于是在黄浦口之二英里阔河身，在江阴应阔一英里半。（参观第六图）

此段左岸即北岸筑河堤，起自崇宝沙，与海堤相连，作一凸曲线，以至崇明岛，在崇明城西北约六英里处，接于滩边。然后沿崇明滩边，直至马孙角（译音），然后转而横过北水道，离北岸约三四英里，作一平行线，直抵金山角（译音）。在此处截断近年新成之深水道，向西南，以与靖江县城东北河岸相接。沿此岸再筑七八英里，又挖开陆地，以增河身之阔。令其自江阴炮台脚下起，算至对岸，常有一英里半之距离。此自崇宝沙至江阴对面之靖江，河堤共长约一百英里。

formed in recent years and curves southwestward to join the shore northeast of Tsingkiang and follows the shore line for a distance of about seven or eight miles, then cuts into the land side to give this part of the river a width of one and a half miles from the fort at the Kiangyin side. This embankment from Tsungpao Sha to Tsingkiang Point opposite Kiangyin fort is about one hundred miles in length.

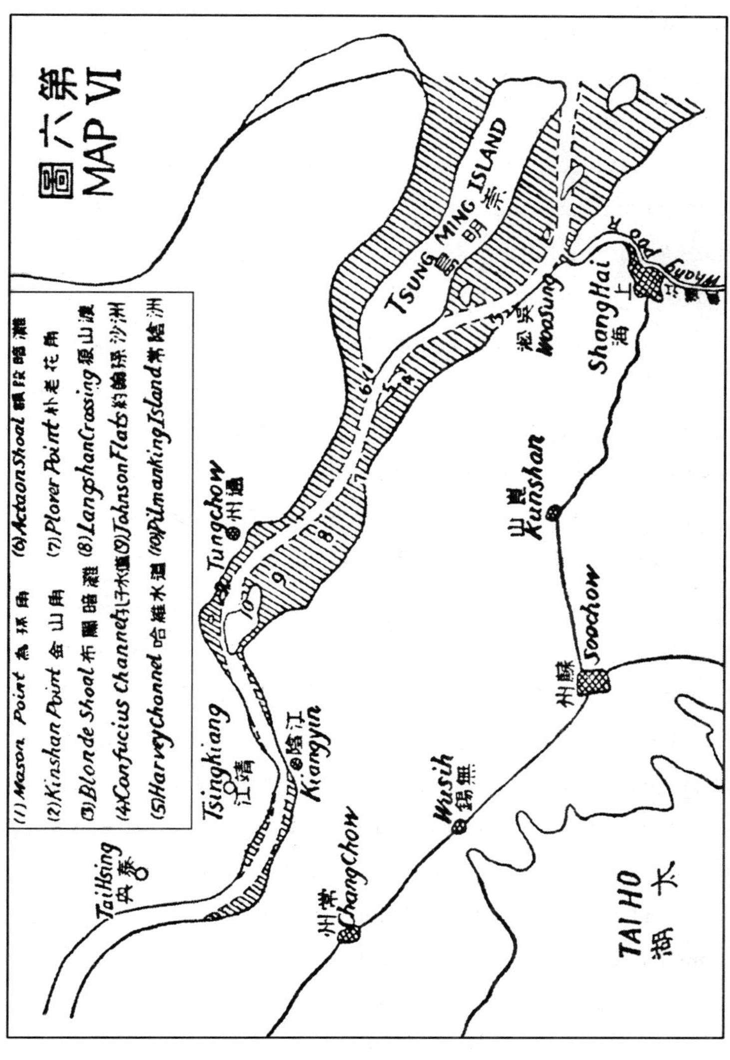

South of Tsungming Island a part of this embankment and a part of the wall that projects into the sea together inclose a shallow space of about 160 square miles good for reclamation purposes. The other part of the embankment, which runs from Mason Point at the head of Tsungming Island to Tsingkiang shore, incloses another space of about 130 square miles.

The right embankment starts at the end of the left jetty of Whangpoo Junction and, skirting along the Paoshan shore and passing the Blonde Shoal into the deep, crosses the Confucius Channel on into Actaon Shoal and follows the right side of Harvey Channel on to Plover Point. Then it turns northwest across the deep channel into Langshan Flats, thence recrosses the deep channel at Langshan crossing into Johnson Flats, then joins the Pitman King Island, and thence skirts along the shore right into the foot of the hills at Kiangyin forts. This embankment incloses two shallow spaces: one above and the other below Plover Point, together about 160 square miles. Alongside of both of these embankments there are shallow spaces amounting to about 450 square miles, a great part of which having already formed land and a part already appearing in low water. When these spaces are cut off from the moving current the process of reclamation would be made to work more rapidly so it is not extravagant to hope that within the course of twenty years the whole of these 450 square miles would be completely reclaimed and ready for cultivation. The profits from the new lands thus reclaimed would amount to about $29,760,000 if only taken at $20 per mow. The profits from the new lands would be netted from the beginning of the work and would increase every year up to the completion of the reclamation process.

With a profit of $30,000,000 in the course of twenty years before us, it is a worth-while proposition to take up. Now let us see what amount of capital should be invested before the whole project of our reclamation work could be completed. In order to reclaim this 450 square miles of land two hundred miles of embankments have to be built. Part of these projected embankments will be along the shore line, a greater part will be in midstream, and a small part in deep channel. Those along the shore line need not be bothered with except that the concave surface must be protected with stone or concrete work. Those in midstream should be filled up with stone ten feet or less below low-water level just enough to give a resistance to the undercurrent in order to prevent it from running sideward. Thus the main current would follow the line of least resistance and cut the channel, as directed by the rudimental embankment, by its own force.

在崇明岛迤南，此河堤之一部及海堤，共围有浅滩约一百六十英方里，可以填为实地。其河堤之他一部，自崇明岛上头马孙角起，至靖江河岸止，另围有浅滩一百三十英方里。

右边河堤，自黄浦江口石坝尽处起，循宝山岸边，过布兰暗滩，直到深处，横过“孔夫子水道”，穿入额段暗滩（译音），随哈维水道（译音）右边，溯流筑至朴老花角（译音）。再在狼山渡，横截深水道，穿过约翰孙沙洲（译音），与常阴洲相接续。再循此岸，直筑至江阴炮台山脚下。此段河堤围有浅滩两处，一在朴老花角上游，他一则在其下游，共约有一百六十英方里。此两边河堤之所围浅滩，共约四百五十英方里，其中大部分已成陆地，亦有一部已于低潮时露出。此等地方，若令不与湍流相遇，则其填塞之进行更速。所以谓二十年之内，此四百五十英方里之地，当完全填成实地，可供耕作，亦非奢望也。如使此种新地每亩仅值二十元，则此新填地所生利益，已约有二千九百七十六万元矣。而此近三千万之利益，固从新地而生。此新地之利益，自起工以后，则每年增长，直至其填塞完成而后已者也。

以后此二十年间可得三千万元利益而论，此种提案，自可采供讨议。今先计须投资本若干，然后我填筑之全计划可以完成。将欲填此四百五十英方里之地，须筑二百英里之河堤。此所计划之河堤，有一部分为沿河岸线者，而大部分须在中流，更有一小部分须筑在深水道之中。沿河岸线者，惟有在凹曲线面之一部须以石建，或用士敏土坚结，以保护堤面，此外无须费力。在中流者，须用石叠起，至离低潮水面下不及十英尺为止，适足以抵抗下层水流，令不轶出正路之外。如此则大股流水，将循此抵抗最少之线，以其自力，从其初级河堤所诱导，

This rudimental embankment would cost less than the sea wall which I estimated at $200,000 per mile. Except at one point, that is, the junction of the North Channel at Mason Point, which has to be blocked up entirely, the cost for which, as has been estimated by experts, would amount to over a million dollars for a distance of two or three miles. Thus the profits accruing from the reclaimed lands would be quite sufficient to pay for the embankments. So far we see that the regulating of the Yangtze from the sea to Kiangyin is a self-paying proposition from the reclamation of land alone, aside from the improvement of the navigation of the Yangtze River.

c. From Kiangyin to Wuhu

This part of the river is quite different in nature from that below Kiangyin. Its channel is more stable and only in a few places sharp curves occur and the water has cut into the concave sides of the land, thus occasionally making new channels along the sides of the two shores. This section of the river is about 180 miles in length. See Map VII.

开一水道。此种初级河堤所费，比之海堤较廉，而海堤所费，依吾前计算为二十万元一英里而已。惟有在马孙角、北水道分流点一处，须将该水道完全闭塞，其费已经专门家估算，当在百万元以外，方能填筑此二三英里之堤。是故由新填地所生利益，必足以回复其所筑河堤所费。可知即此填新地一节，已足令自海口到江阴两段导江工程不致亏本，而又有改良扬子江航路之益也。

丙 自江阴至芜湖

此段河流，性质与江阴以下全异。其水道较为巩固，惟有三数处现出急曲线，河流蚀入凹曲线方面之陆地，因此时时于两岸另开新水道而已。此段长约一百八十英里。（参观第七图）

此处整治之工，比之江阴以下更为困难。盖其泛滥之地，应填筑者，仍与长江下游景况正同。其急曲线须修之使直，旁支水道应行闭塞，中流小岛应行削去，窄隘水路应行浚广，令全河上下游一律。

The regulating works here would be more complicated than those below Kiangyin. For besides the dilated parts which have to be reclaimed in the same manner as those of the lower part of the river, the sharp curves have to be straightened and side channels have to be blocked, and midstream islands have to be removed, and narrows have to be widened to give uniform width to the river.

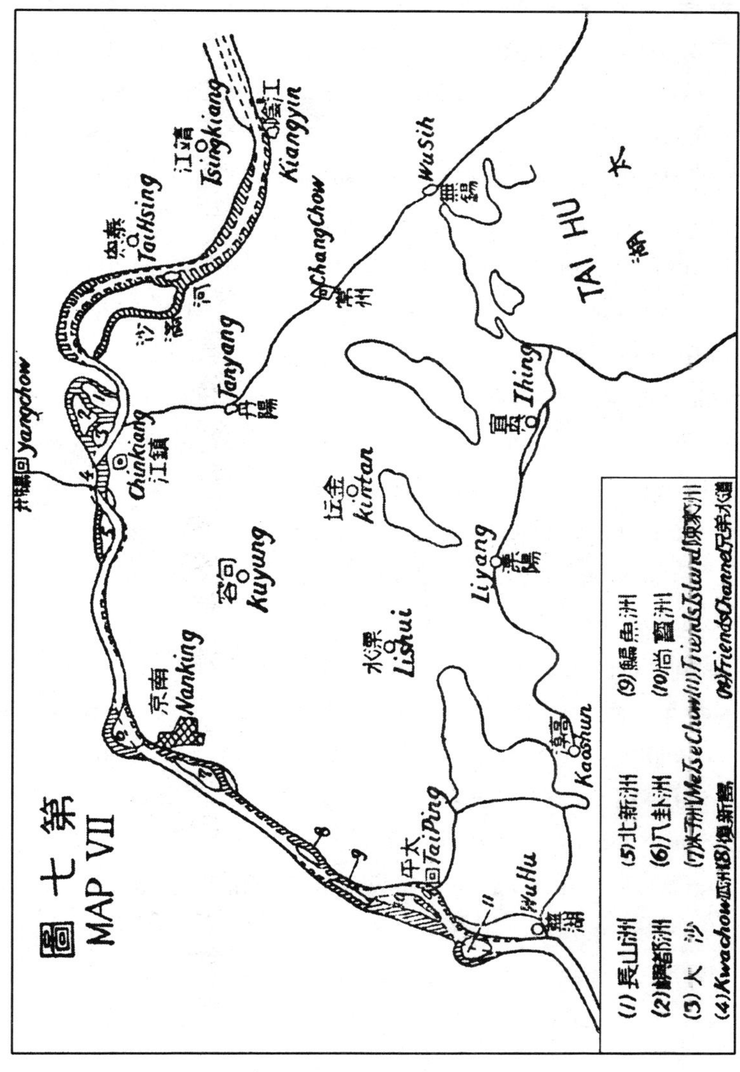

However, most of the exist- ing embankments in this part could be left as they are except some of the concave surfaces of the shores have to be protected by either stone or concrete work. The regulating works of the channel and the embankments can be done by artificial means as well as by natural processes so as to economize as much as possible. The cost of the whole works of this part of the river cannot be accurately estimated until a detail survey is made; but in a rough guess $400,000 per mile may not be very far from the mark. Thus 180 miles will cost $72,000,000 exclusive of the expenses for the widening of the point between Nanking and Pukow, in which case valuable properties will have to be removed.

The Kwachow cut is to straighten the three sharp curves in front of and above Chinkiang by converting them into one. Two and a half miles of the land in the northern shore opposite Chinkiang will have to be cut into in order to form a new channel of a mile or more in width. The part of the river in front of, and above and below Chinkiang has to be reclaimed. The new land thus reclaimed would form the water front of Chinkiang city, the value of which may be sufficient to defray the cost of the work and compensate for the land taken away on the northern shore, to form the new channel. So the works of this part will be at least a self-paying proposition.

The narrow between Pukow and Hsiakwan from pier to pier is barely six cables wide. The depth of the water in this narrow from the shallowest to the deepest is six to twenty-two fathoms. The land of the Hsiakwan side had occasionally sunk away on account of the too rapid current and the depth of the water. This indicates that this part is too narrow for the volume of the Yangtze water to pass. Therefore a wider passage must be provided for. In order to do so, the whole town of Hsiakwan must be sacrificed as the river must be widened right up to the foot of the Lion Hill, so as to provide a passage of a mile wide at this point. What the cost for the compensation of this valuable property of Hsiakwan will be will have to be submitted to the experts for a careful investigation before it can be determined. This will be the most costly part of the whole project for the regulating of the Yangtze. But undoubtedly some equally valuable property can be created along the riverside near by in place of Hsiakwan, so that a balance may be realized by the work itself.

The channel below the Nanking Pukow Narrow will follow the short passage alongside of the foot of the Mofushan to Wulungshan. The loop around the island north of Nanking will have to be blocked up in order to straighten the course of the river.

然而此部分原有河堤，大抵可以听其自然，惟其河岸凹曲线面，有数处应用石或士敏土坚结以保护之耳。以力求省费之故，此段水道及河堤整治工程，可以一面用人为之工作，一面助以自然之力。此一段河流工程全部所费，不能于测量未竣以前精密计出，但粗为计算，则四十万一英里之数，总相去不远。故全段一百八十英里，应费七千二百万元。此外尚有开阔南京、浦口中间河面之费，未计有内；此处有多数高价之产业须全毁去，其费颇多也。

瓜洲开凿一事，所以令镇江前面及上下游三处急曲线改为一处，使河流较直也。此处沿江北岸约二英里半陆地，正对镇江，必须凿开，令成新水道，阔一英里有余。其旧道在镇江前面及上下游者，则须填塞之。所填之地，即成为镇江城外沿江市街，估其价值，优足以偿购取瓜洲陆地，及开凿工程之费。故此一部分，至少总可认为不亏本之提案。

浦口、下关间窄处，自此码头至彼码头，仅得五分英里之三，即一千二百码而已。而此处水深最浅处为三十六英尺，最深处为一百三十二英尺。下关一边陆地，时时以水流过急、河底过深之故而崩陷，斯即显然为此部分河道太窄，不足以容长江洪流通过也。然则非易以广路不可矣。为此之故，必以下关全市为牺牲，而容河流直洗狮子山脚，然后此处河流有一英里之阔。以赔还下关之高价财产而论，须费几何，必须提交专门家详细调查，乃能决定。要之，此为整治扬子江全计划中最耗费之部分。但亦有附近下关沿岸之地，可以成为高价财产无疑，故此工程或可望得自相弥补也。

南京、浦口间窄路下游之水道，应循其最短线路，沿幕府山脚，以至乌龙山脚。其绕过八卦洲后面之干流，应行填塞，俾水流直下无滞。

The section of the river from Nanking to Wuhu is almost in a straight line with three dilatations along its course one just above Nanking the other two just above and below the East and West pillars. To regulate the first dilatation the channel above Me-tse-chow should be blocked up and the island outside of it should be partly cut to widen the proper channel. To regulate the other two dilatations the river should be made to curve toward Taiping Fu to follow the deep channel on the right bank. The left channel should be blocked up. The islands along this curve should be partly or wholly removed. To regulate the dilatation above the Pillars, the Friends Channel should be blocked up and Friends Island be partly cut away. And the left bank below Wuhu should also be cut to give the channel a uniform width.

d. From Wuhu to Tungliu

This part of the river is about 130 miles in length. Along its course there are six dilatations, the most prominent of which is the one that lies immediately below Tungling, which extends over ten miles from side to side. In each of these dilatations there are usually two or three channels with newly formed islands between them. The deep passage often changes from one side to the other, and it is not uncommon that all of the channels are filled up at the same time, thus stopping navigation altogether for a considerable period. See Map VIII.

由南京至芜湖一段河流，殆成一直线，其中有泛滥三处，一处刚在南京上游，余二则在东西梁山之上下游。其第一泛滥之米子洲上游支流，应行闭塞，另割该洲外面一幅，使本流河幅足用。至欲整治余二泛滥，则应循其右岸深水道作曲线，向太平府城，而将左边水道锁闭。此曲线所经各沙洲，有须全行削去者，亦有须削其一部者。而在东西梁山上游之泛滥，须将兄弟水道完全闭塞，并将陈家洲削去一部。而芜湖下游左岸，亦须稍加割削，令河流广狭上下一律。

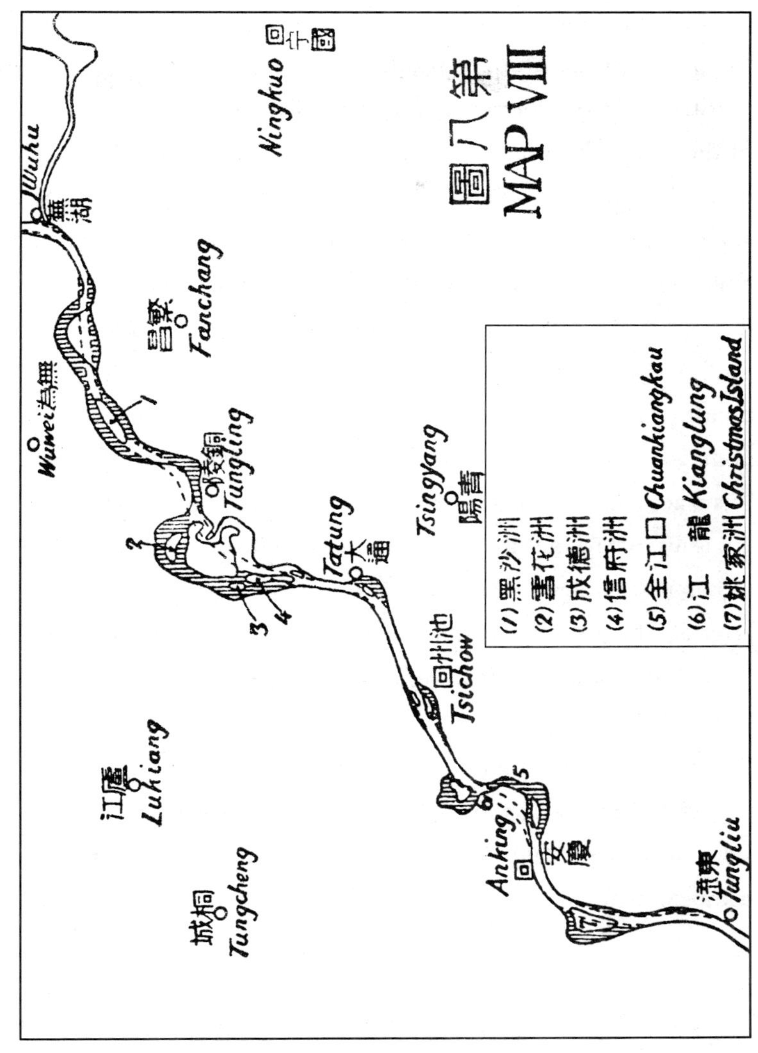

丁　自芜湖至东流

此段大江约长一百三十英里，沿流有泛滥六处。其中最显著者，即在铜陵下之泛滥也。此泛滥，两岸相距在十英里以上。第一泛滥，常分为两三股水道，其间夹有新涨之沙洲。其深水道时时变迁，忽在此股，忽在彼股，有时竟至数股同时淤塞，逼令航行暂时停止，亦非希觏[43]之事也。（参观第八图）

In regulating the part of the river from ten miles above Wuhu to ten miles below Tatung, I propose to cut a new channel through the midstream islands formed by the three dilatations and the sharp corners of the shore, in order to straighten as well as to shorten the river, as marked by the dotted lines in the map attached here. The cost of the cut could not be estimated until a detail survey is made. But as soon as the embankments are laid out the natural force of the river's own current will do a great part of the dredging work, so that the expenses of the cutting for the new channel will be much less than usual. Above Tatung there are two sharp turns of the left shore to be cut. One is on the left shore at the point where the beacon now stands about twelve miles from Tatung. In this place a few miles of the left shore will have to be cut away. The other cut is just below the city of Anking hence to Kianglung beacon, a distance of about six miles. By this cut we do away with the sharp turns of the river at Chuan Kiang Kau. These cuttings would cost much more than the piling of stone at the lower reach of the river. It is quite certain that the reclamation of the side channels of this part will not cover the cost of the cuttings. Therefore this part of the regulating work will not be self-paying, but the navigation of the Yangtze, the protection it gives to both sides of the land, and the prevention of floods in the future will amply compensate for such work.

e. From Tungliu to Wusueh

This part of the river is about eighty miles in length. The land along the right bank is generally hilly while that along the left is low. Along its course there are four dilatations. In three of these dilatations the current has cut into the left or northern bank of the river and then turns back into its main course again almost at right angles. At such points the bank is very unstable. Between the channels of these dilatations islands are being formed. See Map IX.

The regulating works of this part are much easier to construct than those of the lower part. The three diverting semicircular channels have to be blocked up at the upper ends, and the lower openings left open for silt to go into at flood seasons in order to reclaim them by the natural process. The other dilatations should be narrowed in from both sides by jetties. A few places will have to be cut, the most important being the Pigeon Island and the turn above Siau Ku Shan. Some of the midstream islands will have to be removed, and a few wide places filled up in order to make the channel uniform, so as to give a regular minimum depth of six fathoms right along the whole course.

为整治此自芜湖上游十英里至大通下游十英里一段河流，吾拟凿此三泛滥中流之沙洲及岸边之突角，为一新水道，直贯其中，使成一较短较直之河身，即附图中点线所示之路是也。此项费用，亦须详细测量之后，始能算定。但若两边河堤筑定之后，则浚渫工程之大部分，将以河流之自然势力行之，故开凿新河之费，必较寻常大为减少。大通以上，左岸有急度弯曲两处，须行凿开。第一处即大通上游十二英里，现设塔灯水标处之左岸，此处左岸陆地有二三英里，须略加刊削。次一处则应在安庆下游，凿至江龙塔灯水标，计长六英里左右。既凿此河，则免去全江口急度之转湾矣。此项开凿工程，比之下游叠石为堤之费更多。其旁支水路，虽能填为耕地，究不能补其开凿所费。是以此一部分整治之工程，不免为亏本，但以其通长江航道，与保护两岸陆地，又防止将来洪水为患，则此种工程必为有益明也。

戊　自东流至武穴

此段长约八十英里，沿右岸皆山地，左岸则大抵低地也。沿流有泛滥四处，此中有三处，以水流之蚀及左岸，成一支流，复至下游，与正流相会，其会合处殆成直角。在此等地方，河岸殊不巩固，而此泛滥各股水道之间，正在堆积，将成沙洲矣。（参观第九图）

此段整治工程，比之下游各段，施工较易。此三处成半圆形时时转变之支流，应从其分支口施以闭塞，仍留其下游会流之口，任令洪水季节之沙泥随水泛入，自然填塞之。其他一处泛滥，则须于两边筑坝，束而窄之。更有数处须行削截，而小孤山上游及粮洲两处尤为重要。江心沙洲有一部分须削去，而河幅阔处亦有须填窄者。总令水道始终一律，期于全航道常有三十六英尺以上之水深也。

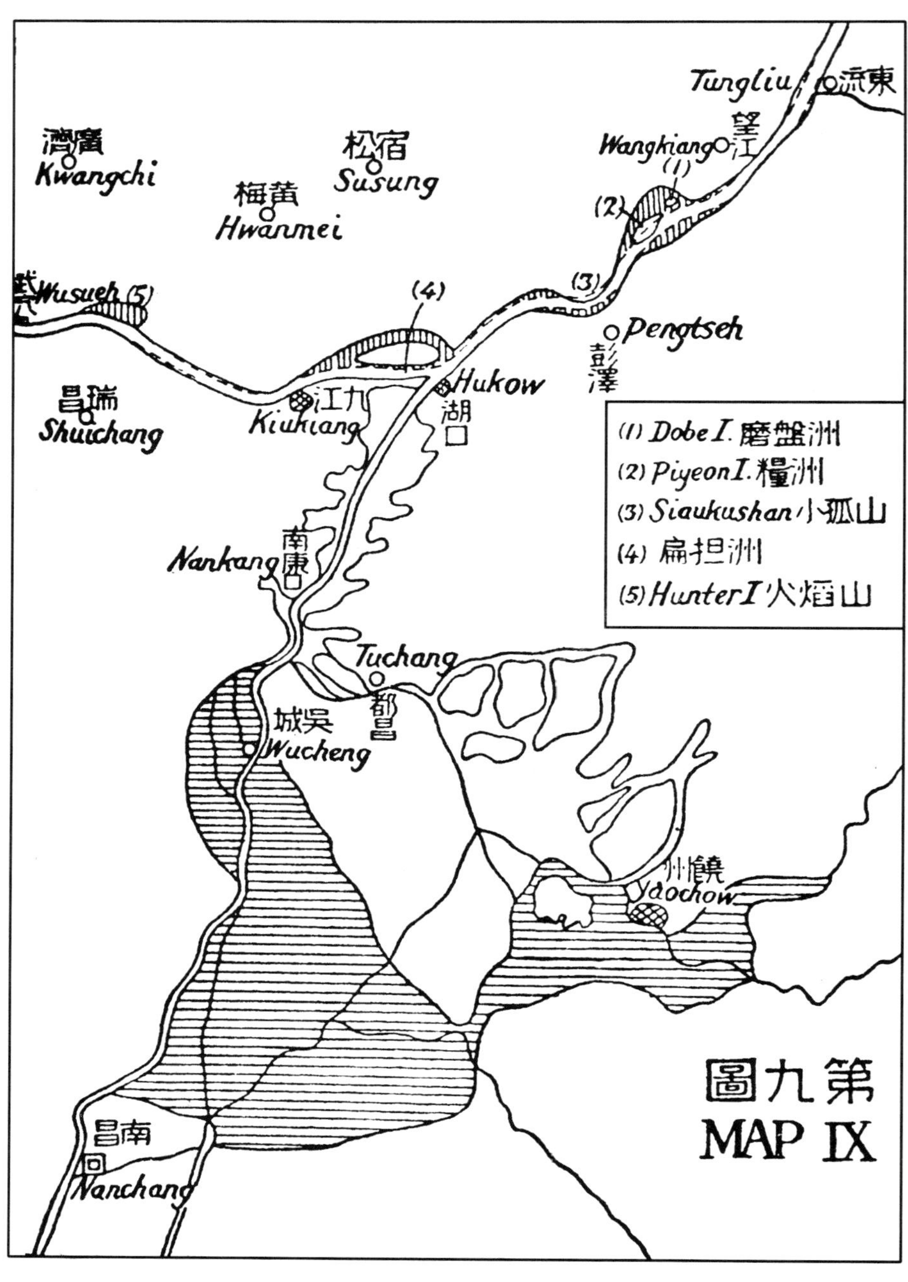
Tungliu 東流
Wangkiang 望江
廣濟 Kwangchi
宿松 Susung
黃梅 Hwanmei
Wusueh (5)
(1)
(2)
(3)
(4)
Pengtseh 彭澤
瑞昌 Shuichang
九江 Kiukiang
Hukow 湖口
Nankang 南康
Tuchang 都昌
吳城 Wucheng
饒州 Yaochow
南昌 Nanchang
(1) Dobe I. 磨盤洲
(2) Piyeon I. 糧洲
(3) Siaukushan 小孤山
(4) 扁担洲
(5) Hunter I 火焰山
第九圖
MAP IX

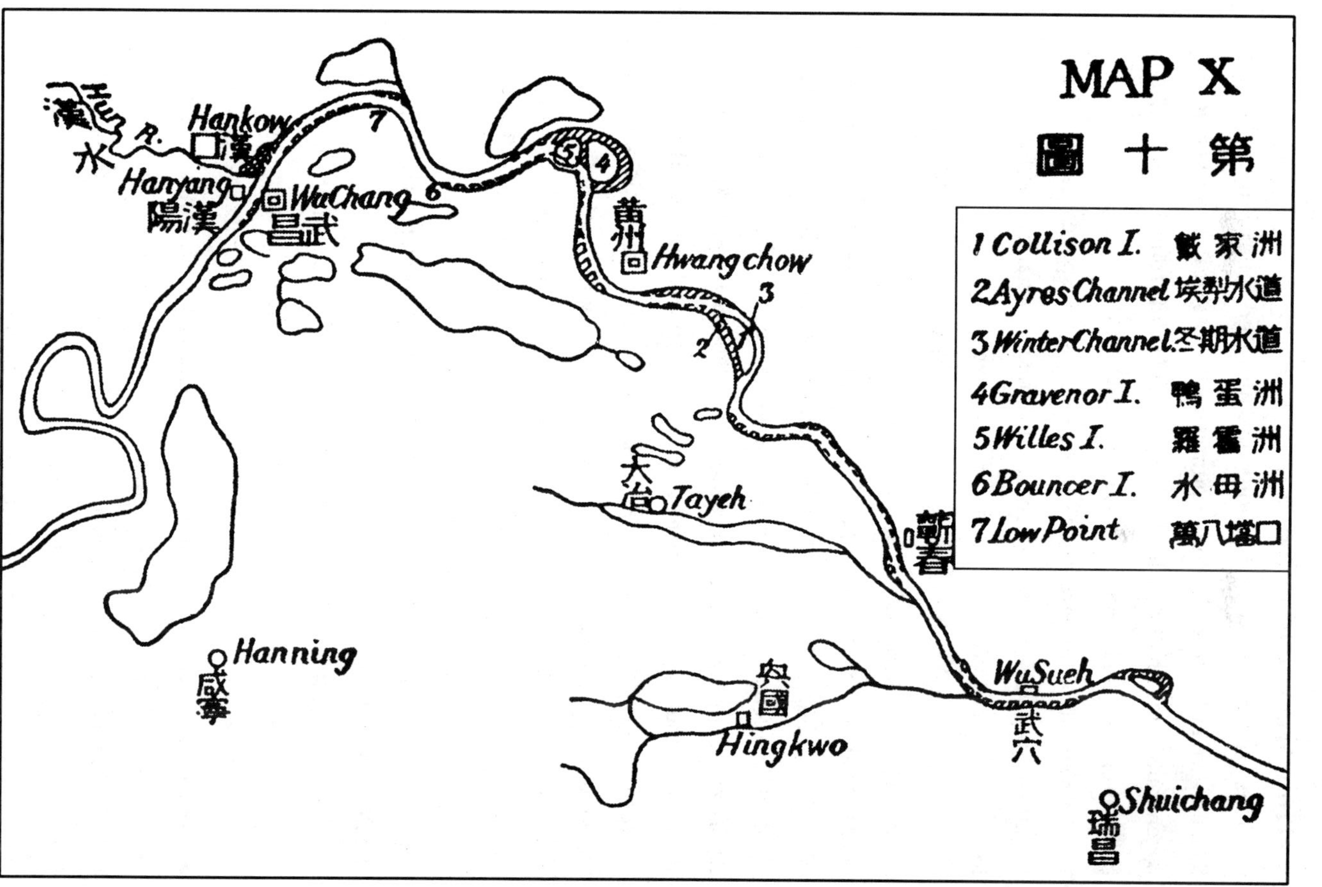

MAP X
第十圖
1 Collison I. 戴家洲
2 Ayres Channel
3 Winter Channel 冬期水道
4 Gravenor I. 鴨蛋洲
5 Willes I.
6 Bouncer I.
7 Low Point
Hun R. 漢水
Hankow 漢口
Hanyang 漢陽
WuChang 武昌
Hwangchow 黃州
Tayeh 大冶
Hanning 咸寧
Hingkwo 興國
WuSueh 武穴
Shuichang 瑞昌

f. From Wusueh to Hankow

This part of the river is about one hundred miles long. Above Wusueh we enter into the hilly country on both sides. The river here is generally about half a mile wide, with a depth of from five to twelve fathoms or sometimes more in certain places. See Map X.

To regulate this part of the river a few wide spaces have to be reclaimed to give a uniform channel, and the side channels at three or four places closed up. Then we can make a channel with a uniform depth of from six to eight fathoms at all seasons. At Collison Island section of the river the Ayres Channel has to be closed up, leaving the winter channel alone so as to give a gentle curve above and below this island. At Willes Island and Gravenor Island point the Round Channel and the channel between these two islands must be blocked up. The river must be made to cut through Willes Island to make a shorter curve. At Bouncer Island the South channel must be blocked up and above this the Low Point turn must be cut away to form a gentler curve. From this point to Hankow the river should be made narrower first by reclaiming the right side as far as the meeting of the southwest curve with the right bank then the reclamation should start at the opposite side of the left bank and right up along the front of Hankow Settlement until the Han River Mouth is reached. Thus a depth of six to eight fathoms can be secured right up to the Bund of Hankow.

To sum up, the whole length of the regulating course of the river from the deep sea to Hankow is about 630 miles. The embankments will be twice this length; that is, 1,260 miles. I have estimated that the sea wall at the mouth of the river could be built at $200,000 a mile, thus for both sides $400,000 a mile will be sufficient or the 140 miles from the deep sea to Kiangyin. For, in this part we have only the two embankments to deal with, which merely requires the tumbling of stones into the water until the pile is strong enough to hold the current to a directed course. As soon as these stone ridges on both sides of the river are formed, nature will do the rest to make the channel deep. The work for this part, therefore, is simple.

But the work for certain sections of the upper part of the river is more complicated as about fifty or sixty miles of solid land of from ten to twenty feet above water level and thirty to forty feet below have to be cut in order to straighten the river's course. Of this cutting and removing work, how much will have to be done artificially and how much can be done by nature, I leave to the experts to estimate. Excepting this,

己　自武穴至汉口

此段约长一百英里，自武穴而上，夹岸皆山地，河幅常为半英里内外。水深自三十英尺至七十二英尺，有数处尚在七十二英尺以上。（参观第十图）

整理此段，须填塞其宽广之河面三数处。令水道整齐，有三四处支流须行闭塞。如此，然后冬季节俱有三十六英尺至四十八英尺水深之水道，可得而成也。在戴家洲一段河流，应将埃梨水道（译音）闭塞，独留冬季水道，则此岛上游下游曲线均较缓徐。在鸭蛋洲及罗霍洲之处，其大弯曲水道及两岛间水道均应闭塞，而另开一新水道，穿过罗霍洲以成为较短之曲线。在水母洲，其南水道务须闭塞，而此洲之上万八墙口曲处，亦须挖成较缓徐之曲线。由此处以至汉口，则须先填右岸，收窄河身，至与右岸向西南曲处相接而止。再从对面左岸填起，直过汉口租界面前，以至汉水口。则汉口堤岸面前，可以常得三十六英尺至四十八英尺深之水道矣。

总计自海中至汉口，治河长约六百三十英里，河堤之长当得其二倍，即一千二百六十英里也。在江口之堤，吾尝约计每英里费二十万元，两堤四十万。此项数目，自深海以迄江阴一百四十英里，均可适用，充足有余。因此部分惟须建两堤，此堤亦惟须于水中堆石，令其坚足以约束河流，使从其所导而行，斯已足矣。此两岸列石既成之后，水道可因于自然之力以成，所以此部工程尚为简单。

然而在上游有数处为困难，其中有五六十英里之实地，水面上有一二十英尺之高，水面下尚有三四十英尺之深，须行削去，以使河身改直。此凿开及削去之工程，有若干须用人工，有若干可借天然之力，仍须待专门家预算。除此不计外，工程全部每一英里所费

the other parts of this work, I think, cannot cost much more than $400,000 a mile. So that the whole work from the sea to Hankow, a distance of 630 miles will cost about $252,000,000, or let us say, including the unknown part, $300,000,000 for the completion of the entire project for the regulating of the Yangtze River. By this regulating of the Yangtze River, we secure an approach of 600 miles inland for ocean-going vessels into the very center of a continent of two hundred millions of people of which half or one hundred million is located immediately along 600 miles of the great water highway. As regards remuneration for the work, this project will be more profitable than either the Suez or Panama Canal.

Although we could not find means whereby the works above Kiangyin may be made self-paying as those of the sections below by the reclamation of land, profit from city building along the course of the river can be realized after the regulating work is completed.

In conclusion, I must say that the figures given concerning the harbor works and the Yangtze regulation are merely rough estimates which must be in the nature of the case. As regards the costs of building the rudimental dikes at the estuary of the Yangtze as well as along the dilating parts of the river, the estimation may seem too low. But the data on which I base my estimate are as follows: First, my own observation of the private enterprise of reclamation by building dikes at the Canton delta around my native village; second, the cheap stone that can be obtained at the Chusan Archipelago; third, the estimation of Mr. Tyler, Coast Inspector of the Maritime Customs for the blocking up of the North Channel at the upper end of Tsungming Island, where the narrowest part is about three miles. He says that a million taels or more is necessary for the work. Or, let us say, in round figures, five hundred thousand dollars (Mex.) a mile. This is two and a half times my estimate. Now, let us compare the difference. The three-mile channel at the upper end of Tsungming has an average depth of twenty feet of water, while in my project the sea wall or dikes will be built in water having an average of less than two thirds of this depth. Moreover, the work of blocking up the North Channel entirely at a right angle is many times more costly than that of building a rudimental dike of the same length in a parallel line with the current. Since five hundred thousand dollars are enough to block up cross-wise a mile of river twenty feet deep, two fifths of that sum should be quite sufficient to finance the work that I have projected. While writing this, I came across an article in the *Chicago Railway*

不过四十万元。故自海面至汉口，相距六百三十英里，所费当不过二万五千二百万元。今姑假定整治扬子江全盘计划并未知之部分算在其内，须费三万万元。由此计划，吾人辟一通路深入内地六百英里，容航洋巨船驶至住居二万万人口之大陆中心，而此中有一万万人住居于此最大水路通衢之两旁。以工程之利益而论，此计划比之苏彝士[44]、巴拿马两河更可获利。

虽在江阴以上各段，吾人不能发见不亏本之方法，不如江阴下游各段可以新填之地补其所费，但在竣工之后，仍可在沿江建立商埠，由之以得利益也。此建设商埠之计划，将于次部论之。

结　论

当结论此二部，吾更须申言关于筑港及整治扬子江之工程数目，仅为粗略之预算，盖事势上自然如此也。关于在长江出海口及诸泛滥地建筑初步河堤之预算，或者有太低之迹，但吾所据之资料以为计算根源者，在下列各层：第一、为吾所亲见在广东河汊环吾本村筑堤填地之私人企业；第二、为廉价之石，可求之于舟山列岛者；第三、为海关沿岸视察员泰罗君之计算。在崇明岛上端闭塞北水道所费，该水道以此处为最狭，约计有三英里，而泰罗君谓所费约须一百万两有余，然则约五十万元一英里也；比之吾所计算，已为两倍有半，此其差异可得比较而知。盖此崇明岛上端三英里之水道，平均水深二十英尺，而我所计划之海堤江堤，建于水中者，平均比此段少三分之二，且闭塞北水道之工程完全与河流成为直角，则其所费较之建此初步河堤与水流成平行线者，纵使长短相同，所差亦应数倍。而五十万元可以建横截深二十英尺之河，而闭塞之之一英里工程，则其五分之二之经费，亦必足以供吾所规划之工程之用矣。当吾草此文之际，《芝加高[45]

Review, May 17, 1919, dealing with the same subject, which states that steel skeleton is a better and cheaper substitute for stone or other materials for building dikes and jetties in a muddy river like ours. Thus, by this new method, we may be able to construct embankments, with cheaper material than I have hitherto known. So, although the estimate which I have made may be somewhat low, yet it is not so far from correct as it seems at first sight.

● Part III The Construction of River Ports

The construction of river ports along the Yangtze between Hankow and the sea will be one of the most remunerative propositions in our development scheme. For this part of the Yangtze Valley is richest in agricultural and mineral products in China and is very densely populated. With the cheap water transportation provided by the completion of the regulating work both sides of this water highway will surely become industrial beehives. And with cheap labor near by, it will not be a surprise if in the near future both banks will become two continuous cities, as it were, right along the whole extent of the river from Hankow to the sea. In the meantime a few suitable spots should be chosen for profitable city development. For this purpose I will start from the lower part of the river as follows:

a. Chinkiang and North Side.
b. Nanking and Pukow.
c. Wuhu.
d. Anking and South Side.
e. Poyang Port.
f. Wuhan.

a. Chinkiang and North Side

Chinkiang is situated at the junction of the Grand Canal and the

Yangtze. It was an important center of inland water traffic between the north and the south before the steam age. But it will resume its former grandeur and become more important when the old inland waterway is improved, and new ones are constructed. For it is the gateway between the Hoangho and Yangtze valleys. Besides, by the southern portion of the Grand Canal, Chinkiang is connected with the Tsientang valley—

铁路批评》五月十七日所出之报，适有一论文道及此事。彼谓用钢铁骨架以筑河堤及坝，于浊泥河流，如吾辈今所欲治者，比之用石及用其他材料较佳，而又较廉。然则若采此新法，吾等可以用吾前此未知之更廉材料，以建河堤矣。所以吾前所计算或者不免稍低，而仍离正确之数目不远，决不如骤见所觉之过低也。

第三部　建设内河商埠

在扬子江此一部建设内河商埠，将为此发展计划中最有利之部分，因此部分在中国为农矿产最富之区，而居民又极稠密也。以整治长江工程完成之后，水路运送，所费极廉，则此水路通衢两旁，定成为实业荟萃之点，而又有此两岸之廉价劳工附翼之。则即谓将来沿江两岸，转瞬之间变为两行相连之市镇，东起海边、西达汉口者，非甚奇异之事也。此际应先选最适宜者数点，以为获利的都市发展。依此目的，吾人将从下游起，溯江逐港论之如下：

甲　镇江及其北岸。
乙　南京及浦口。
丙　芜湖。
丁　安庆及其南岸。
戊　鄱阳港。
己　武汉。

甲　镇江

镇江位于运河与江会之点，在汽机未用以前，为南北内地河运中心重要之地。而若将旧日内地运河浚复，且增浚新运河，则此地必能恢复其昔日之伟观，且更加重要。因镇江为挈合黄河流域与长江流域中间之联锁，而又以运河之南端直通中国最富饶之钱塘江流域。

the richest part of China. Thus, this city is bound to grow into a great commercial center in the near future.

In our regulation work of the Yangtze, we shall add a piece of new land, over six square miles, in front of Chinkiang. This land on the south side of the river will be utilized for city-planning for our new Chinkiang. On the north side, land should also be taken up by the state to build another city. The north side will be bound to outgrow that of the south for the whole of Hoangho Valley could only emerge into the Yangtze by waterway through this point. Docks should be built between here and Yangchow for accommodation of inland vessels, and modern facilities should be provided for transhipment between inland vessels and ocean-going steamers. This port should be made as a distributing center as well as a collecting center for the salt of the eastern coast. This, with the help of modern methods, will reduce transportation expenses. Stone or concrete bunds or quays should be built on both sides of the river and tidal jetties should be provided for train ferries. In time, when commerce grows, tunnels or bridges may be added to facilitate traffic of the two sides. The streets should be wide so as to meet modern demands. The water front and its neighborhood should be planned for industrial and commercial uses and the land beyond should be planned for residential purpose. Every modern public utility should be provided. In regard to the details of planning the city, I must leave them to the expert.

b. Nanking and Pukow

Nanking was the old capital of China before Peking, and is situated in a fine locality which comprises high mountains, deep water and a vast level plain—a rare site to be found in any part of the world. It also lies at the center of a very rich country on both sides of the lower Yangtze. At present, although ruined and desolate, it still has a population of over a quarter of a million. Once it was the home of many industries especially silk and now the finest satin and velvet are still produced here. Nanking has yet a greater future before her when the resources of the lower Yangtze Valley are properly developed.

In the regulation of the Yangtze I propose to cut away the town of Hsiakwan, so that the wharf of Nanking could be removed into the deep channel between Metsechow and the outskirt of Nanking. This channel should be blocked up, thereby a wet dock could be formed to

所以此镇江一市，将来欲不成为商业中心，亦不可得也。

依吾整治长江计划，则在镇江前面，吾人既以大幅余地，在六英方里以上者，加入镇江。此项大江南面新填之余地，当利用以为吾人新镇江之都市计划。而江北沿岸之地，亦当由国家收用，以再建一都市。盖以黄河流域全部，欲以水路与江通，惟恃此一口，故江北此一市当然超越江南之市也。镇江、扬州之间，须建船坞，以便内地船舶；又当加最新设备，以便内地船只与航洋船之间，盘运货物之用。此港既用以为东海岸食盐收集之中心，同时又为其分销之中心，如此则可用新式方法，以省运输之费。江之两岸须以石或士敏土坚结筑成堤岸，而更筑应潮高下之火车渡头，以便联络南北两岸铁路客车、货车之往来。至于商业发达之后，又需建桥梁于江上，且凿地道于江下，以便两岸货物来往。街道须令宽阔，以适合现代之要求。其临江街道及其附近，应预定为工商业所用。此区之后面，即为住宅，各种新式公共营造均应具备。至于此市镇计划详细之点，吾则让之专门家。

乙　南京、浦口

南京为中国古都，在北京之前，而其位置乃在一美善之地区。其地有高山，有深水，有平原，此三种天工，钟毓一处，在世界中之大都市诚难觅如此佳境也。而又恰居长江下游两岸最丰富区域之中心，虽现在已残破荒凉，人口仍有一百万之四分一以上。且曾为多种工业之原产地，其中丝绸特著，即在今日，最上等之绫及天鹅绒尚在此制出。当夫长江流域东区富源得有正当开发之时，南京将来之发达，未可限量也。

在整治扬子江计划内，吾尝提议削去下关全市，如是则南京码头当移至米子洲与南京外郭之间，而米子洲后面水道自应闭塞，如是

accommodate all ocean-going vessels. This point is much nearer the inhabited parts of the city than Hsiakwan. And the land between this projected wet dock and the city could form a new commercial and industrial quarter which would be many times larger than Hsiakwan. Metsechow in time, when commerce grows, may also be developed into city lots and business quarters. For the future development of Nanking the land within and without the city should be taken up at the present price under the same principle which I have proposed for the Projected Port at Chapu.

Pukow, opposite Nanking, on the other side of the river, will be the great terminus of all the railways of the great northern plain to the Yangtze. It will be the nearest river port for the rich coal and iron fields of Shansi and Honan, giving access to the lower Yangtze district and hence to the sea. As the great transcontinental trunk line to the sea whether terminating at Shanghai or at our Projected Port, would pass through this point, the construction of a tunnel under the Yangtze to connect Nanking and Pukow by rail at the same time when the cities are being constructed, will not be at all premature. This will at once make possible a through train journey from Shanghai to Peking.

Concrete or stone embankment should be built along the shore above and below the present Pukow point many miles in each direction. Modern streets should be laid out on the land within the embankment so as to be ready for various building purposes. The land on the north side of the river should be taken up by the state for public uses of this international development scheme on the same basis as at our Projected Ports.

c. Wuhu

Wuhu is a town of 120,000 inhabitants and is the center of the rice trade in the lower part of the Yangtze. It is at this point that I propose to make an intake of the water which will go to flush the Whangpoo River at Shanghai, and which will form the upper end of a canal to the sea at Chapu. In the regulating work of the Yangtze the concave part above the junction of the Yangki Ho has to be filled up and the convex part of the opposite side has to be cut away. The junction of the projected canal and the river will be at about a mile or so below the Lukiang junction. The projected canal will run northeast to a point between the southeast corner of Wuhu city and the foot of the hill. There it joins the Yangki Ho and, following the course as far as Paichiatien, branches off in the

则可以作成一泊船坞，以容航洋巨舶。此处比之下关，离南京市宅区域更近，而在此计划之泊船坞与南京城间旷地，又可以新设一工商业总汇之区，大于下关数倍。即在米子洲，当商业兴隆之后，亦能成为城市用地，且为商业总汇之区。此城市界内界外之土地，当照吾前在乍浦计划港所述方法，以现在价格收为国有，以备南京将来之发展。

南京对岸之浦口，将来为大计划中长江以北一切铁路之大终点。在山西、河南煤铁最富之地，以此地为与长江下游地区交通之最近商埠，即其与海交通亦然。故浦口不能不为长江与北省间铁路载货之大中心，犹之镇江不能不为一内地河运中心也。且彼横贯大陆直达海滨之干线，不论其以上海为终点，抑以我计划港为终点，总须经过浦口。所以当建市之时，同时在长江下面穿一隧道以铁路联结此双联之市，决非躁急之计。如此，则上海、北京间直通之车，立可见矣。

现在浦口上下游之河岸，应以石建或用士敏土坚结，成为河堤，每边各数英里。河堤之内应划分为新式街道，以备种种目的建筑所需。江之此一岸陆地，应由国家收用，一如前法，以为此国际发展计划中公共之用。

丙 芜湖

芜湖为有居民十二万之市镇，且为长江下游米粮市易之中心，故吾择取此点为引水冲刷上海黄浦江底之接水口，而此口亦为通上海或乍浦之运河之上口。在整治长江工程之内，青弋河合流点上面之凹曲部分应行填塞，而对岸突出之点则应削去。此所计划之运河，起于鲁港合流点下游约一英里之外。此运河应向北东走，至芜湖城东南角，与山脚中间一点，与青弋河相合；更于濮家店，循此河之支流以行。

northeastern direction. This gives Wuhu a southeast waterfront along the left side of the canal. New bunds should be built along both sides of the canal as well as alongside the Yangtze and at the junction of the canal docks for inland vessels should be constructed with modern plants for transhipment of goods. Wide streets should be laid out from the Bund of the Yangtze far into the inland following the direction of the canal. The bund alongside the Yangtze should be reserved for commercial purposes and those alongside the canal for factories. Wuhu is in the midst of a rich iron and coal field, so it will surely become an industrial center when this iron and coal field is properly developed. Cheap materials, cheap labor, and cheap foodstuffs are abundant at the spot waiting for modern science and machinery to turn them into greater wealth for the benefit of mankind.

d. Anking and South Side

Anking, the capital of Anhwei, was once a very important city but since its destruction by the Taiping war it has never recovered its former greatness. Its present population is about 40,000 only. Its immediate neighborhood is very rich in mineral and agricultural products. The great tea district of Liu-an and the rich mineral district in the southeastern corner of Honan province will have to make Anking their shipping port when railways are developed. In the Yangtze Conservancy work, the concave turn of the river in front and west of the city has to be filled up. This reclaimed land should be for the extension of a new city, where modern transportation plants should be built.

Eagle Point, on the south side opposite Anking should be cut away to make the river curve more gently and to give the channel a uniform width. A new city should be laid out at this point, for from here we command the vast tea districts of southern Anhwei and western Chekiang. The rich inland city of Hweichow, with the highly productive country around it, will have to make this port its shipping station. As Wuhu is the center of the rice trade these twin cities of Anking will be the centers of the tea trade. Like Wuhu, these twin cities are also situated in the midst of rich iron and coal fields which will assist them to become important industrial centers in the near future. So to build twin cities at this point of the river will be a very profitable undertaking.

如此，则芜湖东南循此运河左岸，得一临水之地。运河两旁，应建新堤，一如长江两岸。且建船坞于运河通大江之处，以容内地来往船只，加以近代之机械，供盘运货物过船之用。自江岸起，向内地，循运河之方向，规划广阔之街道，其近江者留以供商业之需，其沿运河者则留为制造厂用地。芜湖居丰富铁矿区之中心，此铁矿既得相当开发之时，芜湖必能成为工业中心也。芜湖有廉价材料、廉价人工、廉价食物，且极丰裕，专待现世之学术与机器，变之以为更有价值之财物，以益人类耳。

丁　安庆及南岸

安庆者，安徽之省城，自从经太平天国战争破坏之后，昔日之盛不可复睹矣。现在人口仅有四万。其直接邻近之处，农产、矿产均富。若铁路既成，则六安大产茶区，与河南省之东南角矿区，均当以安庆为其货物出入之港。在治江工程中，安庆城前面及西边之江流曲处，应行填筑。此填筑之地，即为推扩安庆城建新市街之用。所有现代运输机械，均应于此处建之。

在安庆城对面上游江岸最突出之地角，应行削去，使江流曲度更为和缓，而全河之广亦得一律。新市街即当在此处建造，因皖南、浙西之大产茶区，将于此处指挥掌握之也。如以徽州之内地富饶市镇，又有产出极盛之乡土环绕之，则必求此地以为其载货出入之中站明矣。以芜湖为米市中心言，则此安庆之双联市将为茶市中心，而此双联市之介在丰富煤铁矿区中心，又恰与芜湖相等。此又所以助兹港使于短期之间成为重要工业中心者也。故在长江此部建此双联市，必为大有利益之企业。

e. The Poyang Port

I propose to construct a port at a point between the Poyang Lake and the Yangtze River. This will be the sole port of the Kiangsi province. Every city of this province is connected by natural waterways which, if improved, will become a splendid water transportation system. The province of Kiangsi has a population of 30,000,000 and is extremely rich in mineral resources. A modern port acting as a commercial and industrial center for the development of this resourceful province would be a most remunerative proposition in our project.

The site of the port will be on the west side of the entrance to the Poyang Lake and the right bank of the Yangtze. It will be an entirely new city built on new ground, part of which will be reclaimed from the shallow side of the lake. In the regulating work of the Poyang Channel, a training wall should be built from the foot of the Taku Tang Hill to Swain Point opposite to Stone Bell Hill of Hukow. A closed dock should be constructed within this training wall for the accommodation of inland water vessels. The city should be laid out on the triangular space formed by the right bank of the Yangtze, the left side of the Poyang Lake and the foot hill of the Lushan Mountain. This triangle is about 10 miles on each side, excellent for city development. The porcelain industry should be established here instead of at Kingteh Chen, for great damages often occur owing to the lack of transportation facilities, and to the necessity of transhipment for the export of the finished articles from the latter place. Modern plants on a large scale should be adopted for the manufacturing of cheap wares as well as fine articles in our projected Poyang Port, for here we shall have the greater advantage of collecting raw materials than at Kingteh Chen. Thus the concentrating of the various manufactures in an advantageous center will result in quickening the growth of our new city. This Poyang Port is bound to grow into one of the great commercial and manufacturing centers in China, judging from the possibilities of Kiangsi alone. It will not only be a great shipping port of the Yangtze but will also be a railway center between North and South China. Thus to develop this port on a large scale is quite justifiable from an economic point of view.

f. Wuhan

Wuhan signifies the three cities of Wuchang, Hankow, and Hanyang. This point is the headwater of our projected ocean passage, the pivot of the railway system of China Proper, and will become the most

戊 鄱阳港

吾欲于长江与鄱阳湖之间，建设一鄱阳港，此港将成为江西富省之惟一商埠矣。江西省每县均有自然水路联络之，若更加以改良，则必成宏伟之水路运输系统。江西有人民三千万，矿源最富，如有一新式商埠以为之工商业中心，以发展此富源饶裕之省分，则必为吾计划中最获利之一部分矣。

此港位置，应在鄱阳湖入口西端，长江右岸之处。此港应为新地之上所建之新市，其中一部之地，须由填筑湖边低地成之。在鄱阳湖水道整治工程之中，应建一范堤，起自大姑塘山脚，迄于湖口石钟山对面之低沙角。此范堤之内，应建造一有闸船坞，以便内河船舶寄泊。而此港市街则应设在长江右岸、鄱阳湖左侧、庐山山麓，合成之三角地。此三角地，每边约有十英里，以供市街发展，优良已极。景德镇磁器工业应移建之于此地。盖以运输便利缺乏之故，景德之磁常因之大受损坏，而出口换船之际，尤常使制成之磁器碰损也。此地应采用最新大规模之设备，以便一面制造最精良之磁器，一面复制廉价之用具。盖此地收集材料，比之在景德镇更为便宜也。以各种制造业集中于一便利之中心，其结果不特使我计划之港长成迅速，且于所以奉给人者亦可更佳良。但以江西一省观之，鄱阳湖已必为世界商业制造之大中心。鄱阳湖非特长江中一泊船港，又为中国南北铁路之一中心。所以从经济上观之，以大规模发展此港者，全然非不合宜者也。

己 武汉

武汉者，指武昌、汉阳、汉口三市而言。此点实吾人沟通大洋计划之顶水点，中国本部铁路系统之中心，而中国最重要之商业中心也。

important commercial metropolis in the country. The population of these three cities is over a million and could be easily doubled or trebled if improvements would be made. At present, Hanyang possesses the largest iron works in China, and Hankow, many modern industries, while Wuchang is becoming a great cotton manufacturing city. Besides, Hankow is the trade center of Central and West China, and the greatest tea market we have. The provinces of Hupeh, Hunan, Szechuen, and Kweichow and a part of Honan, Shensi, and Kansu all depend upon Hankow as their only port in the outside world. When railways are developed in China, Wuhan will be still more important and will surely become one of the greatest cities in the world. So in planning the future city of Wuhan we must adopt for its development a scale as large as that of New York or London.

In the regulation of the Yangtze embankments, we have to reclaim the front of Hankow from the jetty of Lungwangmiao at the junction of the Han River right along the left bank to the point where the Yangtze turns eastward. This reclaimed space will be at an average of about 500 to 600 yards wide. This will narrow down the river at this part to give a uniform channel of 5 to 6 cables in width and to give the Hankow settlement a strip of valuable land along its waterfront. This will also help to pay a part of the expenses for city construction. The sharp bend of the Han River just before it joins the Yangtze should be straightened so as to make a gentler curve around Lungwangmiao Point and thus enable the currents of both rivers to flow in the same direction at their junction. The Hanyang embankment will follow pretty closely the present shore line but not beyond the iron works jetty. The wide space of the river above Wuchang city should be walled in to make a closed dock for inland water as well as ocean going vessels. Below Wuchang, an embankment parallel to that of the left side should be built so as to make the future city extend far below the present one. A tunnel should be constructed to connect both embankments at a point where the Kinghan railway makes its first turn when it comes to the Yangtze River. And another tunnel or bridge should be constructed between Hankow and Hanyang on one side and Wuchang on the other at the junction of the Han River and the Yangtze. Additional tunnels or bridges may be constructed at different points when the city grows larger in the future. All the outlying land of these trio-cities should be taken up on the same basis as at our projected seaports, so that private monopoly and speculation in land may be prevented, and that the unearned increment will go to the State to help the payment of capital and interest on the foreign loans which are to be made in this international development scheme.

三市居民数过百万，如其稍有改进，则二三倍之，决非难事。现在汉阳已有中国最大之铁厂，而汉口亦有多数新式工业，武昌则有大纱厂。而此外，汉口更为中国中部、西部之贸易中心，又为中国茶之大市场。湖北、湖南、四川、贵州四省，及河南、陕西、甘肃三省之各一部，均恃汉口以为与世界交通唯一之港。至于中国铁路既经开发之日，则武汉将更形重要，确为世界最大都市中之一矣。所以为武汉将来立计划，必须定一规模，略如纽约、伦敦之大。

在整治长江堤岸，吾人须填筑汉口前面，由汉水合流点龙王庙渡头起，迄于长江向东屈折之左岸一点。此所填之地，平均约阔五百码至六百码。如是，所以收窄此部分之河，全河身一律有五六链（每链为一海里十分之一）之阔，又令汉口租界得一长条之高价土地于其临江之处也。此部之价，可以偿还建市所费之一部分。汉水将入江处之急激曲折，应行改直，于是以缓徐曲线绕龙王庙角，且使江汉流水，于其会合处向同一方面流下。汉阳河岸应密接现在之河边，沿岸建筑，毋突过于铁厂渡头之外。武昌上游广阔之空处，当圈为有闸船坞，以供内河外洋船舶之用。武昌下游应建一大堤，与左岸平行，则将来此市可远扩至于现在市之下面。在京汉铁路线，于长江边第一转变处，应穿一隧道过江底，以联络两岸。更于汉水口以桥或隧道，联络武昌、汉口、汉阳三城为一市。至将来此市扩大，则更有数点可以建桥，或穿隧道。凡此三联市外围之地，均当依上述大海港之办法收归国有，然后私人独占土地与土地之投机赌博，可以预防。如是则不劳而获之利，即自然之土地增价，利可尽归之公家，而以之偿还此国际发展计划所求之外债本息也。

• Part IV The Improvement of the Existing Waterways and Canals

The existing waterways and canals in connection with the Yangtze may be enumerated as follows:

a. The Grand Canal.
b. The Hweiho.
c. The Kiangnan Waterway System.
d. The Poyang Waterway System.
e. The Han River.
f. The Tungting System.
g. The Upper Yangtze.

a. The Grand Canal

The Grand Canal connects with the Yangtze at a point opposite Chinkiang and runs northward right up to Tientsin, a distance of over 600 miles. We understand that a detailed survey of the Kiangpeh part of the canal has begun and the work of improving it will commence soon. In our project, I propose to substitute the Kiangpeh portion of the Grand Canal by the Yangtze outlet of the Hweiho.

b. The Hweiho

The Hweiho rises in the northwest corner of Honan and runs southeast and east to the north of Anhwei and Kiangsu. Its outlets have been sealed up in recent years so its water has accumulated in the Hungtse Lake and it depends upon evaporation as its only means of disposing the water. Thus in the heavy rainy season, it floods a vast extent of the country surrounding the lake and causes great misery to millions of people. So the conservancy of the Hweiho is a very urgent question of China to-day. Recently many investigations have been made and many plans proposed. Mr. Jameson, chief engineer for the American Red Cross

Society, has proposed two outlets for the Hweiho: one following the old course of the Yellow River to the sea and another through Paoying and Kao-yu Lakes to the Yangtze. In this project I propose to follow Mr. Jameson's plan for the sea outlet only as far as the old Yellow River and for the Yangtze outlet only as far as Yangchow. When the sea outlet or north branch reaches the old Yellow River I will lead it across into the Yenho

• 第四部　改良扬子江之现存水路及运河

兹将现存水路运河、扬子江相联络者，列举如下：

甲　北运河。
乙　淮河。
丙　江南水路系统。
丁　鄱阳水路系统。
戊　汉水。
己　洞庭系统。
庚　扬子江上游。

甲　北运河

北运河在镇江对岸一点与扬子江联络，北走直至天津，其长逾六百英里。在江北之一部运河，现已著手为详细之测量，改良工事不久可以起工，此吾人所共知者也。在吾计划，吾将以淮水注江之一段，代江北一段运河之用。

乙　淮河

淮河出河南省西北隅，东南流，又折而东流，至安徽、江苏两省之北部。其通海之口近年已经淤塞，故其水郁积于洪泽湖，全恃蒸发以为消水之路，于是一入大雨期，洪水泛滥于沿湖广大区域，人民受其荼毒者以百万计。所以修浚淮河，为中国今日刻不容缓之问题。近年迭经调查，屡有改良之提案。美国红十字会技师长詹美生君，曾献议为淮河开两出口，其一循黄河旧槽以达海，其一经宝应、高邮两湖以达扬子江。在此计划，吾赞成詹君通海、通江之方法，但于用黄河旧槽及其经过扬州西面一节，有所商榷。在其出海之口，即淮河北支已达黄河旧槽之后，吾将导以横行入于盐河，循盐河而下，至其北折

and follow the Yenho to its northern turn. From there, we cut across the narrow strip of land into the Kuanho which enters the sea at the nearest deep water line. This saves a great deal of work of excavating the old course of the Hoangho. When the southern branch reaches Yangchow, I propose to make the canal pass east of that city instead of west as Mr. Jameson proposed, so that its current will join the Yangtze in the same direction at the new curve below Chinkiang city.

Both of these outlets or branches of the Hweiho should be made at least twenty feet deep right along, so that coastal vessels from the north to the Yangtze could use them as passage instead of going round the Yangtze estuary, thus shortening the distance by about 300 miles. And with twenty feet depth for both outlets, the Hweiho and the Hungtse Lake would be well drained and the present bottom of the lake, which is sixteen feet above sea level would be converted into agricultural land at once. Thus 6,000,000 mow of land could be reclaimed according to the estimate of Mr. Jameson, from the Hungtse and the neighboring lakes. If twenty dollars a mow be taken for its value, a sum of $120,000,000 could be netted. Besides this direct profit to the Government, there is an area of some 17,000 square miles of occasionally flooded land which would be made flood-proof so that normally we shall have two crops a year instead of two only in five years. That is to say, the 17,000 square miles or 10,880,000 acres will be made to produce five times more than at present. For instance, if the value of the gross production be estimated at fifty dollars an acre, then the total value would be $544,000,000 Mex. and five times this sum would amount to $2,720,000,000 Mex. What an enormous profit to the country!

c. The Kiangnan Waterway System

This system comprises the South Grand Canal, the Whangpoo, the Taihu, and its connections. The most important improvement I intend to make here is to widen and deepen the Wuhu-Ihsing Waterway between the Yangtze and the Taihu, and from there to dredge a deep channel right through the Taihu to a point midway of the Grand Canal between Suchow and Kashing. At Kashing, divide it into two branches:—one following the Kashing Sunkiang Canal to Whangpoo, and the other, to the Projected Port at Chapu. This waterway between the Yangtze and the Whangpoo, before it reaches Shanghai, should be made as wide and deep as possible so as to make it carry sufficient water to flush the Shanghai

一处，复离盐河过河边狭地，直入灌河，以取入深海最近之路，此可以大省开凿黄河旧路之烦也。其在南支在扬州入江之处，吾意当使运河经过扬州城东，以代詹君经城西入江之计划。盖如此则淮河流水，刚在镇江下面新曲线，以同一方向与大江会流矣。

淮河此两支，至少均须得二十英尺深之水流，则沿岸商船自北方赴长江各地，可免绕道经由江口以入，所省航程近三百英里。而两支既各有二十英尺之深，则洪泽与淮河之水流宣畅；而今日高于海面十六英尺之湖底，即时可以变作农田。则以洪泽合之其旁诸湖，依詹美生君之计算，六百万亩之地，咄嗟可致也。如此以二十元为其一亩之价，则此纯粹地价已足一万二千万元，此政府之直接收入也。而又有一万七千英方里地，向苦水潦[46]之灾者，今既无忧，所以昔日五年而仅两获者，今一年而可再获，是一万七千英里者，得一千零八十八万英亩（七千余万中亩），各得五倍奇收获也。假如总生产额一英亩所值为五十元，则此地所产总额原得五万四千四百万元者，今为二十七万二千万元也。其在国家，岂非超越寻常之利益乎！

丙　江南水路系统

此项系统包含南运河与黄浦江、与太湖、及其与为联络之水路而言。此中吾所欲为最重要之改良，乃在浚广浚深芜湖、宜兴间之水路，以联长江与太湖，而又贯通太湖浚一深水道，以达南运河苏州、嘉兴间之一点。其在嘉兴歧为两支，一支循嘉兴、松江之运河，以达黄浦江；他一支则至乍浦之计划港。此项长江、黄浦间水路，当其未达上海之前，应先行浚令广深至其极限，使能载足流水。一面以洗涤上海港面，不容淤积；一面亦使内河船舶来往于江海之间者经此，

harbor as well as to provide a shorter passage for inland water vessels between the Yangtze and the seaports. This waterway will act as silt carrier by which the Taihu and the various lakes alongside of it may be reclaimed in the future. Besides the main object for which this canal is assigned, the reclamation scheme and the local traffic would also add profit to it. This makes its remuneration doubly sure. As no accurate surveys of the shallow Taihu and other lakes and swamps could be obtained, the exact number of mow to be reclaimed could not be given here. But in a rough estimate I should say that the reclaimed space of the Kiangnan Lakes would be about the same in extent as those of Kiangpeh (the North of the Yangtze).

d. The Poyang Waterway System

This system drains the entire area of Kiangzi province. Every hsien, city, and important town is reached by waterway. Waterways are the only means of communication in this province as well as in all the provinces of Southeastern China, before the advent of railways. The lower part of the Kiangsi waterway system suffers the same irregularities as those of the lower Yangtze as both are on low land. So, to regulate it, a similar work as that for the Yangtze should be applied. The Poyang Lake should be divided by deep channels from the junction of each river, and these should join together to form larger channels and finally unite into one main channel at a point near Chuki and, running through the narrow part of the lake, join the Yangtze at Hukow. The sides of the deep channels should be lined with submerged stone ridges as high as the shallow part of the lake, whereby the channels would serve the purpose of draining as well as of navigation.

The shallow space beside those channels will be reclaimed into arable land in due time. So the work of regulating the Poyang channels will be well paid by reclamation.

e. The Han River

This river is navigable for small crafts through its main body up to Hanchung in the southwest corner of Shensi; and through its branches up to Nanyang and Shekichen in the southwest corner of Honan. This navigable stream commands quite a large area of watershed. The upper part, that is above Siangyang, is in mountainous country. From Siangyang to Shayang it is in a wide, open valley and below Shayang it runs into the Hupeh swamp.

大减其路程也。而此水路又可为挟土壤俱来之用，太湖暨其旁诸湖沿水路之各区，将来均可因其填塞，成为耕地。故于建此水路之大目的以外，又有此种填筑计划及本地载货之利益可收，于是其获利之性质，可以加倍确实。现在太湖暨其他诸湖沼地之精确测量尚无可征，则能填筑为田者当有几亩，今亦未可遽言[47]，但以粗略算之，则填筑江南诸湖所得之地，吾意其亩数必不在江北之田以下。

丁 鄱阳水路系统

此一系统，为江西全省排水之用。每县、每城乃至每一重要市镇，均可由水路达到。全省交通，惟恃水路，此乃未有铁路前，中国东南各省所同者也。江西下游水路系统受不规则之害与长江同，皆以其为低地之故，然则其整治之工亦应与长江相同。鄱阳湖应按各水入湖之路，分为多数水道，然后逐渐汇流，卒至渚溪附近乃合而为一。度此湖狭隘之部，而与长江合于湖口。此深水道两旁应各叠水底石堤为一线，使刚与湖中浅处同高，以是其水道可以于排水之外并作航行之用也。水道以外之浅处，将来于相当时间可填为耕地。于是整治鄱阳湖各水道之计划，可以其填筑而得充足之报酬矣。

戊 汉水

此水以小舟溯其正流，可达陕西西南隅之汉中；又循其旁流，可达河南西南隅之南阳及赊旗店。此可航之水流，支配甚大之分水区域：自襄阳以上，皆为山国；其下以至沙洋，则为广大开豁之谷地；由沙洋以降，则流注湖北沼地之间，以达于江。

To improve this river dams should be built above Siangyang in order to utilize water power as well as to make locks for larger crafts to ascend to the navigable point now navigable only for small crafts. Below Siangyang, where the river is very wide and shallow, rudimental dikes should be constructed of stones or piles in order to restrict its channel and to reclaim the shallow space on both sides by natural process. In the swamp, the river should be straightened and deepened. A new canal between the Han and the Yangtze at Shasi should be constructed to provide a shorter passage between Hankow and Shasi and beyond. This canal in the swamp should be open to the lakes along its course so as to let the silt-carrying water enter into them in the flood season, thus filling them up quicker.

f. The Tungting System

This system of waterway drains the whole province of Hunan and beyond. The most important branches are the Siangkiang and the Yuankiang. The former runs through Hunan into the northeast corner of Kwangsi province and connects with the Sikiang system by a canal near Kweilin. The latter runs across the west border of Hunan into the eastern part of Kweichow province. Both could be improved for the navigation of large crafts. The canal between the Yangtze and the Sikiang watersheds should be reconstructed and modern locks should be provided in it as well as along the two waterways. Thus, vessels of ten feet draught may freely pass between the Yangtze and the Sikiang. The Tungting Lake should be drained by deep channels in the same manner as the Poyang Lake, and its shallow space reclaimed by natural process.

g. The Upper Yangtze

I include the part from Hankow to Ichang also in the Upper Yangtze, because it is at Hankow that the ocean navigation ends, and the inland water communication begins. So, in dealing with the improvement of the

Upper Yangtze, I will begin at Hankow. At present the Upper Yangtze is navigable for shallow draught steamers up to Kiating, a point about 1,100 miles above Hankow by river. If improvement be made farther on, than shallow draught steamers could navigate right up to Chengtu, the capital of Szechuen province, and the center of the richest plain in West China, about sixty miles up the Min River.

改良此水，应在襄阳上游设水闸。此一面可以利用水力，一面又使巨船可以通航于现在惟通小舟之处也。襄阳以下，河身广而浅，须用木桩或叠石作为初级河堤，以约束其水道，又以自然水力填筑两岸洼地也。及至沼地一节，须将河身改直浚深。其在沙市，须新开一运河，沟通江汉，使由汉口赴沙市以上各地得一捷径。此运河经过沼地之际，对于沿岸各湖，均任其通流，所以使洪水季节挟泥之水溢入渚湖，益速其填塞也。

己　洞庭系统

此项水路系统，为湖南全省及其上游排水之用。此中最重要之两支流，为湘江与沅江。湘江纵贯湖南全省，其源远在广西之东北隅，有一运河[48]在桂林附近，与西江系统相联络。沅江通布湖南西部，而上流则跨在贵州省之东。两江均可改良，以供大河船[49]航行。其湘江、西江分水界上之运河，更须改造。于此运河及湘江、西江各节，均须设新式水闸，如是则吃水十英尺之巨舶，可以自由来往于长江、西江之间。洞庭湖则须照鄱阳湖例，疏为深水道，而依自然之力，以填筑其浅地为田。

庚　长江上游

自汉口至宜昌一段，吾亦括之入于长江上游一语之中。因在汉口为航洋船之终点，而内河航运则自兹始，故说长江上游之改良，吾将发轫于汉口。现在以浅水船航行长江上游，可抵嘉定，此地离汉口约一千一百英里。如使改良更进，则浅水船可以直抵四川首府之成都。斯乃中华西部最富之平原之中心，在岷江之上游，离嘉定仅约六十英里耳。

To improve the Upper Yangtze from Hankow to Yochow, the work is much similar to that of the lower part. The channel should be regulated by rudimental dikes. The concave embankments in sharp bends should be protected by stone or concrete; obstacles in midstream should be removed. The great loop, called the Farmer Bend, above Kinkow, should be cut through at the neck of Paichow, and the sharp point of Hanchin Kwang should be cut away to make the curve of the river more gentle.

The tortuous part of the Yangtze, north of the Tungting Lake, between Kinho Kow and Skipper Point, should be blocked up altogether and a new channel made through Tungting Lake, returning to the Yangtze by the Yochow Channel. This avoids the crooked passage and shortens the river course considerably. From Skipper Point to Ichang the dilatations should be restricted by dikes of stone or piling, and some sharp points of the shores should be cut away to make the curves more gentle.

The Yangtze River above Ichang enters the Gorges which run about a hundred miles up to the Szechuen depression, known as the Red Basin. This part of the river from Ichang right along to its source is confined by rocky banks, very narrow and deep, having an average depth of six fathoms and at some particular points even thirty fathoms. Many rapids and obstructions occur along its course.

To improve the Upper Yangtze, the rapids should be dammed up to form locks to enable crafts to ascend the river as well as to generate water power. Obstructions should be blasted and boulders removed. Thus, a ten-foot channel right along from Hankow to Chungking could be obtained so that through inland water transportation could be established from Chungking to Peking in the north and to Canton in the south, as well as to all navigable points in China Proper all the year round. In this way, transportation expenses to the richest emporium in West China could be reduced hundredfold. The benefit to the people will be enormous and the encouragement to commerce will indeed be great.

● Part V The Establishment of Large Cement Works

Steel and cement are the basis of modern construction, and the most important factors of the material civilization of the present age. In the various projects of our development scheme, the demand for steel and cement will be so enormous that all manufacturing countries combined will not be able to supply the needs. Therefore, in our first program,

改良自汉口至岳州一段，其工程大类下游各部。当筑初步河堤，以整齐其水道。而急弯曲之凹岸，当护以石堤，或用士敏土坚结。中流洲屿，均应削去。金口上游大湾，所谓簰州曲者，应于簰州地颈开一新河以通航。至后金关之突出地角，则应削除，使河形之曲折较为缓徐。

洞庭之北、长江屈曲之部，自荆河口起以至石首一节，吾意当加闭塞。由石首开新道，通洞庭湖，再由岳州水道归入本流。此所以使河身径直，抑亦缩短航程不少。自石首以至宜昌，中间有泛滥处，当以木石为堤约束之；其河岸有突出点数处，须行削去，而后河形之曲折可更缓也。

自宜昌而上，入峡行，约一百英里而达四川之低地，即地学家所谓红盆地也。此宜昌以上迄于江源一部分河流，两岸岩石束江，使窄且深，平均深有六英寻（三十六英尺），最深有至三十英寻者。急流与滩石，沿流皆是。

改良此上游一段，当以水闸堰其水，使舟得溯流以行，而又可资其水力。其滩石应行爆开除去。于是水深十英尺之航路，下起汉口，上达重庆，可得而致。而内地直通水路运输，可自重庆北走直达北京，南走直至广东，乃至全国通航之港无不可达。由此之道，则在中华西部商业中心，运输之费当可减至百分之十也。其所以益人民者何等巨大，而其鼓舞商业何等有力耶！

• 第五部　创建大士敏土厂

钢铁与士敏土为现代建筑之基，且为今兹物质文明之最重要分子。在吾发展计划之种种设计，所需钢铁与士敏土不可胜计，即合世界以制造著名之各国所产，犹恐不足供此所求。所以在吾第一计划，

I have proposed to establish large steel works in the rich iron and coal fields in the provinces of Shansi and Chihli; so in this second program I propose to establish large cement works along the shores of the Yangtze River. The Yangtze Valley is exceptionally rich in materials for cement,—limestone and coal lying side by side at the water edge along the navigable channel from Chinkiang upward. Thus, local supplies could be created for local needs.

At present, there is one cement works at Shihuiyau near Hoangshikang at the upper reach. It is situated between a deep water wharf and a limestone hill. The limestone is so near by that it can be cut and shoveled into the kilns immediately. Between Hankow and Kiukiang there are many places possessing the same advantage. Below Kiukiang, there are also many such advantageous positions as Matang, Wushiki and many others between Kiukiang and Anking. Between Anking and Nanking there are exceptionally good locations for putting up cement works such as Tatung, Tikang, and Tsaishisze, all these places being provided abundantly with limestone and coal and iron, lying side by side.

With the huge harbor works, city building, and embankment construction, the market for cement will be so great that a capital of one to two hundred million dollars should be invested for the supply. This work should be started gradually in accord with the acceleration of the other works of the general development so that one project will further the other, and over-production and waste of capital individually in any of the parts of the general scheme will be guarded against. This will help make each of them a profitable business by itself.

吾提议建一大炼钢厂于煤铁最富之山西、直隶。则在此第二计划，吾拟欲沿扬子江岸建无数士敏土厂。长江谷地特富于士敏土原料，自镇江而上可航之水道，夹岸皆有灰石及煤，是以即为其本地所需要，还于其地得有供给也。今日已有制士敏土之厂在黄石港上游不远之石灰窑，其位置刚在深水码头与灰石山之间。其山既若是近，故直可由山上以锹锄起石，直移之窑中，无须转运。而在汉口、九江之间，与此相类之便利，尚复多有。九江以下，马当、黄石矶以及九江、安庆间诸地，又有极多之便利相同之灰石山。其安庆以下至南京之间，多为极有利于制士敏土之地区，即如大通、荻港、采石矶，均有丰裕之灰石及煤铁矿，夹江相望也。

筑港、建市街、起江河堤岸诸大工程同时并举，士敏土市场既如斯巨大，则应投一二万万之资本，以供给此士敏土厂矣。而此业之进行，即与全盘其他计划相为关连，徐徐俱进，则以一规划奖进其他规划，各无忧于生产过剩与资本误投，而各计划俱能自致其为一有利事业矣。

PROGRAM III

The main feature of the third program will be the construction of a great southern port which will complete the plan for three first-class seaports in China as proposed in the preliminary part of this International Development Scheme. Our Great Southern Port will naturally be Canton, which is not only the center of commerce in South China but also the largest city in all China. Until recent times it was the largest city on the coasts of the Pacific, and the center of commerce of Asia. With the development of China, Canton will surely resume its former importance. Around this southern metropolis I formulate the third program as follows:

I. The Improvement of Canton as a World Port.
II. The Improvement of the Waterway System of Canton
III. The Construction of the Southwestern Railway System of China.
IV. The Construction of Coast Ports and Fishing Harbors.
V. The Establishment of Shipbuilding Yards.

• Part I The Improvement of Canton as a World Port

Canton's position as a seaport has been taken away by Hongkong since its cession to England after the Opium War. But as a commercial center of South China, Canton still holds its own, despite the advantages of deep-water harbor, the artificial improvements of Hongkong, and the political dominance of England. The loss of its position as a seaport is entirely due to the ignorance of the Chinese people who never made any combined effort to improve the welfare of the country, and also to the corrupt government and officials of the Manchu dynasty. Since the establishment of the Republic, the people have begun to awake very rapidly and many schemes have been suggested to make Canton a seaport. This awakening of the millions of Chinese has caused much apprehension to the Hongkong Government. The authorities of that colony have been doing their utmost to hinder every move to restore Canton as a seaport and try to nip every scheme in the bud. Of course, if Canton is improved and made into a world port, then all the services that Hongkong performs for her as a shipping stage would be dispensed with altogether. But a developed Canton and a prosperous China will recompense Hongkong in various ways a hundred times more than its present position as the monopolized ocean port of a backward and

叁 第三计划

第三计划主要之点，为建设一南方大港，以完成《国际发展计划》篇首所称中国之三头等海港。吾人之南方大港，当然为广州。广州不仅中国南部之商业中心，亦为通中国最大之都市。迄于近世，广州实太平洋岸最大都市也，亚洲之商业中心也。中国而得开发者，广州将必恢复其昔时之重要矣。吾以此都会为中心，制定第三计划如下：

一、改良广州为一世界港。

二、改良广州水路系统。

三、建设中国西南铁路系统。

四、建设沿海商埠及渔业港。

五、创立造船厂。

• 第一部 改良广州为一世界港

广州之海港地位，自鸦片战争结束，香港归英领后，已为所夺。然香港虽有深水港面之利益，有技术之改良，又加以英国政治的优势，而广州尚自不失为中国南方商业中心也。其所以失海港之位置也，全由中国人民之无识，未尝合力以改善一地之公共利益，而又益之以满洲朝代之腐败政府及官僚耳。自民国建立以来，人民忽然觉醒，于是提议使广州成为海港之计划甚多。以此亿兆中国人民之觉醒，使香港政府大为警戒。该地当局，用其全力以阻止一切使广州成为海港之运动；凡诸计划，稍有萌芽，即摧折之。夫广州诚成为一世界港，则香港之为泊船载货站头之一切用处，自然均将归于无有矣。但以此既开发之广州与既繁荣之中国论，必有他途为香港之利，而比之现在仅为一退化贫穷之中国之独占海港，利必百倍可知。试征之

poor China. Just look at the port of Victoria in British Columbia, which was once the only seaport of West Canada as well as the Northwestern region of the United States, but it prospered very little then with an undeveloped hinterland despite its monopolistic character. Whereas as soon as the rival ports arose, Vancouver on its own side, and Seattle and Tacoma on the American side, all within the same distance as Hongkong is to Canton, all of them because of a developed hinterland prospered wonderfully, despite the keen competition between them as seaports. Thus, we see that competitive seaports like Vancouver, Seattle, and Tacoma instead of killing Victoria, as was once supposed by shortsighted people, have made it more prosperous than ever. Then, why doubt that a prosperous Canton and a developed China would not give the same result to Hongkong? This is but a natural outcome. Therefore, there should be no fear that a prosperous Canton and a developed China would be harmful to Hongkong as a free port. So, instead of doing the utmost as hitherto to hinder the development of Canton as a seaport, the Hongkong authorities should do their utmost to encourage such a project. Besides, the development of Canton and South China will benefit the English as a whole commercially a hundred times more than Hongkong can do at present. Although the local authorities of that crown colony do not see far enough to realize it, however, I believe that the great statesmen and captains of industries in the now mightiest empire of the world would surely see it. With this belief in my mind I feel quite safe in giving publicity to the scheme of my international development of Canton as a world port in South China.

Canton is situated at the head of the Canton Delta, which is formed by the junction of three rivers—the Sikiang or West River, the Peikiang or North River, and the Tungkiang or East River. The area of this delta is about 3,000 square miles and it has the most fertile alluvial soil known in China. The land yields three crops a year—two crops of rice and one crop of other products such as potatoes or beets. In silk culture, it gives eight crops every year. The most delicious fruits of many varieties are produced in this delta. This is the most thickly populated district of all China. Within this delta and its immediate neighborhood, more than half of the population of Kwangtung province is found. This is the reason why, despite the great productivity of this fertile delta, large quantities of foods have to be supplied by the surrounding country as well as by foreign imports. Before the age of machinery Canton for centuries was well known as an industrial center of Eastern Asia. The workmanship and

英领哥伦比亚域多利港[50]之例，彼固尝为西坎拿大[51]与美国西北区之唯一海港矣。然而即使有独占之性质，而当时腹地贫穷，未经开发，其为利益，实乃甚小。乃至一方有温哥华起于同国方面，他方美国又有些路与打金麻并起为其竞争港，[52]此诸港之距域多利远近恰与香港之距广州相似，而以其腹地开发之故，即使其俱为海港，竞争之切有如是，仍各繁荣非常。所以吾人知竞争海港，有如温哥华、些路、打金麻者，不惟不如短见者所尝推测，以域多利埠置之死地，且又使之繁荣有加于昔。然则何疑于既开发之广东、既繁荣之中国，不能以与此相同之结果与香港耶？实则此本自然之结果而已，不必有虑于广东之开发、中国之繁荣，伤及香港之为自由港矣。如是，香港当局正当以其全力，鼓励此改良广州以为海港一事，不应复如向日以其全力阻止之矣。抑且广州与中国南方之发展，在于商业上所以益英国全体者，不止百倍于香港今日所以益之者。即使此直辖殖民地之地方当局，无此远见以实行之，吾信今日寰球最强之帝国之各大政治家、各实业首领必能见及于此。吾既怀此信念，故吾以为以我国际共同发展广州以为中国南方世界大港之计划，布之公众，绝无碍也。

广州位于广州河汊之顶，此河汊由西江、北江、东江三河流会合而成，全面积有三千英方里，而为在中国最肥饶之冲积土壤。此地每年有三次收获，二次为米作，一次为杂粮，如马铃薯或甜菜之类。其在蚕丝每年有八次之收成。此河汊又产最美味之果实多种。在中国，此为住民最密之区域，广东全省人口过半住于此河汊及其附近。此所以纵有河汊沃壤所产出巨额产物，犹须求多数之食料于邻近之地与外国也。在机器时代以前，广州以东亚实业中心著名者几百年矣。其人

handicraft of its people are still unequaled in many parts of the world. If machinery will be introduced in its industries under our international development scheme, Canton will soon recover its former grandeur as a great manufacturing center.

As a world port, Canton is in a most advantageous position. Being situated at the junction of three navigable rivers and at the head of the ocean navigation it is a pivot of inland water as well as ocean communication in South China. If the Southwestern railway system is completed, then Canton will be equal in importance to the two great ports in North and East China, in regard to transportation facilities. The ocean approach of Canton is generally deep excepting at two points which can be easily trained and dredged to enable modern liners to pass in and out at any hour. The deep water line of the ocean reaches up to Lingting Island, where the depth is from 8 to 10 fathoms. Above Lingting, the channel gets shallower (about 3 or 4 fathoms) and runs about 15 miles up to the Fumen Entrance. From this point the water becomes deep again (between 6 and 10 fathoms) right up to the Second Bar—a distance of 20 miles. At the Second Bar, the water is about 18 to 20 feet deep for only a few hundred yards. After crossing the Second Bar, the water becomes deep again for a distance of 10 miles averaging about 30 feet deep up to the First Bar which will be the city limit of our future Canton.

To improve the Approach to Canton, I suggest that two submerged training walls be built at the left side of Canton Estuary above Lingting Island—one from the shore to the head of the Kongsu Bank, and another from the end of the same bank to the head of the Lingting Bank. The first training wall will be 3 to 4 feet under water just at the same level of the bank. The second wall will be from 4 feet at one end to 16 feet at the other, which are the levels of the respective banks which it connects. (See (1) (3) Map XI.) It will cross a channel of 24 feet deep between them. These two walls together with the four-foot Kongsu Bank will act as one continuous wall and will direct the undercurrent which now runs between the left shore and Lingting Bank, into the middle part of the estuary, thus cutting a channel between the bar and the bank of the same name to meet the deep water on the west side of Lingting Island. On the right side of the Canton Estuary, a training wall should be built from the lower part of Fraser Bank in a southeasterly direction across the 24-foot channel into the Lingting Bar ending at the east edge of that bar.

民之工作手艺，至今在世界中仍有多处不能与匹。若在吾国际共同发展实业计划之下，使用机器，助其工业，则广州不久必复其昔日为大制造中心之繁盛都会矣。

以世界海港论，广州实居于最利便之地位。既已位于此可容航行之三江会流一点，又在海洋航运之起点，所以既为中国南方内河水运之中轴，又为海洋交通之枢纽也。如使西南铁路系统完成，则以其运输便利论，广州之重要将与中国北方、东方两大港相侔[53]矣。广州通大洋之水路大概甚深，惟有二处较浅，而此二处又甚易范之以堤，且浚渫之，使现代航海最大之船可以随时出入无碍也。海洋深水线，直到零丁岛边，该处水深自八英寻至十英寻。自零丁以上，水道稍浅（其深约三四英寻），以达于虎门，凡十五英里。自虎门起，水乃复深，自六英寻至十英寻。直至莲花山脚之第二闩洲，其长二十英里；在第二闩洲处，仅有数百码水深自十八英尺至二十英尺而已。过第二闩洲后，其水又深，平均得三十英尺者约十英里，以至于第一闩洲，此即吾人所欲定为将来广州港面水界之处也。将改良此通广州之通海路，吾意须在广东河口零丁岛上游左边建两水底范堤：其一，由海岸筑至东新坦头，他一则由该坦尾起筑至零丁坦顶上。此第一范堤之顶，应在水面下三四英尺，约与该坦同高。第二范堤一端低于水面四英尺，一端低十六英尺，各按所联之坦之高低（参照第十一图之1及3），此堤须横断两坦间深二十四英尺之水道。合此两堤与此四英尺高之东新坦，将成为一连续海堤之功用，可以导引现在冲过左边海岸与零丁岛之间之下层水流，入于河口当中一部。于是可以在零丁横沙与同名之坦中间，开一新水道，而与零丁岛右边深水相接。在广东河口右边须建一范堤，自万顷沙外面沙堤下面起，向东南行，横断二十四英尺深之水道，直穿过零丁横沙至其东头尽处为止（参照第十一图之2）。

(See (2) Map XI.) Thus, with these submerged walls on both sides of the estuary to confine the undercurrent in the middle, a very deep channel can be formed to connect with the Fumen Entrance at one end and the Lingting trough at the other both of which are about 50 feet deep so that a thoroughfare from deep sea right up to the Second Bar of the Pearl River will be created.

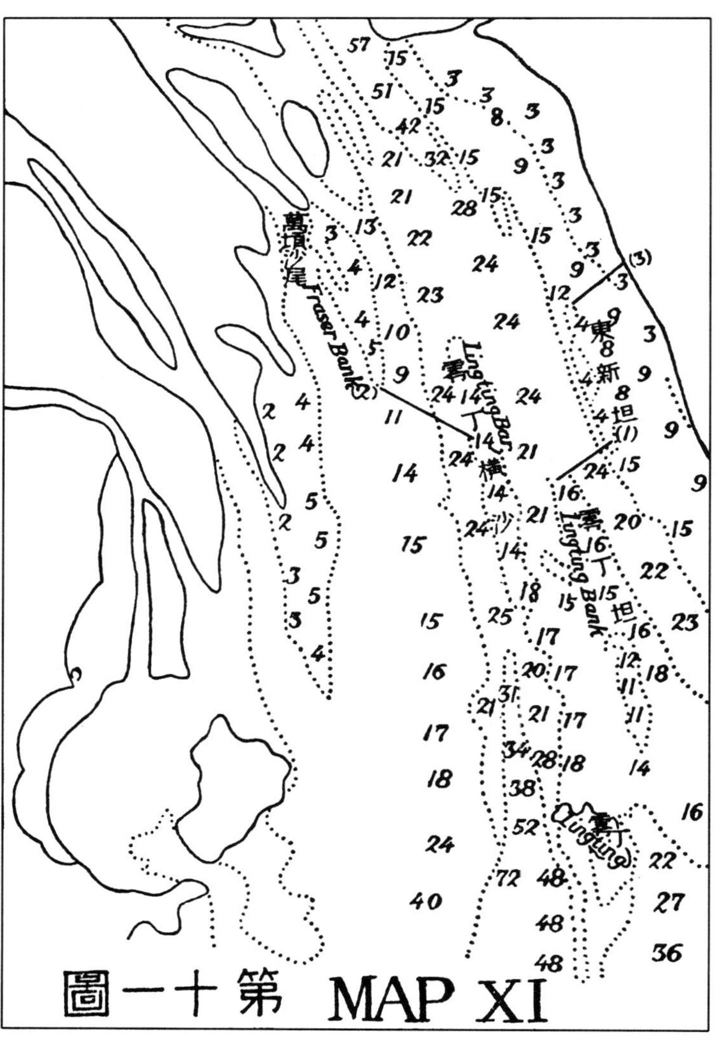

第十一圖 MAP XI

These submerged sea walls taken together are about 8 miles in length and will be built only 6 to 12 feet from the bottom of the sea. The expenses will not be much while the acceleration of the natural reclamation process will be very great. Thus, the lands that will be formed on both sides by these walls will far more than repay the expenses of the work of building these walls.

To regulate the Approach of Canton, in that part of the Pearl River from the Fumen Entrance to Whampoa, I suggest that the East River Estuaries be concentrated in a single outlet by using the uppermost channel which joins the Pearl River at the lower point of Davids Island. The other outlets of the East River, which joins the Pearl River below the Second Bar, should be closed up by dams built to the height of the normal water level so as to permit them to serve as flood channels in the rainy season. By concentrating the whole volume of water of the East River above the Second Bar, a stronger current could be obtained to flush the upper part of this section of the river.

如是，以此河口两边各水底堤，限制下层水流，使趋中央一路，则可得一甚深之水道。自虎门起，直通零丁口，约五十英尺深。于是可得创造一自深海直达珠江之第二闩洲之通路矣。

合此各水底堤计之，其长约八英里，而其高只须离海底六英尺至十二英尺而已。其所费者应不甚多，而其使自然填筑进行加速之力则甚大。故因此诸堤两岸新成之地，必能偿还筑此诸堤之工程所费，且大有余裕也。

整治此广州通海之路，自虎门至黄埔一段珠江，吾意须使东江出口集中于一支，即用其最上之水道，于鹿步墟岛下游一点与珠江合流者。其他在第二闩洲以下与珠江会流各支，概须筑与寻常水面同高之堰，以截塞之，至入雨期则仍以供宣泄洪水之水道之用。此集会东江全流于第二闩洲上面，可以得更强之水，以冲洗珠江上部也。

In the training works of this section, I propose that several jetties should be built as follows: First, a jetty from Elliot Island at point (A) to the farther side of Calcutta Shoal opposite the lower point of Parker Island. This will block the current between Elliot Island and Calcutta Shoal and divert it into the present 36-foot channel thus making it deeper by its natural force. Second, another jetty from Bolton Island, at point (B) to midstream terminating at the lower side of the Second Bar, on the right side of the river. Third, a jetty from the lower point of Pattinger Island at (C) to midstream terminating at the lower side of the same bar on the left side of the river. Thus the Second Bar would be flushed by the concentrated current created by these two jetties. The shallow bottom above these jetties should be dredged to the required depth. If a rocky bottom is found at this bar it should be blasted and removed, so as to give a uniform depth to the whole approach. Fourth, the channel between the right bank of the river and Bolton Island should be blocked up at (D). Fifth, a jetty from Pattinger Island at (E) to the head of the Second Bar Bank in midstream so as to cut off the current at the left side of the river and to increase the velocity in the middle channel. Sixth, a jetty from the right shore at (F) about midway between Danes Island and the Second Bar, should be built to the head of the Midstream Shoal so as to cut off the current at the right side of the river. And seventh, another jetty from the lower point of Davids Island at (G) to midstream opposite to the end of jetty (F). Jetties (G) and (F) will concentrate the current of the upper Pearl River while at the same time jetty (G) will also turn the East River current into the same direction as that of the Pearl River. (See Map XII.)

By these seven jetties, the current between Whampoa and Fumen could be controlled and the bottom of the river flushed to a depth of 40 feet or more, thus creating a thoroughfare for ocean-going steamers from the open sea right up to the city of Canton. These jetties taken together will be not more than 5 miles in length and mostly in very shallow water. After the building of these jetties, land will be rapidly formed between jetties along both sides of the channel by natural process. The reclaimed land alone will be quite enough to pay the expenses of constructing these jetties, aside from the fact that the main object of regulating the river and opening up a deep channel for ocean transportation will have been realized.

此一段范水工程，吾意须筑多数之坝如下：第一，自江鸥沙之 A 点筑一坝，至攋沙岛低端对面加里吉打滩边。此坝所以堵截江鸥沙与加里吉打滩中间之水流，而转之入于现在三十六英尺深之水道，以其自然之力浚使更深。第二，于此河右岸，由海心沙之 B 点起另筑一坝，至中流第二闩洲下端为终点。第三，于此河左岸，自漳澎尾沙下头 C 点筑一坝，至中流，亦以第二闩洲下端为终点。以是借此两坝所束集中水流之力，可以刷去第二闩洲，其两坝上面浅处，则可浚之至得所求之深为止。若发现河底有岩石，则应炸而去之，然后全部通路可得一律之水深也。第四，在此河右岸与海心沙中间之水道，须堵塞之于 D 点（即瑞成围头）。第五，在漳澎常安围上游之 E 点起筑一坝，至第二闩洲坦之上端中流。如是，则此河左边水流截断，而中央水道之流速可以增加也。第六，在右岸长洲岛与第二闩洲之间适中之处 F 点起筑一坝，至中流滩之顶上，以截断此河右边之水流。第七，于鹿步墟岛下端 G 点起筑一坝，至中流，与前述之 F 坝相对。此 EG 两坝所以集中珠江上段水流，而 G 坝同时又导引东江，使其流向与珠江同一也。（参照第十二图）

以此七坝，自黄埔以迄虎门之水流可得有条理，而冲刷河底可致四十英尺以上之深，如是则为航洋巨舶开一通路，自公海直通至广州城矣。合此诸坝，其长当不过五英里，而又大半建于浅水处。自建坝以后，水道两旁各坝之间，以其自然之力，新填地出现必极速。单以所填之地而论，必足以偿还筑坝所费。况又有整治珠江与为海洋运输开一深水道之两大目的，可由此而实现乎！

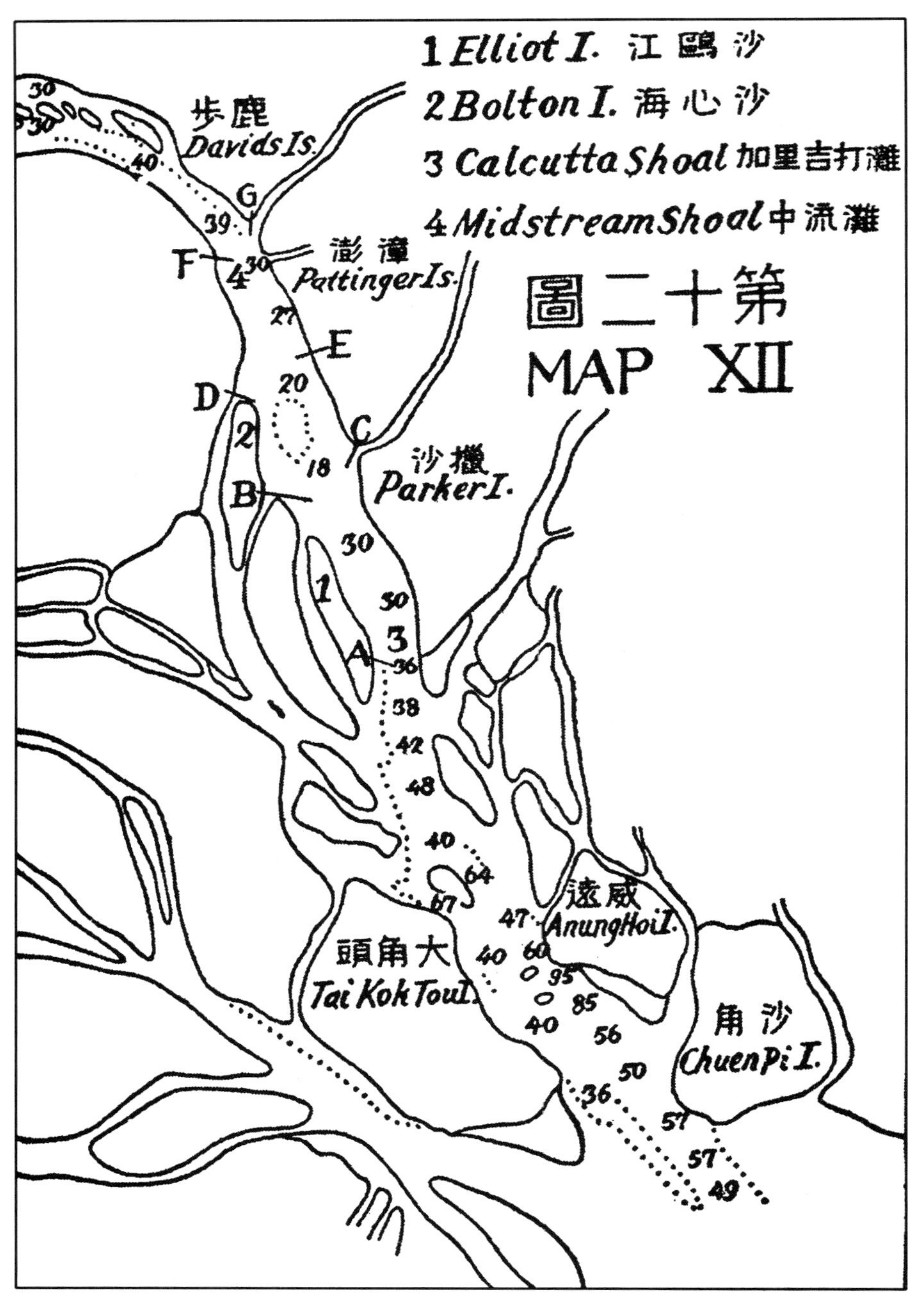
1 Elliot I. 江鷗沙
2 Bolton I. 海心沙
3 Calcutta Shoal 加里吉打灘
4 Midstream Shoal 中流灘
圖二十第
MAP XII
步鹿
Davids Is.
G
F
Pattinger Is.
E
D
C
B
A
Parker I.
遠威
Anunghoi I.
頭角大
Tai Kok Tou I.
角沙
Chuen Pi I.

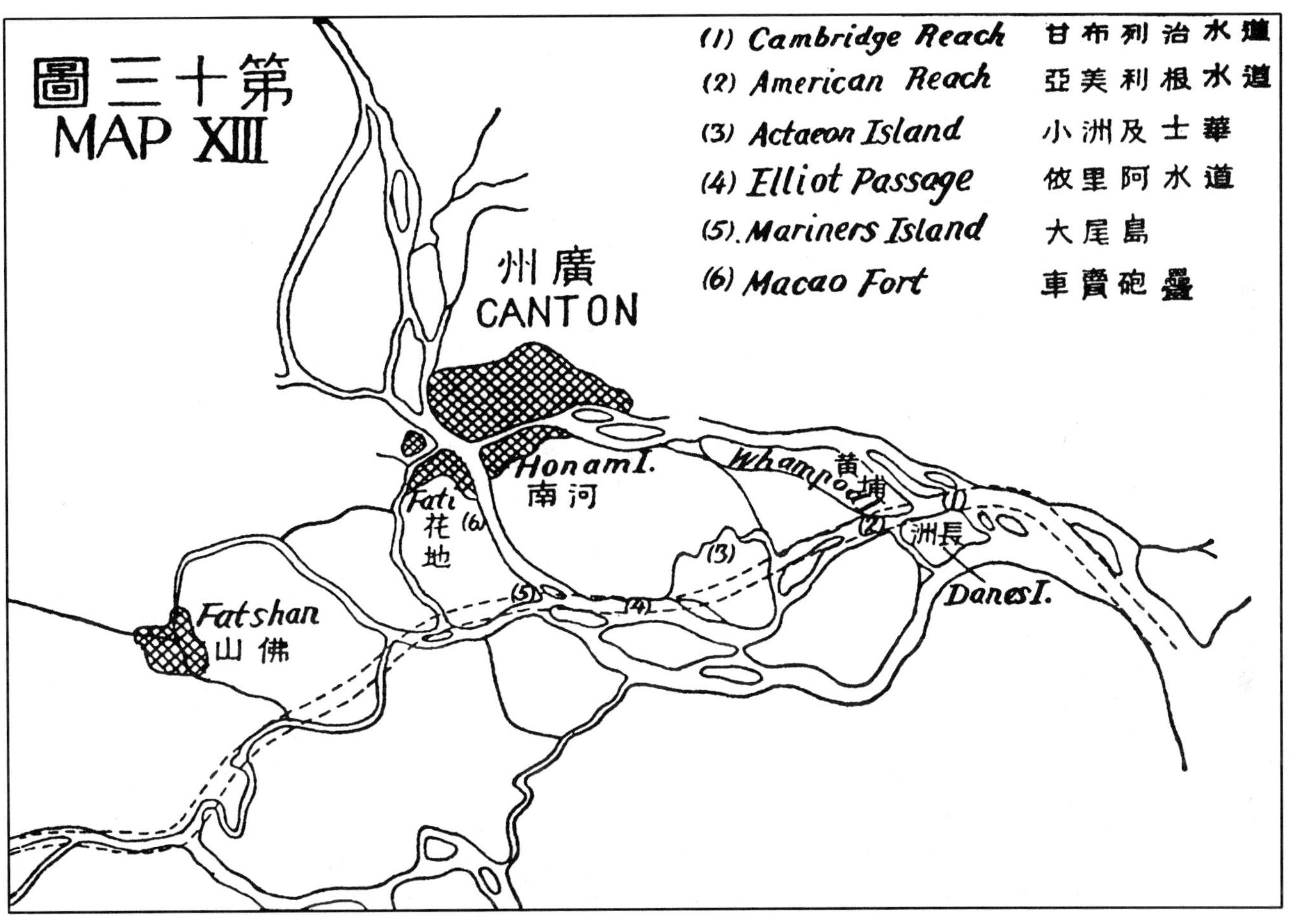

第十三圖
MAP XIII
(1) Cambridge Reach 甘布利治水道
(2) American Reach 亞美利根水道
(3) Actaeon Island 小洲及士華
(4) Elliot Passage 攸里阿水道
(5). Mariners Island 大尾島
(6) Macao Fort 車賣砲壘
廣州
CANTON
Honam I.
南河
Whampoa
黃埔
洲長
Danes I.
Fati
花地
Fatshan
佛山
(1)
(2)
(3)
(4)
(5)
(6)

Having dealt with the approach to Canton, we may now take up the improvement of Canton City itself as a world port. The harbor limit of Canton will be at the First Bar. From there, the harbor will follow the deep water of Cambridge Reach and the water between Whampoa and Danes Island into American Reach. At this point it will cut through Actaeon Island to the south of Honam Island and follow the Elliot Passage to Mariners Island. From Mariners Island following the Fatshan Creek, a straight channel should be cut in a southwesterly direction to the Tamchow Channel. Thus, a new waterway will be made from the First Bar to Tamchow Channel, a distance of about 25 miles. This waterway will be the main outlet of the North River as well as a thoroughfare for the West River, and will also serve as the harbor of Canton. By conveying all the water of the North River and a part of that of the West River through this waterway, the current will be strong enough to flush the harbor to a depth of 40 feet or more. (See Map XIII.)

The new city of Canton will be extended from Whampoa to Fatshan, separated by the Macao Fort and Shameen Reaches. The section that lies east of this water should be developed into commercial quarters and that west of it into factory quarters. The factory section should be transected by canals connecting with the Fati and Fatshan creeks so as to give cheap transportation facilities to every factory. In the commercial section, tidal wharves with modern plants and warehouses should be provided. A bund should be built from the First Bar Island along the north side of the new waterway, the west side of Honam to connect with the bund of Shameen, and the northwestern side of Canton city. Another bund should be built from above Fati along the east side of Fati Island to Mariners Island thence turning southwest along the left bank of the new waterway. The Front Reach, that is, the river between the present Canton city and Honam Island should be filled up from the upper point of Honam to Whampoa for city building.

In regard to the question of remuneration, the development of Canton as a world port will be the most profitable undertaking of the kind in the

International Development Scheme. Because, besides its commanding position as a commercial metropolis and its possession of advantageous facilities as a manufacturing center of South China, a modern residential city is in great demand in this part of the country. The well-to-do people and merchants of this rich delta as well as those retired Chinese merchants and millionaires abroad all over the world are very eager to spend their remaining days at home. But owing to the lack of modern conveniences and comforts they reluctantly remain in foreign countries. Thus to build a new

吾人既为广州通海水路作计，则可次及改良广州城以为世界商港一事矣。广州港面水界应至第一闩洲为止。由此处起，港面应循甘布列治水道（乌涌与大吉沙之间），经长洲、黄埔两岛之间，以入亚美利根水道（深井与仑头之间）。于是凿土华、小洲之间，开一新路，以达于河南岛之南端，复循依里阿水道（沥滘[54]、下滘之间），以至大尾岛（三山对面）。于是循佛山旧水道，更凿一新水道，直向西南方，与潭洲水道会流。如是，由第一闩洲起以达潭洲水道，成一新水路矣，其长当有二十五英里。此水路将为北江之主要出口，又以与西江相通连。一面又作为广州港面，以北江水量全部及西江水量一部，经此水路以注于海。故其水流之强，将必足以刷洗此港面，令有四十英尺以上之深也。（参观第十三图）

新建之广州市，应跨有黄埔与佛山，而界之以车卖炮台及沙面水路。此水以东一段地方，应发展之以为商业地段；其西一段，则以为工厂地段。此工厂一区，又应开小运河以与花地及佛山水道通连，则每一工厂均可得有廉价运送之便利也。在商业地段，应副之以应潮高下之码头，与现代设备及仓库，而筑一堤岸。自第一闩洲起，沿新水路北边及河南岛西边，与沙面堤岸联为一起。又另自花地上游起筑一堤岸，沿花地岛东边，至大尾乃转向西南，沿新水路左岸筑之。其现在省城与河南岛中间之水道，所谓省河者，应行填塞。自河南头填起，直至黄埔岛，以供市街之用。从利益问题论之，开发广州以为一世界商港，实为此国际共同发展计划内三大港中最有利润之企业。所以然者，广州占商业中枢之首要地位，又握有利之条件，恰称为中国南方制造中心，更加以此部地方之要求新式住宅地甚大也。此河汊内之殷富商民与华人在外国经商致富暮年退隐者，无不切盼归乡，度其余年；但坐缺乏新式之便宜与享乐之故，彼等不免踌躇，仍留外国。

city with modern equipments for residential purposes alone, in Canton, would pay splendidly. The land outside of Canton is at present about 200 dollars a mow. If the land marked off for the future city of Canton should be taken up by the State on the same basis as elsewhere in this International Development Scheme, immediately after the streets are laid out and improvements made, the price of land would rise from ten to fifty times its original value.

The landscape of the environment of Canton is exceptionally beautiful and charming. It is an ideal place for planning a garden city with attractive parks. The location of the city of Canton resembles that of Nanking but is of greater magnitude and beauty. It possesses three natural elements—deep water, high mountains, and vast extent of level land which furnish facilities for an industrial and commercial center and provide as well natural scenery for the enjoyment of man. The beautiful valleys and hills of the northern shore of the Pearl River could be laid out for ideal winter resorts and the high mountain tops could be utilized for summer resorts.

Within the city limits at the northwest corner, a rich coal field has been found. When the coal is mined and modern plants for generating electricity and producing gas are provided, then cheap electricity and gas could be had for transportation, for manufacturing, for lighting, heating, and cooking purposes. And so the present wasteful methods of transportation, and expensive fuels for manufacturing and cooking for the populous city of Canton can be done away with entirely. Thus great economic wonders could be wrought by such improvements. The present population of Canton is over a million and if our development plan is carried out, this city would grow in leaps and bounds within a very short time. The population will become greater than any other city and the profit of our undertaking will become correspondingly large.

然则建一新市街于广州，加以新式设备，专供住居之用，必能获非常之利矣。广州城附近之地，今日每亩约值二百元，如使划定以为将来广州市用之地，即应用前此所述方法收用之，则划定街道加以改良之后，地价立可升高至原价之十倍至五十倍矣。

广州附近景物，特为美丽动人，若以建一花园都市，加以悦目之林囿，真可谓理想之位置也。广州城之地势，恰似南京，而其伟观与美景，抑又过之。夫自然之原素有三：深水、高山与广大之平地也。此所以利便其为工商业中心，又以供给美景以娱居人也。珠江北岸美丽之陵谷，可以经营之以为理想的避寒地，而高岭之巅，又可利用之以为避暑地也。

在西北隅市街界内，已经发现一丰富之煤矿。若开采之，而加以新式设计，以产出电力及煤气供给市中，则可资其廉价之电力、煤气以为制造、为运输，又使居民得光、得热、得以炊爨也。如是则今日耗费至多之运输，与烦费之用薪炊爨制造，行于此人烟稠密之市中者，可以悉免矣。是此种改良，可得经济上之奇效也。现在广州居民一百万，若行吾计划，则于极短时期之中将见有飞跃之进步，其人口将进至超过一切都市，而吾人企业之利益，亦比例而与之俱增矣。

• Part II The Improvement of the Waterway System of Canton

The most important waterway system in South China is the Canton system. Besides this the others are not of much importance and will be dealt with elsewhere with their ports. In dealing with the Canton system of waterways, I have to divide it as follows:

a. The Canton Delta.

b. The West River.

• 第二部　改良广州水路系统

中国南部最重要之水路系统，为广州系统。除此以外皆不甚重要，将于论各商埠时附述之。论广州水路系统，吾将分之为下四项：

甲　广州河汊。

乙　西江。

c. The North River.

d. The East River.

a. The Canton Delta

To improve the Canton Delta we have to consider the proposition from three points of view: First, the problem of flood prevention; second, the problem of navigation; and third, the problem of reclamation. Each of these problems affects the others so the solution of one will help that of the others.

First, the problem of flood prevention. The frequent repetition of floods in recent years has wrought great disasters to the people in the neighborhood of Canton. It has destroyed lives by the thousands and property by the millions. The part which suffers most is the country between Canton and Lupao, lying just immediately north of the Canton Delta. This fatal spot is, I think, created by the silting up of the main outlet of the North River immediately below Sainam. On account of this, the North River has to find its outlets through the West River by the short canal at Samshui and through two small streams, one from Sainam, and another from Lupao. The former runs in a northeasterly direction and the latter in a southeasterly direction and they join at Kuanyao. From this point, the river takes a northeasterly course as far as Kumli, thence, turning southeast, passes the west suburb of Canton. Since the North River is silted up below Sainam, its channel above that spot is also getting shallower every year. At present the river above Samshui city is only about four or five feet deep. When the North River rises its water generally finds its way into the West River through the Kongkun Canal. But if the West River should rise at the same time, then there would be no outlet for the North River and its water would accumulate until it overflowed its dikes above and below Lupao. This would naturally cause the dikes to break at some point and allow the water to rush out and flood the whole country that is meant to be protected by these dikes. The remedy for the North River is to reopen the main outlet below Sainam and have the whole channel dredged deep from Tsingyuen to the sea. Fortunately, in our improvement of the navigation of the Canton Delta, we have to do the same thing; so this one work will serve two purposes.

The remedy for the West River is that the shallow part just at its junction with the sea between Wangkum and Sanchoo Islands should be trained by walls on both sides—a long one on the left, and a short one on the right—so as to concentrate the current to cut the river bed here to

丙　北江。

丁　东江。

甲　广州河汊

吾人论广州河汊之改良，须从三观察点以立议：第一，防止水灾问题；第二，航行问题；第三，填筑新地问题。每一问题皆能加影响于他二者，故解决其一，即亦有裨于其他也。

第一，防止水灾问题。近年水灾频频发生，于广州附近人民实为巨害，其丧失生命以千计，财产以百万计。受害最甚者，为广州与芦包间，其地恰在广州河汊之直北。吾以为此不幸之点，实因西南下游北江正流之淤塞而成。以此之故，北江须经由三水之短河道，以入西江，借为出路；同时又经由两小溪流，一自西南，一自芦包，以得出路。此二溪者，一向东南行，一向东北行，而再合流于官窑。自官窑起，复东北流，至于金利，又折而东南流，经过广州之西关。自北江在西南下游淤塞之后，其淤塞点之上游一段，亦逐年变浅；现在三水县城上游之处，亦仅深四五英尺。当北江水涨之时，常借冈根河（即思贤滘）以泄其水于西江。但若西江同时水涨，则北江之水无从得其出路，惟有停积，至高过芦包上下游之基围[55]而后已。如是，自然基围有数处被水冲决，水即横流，而基围所护之地域全区均受水灾矣。欲治北江，须重开西南下面之北江正流，而将自清远至海一段，一律浚深。幸而吾人改良广州河汊之航行时，亦正有事于此项浚深，故一举而可两得也。

救治西江，须于其入海处横琴与三灶两岛之间两岸，各筑一堤，左长右短以范之。如是则将水流集中，以割此河床，使成深二十英尺

a depth of twenty feet or more. In this way, a uniform depth is secured, for after passing the Moto Entrance the West River has an average depth of 20 to 30 feet right along its whole course through this delta. With a uniform depth all the way to the sea, the undercurrent will run quickly and drain off the flood water more rapidly. Besides the deepening process, both shores should be regulated so as to give a uniform width to the channel. Midstream shoals and islands should be removed.

The East River Valley does not suffer so severely from floods as those of the other two rivers, the West and the North, and its remedy will be provided in the regulation of the river for navigation. This will be dealt with in that connection.

Second, the problem of navigation in the Canton Delta in connection with the three rivers. In dealing with this question we commence with the West River. In former days the traffic between the West River Valley and Canton always passed through Fatshan and Samshui, a distance of about 35 miles. But since the silting up of the Fatshan Channel below Sainam, the traffic has to take a great detour by descending the Pearl River southeastward as far as Fumen, then turn northwest into the Shawan Channel, then southeast into the Tamchow Channel, and then west into the Tailiang Channel and south into the Junction Channel and Maning Reach. Here it enters into the West River and runs a northwesterly direction up to Samshui Junction on this river. The whole journey covers a distance of about 95 miles, which compared with the old route is longer by 60 miles. The traffic between Canton and the West River Valley is very great. At present there are many thousands of steam launches plying between Canton City and the outlying districts, and more than half of that number are carrying traffic to and fro on the West River. Every boat has to run 95 miles on each trip whereas if the channel between Samshui and Canton is improved, the distance would be only 35 miles. What a great saving it will be!

In our project to improve the Canton Approach and Harbor, I

suggested the draining of a deep channel from the sea to Whampoa and from Whampoa to Tamchow Channel. We now have to prolong this channel from its Tamchow Junction up to Samshui Junction on the West River. This Channel should be made at least 20 feet deep so as to join the deeper water of the West River above the Samshui Junction. And the same depth should be maintained in the North River itself some distance above Samshui, so as to give facility for the navigation of larger vessels up the river when the whole waterway is improved.

以上之水道；如是则水深之齐一，可得而致。盖自磨刀门以上，通沿广州河汊之一段，西江平均有二十英尺至三十英尺之深也。如有全段一律之水深，以达于海，则下层水流将愈速，而洪水时泄去其水更速矣。除此浚深之工程以外，两岸务须改归齐整，令全河得一律之河阔；中流之暗礁及沙洲，均应除去。

东江流域之受水灾，不如西、北二江之深重。则整治此河，以供航行，即可得其救治，留俟该项论之。

第二，航行问题。广州河汊之航行问题，与三江相连，论此问题，须自西江始。往日西江流域与广州间往来载货，常经由三水与佛山，此路全长三十五英里。但自佛山水道由西南下游起淤塞之后，载货船只须为大迂回：沿珠江而下以至虎门，转向西北以入沙湾水道，又转向东南入于潭洲水道，西入于大良水路，又南入于黄色水道（自合成围至莺哥嘴）及马宁水路，于此始入西江。西北泝江以至三水西北江合流之处，此路全长九十五英里，比之旧路多六十英里。而广州与西江流域之来往船只，其数甚多，现在广州与近县来往之小火轮有数千艘，其中有大半为载货往来西江者。夫使广州、三水间水道得其改良，则今之每船一往复须行九十五英里者，忽减而为三十五英里也，其所益之大，为何如哉！

在吾改良广州通海路及港面之计划，吾曾提议浚一深水道，自海至于黄埔，又由黄埔以至潭洲水道。今吾人更须将此水道延长，自潭洲水道合流点起，以至三水与西江合流之处。此水道至少须有二十英尺水深，以与西江在三水上游深水处相接。而北江自身，亦须保有与此同一之水深，至于三水上游若干里之处，所以便于该河上流既经改良之后大舶之航行也。

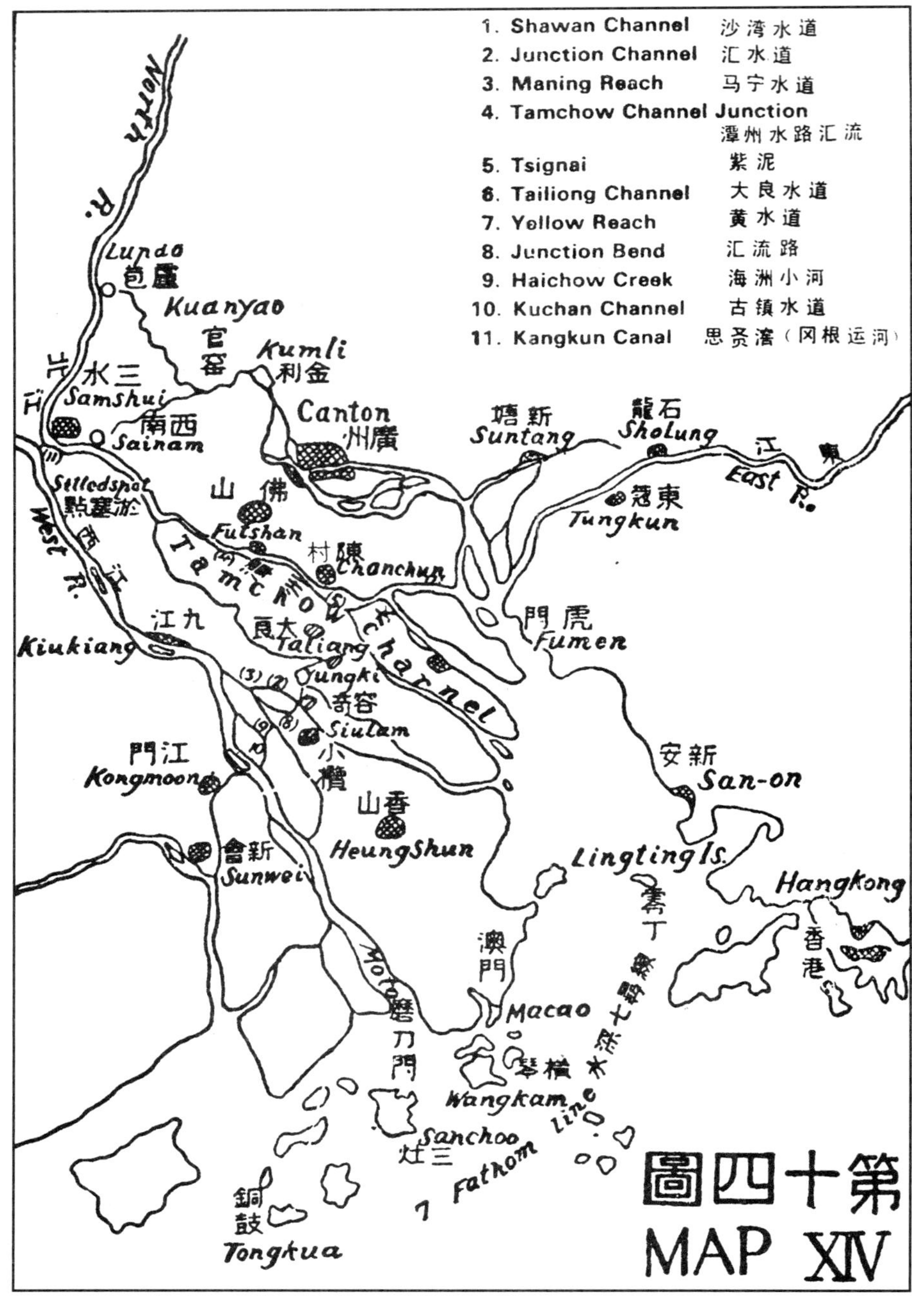
1. Shawan Channel 沙湾水道
2. Junction Channel 汇水道
3. Maning Reach 马宁水道
4. Tamchow Channel Junction 潭州水路汇流
5. Tsignai 紫泥
6. Tailiong Channel 大良水道
7. Yellow Reach 黄水道
8. Junction Bend 汇流路
9. Haichow Creek 海洲小河
10. Kuchan Channel 古镇水道
11. Kangkun Canal 思贤滘（冈根运河）
North R.
Lundo
Kuanyao
Kumli
Samshui
Sainam
Canton
Suntang
Sholung
East R.
Tungkun
Stilledspot
Fatshan
West R.
Tamchow Channel
Chanchun
Fumen
Kiukiang
Taliang
Yungki
Siulam
Kongmoon
San-on
HeungShun
Sunwei
Lingting Is.
Hangkong
Macao
Wangkam
Sanchoo
7 Fathom Line
Tongkua
第十四圖
MAP XIV

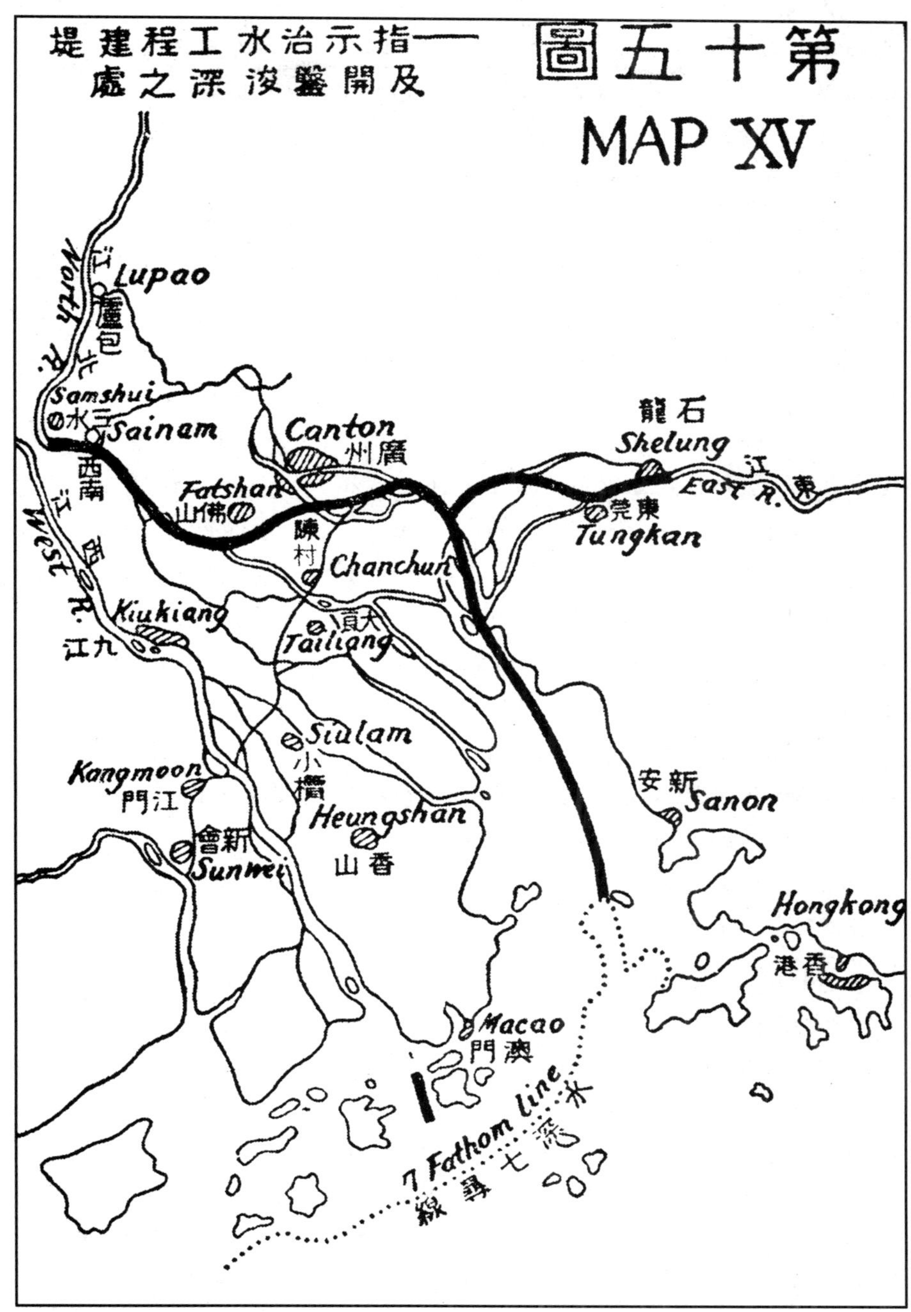

第十五圖
指示治水工程建堤及開鑿浚深之處
MAP XV
North R.
北江
Lupao
蘆包
Samshui
三水
Sainam
西南
Canton
廣州
Fatshan
佛山
陳村
Chanchun
石龍
Shelung
東江
East R.
東莞
Tungkan
West R.
西江
Kiukiang
九江
大良
Tailiang
Siulam
小欖
Kangmoon
江門
新會
Sunwei
Heungshan
香山
新安
Sanon
Hongkong
香港
Macao
澳門
7 Fathom line
七尋深水線

To improve the East River for navigation in the Canton Delta we should concentrate the current of its estuaries into one single outlet by using the right channel which joins the Pearl River at Davids Island, thus deepening the channel as well as shortening the distance between Canton and the East River districts when the upper part of the river is improved.

Another improvement in the Canton Delta for navigation is the opening of a straight canal between Canton City and Kongmoon so as to shorten the passage of the heavy traffic between this metropolis and the Szeyap districts. This canal should begin by straightening the Chanchun Creek south of Canton as far as Tsznai. Then crossing the Tamchow Channel it should enter into the Shuntuck Creek and follow this creek to its end emerging into the Shuntuck Branch at right angles. From there, a new canal must be cut straight to the turn of the Tailiang Channel near Yungki, then the canal should follow this channel through Yellow Reach as far as the Junction Bend. Here another new canal must be cut through to the Hoichow Creek, then it should follow Kuchan Channel to the main channel of the West River, and crossing it enter into the Kongmoon Branch. Thus, a straight canal can be formed between Canton and Kongmoon. In order to understand the improvement of the Canton Delta more clearly see Maps XIV and XV.

Third, the problem of reclamation. A very profitable undertaking in the Canton Delta is the reclamation of new land. This process has been going on for centuries. Many thousands of acres of new land are thus being added to cultivation from year to year. But hitherto all the reclamation has been effected by private enterprise only, and there are no regulations for it. So sometimes this private enterprise causes great detriment to public welfare such as blocking up navigable channels and causing floods. A glaring case is the reclamation work just above the Moto Islands, which blocks more than half of the Main Channel of the West River. In the regulation of the West River, I propose to cut this new land away. In order to protect the public welfare, the reclamation work in this Delta must be taken up by the State and the profits must go to defray the expenses of improving this waterway system for navigation, as well as for the prevention of floods. At present, the area that can be gradually reclaimed is large in extent. On the left side of the Canton Estuary, the available area is about 40 square miles, and on the right side, about 140 square miles. On the estuaries of the West River from Macao to Tongkwa Island, there is an available area of about 200 square miles. Of the 380 square miles, about one fourth would be ready for reclamation within the next ten years. That is to say about 95 square miles could be reclaimed

为广州河汉之航行以改良东江，吾人应将其出口之水流，集中于鹿步墟岛上面之处与珠江合流之最右之一水道。此所以使水道加深，又使异日上流既经改良之日，广州与东江地区路程更短也。

为航行计，广州河汉更须有一改良，即开一直运河于广州与江门之间，此所以使省城与四邑间之运输得一捷径也。此运河应先将陈村小河改直，达天紫泥，于是横过潭洲水道，以入于顺德小河。循此小河，从直角入于顺德支流。由此处须凿新运河一段，直至大良水道近容奇曲处（竹林）。又循此水道，通过黄水道，至汇流路（南沙、小揽之间起莺哥嘴至冈美之对岸）为止。于此处须更凿一段新运河，以通海洲小河，循古镇水道，以达西江正流，横过之以入于江门支流。此即为广州、江门间直达之运河矣。欲更清晰了解广州河汉之改良，可观附图第十四、第十五。

第三，填筑新地问题。在广州河汉，最有利之企业，为填筑新地。此项进行，已兆始于数百年前。于是其所增新地供农作之用者，岁逾百十顷。但前此所有填筑，仅由私人尽力经营，非有矩矱[56]。于是有时私人经营，有阻塞航路、诱致洪水等等事情，危及公安；如在磨刀岛上游之填筑工事，闭塞西江正流水路过半，其最著者也。论整治西江，吾意须将此新坦削去。为保护公安计，此河汉之填筑工作，必须归之国家。而其利益，则须以偿因航行及防水灾而改良此水路系统之所费。现在可徐徐填筑之地区，面积极广。在广州河口左岸，可用之地有四十英方里，其右岸有一百四十英方里；在西江河口，东起澳门，西至铜鼓洲，可用之地约二百英方里。此三百八十英方里之中，四分之一可于十年之内填筑成为新坦，即十年之内有九十五英方

and put to cultivation within a decade. As one square mile contains 640 acres and one acre six mow, so 95 square miles will be equal to 364,800 mow. As cultivated land in this part of China generally costs more than fifty dollars a mow, so, if fifty dollars be taken as the average rate, the value of these 364,800 mow would amount to $18,240,000. This will help a great deal to defray the expenses of improving the waterway for navigation and for preventing floods in this Delta.

b. The West River

The West River is at present navigable for comparatively large river steamers up to Wuchow, a distance of 220 miles by water from Canton, and for small steamers up to Nanning, a distance of 500 miles from Canton, at all seasons. As for small crafts, the West River is navigable in most of its branches, west to the Yunnan frontier, north to Kweichow, northeast to Hunan and the Yangtze Valley by the Shingan Canal.

In improving the West River for navigation I shall divide the work into subsections as follows:

(1) From Samshui to Wuchow.
(2) From Wuchow to the junction of the Liukiang.
(3) Kweikiang or the North Branch of the West River from Wuchow to Kweilin and beyond.
(4) The South Branch from Shunchow to Nanning.

(1) From Samshui to Wuchow. This part of the West River is generally deep and does not need much improvement for vessels up to ten-foot draught excepting at a few points. The midstream rocks should be blasted and removed and sand banks and dilating parts should be regulated by submerged dikes to secure a uniform channel and to make the velocity of the current even, so that a stable fairway could be maintained all the year round. The traffic of this river would be sufficiently great to pay for all the improvements which we propose to make.

(2) From Wuchow to the Junction of the Liukiang. At this junction, a river port should be built to connect the deep navigation from the sea and the shallow navigation of Hungshui Kiang and the Liukiang which penetrate the rich mineral districts of Northwest Kwangsi and Southwest Kweichow. This port will be about fifty miles from Shunchow which is the junction of the Nanning branch of the river. So here we have only to improve a distance of fifty miles, for the improvement of

里之地可以填筑，变为耕地也。以一英方里当六百四十英亩，而一英亩当六亩计，九十五英方里将等于三十六万四千八百亩。而中国此方可耕之地，通常不止值五十元一亩，假以平均五十元一亩算，则此三十六万四千八百亩，已值一千八百二十四万元矣。此大有助于偿还此河汉为航行及防水灾所为改良水路之费也。

乙 西江

现在西江之航行，较大之航河汽船可至距广州二百二十英里之梧州，而较小之汽船则可达距广州五百里之南宁，无间冬夏。至于小船，则可通航于各支流，西至云南边界，北至贵州边界，东北则以兴安运河通于湖南以及长江流域。

为航行计改良西江，吾将以其工程细分为四：

一、自三水至梧州。

二、自梧州至柳江口。

三、桂江（即西江之北支）由梧州起，溯流至桂林以上。

四、南支自浔州至南宁。

一、自三水至梧州。西江此段，水道常深，除三数处外，为吃水十英尺以下之船航行计，不须多加改良。其中流岩石须行爆去，其沙质之岸及泛滥之部分应以水底堤范之，使水深一律，而流速亦随之。于是有一确实航路，终年保持不替矣。西江所运货载之多，固尽足以偿还吾今所提议改良之一切费用也。

二、自梧州至柳江口。在柳江口应建一商埠，以联红水江及柳江之浅水航运，与通海之航运。此两江实渗入广西之西北部与贵州之东南部丰富之矿产地区者也。此商埠应设于离浔州五十英里之处，浔州即此江与南宁一支合流处也。是故在此项改良，所须着力之处只有

the river between Shunchow and Wuchow will be included in the plan for the Nanning Port. Dams and locks would be necessary to make this part of the river navigable for ten-foot draught vessels. But these dams at the same time would serve the purpose of producing water power.

(3) Kweikiang or the North Branch of the West River from Wuchow to Kweilin and beyond. As Kweikiang is smaller, shallower and has more rapids along its course, so its improvement will be more difficult than that of the other parts of the waterway. But this will be a very profitable proposition in this Southern waterway project, for this river not only serves the purpose of transportation in this rich territory but will also serve as a passage for through traffic between the Yangtze and the West River valleys. The improvement should commence from the junction at Wuchow up to Kweilin, and thence upward to the Shingan Canal, then downward to the Siang River, and thereby connecting with the Yangtze River. A series of dams and locks should be built for vessels to ascend to the inter-watershed canal and another series should descend on the other side. The expenses of building these two series of dams and locks could not be estimated until accurate surveys are made. But I am sure this project will be a paying one.

(4) From Shunchow to Nanning. This portion of the Yuhkiang is navigable for small steamers up to Nanning, the center of commerce in South Kwangsi. From Nanning small crafts can navigate through the Yuhkiang as far as the east border of Yunnan, and through Tsokiang as far as the north border of Tongking. If this waterway be improved up to Nanning, then it would be the nearest deep river port for the rich mineral districts of the whole southwest corner of China, which includes the whole province of Yunnan, a greater part of Kweichow and half of Kwangsi. The immediate neighborhood of Nanning is also very rich in minerals, such as antimony, tin, iron, coal and also in agricultural products. So to make Nanning the head of a deep water communication system will be a paying proposition. To improve the waterway up to

Nanning, a few dams and locks along its course will have to be built for vessels of ten-foot draught to go up as well as for water power. The expense for this work cannot be estimated without detailed surveys but it would probably be much less than the improvement of Kweikiang from Wuchow to the Shingan Canal.

五十英里，因梧州至浔州一段，为南宁商埠计划所包括也。为使吃水十英尺以上之船可以航行，必须筑堰，且设水闸于此一部分。而此所设之堰，又同时可借以发生水电也。

三、桂江（即西江之北支）由梧州起溯流至桂林以上。桂江较小较浅，而沿江水流又较速，故其改良，比之其他水路更觉困难。然而，此实南方水路规划中，极有利益之案。因此江不特足供此富饶地区运输之目的而已也，又以供扬子江流域与西江流域载货来往孔道[57]之用。此项改良，应自梧州分歧点起，以迄桂林，由此再溯流至兴安运河，顺流至湘江，因之以达长江。于此当建多数之堰及水闸，使船得升至分水界之运河；他方又须建多数之堰闸，以便其降下。此建堰闸所须之费，非经详细调查，不能为预算也。然而吾有所确信者，则此计划为不亏本之计划也。

四、由浔州至南宁。此右江一部分，上至南宁，可通小轮船。南宁者，广西南部之商业中心也。自南宁起，由右江用小船可通至云南东界，由左江可通至越南东京之北界。如使改良水道，以迄南宁，则南宁将为中国西南隅——云南全省、贵州大半省、广西半省——矿产丰富之全地区之最近深水商埠矣。南宁之直接附近又多产锑、锡、煤、铁等矿物，而同时亦富于农产。则经营南宁，以为深水交通系统之顶点，必不失为有利之计划也。改良迄南宁之水道，沿河稍须设堰及水闸，使吃水十英尺之船可以通航，并资之以生电力。此项工程所费，亦非经详细测量不能预算，但比之改良自梧州至兴安运河一节桂江所费，当必大减矣。

c. The North River

The North River from Samshui to Shiuchow is about 140 miles long. The greater part of its course is confined in the hilly districts, but after it emerges from the Tsingyuen Gorge it comes into a wide, open country, which connects with the plain of Canton. Here the dangerous floods occur most often. Since the silting up of its proper outlet below Sainam, the North River from that point up to the gorge has become shallower every year, so the dikes at the left side, that is, on the side of the plain, often break thus causing the inundation of the whole plain above Canton. Thus the regulation of the river at this part has two aspects to be considered: First, the prevention of floods and second, the improvement for navigation. In dealing with the first aspect nothing could be better than deepening the river by dredging. In the improvement of the Canton Approach and Harbor and also of the Canton Delta, we have to cut a deep channel right from the deep sea up to Sainam. In the improvement of the lower part of the North River, we have simply to continue the cutting process higher up until we have a deep channel, say 15 to 20 feet as far as the Tsingyuen Gorge, either by artificial or natural means. By this deepening of the bottom of the river, the present height of the dikes will be quite enough to protect the plains from being flooded.

In dealing with the second aspect, as we have already deepened the part of the river from Sainam to the Tsingyuen Gorge for flood prevention, we have at the same time solved the navigation question. It has now only the upper part to be dealt with. I propose to make this river navigable up to Shiuchow, the center of commerce as well as the center of the coal and iron fields of Northern Kwangtung. To improve the part above the gorge for navigation, dams and locks should be built in one or two places before a ten-foot draught vessel can ascend up to that point. Although this river is parallel with the Hankow-Canton Railway, yet if the coal and iron fields of Shiuchow are properly developed, a deep waterway will still be needed for cheap transportation of such heavy freight as iron and coal to the coast. So to build dams for water power and to construct locks for navigation in this river will be a profitable undertaking as well as a necessary condition for the development of this part of the country.

d. The East River

The East River is navigable for shallow crafts up to Laolung Sze, a distance of about 170 miles from the estuary at the lower point of Davids Island near Whampoa. Along its upper course, rich iron and coal deposits

丙 北江

北江自三水至韶州，约长一百四十英里，全河中有大部分为山地所夹。但自出清远峡以后，河流入于广豁之区，其地与广州平原相联，此处危险之水灾常见。自西南下游水道淤塞之后，自峡至西南一段河身逐年变浅，左岸靠平原之基围时时崩决，致广州以上之平原大受水灾。所以整治一部分河流，有二事须加考察：第一，防止洪水；第二，航运改良。关于第一事，无有逾于浚深河身一法者。在改良广州通海路及港面并广州河汊时，吾人应开一深水水路，从深海起，直达西南。在改良北江下段时，吾人只须将此工程加长，溯流直至清远峡，拟使有水深自十五英尺至二十英尺之深水道。其浚此水道，或用人工，或兼用自然之力。既已浚深此河底矣，则即以今日基围之高言，亦足以防卫此平原不使其遭水患矣。

论及此第二事，则既为防止水灾，将西南至清远峡一节之北江浚深，即航行问题同时解决矣。然则今所须商及者，只此上段一部而已。吾欲提议将此北江韶州以下一段改良，令可航行。韶州者，广东省北部之商业中心也，又其煤铁矿之中心也。欲改良此峡上一部令可航行，则须先建堰与水闸于一二处，然后十英尺吃水之船可以航行无碍，直至韶州。虽此江与粤汉铁路平行，然而若此地矿山得有相当开发之后，此等煤铁重货仍须有廉值之运输以达之于海，即此水路为不可缺矣。然则于此河中设堰以生水电，设水闸以利航行，固不失为一有利之企业也，况又为发展此一部分地方之必要条件也。

丁 东江

东江以浅水船航行可达于老龙市，此地离黄埔附近鹿步墟岛东江总出口处约一百七十英里。沿此江上段，所在皆有煤铁矿田。铁矿之

are found. Iron has been mined here since time immemorial. At present most of the utensils used in this province are manufactured from the iron mined. So to make a deep navigable waterway up to these iron and coal fields will be most remunerative.

To improve the East River for navigation as well as for flood prevention, I propose to start the work at the lower point of Davids Island as stated in the improvement of the Canton Approach. From here, a deep channel should be dredged up to Suntang, and a mile above that point a new channel should be opened in the direction of Tungkun city, by connecting the various arms of water between these two places and joining the left branch of the East River immediately above Tungkun city. All other channels leading from this new channel to the Pearl River should be closed up to normal water level so as to make these closed-up channels serve as flood outlets in rainy seasons. Thus by blocking up the rest of the estuaries of the East River, all the water would form one strong current which would dredge the river bottom deeper, and maintain the depth permanently. The body of the river should be trained to a uniform width right along its course up to tidal point, and above this point, the river should be narrowed in proportion to its volume of water. Thus the whole river would dredge itself deep far up above Waichow city. The railway bridge at the south side of Shelung should be made a turning bridge so as to permit large steamers to pass through it. Some sharp turns of the river should be reduced to gentle curves and midstream obstacles should be removed. The portion of the river above Waichow should be provided with dams and locks so as to enable ten-foot draught vessels to ascend as near as possible to the iron and coal fields in the valley.

● Part III The Construction of the Southwestern Railway System of China

The southwestern part of China comprises Szechwan, the largest and richest province of China Proper, Yunnan, the second largest province,

Kwangsi and Kweichow which are rich in mineral resources, and a part of Hunan and Kwangtung. It has an area of 600,000 square miles, and a population of over 100,000,000. This large and populous part of China is almost untouched by railways, except a French line of narrow gauge from Laokay to Yunnanfu, covering a distance of 290 miles.

开采于此地也，实在于久远之往昔，记忆所不及之年代。在今日全省所用各种铁器之中，实有一大部分，为用此地所出之铁制造之者。是故浚一可航行之深水道，直上至于煤铁矿区中心者，必非无利之业也。

改良此东江，一面以防止其水害，一面又便利其航行。吾意欲从鹿步墟岛下游之处着手，于前论广州通海路已述之矣。由此点起，须浚一深水道，上至新塘。自新塘上游约一英里之处，应凿一新水道直达东莞城，而以此悉联东江左边在东莞与新塘间之各支流为一。以此新水道为界，所有自此新水道左岸以迄珠江，中间上述各支流之旧路，悉行闭塞。其闭塞处之高，须约与通常水平相同，而以此已涸之河身，供异日雨期洪水宣流之用。如是，东江之他出口已被一律封闭，则所有之水将汇成强力之水流，此水流即能浚河身使加深，又使全河水深能保其恒久不变也。河身须沿流加以改削，令有一律之河幅，上至潮水能达之处；自此处起，则应按河流之量多寡，以定河身之广狭。如是，则东江将以其自力浚深惠州城以下一段矣。石龙镇南边之铁路桥，应改建为开合铁桥，使大轮船可以往来于其间。东江有急激转弯数处，应改以为缓徐曲线，并将中流沙洲除去。惠州以上一部江流，应加堰与水闸，令吃水十英尺之船，可以上溯至极近于此东江流域煤铁矿田而后已。

• 第三部 建设中国西南铁路系统

中国西南一部，所包含者：四川，中国本部最大且最富之省分也；云南，次大之省也；广西、贵州，皆矿产最丰之地也；而又有广东、湖南两省之一部。此区面积有六十万英方里，人口过一万万，除由老街至云南府约二百九十英里法国所经营之窄轨铁路外，中国广地众民之此一部，殆全不与铁路相接触也。

There are great possibilities for railway development in this part of the country. A network of lines should radiate fan-like from Canton as pivot to connect every important city and rich mineral field with the Great Southern Port. The construction of railways in this part of China is not only needed for the development of Canton but also is essential for the prosperity of all the southwestern provinces. With the construction of railways rich mines of various kinds could be developed and cities and towns could be built along the lines. Developed lands are still very cheap and undeveloped lands and those with mining possibilities cost almost next to nothing even though not state owned. So if all the future city sites and mining lands be taken up by the government before railway construction is started, the profit would be enormous. Thus no matter how large a sum is invested in railway construction, the payment of its interest and principal will be assured. Besides, the development of Canton as a world port is entirely dependent upon this system of railways. If there be no such network of railway traversing the length and breadth of the southwestern section of China, Canton could not be developed up to our expectations.

The southwestern section of China is very mountainous, except the Canton and Chengtu plains, which have an area of from 3,000 to 4,000 square miles each. The rest of the country is made up almost entirely of hills and valleys with more or less open space here and there. The mountains in the eastern part of this section are seldom over 3,000 feet high but those near the Tibetan frontier generally have an altitude of 10,000 feet or more. The engineering difficulties in building these railways are much greater than those of the northwestern plain. Many tunnels and loops will have to be constructed and so the construction costs of the railway per mile will be greater than in other parts of China.

With Canton as the terminus of this system of railroads, I propose that the following lines be constructed:

a. The Canton-Chungking line via Hunan.
b. The Canton-Chungking line via Hunan and Kweichow.

c. The Canton-Chengtu line via Kweilin and Luchow.
d. The Canton-Chengtu line via Wuchow and Suifu.
e. The Canton-Yunnanfu-Tali-Tengyueh line ending at the Burma border.
f. The Canton-Szemao line.
g. The Canton-Yamchow line ending at Tunghing, on the Annam border.

于此一地区，大有开发铁路之机会。应由广州起，向各重要城市、矿产地引铁路线，成为扇形之铁路网，使各与南方大港相联结。在中国此部建设铁路者，非特为发展广州所必要，抑亦于西南各省全部之繁荣为最有用者也。以建设此项铁路之故，种种丰富之矿产可以开发，而城镇亦可于沿途建之。其既开之地，价尚甚廉，至于未开地及含有矿产之区，虽非现归国有，其价之贱，去不费一钱可得者亦仅一间耳。所以若将来市街用地及矿产地，预由政府收用，然后开始建筑铁路，则其获利必极丰厚。然则不论建筑铁路投资多至若干，可保其偿还本息，必充足有余矣。又况开发广州以为世界大港，亦全赖此铁路系统，如使缺此纵横联属西南广袤之一部之铁路网，则广州亦不能有如吾人所预期之发达矣。

西南地方，除广州及成都两平原地各有三四千英方里之面积外，地皆险峻。此诸地者，非山即谷，其间处处留有多少之隙地。在此区东部，山岳之高，鲜逾三千英尺；至其西部与西藏交界之处，平均高至一万英尺以上。故建此诸铁路之工程上困难，比之西北平原铁路系统，乃至数倍。多数之隧道与凿山路，须行开凿，故建筑之费，此诸路当为中国各路之冠。

吾提议以广州为此铁路系统终点，以建下列之七路：

甲 广州重庆线，经由湖南。
乙 广州重庆线，经由湖南、贵州。
丙 广州成都线，经由桂林、泸州。
丁 广州成都线，经由梧州、叙府。
戊 广州云南大理腾越线，至缅甸边界为止。
己 广州思茅线。
庚 广州钦州线，至安南界东兴为止。

a. The Canton-Chungking Line via Hunan

This line will start from Canton and follow the same direction as the Canton-Hankow line as far as the junction of the Linkiang with the North River. From that point the railroad turns into the valley of Linkiang, and follows the course of the river upward above the city of Linchow. There it crosses the watershed between the Linkiang and the Taokiang and proceeds to Taochow, Hunan. Thence it follows the Taokiang to Yungchow, Paoking, Sinhwa, and Shenchow, and up to Peiho across the boundary of Hunan into Szechwan by Yuyang. From Yuyang the line proceeds across the mountain to Nanchuen, thence to Chungking after crossing the Yangtze. This railway which has a total length of about 900 miles passes through a rich mineral and agricultural country. In the Linchow district north of Kwangtung, rich coal, antimony, and wolfram deposits are found; in southwestern Hunan, tin, antimony, coal, iron, copper and silver; and at Yuyang, east of Szechwan, antimony and quicksilver. Among agricultural products found along this line we may mention sugar, groundnuts, hemp, tung oil, tea, cotton, tobacco, silk, grains, etc. There is also an abundance of timber, bamboo and various kinds of forest products.

b. The Canton-Chungking Line via Hunan and Kweichow

This line is about 800 miles in length, but as it runs in the same track with line (a) from Canton to Taochow, a distance of about 250 miles, it leaves only 550 miles to be accounted for. This line, therefore, actually begins at Taochow, Hunan, and goes through the northeastern corner of Kwangsi passing by Chuanchow, and then through the southwestern corner of Hunan passing by Chengpu and Tsingchow. Thence it enters into Kweichow by Sankiang and Tsingkiang and crosses a range of hill to Chengyuan. From Chengyuan this line has to cross the watershed between Yuan Kiang and Wukiang to Tsunyi. From Tsunyi it will follow the trade route which leads to Kikiang and then crosses the Yangtze by the same bridge as line (a) to Chungking. This railway will also pass through rich mineral and timber districts.

c. The Canton-Chengtu Line via Kweilin and Luchow

This line is about 1,000 miles long. It runs from Canton directly west to Samshui, where it crosses the North River to the mouth of Suikong. Then, it ascends the valley of the same name to Szewui and Kwongning. Next, it enters into Kwangsi at Waisap, thence to Hohsien and Pinglo. From there it follows the course of the Kweikiang up to Kweilin. Thus the rich iron and coal fields that lie between these two provincial capitals, Canton and Kweilin,

甲　广州重庆线经由湖南

此线应由广州出发，与粤汉线同方向，直至连江与北江会流之处。自此点起，本路折向连江流域，循连江岸上至连州以上，于此横过连江与道江之分水界，进至湖南之道州。于是随道江以至永州、宝庆、新化、辰州，溯酉水过川、湘之界入于酉阳，由酉阳横过山脉而至南川，从南川渡扬子江而至重庆。此路全长有九百英里，经过富饶之矿区与农区。在广东之北连州之地，已发见丰富之煤矿、铁矿、锑矿、钨矿；于湖南之西南隅，则有锡、锑、煤、铁、铜、银；于四川之酉阳，则有锑与水银。其在沿线之农产物，则吾可举砂糖、花生、大麻、桐油、茶叶、棉花、烟叶、生丝、谷物等等；又复多有竹材、木材及其他一切森林产物。

乙　广州重庆线经由湖南、贵州

此线约长八百英里，但自广州至道州一段即走于甲线之上，凡二百五十英里，故只有五百五十英里计入此线。所以实际从湖南道州起筑，横过广西省东北突出一段，于全州再入湖南西南境，过城步及靖州。于是入贵州界，经三江及清江两地，横过山脉，以至镇远。此线由镇远须横过沅江、乌江之分水界，以至遵义；由遵义则循商人通路，直至綦江，以达重庆。此铁路所经，皆为产出木材、矿物极富之区域。

丙　广州成都线经由桂林、泸州

此线长约一千英里。由广东西行，直至三水在此处之绥江口地点，渡过北江。循绥江流域，经过四会、广宁，次于怀集入广西。经过贺县及平乐，由此处循桂江水流，上达桂林。于是广东、广西两省省城之间，各煤铁矿田可得而开凿矣。自桂林起，路转而西，至于永

will be tapped. From Kweilin the road turns west to Yungning and then proceeds to follow the Liukiang valley into Kweichow province at Kuchow. From Kuchow it goes to Tukiang and Pachai and following the same valley it crosses a range of hills into Pingyueh, thence it goes across the Yuankiang watershed into the Wukiang valley at Wengan and Yosejen. From Yosejen it follows the trade route through Luipien hills to Jenhwai, Chishui, and Nachi. Then it crosses the Yangtzekiang to Luchow. From Luchow, it runs through Lungchang, Neikiang, Tzechow, Tseyang and Kienchow to Chengtu. The last part of the line traverses very rich and populous districts of the famous Red Basin of Szechwan province. The middle portion of this line between Kweilin and Luchow lies in a very rich mineral country which possesses great possibilities for further development. This line will open up a thinly populated part for the crowded districts at both ends of the line.

d. The Canton-Chengtu Line via Wuchow and Suifu

This line is about 1,200 miles in distance. It commences at the west end of the Samshui bridge which crosses the North River at that point for line (c), and following the left bank of the West River enters the Shiuhing Gorge to the Shiuhing city. It passes Takhing, Wuchow, and Tahwang along the same bank. While the river here turns southwestwards the line turns northwestwards to Siangchow and then crosses Liukiang to Liuchow and Kingyuan. Then it goes to Szegenhsien and across the Kwangsi and Kweichow border to Tushan and Tuyun. From Tuyun the line turns more westerly to Kweiyang, the capital of Kweichow Province. Next, it proceeds to Kiensi and Tating and then leaving the Kweichow border at Pichieh it enters Yunnan at Chenhiung. Turning northward to Lohsintu and crossing the Szechwan border at that point, it proceeds to Suifu. From Suifu the road follows the course of the Minkiang, passes by Kiating and enters the Chengtu plain to Chengtu, the capital of Szechwan. This line runs from one densely populated district to another and passes through a wide strip of thinly populated and undeveloped country in the middle. Along its course many rich iron and coal fields, silver, tin, antimony, and other valuable metal deposits are found.

e. The Canton-Yunnanfu-Tali-Tengyueh Line

This line is about 1,300 miles in length from Canton to the Burma border at Tengyueh. The first 300 miles of the line from Canton to Tahwang will be the same as line (d). From the Tahwang junction this

宁，又循柳江流域，上至贵州边界。越界至古州，由古州过都江及八寨，仍循此河谷而上，逾一段连山至平越。由平越横渡沅江分水界，于瓮安及岳四城，入乌江流域。自岳四城循商人通路逾雷边山至仁怀、赤水、纳溪。于是渡扬子江，以至泸州。自泸州起，经过隆昌、内江、资州、资阳、简州，以达成都。此路最后之一段，横过所谓“四川省之红盆地”，有名富庶之区也。其在桂林、泸州之间，此路中段则富于矿产，为将来开发希望最大者。此路将为其两端人口最密之区，开一土旷人稀之域，以收容之者也。

丁　广州成都线经由梧州与叙府

此线长约一千二百英里。自丙线渡北江之三水铁路桥之西端起，循西江之左岸，以入于肇庆峡，至肇庆城。即循此岸，上至德庆、梧州、大湟。在大湟，河身转而走西南，路转而走西北，至象州，渡柳江，至柳州及庆远。于是进至思恩，过桂、黔边界，入贵州，至独山及都匀。自都匀起，此路再折偏西走，至贵州省城之贵阳，次进至黔西及大定。离贵州界于毕节，于镇雄入云南界。北转而至乐新渡，过四川界，入叙府。自叙府起，循岷江而上，至嘉定，渡江，入于成都平原，以至成都。此路起自富庶之区域，迄于富庶之区域，中间经过宽幅之旷土未经开发、人口极稀之地。沿线富有煤、铁矿田，又有银、锡、锑等等贵金属矿。

戊　广州云南大理腾越线

此线长约一千三百英里。起自广州，迄于云南、缅甸边界之腾越。其首段三百英里，自广州至大湟，与丁线相同。自大湟江口分支

line branches off to Wusuan and following in a general way the course of the Hungshui Kiang passes through Tsienkiang and Tunglan. Then it cuts across the southwestern corner of Kweichow province passing by Sinyihsien and thence enters Yunnan province at Loping and by way of Luliang to Yunnanfu, the capital of the province. From Yunnanfu this line runs through Tsuyung to Tali, then turns southwestwards to Yungchang and Tengyueh ending at the Burma border.

At Tunglan, near the Kweichow border in Kwangsi, a branch line of about 400 miles should be projected. This line should follow the Pepan Kiang valley, up to Kotuho, and Weining. Thence it enters Yunnan at Chaotung, and crosses the Yangtze River at Hokeow, where it enters Szechwan. Crossing the Taliang mountain, it goes to Ningyuan. This branch line taps the famous copper field between Chaotung and Ningyuan, the richest of its kind in China.

The main line running through the length of Kwangsi and Yunnan from east to west, will be of international importance, for at the frontier it will join the Rangoon Bhamo line of the Burmese Railway System. It will be the shortest road from India to China. It will bring the two populous countries nearer to each other than now. By the new way the journey can be made in a few days, whereas by the present sea-route it takes as many weeks.

f. The Canton-Szemao Line

This line to the border of Burma is about 1,100 miles long. It starts from south of Canton, passes Fatshan, Kunshan, and crosses the West River from Taipinghü to Samchowhü. Thence it proceeds to Koming, Sinhing, and Loting. After passing Loting it crosses the Kwangsi border at Pingho, and proceeds to Junghsien and then westward, crossing the Yukiang branch of the West River, to Kweihsien. Thence it runs north of Yukiang to Nanning. At Nanning a branch line of 120 miles should be projected. Following the course of the Tsokiang it goes to Lungchow where it turns southward to Chennankwan on the Tongking border to join the French line at that point. The main line from Nanning proceeds in the same course as the upper Yukiang to Poseh. Then it crosses the border into Yunnan at Poyai, and by way of Pamen, Koukan, Tungtu and Putsitang to Amichow, where it crosses the French Laokay-Yunnan line. From Amichow it proceeds to Linanfu, Shihping and Yuankiang where it crosses the river of the same name. Thence it passes through Talang, Puerhfu and Szemao and finally ends at the border of Burma near the Mekong River. This line taps the rich tin, silver, and antimony deposits of

至武宣，循红水江常道，经迁江及东兰。于是经兴义县，横过贵州省之西南隅入云南省，至罗平，从陆凉一路以至云南省城。自省城经过楚雄，以至大理。于是折而西南，至永昌，遂至腾越，终于缅甸边界。

在广西之东兰，近贵州边界处，此路应引一支线，约长四百英里。此线应循北盘江流域，上至可渡河与威宁，于昭通入云南，在河口过扬子江。即于此处入四川，横截大凉山，至于宁远。此路所以开昭通、宁远间有名铜矿地之障碍，此项铜矿为中国全国最丰之矿区也。

此路本线，自东至西，贯通桂、滇两省，将来在国际上必见重要。因在此线缅甸界上，当与缅甸铁路系统之仰光、八莫一线相接，将来此即自印度至中国最捷之路也。以此路故，此两人口稠密之大邦，必比现在更为接近。今日由海路，此两地交通须数礼拜者，异时由此新路，则数日而足矣。

己 广州思茅线

此线至缅甸界止，约长一千一百英里。起自广州市西南隅，经佛山、官山，由太平墟渡过西江，至对岸之三洲墟。于是进入高明、新兴、罗定。既守罗定，入广西界，至平河，进至容县。于是西向，渡左江，至于贵县，即循左江之北岸以达南宁。在南宁应设一支线，约长一百二十英里，循上左江水路以至龙州，折而南，至镇南关、安南东京界上止，与法国铁路相接。其本线，由南宁循上右江而上，至于百色。于是过省界入云南，到剥隘，经巴门、高甘、东都、普子塘一路，至阿迷州，截老街、云南铁路而过。由阿迷州进至临安府、石屏、元江。于是渡过元江，通过他郎、普洱及思茅，至缅甸边界近澜沧江处为止。此线穿入云南、广西之南部锡、银、锑三种矿产最富之地，

south Yunnan and Kwangsi, while rich iron and coal fields are found right along the whole line. Gold, copper, mercury, and lead are also found in many places. As regards agricultural products, rice and groundnuts are found in great abundance, also camphor, cassia, sugar, tobacco, and various kinds of fruits.

g. The Canton-Yamchow Line

This line is about 400 miles long measuring from the west end of the Sikiang bridge. Starting from Canton it runs on the tracks of line (f) as far as the farther side of the bridge over the West River. Thence it branches off to the southwest to Hoiping and Yanping, and by way of Yeungchun to Kochow and Fachow. At Fachow, a branch line of 100 miles should be projected to Suikai, Luichow and Haian on the Hainan Straits where, by means of a ferry, it connects with Hainan Island. The mainline continues from Fachow westward to Sheshing, Limchow, Yamchow and ends on the Annam border at Tunghing, where it may connect with a French line to Haiphong. This line is entirely within the Kwangtung province. It passes through a very populous and productive country. Coal and iron are found along the whole line, while gold and antimony, in some parts. Agricultural products, as sugar, silk, camphor, ramie, indigo, groundnuts, and various kinds of fruits are raised here.

The total length of this system as outlined above is about 6,700 miles. In addition there will be two connecting lines between Chengtu and Chungking; another from east of Tsunyi on line (b) southward to Wengan on line (c); another from Pingyueh on line (c) to Tuyun on line (d); another from the border of Kweichow on line (d) through Nantan and Noti to Tunglan on line (e), thence through Szecheng to Poseh on line (f). These connecting lines total about 600 miles. So the grand total will be about 7,300 miles.

This system will be intersected by three lines. First, the existing French line from Laokay to Yunnanfu with a projected line from Yunnanfu to Chungking crosses line (f) at Amichow, line (e) at Weining, line (d) at Suifu, line (c) at Luchow, and meets lines (a) and (b) at Chungking. Second, the projected British line from Shasi to Sinyi crosses line (a) at Shenchow, line (b) at Chenyuen, line (c) at Pingyueh, line (d) at Kweiyang and a branch of line (e) at a point west of Yungning. Third, the projected American line from Chuchow to Yamchow crosses line (a) at Yungchow, line (b) at Chuanchow, line (c) at Kweilin, line (d) at Liuchow,

同时沿线又有煤铁矿田至多，复有多地产出金、铜、水银、铅。论其农产，则米与花生均极丰饶，加以樟脑、桂油、蔗糖、烟叶，各种果类。

庚 广州钦州线

此线从西江铁路桥西首起算，约长四百英里。自广州起，西行至于太平墟之西江铁路，与己线同轨。过江始分支，向开平、恩平，经阳春，至高州及化州。于化州须引一支线，至遂溪、雷州，达于琼州海峡之海安，约长一百英里。于海安再以渡船与琼州岛[58]联络。其本线，仍自化州西行，过石城、廉州、钦州，达于与安南交界之东兴为止。东兴对面芒街至海防之间，将来有法国铁路可与相接。此线全在广东省范围之内，经过人口多、物产富之区域，线路两旁皆有煤铁矿，有数处产金及锑，农产则有蔗糖、生丝、樟脑、苎麻、靛青、花生及种种果类。

此系统内各线，如上所述，约六千七百英里。此外须加以联络成都、重庆之两线。又须另设一线，起自乙线遵义之东，向南行至瓮安，与丙线接；又一线自丙线之平越起，至丁线之都匀；又一线由丁线贵州界上一点，经南丹、那地，以至戊线之东兰，再经泗城，以至己线之百色。此联络各线，全长约六百英里。故总计应有七千三百英里。

此系统将于下文所举三线经济上大有关系：一、法国经营之老街、云南府已成线，及云南府、重庆计划线。此线与己线交于阿迷州，与戊线交于威宁，与丁线交于叙府，与丙线交于泸州，而与甲乙两线会于重庆。二、英国经营之沙市、兴义计划线。此线与甲线交于辰州，与乙线交于镇远，与丙线交于平越，与丁线交于贵阳，而于戊线之支线交于永定西方之一点。三、美国经营之株洲、钦州计划线。此线与甲线交于永州，乙线交于全州，丙线交于桂林，丁线交于柳州，

line (e) at Tsienkiang, line (f) at Nanning, and meets line (g) at Yamchow. Thus, if this system and the three projected French, British, and American lines are completed, Southwestern China would be well provided with railway communications.

All these lines will run through the length and breadth of a vast mineral country, in which most of the essential and valuable metals of the world are found. There is no place in the world which possesses as here so many varieties of rare metals, such as wolfram, tin, antimony, silver, gold, and platinum and at the same time so richly provided with the common but essential metals, such as copper, lead, and iron. Furthermore, almost every district in this region is abundantly provided with coal, so much so that there is a common saying: "Mu mei pu lih cheng," that is, "Nobody would build a city where there is no coal underneath." The idea was that in case of a siege those within the city might obtain fuel from under the ground. In Szechwan, petroleum and natural gas are also found in abundance.

Thus, we see that this Southwestern Railway System for the development of mineral resources in the mountainous regions of Southwestern China is just as important as the Northwestern Railway System is for the development of agricultural resources in the vast prairies of Mongolia and Turkestan. These railway systems are a necessity to the Chinese people and a very profitable undertaking to foreign capitalists. They are of about equal length, viz.—about 7,000 miles. The cost per mile of the Southwestern System will be at least twice that of the Northwestern System, but the remuneration from the development of mineral resources will be many times that from the development of agricultural resources.

● Part IV The Construction of Coast Ports and Fishing Harbors

After planning the three world ports on the coast of China, it is time for me to go on and deal with the development of second- and third-class seaports and fishing harbors along the whole coast in order to complete a system of seaports for China. Recently, my projected plan of the Great Northern Port was so enthusiastically received by the people of Chihli Province that the Provincial Assembly has approved the project and decided to carry it out at once as a provincial undertaking. For this object, a loan of $40,000,000 has been voted. This is an encouraging sign and doubtless the other projects will be taken up sooner or later by either the provinces or the Central Government, when the people begin to realize their necessity. I propose that four second-class seaports and nine third-class seaports and numerous fishing harbors should be constructed.

戊线交于迁江，己线交于南宁，而与庚线会于钦州。所以此法、英、美三线，与本系统各线，一律完成之后，中国西南各省之铁道交通可无缺少矣。

此诸线皆经过广大且长之矿产地，其地有世界上有用且高价之多种金属。世界中无有如此地含有丰富之稀有金属者，如钨、如锡、如锑、如银、如金、如白金等等；同时又有虽甚普通而尤有用之金属，如铜、如铁、如铅。抑且每一区之中，均有丰裕之煤。南方俗语有云："无煤不立城。"盖谓预计城被围时，能于地中取炭，不事薪采，此可见其随在有煤产出也。四川省又有石油矿及自然煤气（火井），极为丰裕。

是故吾人得知，以西南铁路系统开发西南山地之矿产利源，正与以西北铁路系统开发蒙古、新疆大平原之农产利源，同其重要。此两铁路系统，于中国人民为最必要，而于外国投资者又为最有利之事业也。论两系统之长短，大略相同，约七千英里。此西南系统，每英里所费平均须在彼系统两部以上，但以其开发矿产利源之利益言，又视开发农产利源之利益更多数倍也。

• 第四部 建设沿海商埠及渔业港

既于中国海岸为此三世界大港之计划，今则已至进而说及发展二三等海港及渔业港于沿中国全海岸，以完成中国之海港系统之机会矣。近日以吾北方大港计划为直隶省人民所热心容纳，于是省议会赞同此计划，而决定作为省营事业立即举办，以此目的，经已票决募债四千万元。此为一种猛进之征兆。而其他规划，亦必或早或晚，或由省营，或由国营，随于民心感其必要，次第采用。吾意则须建四个二等海港、九个三等海港及十五个渔业港。

The four second-class seaports will be arranged so as to be placed in the following manner: one on the extreme north, one on the extreme south, and the other two midway between the three great world ports.

I shall deal with them according to the order of their future importance as follows:

a. Yingkow.
b. Haichow.
c. Foochow.
d. Yamchow.

a. Yingkow

Yingkow is situated at the head of the Liaotung Gulf and was once the only seaport of Manchuria. Since the improvement of Talien as a seaport, the trade of Yingkow has dwindled and lost half of its former business. As a seaport, Yingkow has two disadvantages, first, the shallowness of its approach from the sea and second, the blocking up by ice for several months in winter. Its only advantages over Talien is that it is situated at the mouth of the Liaoho and has inland water communication throughout the Liao valley in south Manchuria. The half of the former trade that it still holds at present against Talien is entirely due to the inland water facility. To make Yingkow outmatch Talien again in the future and become first in importance after the three great world ports, we must improve its inland water communication, as well as deepen its approach from the sea. In regard to the improvement of the approach work similar to the improvement of the Canton Approach should be adopted. Besides the construction of a deep channel, about twenty feet in depth, reclamation work should be carried out at the same time. For, the shallow and extensive swamp at the head of the Liaotung Gulf could be turned into rice-producing land from which great profit could be derived. Regarding the inland water communication, not only the water system in the Liao valley but also the Sungari and the Amur Systems have to be improved. The most important work is the construction of a canal to connect these systems and this I shall now discuss in the next paragraph.

The Liaoho-Sungari Canal is the most important factor in the future prosperity of Yingkow. It is by this canal only that this port can be made the most important of the second-class seaports in China and further the vast forest lands, the virgin soil and the rich mineral resources of North Manchuria can be connected by water communication with Yingkow.

此四个二等海港，应以下列之情形配置之，即一在北极端，一在南极端，其他之港则间在此三世界大港之间。

此项港口，按其将来重要之程度排列之如下：

甲　营口。

乙　海州。[59]

丙　福州。

丁　钦州。

甲　营口

营口位于辽东湾之顶上，昔者尝为东三省之唯一海港矣。自改建大连为一海港以后，营口商业大减，昔日之事业殆失其半。以海港论，营口之不利有二：一为其由海入口之通路较浅，二为冬期冰锢至数月之久。而其胜于大连唯一之点，则为位置在辽河之口，拥有内地交通遍及于南满辽河流域之内；其所以仍保有昔时贸易之半与大连抗者，全以其内地水路之便也。欲使营口将来再能凌驾大连而肩随[60]于前言三世界大港之后，吾人必须一面改良内地水路交通，一面浚深其达海之通路。关于通路改良之工程，当取与改良广州通海路相同的方法，既设一水深约二十英尺之深水道，而又同时行填筑之工程。盖以辽东湾头广而浅之沼地，可以转为种稻之田，借之可得甚丰之利润也。至于内地水路交通，则不独辽河一系，即松花江、黑龙江两系统亦应一并改良。其最重要之工程，则为凿一运河，联此各系统，此则吾当继此有所讨论。

辽河与松花江间之运河，于将来营口之繁荣，实为最要分子。惟有由此运河，此港始能成为中国二等海港中最重要者。而在将来，此北满之伟大森林地及处女壤土丰富矿源，可以以水路交通与营口相衔接也。

So this canal is all important for Yingkow, without which Yingkow as a seaport could at most hold her present position, a town of 60,000 to 70,000 inhabitants and an annual trade of $30,000,000 to $40,000,000 only and could never gain a place as the first of the second-class seaports in China. This canal can be cut either south of Hwaiteh in a line parallel to the South Manchurian Railway between Fan Kia Tun and Sze Tung Shan, a distance of less than ten miles, or north of Hwaiteh in a line between Tsing-shan-pao and Kaw-shan-tun, a distance of about fifteen miles. In the former case the canal is shorter but it makes the waterway as a whole longer, while in the latter case, the canal is about twice as long but it makes the waterway as a whole shorter between the two systems. In either line, there are no impassable physical obstacles. Both lines are on the plain but the elevation of the one may be higher than that of the other, which is the only factor that will determine the choice between the two. If this canal is constructed, then the rich provinces of Kirin and Heilungkiang and a portion of Outer Mongolia will be brought within direct water communication with China Proper. At present, all water traffic has to go by way of the Russian Lower Amur, then round a great detour of the Japan Sea before reaching China Proper. This canal will not only be a great necessity to Yingkow as a seaport, but will also have a great bearing on the whole Chinese nation economically and politically. With the Liaoho-Sungari Canal completed Yingkow will be the grand terminus of the inland waterway system of all Manchuria and Northeastern Mongolia; and with the approach from the sea deepened it will also be a seaport next in importance only to the three first-class world ports.

b. Haichow

Haichow is situated on the eastern edge of the central plain of China. This plain is one of the most extensive and fertile areas on earth. As a seaport, Haichow is midway between the two great world ports along the coast line, namely the Great Northern and the Great Eastern Ports. It has been made as the terminus of the Hailan railway, the trunk line of central China from east to west. Haichow also possesses the facility of inland water communication. If the Grand Canal and the other waterway systems are improved, it will be connected with the Hoangho Valley in North China, the Yangtze Valley in Central China, and the Sikiang Valley in South China. Its deep sea approach is comparatively good, being the only spot along the 250 miles of the North Kiangsu coast that could be reached by ocean steamers to within a few miles of the shore. To make

所以为营口计，此运河为最重要；使其缺此，则营口之为一海港也，最多不过保其现在之位置，人口六、七万，全年贸易三、四千万元，极矣，无由再占中国二等海港首位之益矣。此运河可凿之于怀德以南，范家屯与四童山之间，与南满铁路平行，其长不及十英里；亦可凿之于怀德以北，青山堡与靠山屯之间，其长约十五英里。在前一线，所凿者短，而以全水路计则长；在后一线，运河之长几倍前者，而计此两江系统间之全水路则较短。两线均无不可逾越之物质的障碍，二者俱在平原，但其中一线高于海面上之度或较他一线为多，则将来择用于二者间唯一之取决点也。若此运河既经开竣，则吉林、黑龙江两富省及外蒙古之一部，皆将因此与中国本部可以水路交通相接，然则此运河不特营口之为海港大有需要焉也，又与中国全国国民政治上、经济上亦大有关系。辽河、松花江运河完成以后，营口将为全满洲与蒙古东北部内地水路系统之大终点。而通海之路既经浚深以后，彼又将为重要仅亚于三大港之海港矣。

乙 海州

海州位于中国中部平原东陲，此平原者，世界中最广大肥沃之地区之一也。海州以为海港，则刚在北方大港与东方大港二大世界港之间，今已定为东西横贯中国中部大干线海兰铁路之终点。海州又有内地水运交通之利便，如使改良大运河其他水路系统已毕，则将北通黄河流域，南通西江流域，中通扬子江流域。海州之通海深水路，可称较善。在沿江北境二百五十英里海岸之中，只此一点，可以容航洋巨舶

Haichow a seaport for 20 feet draught vessels, the approach has to be dredged for many miles from the mouth of the river before the four fathom line could be reached. Although possessing better advantages than Yingkow, in being ice free, Haichow, as a second-class seaport, has to be content to take a second place after Yingkow, because she does not have as vast a hinterland as Yingkow, nor such a monopolistic position in regard to inland water communication.

c. Foochow

Foochow, the capital of Fukien Province, ranks third among our second-class seaports. Foochow is already a very large city, its inhabitants being nearly a million. It is situated at the lower reach of the Min River, about 30 miles from the sea. The hinterland of this port is confined to the Min Valley with an area of about 30,000 square miles. The territory beyond this valley will be commanded by other coast or river ports, so the area commanded by this port is much smaller than that by Haichow. Consequently, it could be given only the third place in the category of second-class seaports. The Foochow approach from the Outer Bar to Kinpei Entrance is very shallow. After this Entrance is passed, the river is confined on both sides by high hills and becomes narrow and deep right up to Pagoda Anchorage.

I propose that a new port should be constructed at the lower part of Nantai Island. For here land is cheap and there will be plenty of room for modern improvement. A locked basin for shipping could be constructed at the lower point of Nantai Island, just above Pagoda Anchorage. The left branch of the Min River above Foochow City should be blocked up so as to concentrate the current to flush the harbor at the south side of Nantai. The blocked-up channel on the north side of that island should be left to be reclaimed by natural process or may be used as a tidal basin to flush the channel below Pagoda Anchorage, if it is found necessary. The upper Min River must be improved as far as possible for inland water traffic. Its lower reach from Pagoda Anchorage to the sea must be trained and regulated to secure a through channel of 30 feet or more to the open sea. Thus Foochow could also be made a calling port for ocean liners that ply between the world ports.

d. Yamchow

Yamchow is situated at the head of Tongking Gulf in the extreme south of the China Coast. This city is about 400 miles west of Canton—the Great Southern Port. All the districts lying west of Yamchow will find

逼近岸边数英里内而已。欲使海州成为吃水二十英尺之船海港，须先浚深其通路至离河口数英里外，然后可得四英寻深之水。海州之比营口，少去结冰，大为优越；然仍不能不甘居营口之下者，以其所控腹地不如营口之宏大，亦不如彼在内地水运上有独占之位置也。

丙 福州

福建省城在吾二等海港中居第三位。福州今日已为一大城市，其人口近一百万，位于闽江之下游，离海约三十英里。此港之腹地，以闽江流域为范围，面积约三万方英里。至于此流域以外之地区，将归他内河商埠或他海港所管，故此港所管地区又狭于海州。所以以顺位言，二等海港之中，此港应居第三位。福州通海之路，自外闩洲以至金牌口，水甚浅；自金牌口而上，两岸高山夹之，既窄且深，直至于罗星塔下。

吾拟建此新港于南台岛之下游一部，以此地地价较贱，而施最新改良之余地甚多也。容船舶之锁口水塘，应建设于南台岛下端，近罗星塔处。闽江左边一支，在福州城上游处应行闭塞，以集中水流，为冲刷南台岛南边港面之用。其所闭故道，绕南台岛北边者，应留待自然填塞，或遇有必要，改作蓄潮水塘（收容潮涨时之水，俟潮退时放出，以助冲洗港内浮沙），以冲洗罗星塔以下一节水道。闽江上段，应加改良，人力所能至之处为止，以供内地水运之用。其下一段，自罗星塔以至于海，必须范围整治之，以求一深三十英尺以上之水道，达于公海。于是福州可为两世界大港间航洋汽船之一寄港地矣。

丁 钦州

钦州位于东京湾之顶，中国海岸之最南端。此城在广州即南方大港之西四百英里。凡在钦州以西之地，将择此港以出于海，则比经广州可

their way to the sea by this port 400 miles shorter than by Canton. As sea transportation is commonly known to be twenty times cheaper than rail transportation, the shortening of a distance of 400 miles to the sea means a great deal economically to the provinces of Szechuan, Yunnan, Kweichow, and a part of Kwangsi. Although Nanning, an inland water port, lying northwest of Yamchow, is much nearer to the hinterland than Yamchow, yet it could not serve this hinterland as a seaport. So all the direct import and export trade will find Yamchow the cheapest shipping stage.

To improve Yamchow as a seaport the Lungmen River should be regulated in order to secure a deep channel to the city, and the estuary should be deepened by dredging and training to provide a good approach to the port. This port has been selected as the terminus of the Chuchow Yamchow Railway (Chu-Kin line) which will run from Hunan through Kwangsi into Kwangtung. Although the hinterland of this port is much larger than that of Foochow, yet I still rank it after that city because the area commanded by it is also commanded by Canton, the southern world port, and by Nanning, the river port, and so all internal as well as indirect import and export trade must go to the other two ports. It is only the direct foreign trade that will use Yamchow. Thus, in spite of its extensive hinterland it is very improbable that it could outmatch Foochow in the future as a second-class port.

Besides the three great world ports, and the four second-class ports, I propose to construct nine third-class ports along the China coast, from north to south, as follows:

a. Hulutao.	b. Hoangho Port.	c. Chefoo.
d. Ningpo.	e. Wenchow.	f. Amoy.
g. Swatow.	h. Tienpak.	i. Hoihou.

a. Hulutao

Hulutao is an ice-free and deep-water port, situated on the west side of the head of Liaotung Gulf, about 60 miles from Yingkow. As a winter port for Manchuria, it is in a more advantageous position than Talien for it is about 200 miles shorter by rail to the sea than the latter and is on the edge of a rich coal field. When this coal field and the surrounding mineral resources are developed, Hulutao will become the first of the third-class ports and a good outlet for Jehol and Eastern Mongolia. This port may be projected as an alternative to Yingkow, as the sole port of Manchuria and Eastern Mongolia, if a canal could be constructed to connect it with

减四百英里。通常皆知海运比之铁路运价廉二十倍，然则节省四百英里者，在四川、贵州、云南及广西之一部言之，其经济上受益为不小矣。虽其北亦有南宁以为内河商埠，比之钦州更近腹地，然不能有海港之用，所以直接输出入贸易，仍以钦州为最省俭之积载地也。

改良钦州以为海港，须先整治龙门江，以得一深水道直达钦州城。其河口当浚深之，且范之以堤，令此港得一良好通路。此港已选定为通过湘、桂入粤之株钦铁路之终点。虽其腹地较之福州为大，而吾尚置之次位者，以其所管地区，同时又为广州世界港、南宁内河港所管，所以一切国内贸易及间接输出入贸易皆将为他二港所占，惟有直接贸易始利用钦州耳。是以腹地虽广，于将来二等港中，欲凌福州而上，恐或不可能也。

此三个世界大港、四个二等港之外，吾拟于中国沿海，建九个三等港，自北至南如下：

甲　葫芦岛。　乙　黄河港。　丙　芝罘[61]。
丁　宁波。　戊　温州。　己　厦门。
庚　汕头。　辛　电白。　壬　海口。

甲　葫芦岛

此岛为不冻深水港，位于辽东湾顶西侧，离营口约六十英里。论东三省之冬期港，此港位置远胜大连，以其到海所经铁路较彼短二百英里，又在丰富煤田之边沿也。当此煤田及其附近矿产既开发之际，葫芦岛将为三等港中之首出者，为热河及东蒙古之良好出路。此港又可计划之，以为东蒙古及满洲全部之商港，以代营口，但须建一运河

the Liaoho. It is only by inland water communication that Yingkow could be made the important port of Manchuria in the future and it will be the same in the case of Hulutao. So if inland water communication could be secured for Hulutao it will entirely displace Yingkow. If it is found to be economically cheaper in the long run to construct a Hulutao-Liaoho Canal than to construct a deep harbor at Yingkow, the Hulutao harbor will have to be placed on the northwest side of the peninsula instead of on the southwest as at present projected. For the present site has not enough room for anchorage without building an extensive breakwater into the deep sea, which will be a very expensive work. Furthermore, there would not be room enough for city planning on the narrow peninsula, whereas on the other side, the city could be built on the mainland with unlimited space for its development.

I suggest that a sea wall be built from the northern point of Lienshanwan to the northern point of Hulutao to close up the Lienshan Bay and make it into a closed harbor, and an entrance be opened in the neck of Hulutao to the south side where deep water is found. This closed harbor will be over 10 square miles in extent but only some parts need to be dredged to the required depth at present. On the north side of the harbor, another entrance into the neighboring bay should be left open between the sea wall and the shore, and another breakwater should be built across the next bay. From there, a canal should be constructed either by cutting into the shore or by building a wall parallel with the coast line until it reaches the lowland from where a canal should be cut to connect with the Liaoho. If a canal is thus constructed for Hulutao, then it will at once take the place of Yingkow and become the first of the second-class ports.

b. The Hoangho Port

The Hoangho Port will be situated at the estuary of the Hoangho on the southern side of the Gulf of Pechihli, about 80 miles from our Great

Northern Port. When the Hoangho regulation is completed its estuary will be approachable by ocean steamers, and a seaport will naturally spring up there. As it commands a considerable part of the northern plain in the provinces of Shantung, Chihli, and Honan and possesses the facility of inland water communication, this port is bound to become an important third-class port.

以与辽河相连耳。将来惟有由内地水路交通可以成一重要商港，而葫芦岛恰亦与之相同，所以葫芦岛若得内地水路交通，自然可代营口而兴。如使确知于此凿长距离运河，以通葫芦岛于辽河，比之建一深水港面于营口，经济上更为廉价，则葫芦岛港面应置之于此半岛之西北边，不如今之计划置之半岛之西南。盖今日之位置，不足以多容船舶碇泊，除非建一广大之防波堤直入深海中，此工程所费又甚多也。且此狭隘之半岛，又不足以容都市规划，若其在他一边，则市街可建于本陆，有无限之空隙容其发展也。

吾意须自连山湾之北角起，筑一海堤，至于葫芦岛之北端，以闭塞连山湾，使成为锁口港面。在葫芦岛之颈部，开一口，向南方深水处；此闭塞港面，应有十英方里之广。但此中现在只有一部分须浚至所求之深。在此港面北方，须另留一出口，介于海堤、海岸之间，以通其邻近海湾。并须另建一防波堤，横过第二海湾。由该处起，应建一运河，或凿之于海岸线内，或建一海堤与海岸线平行，至与易凿之低地连接为止。再由该地开凿运河，与辽河相连。如能为葫芦岛凿此运河，则此岛立能取营口而代之，居二等港首位矣。

乙　黄河港

此港将位于黄河河口北直隶湾之南边，离吾人之北方大港约八十英里。当整治黄河工程已完成之日，此河口将得为航洋汽船所经由，自然有一海港萌芽于是。以是所管北方平原在直隶、山东、河南各省有相当之部分，而又益以内地水运交通，所以此港欲不成为重要三等海港，亦不可得矣。

c. Chefoo

Chefoo is an old treaty port situated on the northern side of the Shantung Peninsula. Once it was the only ice-free port in the whole of North China. Since the development of Talien in the north and the development of Tsingtau in the south its trade has dwindled considerably. As a seaport, it will undoubtedly hold its own when the railroads in the Shantung Peninsula are developed, and the artificial harbor is completed.

d. Ningpo

Ningpo is also an old treaty port, situated on a small river, the Yungkiang, in the eastern part of Chekiang province. It has a good approach, deep water reaching right up to the estuary of the river. The harbor can be easily improved by simply training and straightening two bends along its course up to the city. Ningpo commands a very small but rich hinterland. Its people are very enterprising, and are famed for their workmanship and handicrafts second only to those of Canton. Thus Ningpo is bound to become a manufacturing city when China is industrially developed. But owing to the proximity of the Great Eastern Port, Ningpo will not likely have much import and export trade directly with foreign countries. Most of its trade will be carried on with the Great Eastern Port. So a moderate harbor for local and coast-wise traffic will be quite sufficient for Ningpo.

e. Wenchow

Wenchow is situated near the mouth of the Wukiang in south Chekiang. This seaport has a wider hinterland than Ningpo, its surrounding districts being very productive. If railroads are developed it will undoubtedly command considerable local trade. At present the harbor is very shallow, unapproachable by even moderate-sized coastal steamers. I suggest that a new harbor at Panshiwei, north of Wenchow Island be constructed. For this purpose, a dike should be built between the northern bank and the head of Wenchow Island to block up the river entirely on the northern side of that island leaving only a lock entrance. The Wukiang should be led through the channel on the south side of the island for the purpose of reclaiming the vast expanse of the near-by shallows as well as for draining the upper stream. The approach from the southern side of Hutau Island to the port should be dredged. On the right side of the approach, a wall should be built in the shallow between Wenchow Island and Miau Island and in the shallows between Miau

丙 芝罘

芝罘为老条约港[62]，位于山东半岛之北侧，尝为全中国北部之惟一不冻港矣。自其北方有大连开发，南方又有青岛兴起，其贸易遂与之俱减。以海港论，如使山东半岛之铁路得其开发，而筑港之工程又已完毕，则此港自有其所长。

丁 宁波

宁波亦一老条约港也，位于浙江省之东方，甬江一小河之口。此地有极良通海路，深水直达此河之口。此港极易改良，只须范之以堤，改直其沿流两曲处，直抵城边。宁波所管腹地极小，然而极富，其人善企业，其以工作手工知名，肩随于广州。中国之于实业上得发展者，宁波固当为一制造之城市也。但以东方大港过近之故，宁波与外国直接之出入口贸易未必能多，此种贸易多数归东方大港。故以宁波计，有一相当港面以为本地及沿岸载货之用，亦已足矣。

戊 温州

温州在浙江省之南，瓯江之口。此港比之宁波，其腹地较广，其周围之地区皆为生产甚富者，如使铁路发展，必管有相当之地方贸易无疑。现在港面极浅，中等沿岸商船已不能进出。吾意须于盘石卫即温州岛之北（温州岛者，瓯江口之小岛，非温州城）建筑新港。由此目的，须建一堰于北岸与温州岛北端之间，使此岛北之河流完全闭塞，单留一闭锁之入口。至于瓯江，应引之循南水道，经温州岛，使其填塞附近浅地之大区，而又以范上段水流也。其自虎头岛南边以至此港之通路，应行浚深。在此通路右，应于温州岛与尾妖岛之间浅处，

Island and Sanpam Island so as to form a continuous wall to prevent the silt of Wukiang from entering into the approach. Thus a permanent deep channel will be secured for the new port of Wenchow.

f. Amoy

Amoy, an old treaty port, is situated on the island of Siming. It has a great, deep, and fine harbor, commanding a considerable hinterland in southern Fukien and Kiangsi, very rich in coal and iron deposits. This port carries on a busy trade with the Malay Archipelago and the Southeastern Asian Peninsula. Most of the Chinese residents in the southern islands, Annam, Burma, Siam, and the Malay States are from the neighborhood of Amoy. So the passenger traffic between Amoy and the southern colonies is very great. If railways are developed to tap the rich iron and coal fields in the hinterland, Amoy is bound to develop into a much larger seaport than it is at present. I suggest that a modern port be constructed on the west side of the harbor to act as an outlet for the rich mineral fields of southern Fukien and Kiangsi. This port should be equipped with modern plants in order to connect land and sea transportation.

g. Swatow

Swatow is situated at the mouth of the Hankiang at the extreme east of Kwangtung. In relation to emigration, Swatow is much similar to Amoy, for it also supplies a great number of colonists to southeastern Asia and the Malay Archipelago. So its passenger traffic with the south is just as busy as Amoy. As a seaport Swatow is far inferior to Amoy, on account of its shallow approach. But in regard to inland water communication, Swatow is in a better position as the Hankiang is navigable for many hundreds of miles inland by shallow crafts. The country around Swatow is very productive agriculturally, being second only to the Canton Delta along the Southern seaboard. In the upper reaches of the Hankiang there are very rich iron and coal deposits. The approach to the port of Swatow can be improved easily by a little training and dredging, thus making it a fine local port.

h. Tienpak

Tienpak is situated at a point in the coast of Kwangtung province between the estuary of the West River and the island of Hainan. Its surrounding districts are rich in agricultural products and mineral deposits. So a shipping port in this part is quite necessary. Tienpak can be

及尾妖岛与三盘岛各浅处之间建堤。于是成一连堤，可以防瓯江沙泥不令侵入此通路。如此，然后温州新港可以得一恒常深水道也。

己 厦门

此亦一老条约港也，在于思明岛。厦门有深广且良好之港面，管有相当之腹地，跨福建、江西两省之南部，富于煤铁矿产。此港经营对马来群岛及南亚细亚半岛之频繁贸易，所有南洋诸岛、安南、缅甸、暹罗、马来各邦之华侨，大抵来自厦门附近，故厦门与南洋之间载客之业极盛。如使铁路已经发展，穿入腹地煤铁矿区，则厦门必开发而为比现在更大之海港。吾意须于此港面之西方建新式商埠，以为江西、福建南部丰富矿区之一出口。此港应施以新式设备，使能联陆海两面之运输以为一气。

庚 汕头

汕头在韩江[63]口，广东省极东之处。以移民海外之关系，汕头与厦门极相类似，以其亦供大量之移民于东南亚细亚及马来群岛也。故其与南洋来往船客之频繁，亦不亚厦门。以海港论，汕头大不如厦门，以其入口通路之浅也。然以内地水运论，则汕头为较胜，以用浅水船则韩江可航行者数百英里地。围汕头之地，农产极盛，在南方海岸能追随广州河汉者，独此地耳。韩江上一段，煤铁矿极富。汕头通海之路，只须少加范围浚渫之功，易成为一地方良港也。

辛 电白

此港在广东省海岸、西江河口与海南岛间当中之点。其周围地区富于农产、矿田，则此地必须有一商港，以供船运之用矣。如使以堤

made into a fine harbor by entirely walling in the bay from its west side and by opening a new entrance into the deep water in the neck of the peninsula southeast of the bay. Thus a good approach could be secured. The harbor is very wide but only a part need be dredged for large vessels and the rest of the space could be used by fishing boats and other shallow crafts.

i. Hoihou

Hoihou is situated on the north side of Hainan Island on the strait of the same name, opposite Haian on the Luichow Peninsula. Hoihou is a treaty port, similar to Amoy and Swatow, supplying a great number of colonists to the south; Hainan is a very rich but undeveloped island. Only the land along the coast is cultivated, the central part being still covered by thick forests and inhabited by aborigines, and it is very rich in mineral deposits. When the whole island is fully developed, the port of Hoihou will be a busy harbor for export and import traffic. The harbor of Hoihou is very shallow, and so even small vessels have to anchor miles away in the roadstead outside. This is very inconvenient for passengers and cargoes, so the improvement of the Hoihou harbor is a necessity. Furthermore this harbor will be the ferry point between this island and the mainland for railway traffic when the railway systems of the mainland and the island are completed.

Fishing Harbors

As regards fishing harbors all our first-, second-, and third-class ports must also furnish facilities and accommodations for fishery. Thus all of these, i.e., three first-class ports, four second-class ports, and nine third-class ports, will be fishing harbors as well. But besides these sixteen ports there is still room and need to construct more fishing harbors along the coast of China. I propose, therefore, that five fishing harbors be constructed along the northern coast, that is, along the coast of Fengtien, Chihli, and Shantung, as follows:

(1) Antung, on Yalu River, on the border of Korea.

(2) Haiyangtao, on the Yalu Bay, south of Liaotung Peninsula.

(3) Chinwangtao, on the coast of Chihli, between the Liaotung and Pechihli gulfs, the present ice-free port of Chihli province.

(4) Lungkau, on the northwestern side of Shantung Peninsula.

(5) Shitauwan, at the southeastern point of the Shantung Peninsula.

Six fishing harbors should be constructed along the eastern coast, that is, along the coasts of Kiangsu, Chekiang, and Fukien, as follows:

(6) Shinyangkang, on the eastern coast of Kiangsu, south of the old mouth of the Hoangho.

全围绕电白湾之西边，另于湾之东南半岛颈地开一新出入口，以达深海，则电白可成一佳港面，而良好通路亦可获得矣。港面本甚宽阔，但有一部须加浚渫，以容巨船，其余空隙则留供渔船及其他浅水船之用。

壬 海口

此港位于海南岛之北端，琼州海峡之边，与雷州半岛之海安相对。海口与厦门、汕头俱为条约港，巨额之移民赴南洋者，皆由此出，而海南固又甚富而未开发之地也。已耕作者仅有沿海一带地方，其中央犹为茂密之森林，黎人所居，其藏矿最富。如使全岛悉已开发，则海口一港，将为出入口货辐辏[64]之区。海口港面极浅，即行小船，犹须下锚于数英里外之泊船地，此于载客、载货均不大便。所以海口港面必须改良。况此港面，又以供异日本陆及此岛铁路完成之后，两地往来接驳货儎[65]之联络船码头之用也。

于渔业港一层，吾前所述之头二三等海港均须兼为便利适合渔业之设备，即三个头等港、四个二等港、九个三等港皆同时为渔业港也。然除此十六港以外，中国沿岸仍有多建渔业港之余地，抑且有其必要。故吾意在北方奉天、直隶、山东三省海岸，应设五渔业港如下：

一、安东[66]：在高丽交界之鸭绿江。

二、海洋岛：在鸭绿湾辽东半岛之南。

三、秦皇岛：在直隶海岸辽东湾与直隶湾之间，现在直隶省之独一不冻港也。

四、龙口：在山东半岛之西北方。

五、石岛湾：在山东半岛之东南角。

东部江苏、浙江、福建三省之海岸，应建六渔业港如下：

六、新洋港：在江苏省东陲，旧黄河口南方。

(7) Luszekang, at the northern point of the Yangtze Estuary.

(8) Changtukang, in the midst of Chusan Archipelago.

(9) Shipu, north of Sammen Bay, east of Chekiang.

(10) Funing, between Foochow and Wenchow, east of Fukien.

(11) Meichow Harbor, north of Meichow Island, between Foochow and Amoy.

Four fishing harbors should be constructed on the southern coast, that is, along the seaboard of Kwangtung and Hainan Island, as follows.

(12) Sanmei, on the eastern coast of Kwangtung, between Hongkong and Swatow.

(13) Sikiang Mouth. This harbor should be on the northern side of Wangkum Island. When the Sikiang Mouth is regulated, the Wangkum Island will be connected with the mainland by a sea wall, so a good harbor site could thus be provided.

(14) Haian, situated at the end of the Luichow Peninsula opposite to Hoihou, on the other side of Hainan Strait.

(15) Yulinkang a fine natural harbor at the extreme south of the Hainan Island.

These fifteen fishing harbors with the greater ports, numbering 31 in all, will link up the whole coast line of China from Antung, on the Korean border to Yamchow, near the Annam border, providing, on an average, a port for every 100 miles of coast line. This completes my project of seaports and fishing harbors for China.

At first sight objections might be raised that too many seaports and fishing harbors are provided for one country. But I must remind my readers that this one country, China, is as big as Europe and has a population larger than that of Europe. If we take a similar length of the coast line of western Europe we would see that there are many more ports in Europe than in China. Besides, the coast line of Europe is many times longer than that of China, and in every hundred miles of the European coast line there are more than one considerable-sized port. Take Holland, for instance. Its whole area is not larger than the hinterland of Swatow, one of our third-class seaports, yet it possesses two first-class ports, Amsterdam and Rotterdam, and numerous small fishing ports. Let us also compare our country with the United States of America in regard to seaports. America has only one fourth the population of China yet the number of ports on her Atlantic coast alone is many times more than the number provided in my plan. Thus, this number of ports for China for the future is but a bare necessity. And I have considered only those that will pay from the beginning so as to adhere strictly to the principle of remuneration that was laid down at the outset of my first program. See Map XVI.

七、吕四港：在扬子江口北边一点。

八、长涂港：在舟山列岛之中央。

九、石浦：浙江之东，三门湾之北。

十、福宁：在福建之东，介于福州与温州之间。

十一、湄州港：福州与厦门之间，湄州岛之北方。

南部广东省及海南岛海岸，应建四渔业港如下：

十二、汕尾：在广东之东海岸，香港、汕头之间。

十三、西江口：此港应建于横琴岛之北侧。西江口既经整治以后，横琴岛将借海堤以与本陆相连，而有一良好港面地区出现矣。

十四、海安：此港位于雷州半岛之末端，隔琼州海峡与海南岛之海口相对。

十五、榆林港：海南岛南端之一良好天然港面也。

以此十五渔业港，合之前述各较大之港，总三十有一。可以连合中国全海岸线，起于高丽界之安东，止于近越南界之钦州。平均每海岸线百英里，而得一港。吾之中国海港及渔业港计划，于是始完。

瞥见之下，当有致疑于一国而须如是之多海港与渔业港者。然读者须记此中国一国之大与欧洲等，其人则较欧洲为多。如使吾人取西欧海岸线与中国等长之一节计之，则知欧洲海港之多，远过中国。欧洲海岸线之长过中国数倍，而以每百英里计，尚不止有一与此相当形式之港。例如荷兰，其全地域不较大于吾人三等港中汕头一港之腹地，而尚有安斯得坦与洛得坦两头等海港，[67] 又有多数之小渔业港附随之。又使与北美合众国较其海港，美国人口仅得中国四分之一，而单就其大西洋沿岸海港而论，已数倍于吾计划中所举之数。所以此项海港之数，不过仅敷中国将来必要之用而已。且吾亦仅择其自始有利可图者言之，以坚守第一计划中所标定之“必选有利之途”一原则也。（参照第十六图。）

MAP XVI 第十六圖

First Class Port 頭等港
Second Class Port 二等港
Third class Port 三等港
Fishing Port 漁業港
Foreign Occupied Port 外國占領港

(1) Antang 安東
(2) Haiyangtao 海洋島
(3) Chihwangtao 秦皇島
(4) Lungkau 龍口
(5) Shitauwan 石島灣
(6) Sinyangkang 新洋港
(7) Luszekang 呂四港
(8) Changtukang 長塗港
(9) Shipu 石浦
(10) Funing 福寧
(11) Meichow 湄州
(12) Sanmei 汕尾
(13) Sikiang Mouth 西江口
(14) Haian 海安
(15) Yulinkiang 榆林港

北方大港 Great Northern P.
葫蘆島 Hulutao
營口 Yingkow
大連 Talien
芝罘 Chefoo
黃河口 HoangHo
青島 Tsingtau
海州 Haichow
東方大港 Great Eastern P.
寧波 Ningpo
溫州 Wenchow
福州 Foochow
南方大港 Great Southern P.
廈門 Amoy
汕頭 Swatow
Yamchow 欽州
Tunpak 白雹
香港 HongKong
海口 Hoihou

● Part V The Establishment of Shipbuilding Yards

When China is well developed according to my programs, the possession of an oversea mercantile fleet, of ships for coastal and inland water transportation, and of a large fishing fleet will be an urgent necessity. Before the outbreak of the late World War, the world's seagoing tonnage was 45,000,000 tons. If China is equally developed industrially, according to the proportion of her population, she would need at least 10,000,000 tons of oversea and coastal shipping for her transportation service. The building of this tonnage must be a part of our industrial development scheme; for cheap materials and labor can be obtained in the country, and so we could build ships for ourselves much cheaper than any foreign country could do for us. And besides the building of a seagoing fleet, we have to build our inland water crafts and fishing fleets. Foreign shipping yards could not do this service for us on account of the impracticability of transporting such numerous small crafts across the ocean. Thus, in any case, China has to put up her own yards to build her inland water crafts and fishing fleets. So the establishment of ship building yards is a necessary as well as a profitable undertaking from

• 第五部 创立造船厂

当中国既经按吾计划发展无缺之际，其急要者，当有一航行海外之商船队，亦要多数沿岸及内地之浅水运船，并须有无数之渔船。当此次世界大战未开之际，全世界海船吨数为四千五百万吨；使中国在实业上，按其人口比例，有相等之发达，则至少须有航行海外及沿岸商船一千万吨，然后可敷运输之用。建造此项商船，必须在吾发展实业计划中占一位置。以中国有廉价之劳工与材料，固当比外国为吾人所建所费较廉。且除航海船队以外，吾人尚须建造大队内河浅水船及渔船，以船载此等小船远涉重洋，实际不易，故外国船厂不能为吾建造此等船只，则中国于此际必须自设备其船厂，自建其浅水船、渔船船队矣。然则建立造船厂者，必要之企业，又自始为有利之企业者。

the beginning. The shipping yards should be established at such river and coastal ports that have the facility of supplying materials and labor. All the yards should be under one central management. Large capital should be invested in the project so as to procure a yearly output of 2,000,000 tons of various kinds of vessels.

All types of vessels should be standardized both in design and equipment. The old and wasteful types of inland water crafts and fishing boats should be replaced by modern efficient designs. The inland water crafts should be designed on the basis of certain standard draughts such as the 2-foot, 5-foot, and 10-foot classes. The fishing trawlers should be standardized into the one-day, the five-day, and the ten-day service class. The coastal transports should be standardized into the 2,000-, the 4,000-, and the 6,000-ton class, and for oversea transports we should have standardized ships of 12,000-, 24,000-, and 36,000-ton classes. Thus, the many thousands of inland water crafts and fishing junks that now ply the rivers, lakes, and coasts of China may be displaced by new and cheaper crafts of a few standard types which could perform better services at less expense.

此造船厂应建于内河及海岸商埠，便于得材料人工之处。所有船厂应归一处管理，而投大资本于此计划，至年可造各种船只二百万吨之限为止。

一切船舶当以其设计及其设备定有基准，所有旧式内河浅水船及渔船，当以新式效力大之设计代之。内河浅水船当以一定之吃水基准为基础设计之，如二英尺级、五英尺级、十英尺级之类。鱼拖船（船旁拖网者）应以行一日、行五日、行十日分级为基准。沿海船可分为二千吨级、四千吨级、六千吨级。而驶赴海外之船，则当设定一万二千吨级、二万四千吨级、三万六千吨级为基准。于是今日以万计之内河船及渔艇来往中国各江、各湖、各海岸者，将为基准划一，可使费少、功多、较新、较廉之船只所代矣。

PROGRAM IV

In my first and third programs, I have described my plans for the Northwestern Railway System and the Southwestern Railway System. The former is for the purpose of relieving the congestion of population in the coast districts and the Yangtze Valley by opening up for colonization the vast unpopulated territory in Mongolia and Sinkiang, as well as of developing the Great Northern Port. The latter is for the purpose of exploiting the mineral resources of Southwestern China, as well as of developing the Great Southern Port—Canton. More railroads will be needed for the adequate development of the whole country. So in this fourth program, I shall deal entirely with railroads which will complete the 100,000 miles proposed in my introductory part of this International Development Scheme. The program will be as follows:

I. The Central Railway System.
II. The Southeastern Railway System.
III. The Northeastern Railway System.
IV. The Extension of the Northwestern Railway System.
V. The Highland Railway System.
VI. The Establishment of Locomotive and Car Factories.

● Part I The Central Railway System

This will be the most important railway system in China. The area which it serves comprises all of China Proper north of the Yangtze and a part of Mongolia and Sinkiang. The economic nature of this vast region is that the southeastern part is densely populated while the northwestern part is thinly populated, and that the southeastern part possesses great mineral wealth while the northwestern part possesses great potential agricultural resources. So every line of this system will surely pay as the Peking-Mukden line has proved.

With the Great Eastern Port and the Great Northern Port as termini of this system of railroads, I propose that, besides the existing and projected lines in this region, the following be constructed, all of which shall constitute the Central Railway System.

a. The Great Eastern Port-Tarbogotai line.
b. The Great Eastern Port-Urga line.

肆 第四计划

在吾第一、第三两计划，吾已详写吾西南铁路系统、西北铁路系统两规划矣。前者以移民于蒙古、新疆之广大无人境地，消纳长江及沿海充盈之人口为目的，而又以开发北方大港；后者则所以开中国西南部之矿产富源，又以开发广州之南方大港也。此外仍须有铁路多条，以使全国得相当之开发。故于此第四计划，吾于《国际共同发展计划》绪论中所拟十万英里之铁路细加说明，其目如下：

一、中央铁路系统。
二、东南铁路系统。
三、东北铁路系统。
四、扩张西北铁路系统。
五、高原铁路系统。
六、创立机关车、客货车制造厂。

第一部　中央铁路系统

此系统将为中国铁路系统中最重要者，其效能所及之地区，遍包长江以北之中国本部，及蒙古、新疆之一部。论此广大地域之经济的性质，则其东南一部人口甚密，西北则疏；东南大有矿产之富，而西北则有潜在地中之农业富源。所以此系统中每一线，皆能保其能有利如京奉路也。

以此北方、东方两大港为此系统诸路之终点故，吾拟除本区现有及已计划各线之外，建筑下列各线，合而成为中央铁路系统：

天　东方大港塔城线。
地　东方大港库伦线。

c. The Great Eastern Port-Uliassutai line.
d. The Nanking-Loyang line.
e. The Nanking-Hankow line.
f. The Sian-Tatung line.
g. The Sian-Ninghsia line.
h. The Sian-Hankow line.
i. The Sian-Chungking line.
j. The Lanchow-Chungking line.
k. The Ansichow-Iden line.
l. The Chochiang-Koria line.
m. The Great Northern Port-Hami line.
n. The Great Northern Port-Sian line.
o. The Great Northern Port-Hankow line.
p. The Hoangho Port-Hankow line.
q. The Chefoo-Hankow line.
r. The Haichow-Tsinan line.
s. The Haichow-Hankow line.
t. The Haichow-Nanking line.
u. The Sinyangkang-Hankow line.
v. The Luszekang-Nanking line.
w. The Coast line.
x. The Hwoshan-Kashing line.

a. The Great Eastern Port-Tarbogotai Line

This line begins at the Great Eastern Port on the seaboard, and runs in a northwesterly direction to Tarbogotai on the Russian frontier, covering a distance of about 3,000 miles. If Shanghai be the Great Eastern Port, the Shanghai-Nanking Railway will form its first section. But if Chapu be chosen, then this line should skirt the Taihu Lake on the southwest through the cities of Huchow, Changhing, and Liyang to Nanking, then crossing the Yangtze at a point south of Nanking, to Chiantsiao and

Tingyuen. Thence, the line turns westward to Showchow and Yingshang, and enters Honan province at Sintsai. After crossing the Peking-Hankow line at Kioshan, and passing Piyang, Tanghsien, and Tengchow, it turns

玄　东方大港乌里雅苏台线
黄　南京洛阳线。
宇　南京汉口线。
宙　西安大同线。
洪　西安宁夏线。
荒　西安汉口线。
日　西安重庆线。
月　兰州重庆线。
盈　安西州于阗线。
昃　婼羌库尔勒线。
辰　北方大港哈密线。
宿　北方大港西安线。
列　北方大港汉口线。
张　黄河港汉口线。
寒　芝罘汉口线。
来　海州济南线。
暑　海州汉口线。
往　海州南京线。
秋　新洋港南京线。
收　吕四港南京线。
冬　海岸线。
藏　霍山嘉兴线。

天　东方大港塔城线

此线起自东方大港之海边，向西北直走，至俄国交界之塔城为止，全长约三千英里。如使以上海为东方大港，则沪宁铁路即成为此路之首一段。但若择用乍浦，则此线应沿太湖之西南岸，经湖州、长兴、溧阳，以至南京。于是在南京之南，渡长江，至全椒及定远。此时线转而西，经寿州及颍上，于新蔡入河南界。在确山，横截京汉线后，过泌阳、唐县、邓州，转而西北，

northwestward to Sichwan and Kingtsekwan, and enters the province of Shensi. Ascending the Tan Kiang Valley, it passes through Lungkucha and Shangchow, and crosses the Tsinling Pass to Lantien and Sian, the capital of Shensi, formerly the capital of China. From Sian, it goes westward, following the valley of the Weiho. It passes through Chowchih, Meihsien, and Paoki and enters the province of Kansu at Sancha, thence proceeding to Tsinchow, Kungchang, Titao, and Lanchow, the capital of Kansu. From Lanchow it follows the old highway which leads into Liangchow, Kanchow, Suchow, Yumen, and Ansichow. Thence it crosses the desert in a northwesterly direction to Hami, where it turns westward to Turfan. At Turfan this line meets the Northwestern Railway System and runs on the latter's track to Urumochi and Manass where it leaves that track and proceeds northwesterly to Tarbogotai on the frontier, crossing the Shair Mountain on the way. This line runs from one end of the country to the other encountering in its entire length of 3,000 miles only four mountain passes, all of which are not impassable for they have been used from time immemorial, as trade highways of Asia.

b. The Great Eastern Port-Urga Line

This line starts from the Great Eastern Port and uses the same track as line (a) as far as Tingyuen, the second city after crossing the Yangtze River at Nanking. From Tingyuen, its own track begins and the line proceeds in a northwesterly direction to Hwaiyuan, on the Hwai River, thence to Mongcheng, Kwoyang, and Pochow. Turning more northward, it crosses the Anhwei border into Honan, and passing through Kweiteh it crosses the Honan border into Shantung. After passing through Tsaohsien, Tingtao, and Tsaochow, it crosses the Hoangbo and enters Chihli province. Passing through Kaichow it re-enters Honan to Changteh, thence it follows the Tsingchangho valley, in a northwesterly direction, across the Honan border into Shansi. Here the line enters the northeastern corner of the vast iron and coal field of Shansi. After entering Shansi, the line follows the river valley to Liaochow and Yicheng, and crosses the watershed into the Tungkwoshui Valley to Yutse and Taiyuan. From Taiyuan, it proceeds northwestward through another rich iron and coal field of Shansi to Kolan. Thence, it turns westward to Poate, where it crosses the Hoangho to Fuku, in the northeastern corner of Shensi. From Fuku, the line proceeds northward, cuts through the Great Wall into the Suiyuan District and crosses the Hoangho to Saratsi.

至淅川及荆紫关，入陕西界。溯丹江谷地而上，通过龙驹寨及商州，度蓝关至蓝田及西安。西安者，陕西之省城，中国之古都也。由西安循渭河而西行，过盩厔、郿县、宝鸡，于三坌入甘肃界。进向秦州、巩昌、狄道，及于甘肃省城之兰州。自兰州从昔日通路，以至凉州、甘州、肃州、玉门及安西州。由此西北行，横绝沙漠以至哈密。自哈密转而西，达土鲁番[68]。在土鲁番，与西北铁路系统之线会，即用其线路轨，以至迪化及绥来。自绥来与该线分离，直向边界上之塔城，途中切断齐尔山而过。此线自中国之一端至于他一端，全长三千英里，仅经过四山脉。而此四山脉皆非不可逾越者，由其自未有历史以前已成为亚洲贸易路一事，可以知之矣。

地　东方大港库伦线

此线自东方大港起，即用天线路轨迄于定远。定远即在南京渡江后第二城也。自定远起，始自建其路轨，进向西北，达于淮河上之怀远。于是历蒙城、涡阳及亳州，更转迻北，过安徽界，入河南，经归德，又出河南界，入山东界。于是经曹县、定陶、曹州，渡黄河，入直隶界。通过开州，再入河南，至于彰德。自彰德循清漳河谷地西北走，出河南界，入山西界。于是本线通过山西省大煤铁矿田之东北隅矣。既入山西，仍遵此谷地，至辽州及仪城，越分水界，入洞涡水谷地，至榆次及太原。自太原西北进，入山西省之别一煤铁矿区，至于岢岚。又转而西，至保德，于此渡黄河，至府谷，陕西省之东北隅也。此线自府谷北行，截开万里长城，入绥远区，再渡黄河，至萨拉齐。由萨拉齐起西北行，截过此大平原，

From Saratsi, the line runs in a northwesterly direction across the vast prairie to Junction A of the Northwestern Trunk Line, where it joins the common track of the Dolon Nor-Urga line to Urga. This line runs from a thickly populated country at one end in Central China to the vast thinly populated but fertile regions of Central Mongolia, having a distance of about 1,300 miles from Tingyuen to Junction A.

c. The Great Eastern Port-Uliassutai Line

Starting from the Great Eastern Port, this line follows line (a) as far as Tingyuen, and line (b) as far as Pochow. At Pochow, it branches off on its own track and proceeds westward across the border to Luye, in Honan. Thence it turns northwestward to Taikang, Tungsu, and Chungmow where it meets the Hailan line and runs in the same direction with it to Chengchow, Jungyang, and Szeshui. From Szeshui it crosses the Hoangho to Wenhsien, thence to Hwaiking and over the Honan border into Shansi. It now passes through Yangcheng, Chinshui, and Fowshan to Pingyang where it crosses the Fen River and proceeds to Puhsien and Taning, then westward to the border where it crosses the Hoangho into Shensi. Thence it proceeds to Yenchang, and follows the Yenshui Valley to Yenan, Siaokwan, and Tsingpien. Then running along the south side of the Great Wall, it enters Kansu, and crosses the Hoangho to Ninghsia. From Ninghsia, it proceeds northwestward across the Alashan Mountain to Tingyuanying at the edge of the desert. Thence it proceeds in a straight line northwestward to Junction B of the Northwestern Railway System, where it joins that system and runs to Uliassutai. This part of the line passes through desert and grassland both of which could be improved by irrigation. The distance of this line from Pochow to Junction B is 1,800 miles.

d. The Nanking-Loyang Line

This line runs between two former capitals of China, passes through a very populous and fertile country, and taps a very rich coal field at the

Loyang end. It starts from Nanking, running on the common track of lines (a) and (b) and branches off at Hwaiyuan westward to Taiho. After passing Taiho, it crosses the Anhwei border into Honan. Thence it runs alongside the left bank of the Tashaho to Chowkiakow, a large commercial town. From Chowkiakow, it proceeds to Linying where it crosses the Peking-Hankow line thence to Hiangcheng and Yuchow where the rich

至西北干路之甲接合点。在此处与多伦诺尔、库伦间之公线合，以至库伦。此线自中国中部人口最密之地，通至中部蒙古土沃人稀之广大地域。其自定远至甲接合点之间，约长一千三百英里。

玄　东方大港乌里雅苏台线

自东方大港，因用天线路轨，至于定远，再用地线路轨，至于亳州。由亳州起，分支自筑路轨，西向行越安徽省界，至河南之鹿邑。自此处转向西北，逾太康、通许，以及中牟。在中牟与海兰线相会，并行至于郑州、荥阳、汜水。在汜水渡过黄河，至温县。又在怀庆出河南界，入山西界。于是乃过阳城、沁水、浮山，以至平阳。在平阳渡汾水，至蒲县、大宁。转而西，至省界，再渡黄河，入陕西境。于是进至延长，遵延水流域，以至于延安、小关、靖边，然后循长城之南边，以入甘肃。又渡黄河，至宁夏。自宁夏而西北，过贺兰山脉，至沙漠缘端之定远营。于此取一直线向西北走，直至西北铁路系统之乙接合点，与此系统合一线以至乌里雅苏台。此线所经之沙漠及草地之部分，均可以以灌溉工事改善之。其自亳州至乙接合点之距离，为一千八百英里。

黄　南京洛阳线

此线走于中国两古都之间，通过烟户[69]极稠、地质极肥之乡落，又于洛阳一端触及极丰富之矿田。此线自南京起，走于天、地两线公共路轨之上，自怀远起始分支西行，至太和。既过太和，乃逾安徽界，入河南界。又沿大沙河之左岸，至周家口，此一大商业市镇也。自周家口进至于临颖，与京汉线交。更进至襄城、禹州，则河南省大煤矿田所在地也。

coal field of Honan lies. After Yuchow it crosses the Sungshan watershed to Loyang where it meets the Hailan line running from east to west. This line is about 300 miles from Hwaiyuan to Loyang.

e. The Nanking-Hankow Line

This line will run alongside the left bank of the Yangtzekiang, connecting with Kiukiang by a branch line. It starts on the opposite side of Nanking and goes southwest to Hochow, Wuweichow and Anking, the capital of Anwei province. After Anking, it continues in the same direction to Susung and Hwangmei, where a branch should be projected to Siaochikow, thence across the Yangtze River to Kiukiang. After Hwangmei, the line turns westward to Kwangchi, then northwestward to Kishui, and finally westward to Hankow. It covers a distance of about 350 miles through a comparatively level country.

f. The Sian-Tatung Line

This line starts from Sian and runs northward to Sanyuan,Yaochow, Tungkwan, Yichun, Chungpu, Foochow, Kanchuan, and Yenan, where it meets the Great Eastern Port-Uliassutai line. From Yenan, it turns northeastward to Suiteh, Michih, and Kiachow on the right bank of the Hoangho. Thence it runs along the same bank to the junction of the Weifen River with the Hoangho (on the opposite side), where it crosses the Hoaugho to the Weifen Valley and proceeds to Singhsien and Kolan, there crossing the Great Eastern Port-Urga line. From Kolan, it proceeds to Wuchai and Yangfang, where it crosses the Great Wall to Sochow and then Tatung there meeting the Peking-Suiyuan line. This line is about 600 miles long. It passes through the famous oil field in Shensi, and the northern border of the northwestern Shansi coal field. At Tatung, where it ends, it joins the Peking-Suiyuan line and through the section from Tatung to Kalgan it will connect with the future Northwestern System which will link Kalgan and Dolon Nor together.

g. The Sian-Ninghsia Line

This line will start from Sian in a northwesterly direction to Kingyanghsien, Shunhwa, and Sanshui. After Sanshui, it crosses the Shensi border into Kansu at Chengning and then turns west to Ningchow. From Ningchow, it follows the Hwan Valley along the left bank of the river up to Kingyangfu and Hwanhsien, where it leaves the bank and proceeds to Tsingping and Pingyuan, where it meets the Hwan

自禹州而往，过嵩山分水界，以逮洛阳，与自东徂西之海兰线相会。此线自怀远至洛阳，凡三百英里。

宇　南京汉口线

此线应循扬子江岸而行，以一支线与九江联络。自南京对岸起西南行，至和州、无为州及安庆。安庆者，安徽者城也。自安庆起，仍循同一方向至宿松、黄梅。自黄梅别开一支线，至小池口，渡扬子江，以达九江。本线则自黄梅转而西至广济，又转而西北至蕲水，卒西向以至汉口，距离约三百五十英里，而所走之路平坦较多。

宙　西安大同线

此线自西安起，北行至于三原、耀州、同官、宜君、中部、甘泉，以至延安，与东方大港乌里雅苏台线相会。自延安起转而东北，至于绥德、米脂及黄河右岸之葭州，即循此岸而行，至蔚汾河与黄河汇流处（在对岸）。渡黄河至蔚汾河谷地，循之以至兴县、岢岚，在岢岚与东方大港库伦线相交。过岢岚，至五寨及羊房。在羊房截长城而过，至朔州，乃至大同，与京绥线相会。此线约长六百英里。经过陕西有名之煤油矿，又过山西西北煤田之北境，其在终点大同与京绥线合。借大同至张家口一段之助，可与将来西北系统中联络张家口与多伦诺尔之一线相属。

洪　西安宁夏线

此线应自西安起，西北向行，至泾阳县、淳化、三水（今改称栒邑）。过三水后，出陕西界，入甘肃界，于正宁转而西，至宁州。自宁州始入环河谷地，循其左岸，上至庆阳府及环县。乃离河岸，经清平、

River again and follows that valley up to the watershed. After crossing the watershed, it proceeds to Lingchow, then across the Hoangho to Ninghsia. This line covers a distance of about 400 miles and passes through a rich mineral and petroleum country.

h. The Sian-Hankow Line

This is a very important line connecting the richest portion of the Hoangho Valley with the richest portion of the central section of the Yangtze Valley. It starts from Sian on the track of line (a), crosses the Tsingling and descends the Tankiang Valley as far as Sichwan. At this point, it branches off southward across the border into Hupeh, and following the left bank of the Han River, passes Laohokow to Fencheng, opposite Siangyang. After Fencheng, it follows continuously the same bank of the Han River to Anlu, thence proceeding in a direct line southeastward to Hanchwan and Hankow. This line is about 300 miles long.

i. The Sian-Chungking Line

This line starts from Sian almost directly southward, crosses the Tsingling Mountain into the Han Valley, passes through Ningshen, Shihchuan, and Tzeyang, ascends the Jenho Valley across the southern border of Shensi into the province of Szechwan at Tachuho. Then crossing the watershed of the Tapashan into the Tapingho Valley, it follows that valley down to Suiting and Chuhsien. Thence it turns to the left side of the valley to Linshui and follows the trade road to Kiangpeh and Chungking. The entire distance of this line is about 450 miles through a very productive region and rich timber land.

j. The Lanchow-Chungking Line

This line starts from Lanchow southwestward and follows the same route as line (a) as far as Titao. Thence, it branches off and ascends the Taoho Valley across the Minshan watershed into the Heishui Valley following it down to Kiaichow and Pikow. After Pikow, it crosses the Kansu border into Szechwan and proceeds to Chaohwa, where the Heishuiho joins the Kialing. From Chaohwa, it follows the course of the Kialing River down to Paoning, Shunking, Hochow, and Chungking. The line is about 600 miles long, running through a very productive and rich mineral land.

平远后，与环河相会，仍循该谷地，上至分水界。过分水界后，至灵州，渡黄河至宁夏。此线长约四百英里，经过矿产及石油最富之地区。

荒　西安汉口线

此线联络黄河流域最富饶一部与中部长江流域最富饶一部之一重要线路。此线自西安起，用天线路轨，过秦岭，进至丹江谷地。直至淅川，始分线南行，过省界，至湖北。循汉水左岸，经老河口，以至襄阳对岸之樊城。由樊城仍循此岸以至安陆，由此以一直线东南至汉川及汉口。全线约长三百英里。

日　西安重庆线

此线自西安起，直向南行，度秦岭，入汉水谷地。经宁陕、石泉、紫阳，进入任河谷地，逾陕西之南界，于大竹河入四川界。于是逾大巴山之分水界，以入太平河谷地。循此谷地而下，至绥定及渠县，乃转入此谷地之左边，至于邻水。又循商路，以至江北及重庆。此线全长约四百五十英里，经由极多产物之地区及富于材木之地。

月　兰州重庆线

此线从兰州起西南行，用天线之线路，直至狄道为止。由此分支进入洮河谷地，过岷山分水界，入黑水谷地沿之而下，至于阶州及碧口。自碧口而降，出甘肃界，入四川界，进逮昭化黑水河，即在昭化与嘉陵江合。自昭化起，即顺嘉陵江，降至保宁、顺庆、合州以及重庆。此线约长六百英里，经过物产极多、矿山极富之地区。

k. The Ansichow-Iden Line

This line passes through the fertile belt of land between the Gobi Desert and the Altyntagh Mountain. Although this strip of land is well watered by numerous mountain streams yet it is very sparsely populated, owing to the lack of means of communication. When this line is completed, this strip of land will be most valuable to Chinese colonists. The line starts from Ansichow westward to Tunhwang, and skirts the southern edge of the Lobnor Swamp to Chochiang. From Chochiang, it proceeds in the same direction via Cherchen to Iden where it connects with the terminus of the Northwestern System. With this System, it forms a continuous and direct line from the Great Eastern Port to Kashgar at the extreme west end of China. This line from Ansichow to Iden is about 800 miles in length.

l. The Chochiang-Koria Line

This line runs across the desert alongside the lower part of the Tarim River. The land on both sides of the line is well watered and will be valuable for colonization as soon as the railroad is completed. This line is about 250 miles in length and connects with the line that runs along the northern edge of the desert. It is a short cut between fertile lands on the two sides of the desert.

m. The Great Northern Port-Hami Line

This line runs from the Great Northern Port in a northwesterly direction by way of Paoti and Siangho to Peking. From Peking it runs on the same track with the Peking-Kalgan Railway to Kalgan, where it ascends the Mongolian Plateau. Then it follows the caravan road northwestward to Chintai, Bolutai, Sessy, and Tolibulyk. From Tolibulyk, it takes a straight line westward crossing the prairie and desert of both the Inner and Outer Mongolia to Hami where it connects with the Great Eastern Port-Tarbogotai line which runs almost directly west to

Urumochi, the capital of Sinkiang. Thus, it will be the direct line from Urumochi to Peking and the Great Northern Port. This line is about 1,500 miles in length, the greater part of which will run through arable land and so when it is completed it will form one of the most valuable railways for colonization.

盈 安西州于阗线

此线贯通于戈壁沙漠与阿勒腾塔格岭中间一带肥沃之地。虽此一带地方，本为无数山间小河所灌溉，润泽无缺，而人口尚极萧条，则交通方法缺乏之所致也。此线完成之后，此一带地方必为中国殖民最有价值之处。此线起自安西州，西行至敦煌，循罗布泊沼地之南缘端，以至婼羌。自婼羌仍用同一方向，经车城，以至于阗，与西北系统线之终点相接。借此系统之助，得一东方大港与中国极西端之喀什噶尔直接相通之线。自安西州以至于阗，长约八百英里。

昃 婼羌库尔勒线

此线沿塔里木河之下游，截过沙漠，其线路两旁之地给水丰足，铁路一旦完成，即为殖民上最有价值之地。本线长约二百五十英里，与走于沙漠北缘端之线上联属。沙漠两边肥饶土地之间，此为捷径。

辰 北方大港哈密线

此线自北方大港西北行，经宝坻、香河，以至北京。由北京起即用京张路轨，以至张家口，由此以进入蒙古高原。于是循用商队通路，向西北行，以至陈台、布鲁台、哲斯、托里布拉克。自托里布拉克向西，取一直线，横度内外蒙古之平原及沙漠，以至哈密，以与东方大港塔城线相联络。而该线则直通于西方新疆首府之迪化。故此线，即为迪化城与北京及北方大港之直通线。此线长约一千五百英里，其中有大部分走于可耕地之上。然则其完成之后，必为殖民上最有价值之铁路矣。

n. The Great Northern Port-Sian Line

This line will run westward from the Great Northern Port to Tientsin. From here it runs southwestward to Hokien, passing through Tsinghai and Tachen. From Hokien, it runs more westerly to Shentseh, Wuki, and Chengting where it joins the Chengtai line as well as crosses the Kinhan line. From Chengting it takes the same road as the narrow-gauge Chengtai line which has to be reconstructed into standard gauge so as to facilitate through trains to Taiyuan and farther on. From Taiyuan it runs southwestward to Kiaocheng, Wenshui, Fenchow, Sichow, and Taning. After Taning it turns westward and crossing the Hoangho, it turns southwestward to Yichwan, Lochwan, and Chungpu where it joins the Sian-Tatung line and runs on the same tracks to Sian. Its length is about 700 miles over very rich and extensive iron, coal, and petroleum fields, as well as productive agricultural lands.

o. The Great Northern Port-Hankow Line

This line starts from the Great Northern Port skirting the coast to Petang, Taku, and Chikow, thence to Yenshan and crosses the Chihli border into Shantung at Loling. From Loling, it goes to Tehping, Linyi and Yucheng where it crosses the Tientsin-Pukow line, proceeds to Tungchang and Fanhsien, and then crosses the Hoangho to Tsaochow. After Tsaochow it passes the Shantung border into Honan, crossing the Hailan line to Suichow. From Suichow it proceeds to Taikang where it crosses line (c), then to Chenchow and Chowkiakow where it crosses line (d) and thence to Siangcheng, Sintsai, Kwangchow, and Kwangshan. After Kwangshan it crosses the boundary mountain into Hupeh, passing through Hwangan to Hankow. This line is about 700 miles long, running from the Great Northern Port to the commercial center of central China.

p. The Hoangho Port-Hankow Line

This line starts from the Hoangho Port in a southwesterly direction to Pohsing, Sincheng, and Changshan, then across the Kiauchow-Tsinan line to Poshan. Thence it ascends the watershed into the Wen Valley to Taian where it crosses the Tientsin-Pukow line to Ningyang and Tsining. From Tsining it proceeds in a straight line southwestward to Pochow in Anhwei, and Sintsai in Honan. At Sintsai it joins the Great Northern Port-Hankow line to Hankow. The distance of this line from the Hoangho Port to Sintsai is about 400 miles.

宿　北方大港西安线

此线自北方大港西行，至于天津。由该处西行，经过静海、大城，以至河间。由河间更偏西行，至于深泽、无极，又与京汉线交于正定，即于此处与正太线相接。自正定起，即用正太线路。但该线之窄轨，应重新建筑，改为标准轨阔，此所以便于太原以往之通车也。自太原起，此线向西南行，经交城、文水、汾州、隰州，以至大宁。由大宁转而西行，渡黄河。又西南行，至宜川、洛川、中部。在中部，与西安大同线相会，即用其路线以达西安。此线长约七百英里。其所经者，则农产物极多之地区，又煤、铁、石油丰富广大之矿田也。

列　北方大港汉口线

此线自北方大港起，循海岸而行，至北塘、大沽、岐口，又至盐山，出直隶界，入山东界于乐陵。自乐陵而往，经德平、临邑，至禹城，与津浦线相交，进至东昌、范县，于是渡黄河，至曹州。既过曹州，出山东界，入河南界，与海兰线相交，至睢州。由此进至太康，与玄线相交，经陈州及周家口，与黄线相交，又至项城、新蔡、光州及光山。既过光山，逾分界岭，入湖北境，经黄安，至汉口。此线长约七百英里，自北方大港以至中国中部之商业中心。

张　黄河港汉口线

此线自黄河港起，西南行，至于博兴、新城、长山，乃与胶济线相交，至博山。上至分水界，入于汶河谷地，至泰安。与津浦线相交，又至宁阳及济宁。自济宁而进，以一直线向西南，至安徽之亳州、河南之新蔡。自新蔡起，与北方大港汉口线合，以至汉口。自黄河港至新蔡，约四百英里。

q. The Chefoo-Hankow Line

This line starts at Chefoo on the northern side of the Shantung Peninsula and crosses that Peninsula to Tsimo, on the southern side, via Laiyang and Kinkiakow. From Tsimo it proceeds southwestward across the shallow mud flat at the head of Kiauchow Bay in a straight line to Chucheng. After Chucheng it crosses the watershed into the Shuho Valley to Chuchow and Ichow, then proceeds to Hsuchow where it meets the Tientsin-Pukow line and the Hailan line. From Hsuchow it runs on the same track with the Tientsin-Pukow line as far as Suchow in Anhwei, then branches off to Mongcheng and Yinchow, and crosses the border into Honan at Kwangchow, where it meets the Great Northern Port-Hankow line and proceeds together to Hankow. This line from Chefoo to Kwangchow is about 550 miles in length.

r. The Haichow-Tsinan Line

This line starts from Haichow following the Linhung River to Kwantunpu, then turns westward to Ichow. From Ichow it turns first northward then northwestward, passing by Mongyin and Sintai to Tai-an. At Tai-an it joins the Tsinpu line and proceeds in the same track to Tsinan. This line covers a distance, from Haichow to Tai-an, of about 110 miles, tapping the coal and iron fields of southern Shantung.

s. The Haichow-Hankow Line

This line starts at Haichow in a southwesterly direction, goes to Shuyang and Sutsien, probably in the same route as the projected Hailan line. From Sutsien it proceeds to Szechow and Hwaiyuan, where it crosses the Great Eastern Port Urga and Uliassutai lines. After Hwaiyuan it goes to Showchow and Chenyangkwan, thence continuing in the same direction across the southeastern corner of Honan and the boundary mountain into Hupeh, proceeds to Macheng and Hankow, covering a distance of about 400 miles.

t. The Haichow-Nanking Line

This line goes from Haichow southward to Antung then inclining a little south to Hwaian. After Hwaian it crosses the Paoying Lake (which will be reclaimed according to the regulation of the Hwaiho in Part IV, Program II) to Tienchang and Luho, thence to Nanking. Distance, about 180 miles.

寒　芝罘汉口线

此线起于山东半岛北边之芝罘，即横断此半岛，经过莱阳、金家口，以至于其南边之即墨。由即墨起，向西南，过胶州湾顶之洼泥地，作一直线，至于诸城。既过诸城，越分水界以入沭河谷地，至莒州及沂州，进至徐州，与津浦海兰线相会。自徐州起，即用津浦路轨，直至安徽之宿州。乃分路至蒙城、颍州，过省界，入河南光州，即于此处与北方大港汉口线相会，由之以至汉口。此线自芝罘至光州，长约五百五十英里。

来　海州济南线

此线发海州，循临洪河至欢墩埠，转西向，至临沂。由临沂始转北向，次西北向，经蒙阴、新泰，至泰安。在泰安与津浦线会合，取同一轨道，而至济南。此线自海州至泰安，长约一百一十英里，经过山东南部之煤铁矿场。

暑　海州汉口线

此线自海州出发，西南行，至沭阳与宿迁，或与现在海兰线之预定线路相同。自宿迁而往，经泗州、怀远，与东方大港库伦线及乌里雅苏台线相交。既过怀远，乃向寿州及正阳关，即循同一方向，横过河南省之东南角及湖北之分界岭，过麻城，至汉口。长约四百英里。

往　海州南京线

此线从海州向南至安东，稍南至淮安。既过淮安，渡宝应湖（此湖应按第二计划第四部整治淮河，施以填筑），经天长、六合，以至南京。全长一百八十英里。

u. The Sinyangkang-Hankow Line

This line starts from Sinyangkang to Yencheng, then crossing the Tasung Lake (which will be reclaimed) to Hwaian. From Hwaian it turns southwestward passing over the southeastern corner of the Hungtse Lake (which will also be reclaimed) to Suyi, in Anhwei. After Suyi, it crosses the Tientsin-Pukow line near Mingkwang, to Tingyuen, where it meets lines (b) and (c). After Tingyuen, it proceeds to Liu-an and Hwoshan, then crosses the boundary mountain into Hupeh passing through Lotien to Hankow, a distance of about 420 miles.

v. The Luszekang-Nanking Line

This line starts at Luszekang, a fishing harbor to be constructed at the extremity of the northern point of the Yangtze Estuary. From Luszekang it proceeds westward to Tungchow where it turns northwestward to Jukao, and then westward to Taichow, Yangchow, Luho, and Nanking. This line is about 200 miles long.

w. The Coast Line

This line starts at the Great Northern Port, and follows the Great Northern Port-Hankow line as far as Chikow, where it begins its own line. Keeping along the coast, it crosses the Chihli border to the Hoangho Port, in Shantung, then proceeds to Laichow where it takes a straight cut away from the coast to Chaoyuan and Chefoo, thus avoiding the projected Chefoo-Weihsien line. From Chefoo it proceeds southeastward through Ninghai to Wenteng, where one branch runs to Jungcheng and another to Shihtao. The main line turns southwestward to Haiyang and Kinkiakow, where it joins the Chefoo-Hankow line, and follows it as far as the western side of Kiauchow Bay, thence southward to Lingshanwei. From Lingshanwei the line proceeds southwestward along the coast to Jichao, and crosses the

Shantung border into Kiangsu, passing Kanyu to Haichow. Thence it proceeds southeastward to Yencheng, Tungtai, Tungchow, Haimen, and Tsungming Island which will be connected with the mainland by the regulation works of Yangtze embankment. From Tsungming trains can be ferried over to Shanghai. This line from Chikow to Tsungming is about 1,000 miles in length.

秋 新洋港汉口线

此线自新洋港而起，至于盐城，过大纵湖（此亦应填筑），至淮安。自淮安转向西南，渡过洪泽湖之东南角（此湖仍应填筑），至安徽之盱眙。既过盱眙，在明光附近与津浦线相交，又至定远，与地、玄两线相会。过定远后，进至六安、霍山，逾湖北之分界岭，过罗田，以至汉口。全长约四百二十英里。

收 吕四港南京线

此线由吕四港而起。吕四港者，将来于扬子江口北端尽处应建之渔业港也。自吕四港起西行，至于通州，转西北行，至如皋，又西行至泰州、扬州、六合、南京。全长约二百英里。

冬 海岸线

此线自北方大港起，循北方大港汉口线，至于岐口。始自开线路，密接海岸以行，过直隶界，至山东之黄河港，进至于莱州。自莱州离海岸，画一直线，至招远及芝罘，以避烟潍铁路之计划线。由芝罘转而东南，经过宁海及文登。自文登引一支线至荣城，又一线至石岛，其本线转而西南，至海阳及金家口，与芝罘汉口线合。循之直至于胶州湾之西端，折而南至灵山卫。自灵山卫转而西南，循海岸至日照，过山东界，入江苏省，经赣榆，至海州。于是向西南，进至盐城、东台、通州、海门，以达于崇明岛。此岛以扬子江之治水堤之故，将与大陆联为一气矣。其自崇明赴上海，可用渡船载列车而过。此自岐口迄崇明之线，约长一千英里。

x. The Hwoshan-Wuhu-Soochow-Kashing Line

This line starts from Hwoshan to Shucheng and Wuwei, then across the Yangtze River to Wuhu. After Wuhu it goes to Kaoshun, Liyang, and Ihsing, then crosses over the northern end of Taihu (which will be reclaimed) to Soochow, where it meets the Shanghai-Nanking line. From Soochow it turns southward to Kashing on the Shanghai-Hangchow line. This line runs over very populous and rich districts of Anhwei and Kiangsu provinces, covering a distance of about 300 miles, which will form the greater part of the shortest line from Shanghai to Hankow.

● Part II The Southeastern Railway System

This system covers the irregular triangle which is formed by the Coast line between the Great Eastern and the Great Southern Ports, as the base, by the Yangtze River from Chungking to Shanghai, as one side, and by line (a) of the Canton-Chungking Railway as the other side, with Chungking as the apex. This triangle comprises the provinces of Chekiang, Fukien, and Kiangsi, and a part respectively of Kiangsu, Anhwei, Hupeh, Hunan, and Kwangtung. This region is very rich in mineral and agricultural products, especially iron and coal deposits which are found everywhere. And the whole region is thickly populated. So railway construction will be very remunerative.

With the Great Eastern Port and the Great Southern Port and the second- and third-class ports that lie between the two as termini of this system of railroads, I propose that the following lines be constructed:

a. The Great Eastern Port-Chungking Line.
b. The Great Eastern Port-Canton Line.
c. The Foochow-Chinkiang Line.
d. The Foochow-Wuchang Line.

e. The Foochow-Kweilin Line.
f. The Wenchow-Shenchow Line.
g. The Amoy-Kienchang Line.
h. The Amoy-Canton Line.
i. The Swatow-Changteh Line.

藏　霍山芜湖苏州嘉兴线

此线自霍山起，至舒城及无为，乃过扬子江，至芜湖。又过高淳、溧阳、宜兴，过太湖之北端（将来填筑），至苏州，与沪宁线会。过苏州后，转而南，至沪杭线上之嘉兴。此线走过皖、苏两省富庶之区，长三百英里，将成为上海、汉口间之直接路线之大部分。

中央铁路系统各线，全长统共约一万六千六百英里。

• 第二部　东南铁路系统

本系统纵横布列于一不规则三角形之一。此三角形以东方大港与广州间之海岸线为底，以扬子江重庆至上海一段为一边，更以经由湖南之广州重庆甲线为第二边，而以重庆为之顶点。此三角形全包有浙江、福建、江西三省，并及江苏、安徽、湖北、湖南、广东之各一部。此地富有农矿物产，而煤铁尤多，随在有之，且全区人口甚密，故其建铁路，必获大利。

以东方大港、南方大港及其间之二三等港，为此铁路之终点，可建筑下列之各线：

天　东方大港重庆线。
地　东方大港广州线。
玄　福州镇江线。
黄　福州武昌线。
宇　福州桂林线。
宙　温州辰州线。
洪　厦门建昌线。
荒　厦门广州线。
日　汕头常德线。

j. The Nanking-Siuchow Line.
k. The Nanking-Kaying Line.
l. The Coast Line Between the Great Eastern and Great Southern Ports.
m. The Kienchang-Yuanchow Line.

a. The Great Eastern Port-Chungking Line

This line connects the commercial center of western China—Chungking—with the Great Eastern Port in almost a straight route south of the Yangtze River. It starts from the Great Eastern Port and goes to Hangchow, then through Linan, Ghanghwa, to Hweichow, in Anhwei. From Hweichow it proceeds to Siuning and Kimen, then crosses the border into Kiangsi and passing Hukow reaches Kiukiang. From Kiukiang it follows the right bank of the Yangtze, crosses the Hupeh border to Hingkwochow and then proceeds to Tungshan and Tsungyang, where it passes over the border to Yochow in Hunan. From Yochow it takes a straight line across the Tungting Lake (which will be reclaimed) to Changteh. From Changteh it proceeds up the Liu Shui Valley, passing through Tzeli, and crossing the Hunan border to Hofeng, in Hupeh and then to Shinan and Lichwan. At Shinan a branch should be projected northeastward to Ichang, and at Lichwan another branch should be projected northwestward to Wanhsien, both on the left side of the Yangtze River. After Lichwan it crosses the Hupeh border into Szechwan, passing Shihchu to Foochow, then passes the Wukiang and proceeds along the right side of the Yangtze River as far as lines (a) and (b) of the Canton-Chungking Railway and then crosses together on the same bridge to Chungking on the other side of the river. The length of this line including branches, is about 1,200 miles.

b. The Great Eastern Port-Canton Line

This is a straight line from one first-class seaport to another. It starts from the Great Eastern Port and goes to Hangchow, then turning southwestward, follows the left bank of the Tsien Tang River through Fuyang, Tunglu to Yenchow and Chuchow. Then it proceeds across the Chekiang-Kiangsi border to Kwangsin. From Kwangsin it goes through Shangtsing and Kinki to Kienchang, then proceeds to Nanfeng, Kwangchang, and Ningtu. After Ningtu it proceeds to Yutu,

月　南京韶州线。
盈　南京嘉应线。
昃　东方南方两大港间海岸线。
辰　建昌沅州线。

天　东方大港重庆线

此线越扬子江以南，殆以一直线联结中国西方商业中心之重庆与东方大港。此线起于东方大港，至杭州，经临安、昌化，以至安徽省之徽州（歙县）。由徽州进至休宁、祁门，于是越省界，入江西境，过湖口，至九江。自九江起，循扬子江右岸，越湖北界，至兴国州，又进至通山、崇阳。在崇阳逾界至湖南岳州。自岳州起，取一直线，贯洞庭湖（此湖将来进行填塞）至于常德。由常德溯溇水谷地而上，过慈利，再逾省界，入湖北之鹤峰，于是及于施南与利川。在施南应开一支线，向东北界走，至宜昌；在利川应另开一支线，西北行至万县。此宜昌、万县两地，均在长江左岸。自利川而后，入四川界，过石硅，至涪州。遂过乌江，循扬子江右岸而上，至与广州重庆乙线会而后已。此后以同一之桥渡江，至对岸之重庆。连支线，长约一千二百英里。

地　东方大港广州线

此线由一头等海港，以一直线，至他头等海港。自东方大港起，至杭州。折而西南行，遵钱塘江左岸，过富阳、桐卢，至严州及衢州。更进过浙、赣省界，至广信（上饶）。由广信起，经上清、金溪，至建昌，然后进至南丰、广昌、宁都。由宁都而往，至雩都、

Sinfeng, Lungnan, and crossing the boundary mountain of Kiangsi and Kwangtung, to Changning. Thence via Tsungfa it goes to Canton, covering a distance of about 900 miles.

c. The Foochow-Chinkiang Line

This line starts from Foochow, goes by way of Loyuan and Ningteh to Fuan, and then proceeds across the Fukien-Chekiang border to Taishun, Kingning, Yunho, and Chuchow. Thence it proceeds to Wuyi, Yiwu, Chukih, and Hangchow. After Hangchow it goes to Tehtsing and Huchow and then crosses the Chekiang border into Kiangsu. Then it proceeds by way of Ihsing, Kintan, and Tanyang to Chinkiang. This line is about 550 miles in length.

d. The Foochow-Wuchang Line

This line starts from Foochow and following the left bank of the Min River and passing Shuikow and Yenping reaches Shaowu. After Shaowu, it proceeds across the Fukien border into Kiangsi and then passes through Kienchang and Fuchow to Nanchang, the capital of Kiangsi. From Nanchang it proceeds to Hingkwo, in Hupeh, and passes on to Wuchang, the capital of Hupeh. It covers a distance of about 550 miles.

e. The Foochow-Kweilin Line

This line starts from Foochow, crosses the Min River and proceeds by way of Yungfu, Tatien, Ningyang, and Liencheng to Tingchow. Thence it crosses the Fukien-Kiangsi border to Shuikin. From Shuikin it proceeds to Yutu and Kanchow and then to Shangyiu and Chungyi. After Chungyi it crosses the Kiangsi-Hunan border to Kweiyanghsien and Chenchow, where it crosses the Canton-Hankow line to Kweiyangchow. Thence it continues to Sintien, Ningyuan, and Taochow, where it meets lines (a) and (b) of the Canton-Chungking Railway. After Taochow it turns southward following the Taoho Valley to the Kwangsi border and then crossing it, proceeds to

Kweilin. This line covers a distance of about 750 miles.

f. The Wenchow-Shenchow Line

This line begins from the new Wenchow Port and follows the left bank of the Wukiang as far as Tsingtien. From Tsingtien it proceeds to Chuchow and Suenping and turns westward across the Chekiang border to Yushan in Kiangsi. After Yushan it goes to Tehsing, Loping, and

信丰、龙南。过赣、粤界岭，至长宁（新丰）。于是经从化，以至广州。长约九百英里。

玄 福州镇江线

此线起自福州，经罗源、宁德，以至福安。于是进而逾闽、浙边界，以至泰顺、景宁、云和、处州。于是进经武义、义乌、诸暨，以达杭州。杭州以后经德清及湖州，逾浙江省界，以入江苏，循宜兴、金坛、丹阳之路而进，以至镇江。此线长五百五十英里。

黄 福州武昌线

此线自福州起，沿闽江左岸，过水口及延平，至于邵武。邵武以后过福建界，入于江西，经建昌及抚州，以至省城南昌。由南昌而入湖北之兴国，过之，以至湖北省城武昌。全长约五百五十英里。

宇 福州桂林线

此线自福州起，渡过闽江，进而取永福（永泰）、大田、宁洋、连城一路，以至汀州（长汀）。于是过闽、赣省界，入于瑞金。由瑞金进至雩都、赣州，又进至上犹及崇义。崇义以后，过赣、湘边界，至桂阳县（汝城）及郴州，与粤汉线交于彬州，遂至桂阳州。又进至于新田、宁远、道州，与广州重庆甲乙两线相遇。道州以后，转而南，循道江谷地而上，至广西边界，过界直至桂林。此线长约七百五十英里。

宙 温州辰州线

此线由温州新港起，循瓯江左岸而上，至于青田。由青田进向处州及宣平，转而西出浙江省界，入江西之玉山。自玉山经过德兴、乐平，

then skirting the southern shore of Poyang Lake goes through Yukan to Nanchang, the capital of Kiangsi. From Nanchang it proceeds to Juichow, Shangkao, and Wantsai, then crosses the Kiangsi border to Liuyang in Hunan, and Changsha, the capital of Hunan. After Changsha it goes to Ningsiang, Anhwa, and Shenchow where it connects with line (a) of the Canton-Chungking Railway, and with the Shasi-Singyi line. This line covers a distance of about 850 miles.

g. The Amoy-Kienchang Line

This line starts from the new port of Amoy and goes to Changtai, then following the Kiulungkiang to Changping, Ningyang, Tsingliu, and Kienning. After Kienning it proceeds across the Kiangsi border to Kienchang, where it connects with the Great Eastern Port-Canton line, the Foochow-Wuchang line, and the Kienchang-Yuanchow line. This line covers a distance of about 250 miles.

h. The Amoy-Canton Line

This line starts at the new port of Amoy, and proceeds to Changchow, Nantsing, and Siayang, where it crosses the Fukien border to Tapu, in Kwangtung. From Tapu it goes to Tsungkow, Kaying, Hinning, and Wuhwa. After Wuhwa it crosses the watershed between the Hankiang and the Tungkiang rivers to Lungchan, then following the Tungkiang down to Hoyun, it crosses another watershed to Lungmoon, Tsengshin and Canton. This line covers a distance of about 400 miles.

i. The Swatow-Changteh Line

This line starts from Swatow, proceeds to Chaochow, Kaying, and then crosses the Kwangtung border to Changning in Kiangsi. From Changning it crosses the watershed into Kungkiang Valley and follows that river down to Hweichang and Kanchow. From Kanchow it proceeds to Lungchuan, Yungning, and Lienhwa, where it crosses the Kiangsi border into Hunan. After that, it proceeds to Chuchow and Changsha, the capital of Hunan. From Changsha it goes to Ningsiang, Yiyang, and Changteh where it ends, connecting with the Great Eastern Port-Chungking line, and the Shasia-Singyi line. This line covers a distance of about 650 miles.

乃沿鄱阳湖之南岸，经余干，至于南昌。由南昌经过瑞州（高安）、上高、万载，逾江西省界，入湖南之浏阳，遂至长沙。由长沙经宁乡、安化，以至辰州，与广州重庆甲线及沙市兴义线会合。长约八百五十英里。

洪　厦门建昌线

此线自厦门新港起，至长泰。溯九龙江而上，至漳平、宁洋、清流及建宁县。自建宁以后，过省界，至江西之建昌，与东方大港广州线、福州武昌线、建昌沅州线相会。此线长约二百五十英里。

荒　厦门广州线

此线自厦门新港起，进至漳州、南靖、下洋，于此出福建界，至广东之大埔。由大埔过松口、嘉应、兴宁、五华。于五华，过韩江及东江之分水界，至龙川。乃遵东江而下，至河源。又过一分水界，至于龙门、增城，以至广州。长约四百英里。

日　汕头常德线

此线自汕头起，进至潮州、嘉应，出广东界，至江西之长宁（寻邬）。自长宁越分水界，入贡江谷地，循之以下，至于会昌、赣州。由赣州以至龙泉（遂川）、永宁（宁冈）、莲花。在莲花逾江西界，入湖南，于是进至株洲及长沙。由长沙经过宁乡、益阳，终于常德与东方大港重庆线及沙市兴义线相会。此线长约六百五十英里。

j. The Nanking-Siuchow Line

This line starts from Nanking and runs along the right bank of the Yangtze to Taiping, Wuhu, Tungling, Chichow, and Tungliu. After Tungliu it passes over the Anhwei border into Kiangsi, at Pengtseh, and goes to Hukow. At Hukow it meets the Great Eastern Port-Chungking line and crosses the bridge together with that line to the projected Poyang Port. From the Poyang Port it runs along the west shore of the Poyang Lake through Nanking and Wucheng to Nanchang, where it meets the Wenchow-Shenchow and Foochow-Wuchang lines. From Nanchang it proceeds up the Kan Kiang Valley, via Linkiang to Kian, where it crosses the projected Kienchang-Yuanchow line. After Kian, it proceeds to Kanchow where it crosses the Foochow-Kweilin line. Thence it goes to Nankanghsien and Nanan. After Nanan it crosses the boundary mountain, Tayuling, into Kwangtung at Nanyung, thence passes through Chihing to Siuchow, where it meets the Canton-Hankow line. This line covers a distance of about 800 miles.

k. The Nanking-Kaying Line

This line starts from Nanking, proceeds to Lishui and Kaoshun and then crosses the Kiangsu border into Anhwei at Suencheng. From Suencheng it proceeds to Ningkwo and Hweichow. After Hweichow it crosses the Anhwei border into Chekiang, passing through Kaihwa, Changshan, and Kiangshan, and leaving Chekiang enters Fukien at Pucheng. From Pucheng it proceeds via Kienningfu to Yenping where it crosses the Foochow-Wuchang line and then goes through Shahsien and Yungan to Ningyang, where it meets the Foochow-Kweilin and Amoy-Kienchang lines. From Ningyang it proceeds to Lungyen and Yungting, then joining the Amoy-Canton line at Tsungkow proceeds together to Kaying, its terminus. This line runs over a distance of about 750 miles.

1. The Coast Line Between the Great Eastern and the Great Southern Ports

This line starts from the Great Southern Port—Canton—proceeds in the same direction as the Canton-Kowloon line as far as Shelung and then goes its own way following the course of the Tungkiang River to Waichow. From Waichow it proceeds to Samtochuck, Haifung, and Lukfung, then turning northeastward goes to Kityang and Chaochow. After Chaochow it goes to Jaoping, then crossing the Kwangtung-Fukien border to Chaoan. Thence it proceeds to Yunsiao, Changpu,

月 南京韶州线

此线自南京起，循扬子江右岸而上，至于太平、芜湖、铜陵、池州、东流以后，出安徽界，入江西之彭泽，遂至湖口。在湖口与东方大港重庆线会，即用该线之桥，以至鄱阳港。于是沿鄱阳湖之西岸，经过南康（星子）、吴城，以至南昌，与温州辰州线及福州武昌线会于南昌。由南昌溯赣江谷地而上，由临江（江渡）至吉安，与建昌沅州之计划线交于吉安。由吉安至于赣州，复与福州桂林线交焉。于是进向南康县，及南安。南安以后，过大庾岭分界处，入广东之南雄。于是经始兴，至韶州，与粤汉线会。此线长约八百英里。

盈 南京嘉应线

此线自南京起，进至溧水、高淳。于是出江苏界，入安徽之宣城。自宣城进至宁国及徽州（歙县）。徽州以后，出安徽界，入浙江界，经开化、常山及江山。出浙江界，入福建之浦城。自浦城，由建宁（建瓯）以至延平，与福州武昌线交，更过沙县、永安以至宁洋，与福州桂林线及厦门建昌线会。自宁洋复进至龙岩、永定，至松口与厦门广州线合，迄嘉应而止。所经之路约七百五十英里。

昃 东方南方两大港间海岸线

此线自南方大港广州起，与广九铁路采同一方向，行至石龙，乃自择路线，取东江沿岸一路，以至惠州。由惠州经三多祝、海丰、陆丰，转东北行，至揭阳及潮州。潮州以后，经饶平出广东界，入福建

Changchow, and Amoy. From Amoy it proceeds to Chuanchow, Hinghwa, and Foochow, the capital of Fukien. After Foochow it proceeds in the same direction as the Foochow-Chinkiang line, as far as Fuan, then turns eastward to Funing, and northward to Futing. After Futing it crosses the Fukien border into Chekiang and proceeds through Pingyang to Wenchow. At Wenchow it crosses the Wukiang and proceeds to Lotsing, Hwangyen, and Taichow. Thence, it proceeds through Ninghai to Ningpo, its own terminus, where it connects with the Ningpo-Hangchow line, thus linking it up with the Great Eastern Port via Hangchow. This line covers a distance from Canton to Ningpo of about 1,100 miles.

m. The Kienchang-Yuanchow Line

This line starts from Kienchang and runs through Yihwang, Loan, Yungfeng, and Kishui to Kian, where it crosses the Nanking-Siuchow line. After Kian it proceeds to Yungsin and Lienhwa where it meets the Swatow-Changteh line. Thence it crosses the Kiangsi border into Hunan, at Chaling, then through Anjen to Hengchow where it crosses the Canton-Hankow line. From Hengchow the line proceeds to Paoking where it crosses line (a) of the Canton-Chungking Railway then westward to Yuanchow, its terminus, where it joins with the Shasi-Singyi line. This line covers a distance of about 550 miles. The total length of this Southeastern Railway System is about 9,000 miles.

● Part III The Northeastern Railway System

This system will cover the whole of Manchuria, a part of Mongolia, and a part of Chihli province—an area of nearly 500,000 square miles, with a population of 25,000,000. This region is surrounded by mountains on three sides and opens on the south to the Liaotung Gulf. Amidst these three mountain ranges lies a vast and fertile plain drained by three rivers—the Nonni on the north, the Sungari on the northeast, and the Liaoho on the south. This part of China was once regarded as a desert, but since the completion of the Chinese Eastern Railway it has been found to be the most productive soil in China. It supplies the whole of Japan and a part of China with nitrogenous food in the form of soya bean. This bean, the wonderful properties of which were early discovered by the Chinese, contains the richest nitrogenous substance among vegetables and has been used as

之诏安。自诏安经云霄、漳浦、漳州，以及厦门。由厦门，历泉州、兴化，而至福州省城。自福州以后，用与福州镇江线同一之方向抵福安，乃转而东，至福宁，又转而北，至福鼎。过福鼎后，出福建界，入浙江界，经平阳，至温州。于温州渡瓯江，进至乐清、黄岩、台州，又进历宁海，至于宁波，以为终点。即用杭甬铁路，经杭州，以与东方大港相接。此线自广州至宁波，长约一千一百英里。

辰　建昌沅州线

此线自建昌起，行经宜黄、乐安、永丰、吉水，以至吉安，即于该地与南京韶州线相交。由吉安进而及永新、莲花，与汕头常德线会。于是出江西界，入湖南之茶陵，乃经安仁，至衡州，遇粤汉线。于是由衡州更进至宝庆，则与广州重庆甲线交焉。由是西行，至于终点沅州（芷江），与沙市兴义线相遇。此线长约五百五十英里。东南铁路系统各线，全长统共约九千英里。

• 第三部　东北铁路系统

此系统包括满洲之全部，与蒙古及直隶省之各一部分，占有面积约五十万英方里，人口约二千五百万。其地域三面为山所围绕，独于南部则开放，直达至辽东海湾。在此三山脉之中，低落成为一广浩肥美之平原，并为三河流所贯注，嫩江位于北，松花江位于东北，辽河位于南。此之境界，中国前时视之，等于荒漠，但自中东铁路成立后，始知其为中国最肥沃之地。此地能以其所产大豆，供给日本全国与中国一部分为食料之用。此种大豆为奇美物品，在植物中含有最富

a meat substitute for many thousand years. Vegetable milk is extracted from this bean, and from this milk various kinds of preparations are made. The extraction from this bean has been proved by modern chemists to be richer than any kind of meat. The Chinese and the Japanese have used this kind of artificial meat and milk from time immemorial. Recently food administrators in Europe and America have paid great attention to this meat substitute, while the export of soya bean to Europe and America has steadily increased. This Manchu-Mongolian plain is destined to be the source of the world's supply of soya bean. Besides soya bean, this plain also produces a great quantity of various kinds of grains, and supplies the entire Eastern Siberia with wheat. The Manchurian mountains are exceedingly rich in timber and minerals—gold being especially found in great quantities in many localities.

Railway construction in this region has proved to be a most profitable undertaking. At present there are already three railway systems tapping this rich country, viz., the Peking-Mukden line, the best paying railroad in China, the Japanese South-Manchurian Railway, also a very remunerative line, and the Chinese Eastern Railway, the best paying portion of the whole Siberian system. Besides these, there are many lines projected by the Japanese. In order to develop this rich region properly a network of railways should be projected.

Before dealing with the separate lines of this network of railways, I should like to propose a center for them, just as the spider's nest is to a cobweb. I shall name this central city "Tungchin," the Eastern Mart, which should be situated at a point southwest of the junction of the Sungari and Nonni rivers, about 110 miles west by south from Harbin, and will be in a more advantageous position than the latter. This new city will be the center not only of the railway system but also of the inland water communication when the Liaoho-Sungari Canal is completed.

With the projected city of Tungchin as a center, I propose the following lines:

a. The Tungchin-Hulutao line.
b. The Tungchin-Great Northern Port line.
c. The Tungchin-Dolon Nor line.
d. The Tungchin-Kerulen line
e. The Tungchin-Moho line.
f. The Tungchin-Korfen line.

蛋白质之物，早为中国人所发明；经用以代肉品，不下数千年。由此种大豆可以提出一种豆浆，其质等于牛奶，复由此种豆奶制成各种食品，此种食品为近代化学家所证明，其涵肉质比肉类尤为丰富；而中国人与日本人用之以当肉与奶用者，已不知其始自何时矣。近来欧美各国政府之粮食管理官，对于此项用以代肉之物品，其为注意。所以此种大豆之输出于欧美者，亦日见增加。由此观之，满洲平原确可称为世界供给大豆之产地。除此大豆以外，此平原并产各种谷类极多，就麦一类言之，已足供西伯利亚东部需用。至于满洲之山岭，森林、矿产素称最富，金矿之发见于各地者亦称最旺。

敷设铁路于此境域，经已证明其为最有利益之事业。现已成立铁路贯通于此富饶区域者，已有三干线。如京奉线，为在中国之最旺铁路；日本之南满铁路，亦为获利最厚路线；中东铁路，又为西伯利亚系统之最旺部分。除此以外，尚有数线为日本人所计划经营。如欲依次发展此之富庶区域，即应敷设一网式铁路，乃足敷用也。

在未论及此网式铁路之各支线以前，吾意以为当先设立一铁路中区，犹蜘蛛巢之于蜘蛛网也。吾且名此铁路中区曰“东镇”。此东镇当设立于嫩江与松花江合流处之西南，约距哈尔滨之西南偏一百英里，将来必成为一最有利益之位置。此之新镇，不独可为铁路系统之中心，至当辽河、松花江间之运河成立后，且可成为水陆交通之要地。

既以此计划之新市镇“东镇”为中区，吾拟建筑如下之各线：

天　东镇葫芦岛线。
地　东镇北方大港线。
玄　东镇多伦线。
黄　东镇克鲁伦线。
宇　东镇漠河线。
宙　东镇科尔芬线。

g. The Tungchin-Yaoho line.
h. The Tungchin-Yenchi line.
i. The Tungchin-Changpeh line.
j. The Hulutao-Jehol-Peking line.
k. The Hulutao-Kerulen line.
l. The Hulutao-Hailar line.
m. The Hulutao-Antung line.
n. The Moho-Suiyuan line.
o. The Huma-Chilalin or Shihwei line.
p. The Ussuri-Tumen-Yalu-Coast line.
q. The Linkiang-Dolon Nor line.
r. The Chikatobo-Sansing or Ilan line.
s. The Sansing or Ilan-Kirin line.
t. The Kirin-Dolon Nor line.

a. The Tungchin-Hulutao Line

This is the first line that radiates from this projected Manchurian railway center, and is the shorter of the two direct lines that lead to the ice-free ports on the Liaotung-Chihli Gulf. It runs almost parallel to the South Manchurian Railway, the distance between the two lines being about 80 miles at the northern end, converging to 40 miles at Sinmin, and diverging again after that point. According to the original agreement with the former Russian Government, no parallel line within 100 miles was allowed to be built. But such restriction must be abolished under this new International Development Scheme for the benefit of all concerned. This line starts from Tungchin, and proceeds southward across the vast Manchurian plain by Changling, Shuangshan, Liaoyuan, and Kangping, to Sinmin in a straight line covering a distance of about 270 miles. After Sinmin, the line joins the Peking-Mukden Railway and runs on the same track for a distance of about 130 miles to Hulutao.

b. The Tungchin-Great Northern Port Line

This line is the second that radiates from this railway center direct to a deep water ice-free seaport. It starts from Tungchin, proceeding in a southwesterly direction, passes Kwangan, midway between Tungchin

洪　东镇饶河线。
荒　东镇延吉线。
日　东镇长白线。
月　葫芦岛热河北京线。
盈　葫芦克鲁伦线。
昃　葫芦岛呼伦线。
辰　葫芦岛安东线。
宿　漠河绥远线。
列　呼玛室韦线。
张　乌苏里图们鸭绿沿海线。
寒　临江多伦线。
来　节克多博依兰线。
暑　依兰吉林线。
往　吉林多伦线。

天　东镇葫芦岛线

此是由计划中之满洲铁路中区分出之第一线。比较其他直达辽东半岛之不冰口岸之二线为短，路线与南满铁路平行。在两线之北部末尾，相距约八十英里。依据与俄前政府所订原约，不能在南满铁路百里以内建筑并行路线，但当施行国际发展计划，为共同利益起见，此等约束必须废除。此线起自东镇，向南延进，经过满洲大平原，由长岭、双山、辽源、康平而至新民，成为一直线，约有二百七十英里之长。过新民后，即与京奉铁路合轨，约行一百三十英里之长，即至葫芦岛。

地　东镇北方大港线

此是由铁路中区直达不冰之深水港之第二线。起自东镇，向西南方延进，经过广安于东镇与西辽河间之中道。

and the West Liaoho, and many other small settlements before it crosses the Liaoho. After crossing the Liaoho, it enters the mountainous regions of the Jehol district by a valley to Fowsin, a hsien city, and crosses the watershed into the Talingho Valley. After passing through the Talingho Valley, the line crosses another watershed into the Luan Valley by a branch of the same river. Then it penetrates the Great Wall and proceeds to the Great Northern Port by way of Yungping and Loting. The whole length of this line is about 550 miles, the first half of which is on level land and the second half in mountainous country.

c. The Tungchin-Dolon Nor Line

This is the third line that radiates from the railway center and proceeds nearly in a westerly direction across the plain to Taonan where it crosses the projected Aigun-Jehol line (Japanese), and also meets the termini of two other projected lines, the Changchun-Taonan and the Tsengkiatun-Taonan (Japanese). After Taonan, the line turns more southward by skirting along the foothills of the southeastern side of the Great Khingan range where vast virgin forests and rich minerals are found. Then it passes through the upper Liaoho Valley formed by the Great Khingan Mountain on the north, and the Jehol Mountain on the south and through the towns of Linsi and Kingpang to Dolon Nor, where it meets the trunk line of the Northwestern Railway system. This line covers a distance of about 480 miles, a greater part of which is on level land.

d. The Tungchin-Kerulen Line

This is the fourth line that radiates from the Tungchin Railway center. It runs in a northwesterly direction almost parallel with the Harbin-Manchuli line of the Chinese Eastern Railway, the distance between the two lines varying from 100 to 130 miles. The line starts from Tungchin on the north side of the junction of the Nonni and Sungari rivers and proceeds westward across the Nonni River to Talai, and then turns northwestward across the plain into the valley of the north branch of the Guileli River. After entering the valley, it follows the stream up to its source, then crosses the Great Khingan Mountain watershed into the Mongolian Plain by the Khalka River, and follows the right bank of this river to the north end of Bor Nor Lake. Thence it turns directly westward to the Kerulen River, and follows the south bank of the river to Kerulen. This line covers a distance of about 630 miles.

在未到西辽河以前，先须经过无数小村落。当经过辽河之后，即进入热河区域之多山境界。经过一谷地至阜新县城，再经过分水界，进入大凌河谷地。当经过大凌河谷地之后，此线即由此河之支流，再经一分水界而入于滦河谷地。然后通过万里长城，取道永平与乐亭，而至北方大港。此线共长约五百五十英里，前半截所经过者是平地，后半截所经过者是山区。

玄　东镇多伦线

此是由铁路中区分出之第三线。向西方直走，经过平原，至洮南。由此横过日本之计划瑷珲热河线，并与长春洮南及郑家屯洮南两计划路线之终点相合。经过洮南后，此线即沿大兴安岭山脉东南方之山脚转向南走，在此一带山脉，发见有最丰盛之森林与富饶之矿产。然后经过上辽河谷地，此谷地即由在北之大兴安岭与在南之热河山所成。再通过林西与经棚等市镇，至多伦，于是由此处与西北铁路系统之干线相合。此线长约有四百八十英里，大半皆在平地。

黄　东镇克鲁伦线

此由东镇铁路中区分出之第四线。向西北走，几与中东路之哈尔滨满洲里线平行。两线相隔之距离，由一百英里至一百三十英里不等。此线由嫩江与松花江合流处之东镇北部起，复向西渡嫩江，至大赉，转西北向，横过平原，进入奎勒河之北支流谷地。当进入此谷地后，即沿此河流直上至河源处，然后横过大兴安岭分水界，进入蒙古平原。于是从哈尔哈河之右岸至贝尔池北之末端，由彼处转向西走，至克鲁伦河，即循克鲁伦河南岸至克鲁伦。此线约共长六百三十英里。

e. The Tungchin-Moho Line

This is the fifth line that radiates from this railway center. It starts from the north side of the junction of the Nonni and Sungari rivers, and proceeds northwestward across the northern end of the Great Manchurian Plain to Tsitsiha. At Tsitsiha, it joins the projected Kinchow-Aigun line and proceeds together northwestward alongside the left bank of the Nonni River as far as Nunkiang where it separates from the other. Thence it resumes the northwesterly direction and proceeds into the upper Nonni Valley until the headwater is reached. Then it crosses the northern extremity of the Great Khingan Range to Moho, where it joins the terminus of the Dolon Nor-Moho line. This line is about 600 miles long. About a quarter of this length runs on the plain, the second quarter runs along the lower Nonni Valley, the third along the Upper Valley, and the fourth runs in mountainous but gold-bearing regions, where only physical difficulties are to be expected.

f. The Tungchin-Korfen Line

This is the sixth line from the railway center. It also starts on the northern side of the Nonni-Sungari junction, and proceeds across the plain by the cities Chaotung and Tsingkang. After Tsingkang it crosses the Tungkun River, proceeds to Hailun, and then, ascending the Tungkun Valley, crosses the watershed of the Little Khingan Mountain. Thence it descends into the Korfen Valley and proceeds by Chelu to Korfen on the right bank of the Amur River. This line covers a distance of 350 miles, two thirds of which run on comparatively level land and one third in mountainous district. This is the shortest line from Tungchin to the Amur River and the Russian territory on yonder side.

g. The Tungchin-Yaoho Line

This is the seventh line that radiates from this railway center.

It starts from the northern side of the Nonni-Sungari junction and traverses the plain on the left of the Sungari River by Chaochow, then crosses the Chinese Eastern Railway, and the Hulan River to Hulan. After Hulan, it proceeds to Payen, Mulan, and Tungho, then crosses the Sungari River to Sansing, now called Ilan. Thence it proceeds into the Wokan Valley and crosses the watershed by Chihsingshitse and Takokai into the Noloho Valley and passing by various villages and towns along

宇　东镇漠河线

此是由铁路中区发出之第五线。起自嫩江与松花江合流处之北部，向西北行，横过满洲平原之北端，至齐齐哈尔。在齐齐哈尔与计划之锦瑷线相会，同向西北方，沿嫩江左岸走，至嫩江，而后彼此分路。于是再向西北走，进入嫩江上流谷地，至发源处再横过大兴安岭山脉之北部末尾处至漠河，在漠河与多伦漠河线之末站相会。此线约长六百英里。全线首之四分一行经平源，其次之四分一沿嫩江下流走，第三之四分一行经上流谷地，第四之四分一截经山岭。是为金矿产地，但天然险阻亦意中事也。

宙　东镇科尔芬线

此是由铁路中区分出之第六线。起至嫩江与松花江合流处之北边，向平原前行，经肇东、青冈等城镇。到青冈后，渡通肯河，至海伦。然后上通肯河谷地，横过小兴安岭分水界，由此即向下进入科尔芬谷地。经车陆前行，至科尔芬，即黑龙江之右岸也。此线共长约三百五十英里，三分二为平地，三分一为山地。此为由东镇至黑龙江之最短线，黑龙江之对岸即俄境也。

洪　东镇饶河线

此是由铁路中区分出之第七线。起自嫩江、松花江合流处之北边，经肇州，绕松花江左岸行经平原，而后再横过中东铁路，渡呼兰河，而至呼兰。过呼兰后，向巴彦、木兰、通河等地方前进，再渡松花江至三姓，即今名依兰地方也。于是向前进入倭肯河谷地，过分水界，经七星碣子与大锅盖等地方，进入饶河谷地。于是沿此河边经过

this river to Yaohohsien, ends at the junction of the Noloho and the Ussuri River. This line covers a distance of 500 miles in very fertile country.

h. The Tungchin-Yenchi Line

This is the eighth line that radiates from this railway center. It starts from the eastern side of the Nonni-Sungari junction and proceeds in a southeasterly direction on the right side of the Sungari River to Fuyu or Petunai and various towns along the road on the same side of the river until it comes across the Harbin-Talien Railway, then turns away from the road and proceeds eastward to Yushu and Wuchang. After Wuchang, the line turning more southward, proceeds to Fengtechang and then follows the same direction to Omu. At Omu, it crosses the Mutan River, then proceeds to Liangshuichuan and Shehtauho, where it joins the Japanese Hweining-Kirin line and proceeds together to Yenchi. This line covers a length of about 330 miles through very rich agricultural and mineral country.

i. The Tungchin-Changpeh Line

This is the ninth line that radiates from the Tungchin railway center. It starts from the south side of the Nonni-Sungari junction and proceeds in a southeasterly direction across the plain to Nungan. After Nungan, it crosses the Itung River and proceeds continuously in the same direction across several branches of the same river to Kiudaichan, where it joins the Changchun-Kirin line and proceeds together as far as Kirin. After Kirin, it goes its own way following the right bank of the Sungari River in a southeasterly direction to the junction of Lafaho River and turns southward along the same bank of the Sungari to Huatien. After Huatien, it continues in the same course up to Toutaokiang, as far as Fusung, then turns southeastward into the Sunghsiangho Valley and proceeds upward to the Changpeh Shan watershed by skirting the south side of the Celestial Lake, then turns southward following the Aikiang River to Changpeh on the Korean frontier. This line covers a distance of about 330 miles. Some great difficulties are to be overcome in the last portion of the line where it crosses the Changpeh watershed.

无数村落市镇，始至饶河县，以饶河与乌苏里江合流处为终点。此线之距离约有五百英里，所经之处皆为肥美土地。

荒　东镇延吉线

此是第八线，由铁路中区分出。起自嫩江、松花江会流处之东边，循松花江右岸，向东南方前行，至扶余（又名伯都讷），并经过此江边之镇甚多，至横过哈尔滨大连铁路后，即转向东行，至榆树与五常等地方。到五常后，此线转偏南行，向丰德栈前进，而后依同一方向至额穆。于是由额穆渡牡丹江，然后向凉水泉与石头河前行，至此即与日本会宁吉林线合轨，直达于延吉。此线约共长三百三十英里，经过各农产与矿产极丰富之地方。

日　东镇长白线

此是由铁路中区分出之第九线。起自嫩江、松花江相会处之南部，向东南方走，横过平原，至农安。渡伊通河，相继向同一方进行，经过此河之各支流，至九台站。复由此与长春吉林线合轨，直行至吉林。迨至吉林后，则由其本路循松花江右岸，向东南行至拉法河合流处，即沿松花江河岸转南行，至桦甸。即再由此溯流而上，至头道沟，直达抚松。即转东南行，进入松香河谷地。再溯流前行，经长白山分水界，绕天地湖边南部，然后转向循爱江至长白，即近高丽边界地方也。此线之距离约共三百三十英里。最后之一部分，当经过长白分水界时，须历许多困难崎岖之地。

j. The Hulutao-Jehol-Peking Line

With this line I shall begin to deal with a new group of the Northeastern Railway System which will make Hulutao, the ice-free port on the Liaotung Gulf as their center and terminus. This, the first line, starts from Hulutao and proceeds westward up the Shaho Valley to Sintaipienmen. Thence it crosses the mountainous district through Haiting, Mangniuyingtse, and Sanshihkiatse to Pingchuan, and continues in the same direction to Jehol or Chengteh. After Jehol, it proceeds by the old imperial highway to Lwanping, then turns southwestward to Kupehkow where it penetrates the Great Wall. Thence it follows the same highway through Miyun and Shunyi to Peking. This line covers a distance of about 270 miles.

k. The Hulutao-Kerulen Line

This is the second line of the Hulutao radiation. It starts from this seaport and proceeds northward through the mountainous region of Jehol by Kienping and Chihfeng. Thence, the line follows the highway across the Upper Valley of Liaoho to Chianchang, Sitoo, Takinkou, and Linsi. After Linsi, it proceeds up the Lukiako Valley and crosses the watershed at the southern extremity of the Great Khingan Mountain, through Kanchumiao and Yufuchih. Then it proceeds to Payenbolak, Uniket, and Khombukure where it joins with the Dolon Nor-Kerulen line and proceeds together to Kerulen. This line up to Khombukure covers a distance of about 450 miles, tapping a very rich mineral, timber, and agricultural country.

l. The Hulutao-Hailar Line

This, the third line, starts from Hulutao and proceeds by way of Chinchow along the west side on the Talingho River to Yichow, where it crosses the Talingho to Chinghopienmen and Fowsin. After Fowsin, the line goes northward to Suitung, thence, crossing the Siliaoho to Kailu, it proceeds between the Great and Little Fish Lakes to Kinpan and Tachuan. Then it proceeds across the Great Khingan Mountain into the Oman Valley and follows the same river to Hailar. This line covers a distance of about 600 miles passing through rich mineral and agricultural land and virgin forests.

月　葫芦岛热河北京线

由此吾将从而另为计划东北铁路系统之一新组，此组以辽东半岛之不冰口岸葫芦岛为总站。此第一线起自葫芦岛，向西方走进沙河谷地，至新台边门。于是行过海亭、犏牛营子、三十家子之多山境界，至平泉，复依同一方向直达热河（又名承德）。到热河后，由旧官路至滦平，然后转西南向，至古北口，通过万里长城，由彼处循通路经密云与顺义，至北京。此线之距离约有二百七十英里。

盈　葫芦岛克鲁伦线

此是由葫芦岛分出之第二线。起自葫芦岛口岸，向北直走，经建平与赤峰。行过热河之多山地域后，此线循通道而行，过辽河谷地上部，至间场、西图、大金沟与林西等地方。到林西即进至陆家窝谷地，即由甘珠庙、右府迹，经过大兴安岭极南之水分界。然后再进至巴原布拉克、乌尼克特及欢布库列，由此即与多伦克鲁伦线合轨，直达克鲁伦。此线以达至欢布库列计之，约长四百五十英里，经过丰富之矿产、木材、农业等地方。

昃　葫芦岛呼伦线

此是由葫芦岛分出之第三线。取道锦州，循大凌河右边直走至义州，由此渡大凌河，至清河边门与阜新。到阜新后，此线即向北直行至绥东，由此渡西辽至开鲁，再由大鱼湖与小鱼湖之间直达合板与突泉。然后横过大兴安岭，进入阿满谷地，沿河流直达呼伦。此线长约六百英里，所经过地方皆富于矿产与农业，并有未开发之森林。

m. The Hulutao-Antung Line

This, the fourth line, starts from Hulutao and proceeding northeastward, follows the course of the projected Liaoho-Hulutao Canal, and then goes eastward to Newchwang and Haicheng. From there it proceeds southeastward to Sinmuchen, where it joins the Antung-Mukden line and proceeds together to Antung on the Korean border. This line covers a distance of about 220 miles. This together with the Hulutao-Jehol-Peking line will make the shortest line from Antung and beyond, i. e., Korea, to Peking.

n. The Moho-Suiyuan Line

With this as the first I am going to deal with another group of lines in this system. These will be the circumferential lines which link up the radii from the Tungchin center in two semicircles, the outer and the inner. This Moho-Suiyuan line starts from Moho and proceeds along the right bank of the Amur River to Ussuri, Omurh, Panga, Kaikukang, Anlo, and Woshimen. After this point, the river bends more southward and the line follows the same bend to Ankan, Chahayen, Wanghata, and Huma. From Huma, it proceeds to Sierhkenchi, Chila, Manchutun, Heiho, and Aigun where it meets the terminus of the Chinchow-Aigun line. After Aigun, the line turns more eastward to Homolerhchin, Chilirh, and Korfen where it meets the terminus of the Tungchin-Korfen line. Thence it proceeds to Wuyun, Foshan, and Lopeh. After Lopeh, it goes to Hokang at the junction of the Amur and Sungari. At this point, the line crosses the Sungari River to Tungkiang and proceeds to Kaitsingkow, Otu, and Suiyuan where it ends. This line covers a distance of 900 miles running all its way through the gold-producing region.

o. The Huma-Chilalin or Shihwei Line

This is merely a branch of the Moho-Suiyuan line. It starts from

Huma and follows the Kumara River passing by the Taleitse Gold Mine and Wapalakow Gold Mine. Then it proceeds up the Kumara River in a westerly and southwesterly direction to its southern source and there it crosses the watershed into the Halarh Valley, thence descending the valley to Chilalin or Shihwei. This line covers a distance of about 320 miles running in an extremely rich gold district.

辰 葫芦岛安东线

此第四线，自葫芦岛起，向东北方走，循计划中之辽河葫芦岛运河边直上，而后转东南行至牛庄与海城，由此再转东南行至析木城，于是与安东奉天线合轨，直达近高丽境界之安东。此线约长二百二十英里。此线与葫芦岛热河北京线连合，则成为一由安东以外之高丽至北京之至直捷之线矣。

宿 漠河绥远线

此是别一组铁路系统中之第一线，吾且进而论之。此等为环形线，以东镇中区为轴，成二半圆形，一内一外。此之漠河绥远线，起自漠河，沿黑龙江边前进至乌苏里、额木尔苹果、奎库堪、安罗、倭西们等地。过彼处后，此后转折南流，故此线亦循之至安干、察哈颜、望安达、呼玛等处。于是再由呼玛前行，至锡尔根奇、奇拉、满洲屯、黑河、瑷珲，在瑷珲乃与锦瑷线之终点相会。过瑷珲后，此线即渐转而东向，直达霍尔木勒津、奇克勒与科尔芬等处，在科尔芬与东镇科尔芬线相会。然后由彼处再进至乌云、佛山与萝北，由萝北直至同江，此即黑龙江与松花江会流之点也。此线即由此处渡松花江，抵同江。再由此向街津口额图前行，至绥远，即黑龙江与乌苏里河之合流处也。此线长约九百英里，至所经之地方，皆系金矿产地。

列 呼玛室韦线

此本是漠河绥远线之支线。起自呼玛，循库玛尔河，经过大砬子与瓦巴拉沟等金矿。然后溯库玛尔而上，向西行，又西南偏至此河北源。遂由彼处过分水界，进入哈拉尔谷地，于是由此谷地上达室苇。此线约长三百二十英里，经过极丰富之金矿地方。

p. The Ussuri-Tumen-Yalu-Coast Line

This, the second line of the outer semicircle, starts by continuing the first line at Suiyuan, and proceeds along the left bank of the Ussuri River, passing Kaulan, Fuyeu, and Minkang, to Yaoho, where it meets the terminus of the Tungchin-Yaoho line. From Yaoho, it runs parallel to the Russian Ussuri Railway on the east side of the river as far as Fulin. After Fulin, it parts from the Russian line by turning westward following the Mulingho River to Mishan on the northwestern corner of the Hanka Lake. Thence it goes to Pinganchin, turns southward alongside the boundary line and crosses the Harbin-Vladivostok line at Siusuifen Station to Tungning. After Tungning, it continues the same southward course alongside the boundary line to a point between Szetaukow and Wutaukow, then turns westward to Hunchun, and northwestward to Yenchi where it meets the projected Japanese Hweining-Kirin line. From Yenchi, it follows the Japanese line to Holung, and proceeds southwestward by the left side of the Tumen River across the watershed into the Yalu Valley, where it meets the Tungchin-Changpeh line. After Changpeh it turns westward and northwestward following the right bank of the Yalu to Linkiang, thence southwestward, still following the right bank of the Yalu, to Tsianhsien and then continues in the same direction, along the Yalu bank, to Antung, where it meets the Antung-Mukden Railway. After Antung, it proceeds to Tatungkow at the mouth of the Yalu, thence along the coast to Takushan and Chwangho, then westward through Situn and Pingfangtien to join the South Manchurian Railway at Wukiatun. This line covers a distance of 1,100 miles, which runs from end to end right along the southeastern boundary of Manchuria.

q. The Linkiang-Dolon Nor Line

This is the third line of the outer semicircle of the Tungchin railway center, and connects the radiating lines south of the center. It starts from Linkiang at the southwestward turn of the Yalu River, and proceeds across the mountainous region passing by Tunghwa, Hingking, and Fushun, to Mukden, where it crosses the South Manchurian Railway. From Mukden, it goes together with the Peking-Mukden line as far as Sinmin, where it crosses the Tungchin-Hulutao line and proceeds northwestward through Sinlihtun to Fowsin. After Fowsin the line enters the hilly district of the upper Liaoho Valley, and proceeds to Chihfeng, after passing through

张　乌苏里图们鸭绿沿海线

此是外半圆形之第二线。由绥远起与第一线相续，沿乌苏里江前行，经过高兰、富有、民康等处，至饶河，于是此线与东镇饶河线之末站相会。由饶河起南行，则与在乌苏里江东边之俄乌铁路成平行线，直达虎林而止。到虎林后即离俄罗斯线，转向西方，循穆陵河至兴凯湖之西北角之密山县。由此再至平安镇，转南向，循国界在小绥芬车站横过哈尔滨海参威线，直至东宁。到东宁后相继南向，循国界而行，至五道沟与四道沟间之交点。然后转而西行，至珲春，再西北走至延吉，于是与日本之会宁吉林线相会。由延吉循日本线至和龙，离日本线由图们江左岸向西南走，经过分水界，进入鸭绿谷地，即在此处与东镇长白线相会。过长白后即转西向，又西北偏，沿鸭绿江右岸至临江。彼时又复西南偏，仍沿鸭绿江右岸前行，至辑安县。再相继依同一方向，沿鸭绿江右岸直达安乐，由此即与安东奉天铁路相会。过安东后，向鸭绿江口之大东沟前走，循此海岸线至大孤山与庄河等处。然后转而西向，经平西屯、房店，至吴家屯，与南满铁路相会。此线之距离约有一千一百英里，自头至尾皆依满洲东南之国界而行也。

寒　临江多伦线

此是东镇铁路中区外半圆之第三线。与在中区南部分出之支线相接。此线起自临江，即鸭绿江之西南转弯处也。由此处向多山地域前进，经过通化、兴京与抚顺等地方，至奉天，横过南满铁路。于是此线由奉天与京奉线合轨，直达新民。由此横过东镇葫芦岛线，转向西北走，经过新立屯，至阜新。过阜新后，此线进入辽河谷地上部之山地，

numerous small villages and camping places in this vast pasture. After Chihfeng the line proceeds through the Yinho Valley by Sanchotien, Kungchuling, and Tachientse, to Famuku, thence follows the Tulakanho to Dolon Nor, covering a distance of about 500 miles.

r. The Chikatobo-Sansing or Ilan Line

This is the first line of the inner semicircle which connects the radiating lines from the Tungchin railway center on the northeast. It starts from Chikatobo on the upper reach of the Amur, and proceeds eastward and southeastward through many valleys and mountains of the Great Khingan Range to Nunkiang. After Nunkiang, it goes in a more southerly direction to Keshan, thence to Hailun, and then crosses the Sungari to Sansing or Ilan. This line covers a distance of about 700 miles, passing through an agricultural and gold-producing country.

s. The Sansing or Ilan-Kirin Line

This is the second line of the inner semicircle. It starts from Sansing and proceeds southwestward along the right bank of the Mutan River through Tauchan, Erchan, Sanchan, and Szuchan, to Chengtse where it crosses the Harbin-Vladivostok line. Then it goes to Ninguta, after crossing over the Mutan River from right to the left bank. After Ninguta it proceeds southwestward passing through Wungcheng, Lanchichan, Talachan, and Fungwangtien, to Omu. From Omu it joins the Japanese Hweining-Kirin line and proceeds westward to Kirin. This line covers a distance of about 200 miles, along the fertile Mutan Valley.

t. The Kirin-Dolon Nor Line

This is the third line of the inner semicircle in the Tungchin system. It starts from Kirin and follows the old highway westward to Changchun where it meets the termini of the Chinese Eastern Railway from the north and the Japanese South Manchurian Railway from the south. After Changchun, it proceeds across the plain to Shuangshan where it meets the Tungchin-Hulutao line and the Japanese Szupingkai-Chengkiatun-Taonan line. From Shuangshan, it crosses the Liao River to Liaoyuan, thence it traverses the vast plain, crossing the Tungchin-Great Northern Port line and goes to Suitung where it meets the Hulutao-Hailar line.

直向赤峰前行，经过无数小村落与帐幕地，皆大牧场也。此线由赤峰再前行，经三座店、公主陵、大辗子等处，通过银河谷地至发木谷，然后循吐根河至多伦诺尔。此线长五百英里。

来　节克多博依兰线

此是内半圆形之第一线。与东镇铁路中区之东北方所分出之各支线相连。起自黑龙江上游之节克多博，向东前行，又东南偏，经过大兴安岭山脉之谷地、山地数处，即至嫩江。过嫩江后，渐转南向，至克山，由彼处再至海伦，然后渡松花江至三姓，即依兰也。此线长约七百英里，经过农业与金矿地方。

暑　依兰吉林线

此是内半圆之第二线。起自依兰，向西南方，沿牡丹江右岸前行，经过头站、二站、三站、四站，到城子，即由此处横过哈尔滨海参威线。于是由牡丹江右岸渡至左岸，直往宁古塔。过宁古塔后，复向西方前行，经过瓮城、蓝旗站、搭拉站与凤凰店，至额穆。于此与日本之会宁吉林线相合，向西前行，至吉林。此线所行之长度线约二百英里，经过牡丹江之肥美谷地。

往　吉林多伦线

此是在东镇铁路系统中内半圆形之第三线。起自吉林，循旧通路西行至长春，于是在此与中东铁路北来之线及日本南满铁路南来之线之两末站相会。过长春后，即横过平原，至双山，又在此与东镇葫芦岛线及日本之四平街郑家屯洮南线相会。再由双山渡辽河，至辽源，复由彼处行经一大平原，经过东镇北方大港线，直达绥东，与葫芦岛

After Suitung, it proceeds up the Liao Valley where it comes across the Hulutao-Kerulen line and then crosses the watershed to Dolon Nor where it ends. This line covers a distance of 500 miles. This completes the cobweb system of the projected Northeastern Railway. The total length of this entire system is about 9,000 miles.

● Part IV The Extension of the Northwestern Railway System

The Northwestern Railway System covers the region of Mongolia, Sinkiang, and a part of Kansu, an area of 1,700,000 square miles. This territory exceeds the area of the Argentine Republic by 600,000 square miles. Argentina is now the greatest source of the world's meat supply, while the Mongolian pasture is not yet developed, owing to the lack of transportation facilities. As Argentina has superseded the United States in supplying the world with meat, so the Mongolian pasture will some day take the place of Argentina, when railways are developed and cattle raising is scientifically improved. Thus the construction of railroads in this vast food-producing region is an urgent necessity as a means of relieving the world from food shortage. In the first program of this International Development Scheme, I proposed 7,000 miles of railways for this vast and fertile region, for the purpose of developing the Great Northern Port, and relieving the congested population of southeastern China. But this 7,000 miles of railways form merely a pioneer line. In order to develop this virgin continent properly, more railways have to be constructed. Therefore in this plan, namely, the Extension of the Northwestern Railway System, I propose the following lines:

a. The Dolon Nor-Kiakata line.
b. The Kalgan-Urga-Tannu Ola line.
c. The Suiyuan-Uliassutai-Kobdo line.
d. The Tsingpien-Tannu Ola line.
e. The Suchow-Kobdo line.

f. The Northwestern Frontier line.
g. The Tihwa or Urumochi-Ulankom line.
h. The Gaskhiun-Tannu Ola line.
i. The Uliassutai-Kiakata line.
j. The Chensi or Barkul-Urga line.

呼伦线相会。过绥东后，循辽河谷地上行，先横过葫芦岛克鲁伦线，然后过分水界至多伦，是为终站。此线所经之远度约有五百英里。由以上所举，方能完成吾计划中东北铁路之蜘蛛网系统。就全系统路线之长言之，其总数约有九千英里。

• 第四部 扩张西北铁路系统

西北铁路系统包有蒙古、新疆与甘肃一部分之地域，面积约有一百七十万英方里。此幅土地，大于阿根廷共和国约六十万英方里。阿根廷为供给世界肉类之最大出产地，而蒙古牧场尚未开发，以运输之不便利也。以阿根廷既可代美国而以肉类供给世界，如蒙古地方能得铁路利便，又能以科学之方法改良畜牧，将来必可取阿根廷之地位而代之。此所以在此最大食物之生产地方建筑铁路为最要之图，亦可以救济世界食物之竭乏也。在国际共同发展中国之第一计划中，吾曾提议须敷设七千英里铁路于此境域，以为建筑北方大港之目的，而复可以将中国东南部过密之人民逐渐迁移。但此七千英里之铁路不过为一开拓者，如欲从实际上发展此丰富之境域，铁路必须增筑。故在此扩张西北铁路系统之计划中，吾提议建筑下列之各线:

天 多伦恰克图线。
地 张家口库伦乌梁海线。
玄 绥远乌里雅苏台科布多线。
黄 靖边乌梁海线。
宇 肃州科布多线。
宙 西北边界线。
洪 迪化乌兰固穆线。
荒 戛什温乌梁海线。
日 乌里雅苏台恰克图线。
月 镇西库伦线。

k. The Suchow-Urga line.
l. The Desert Junction-Kerulen line.
m. The Khobor-Kerulen-Chikatobo line.
n. The Wuyuan-Taonan line.
o. The Wuyuan-Dolon Nor line.
p. The Yenki-Ili line.
q. The Ili-Hotien line.
r. The Chensi-Kashgar line and its branches.

a. The Dolon Nor-Kiakata Line

This Line starts from Dolon Nor and proceeds in a northwesterly direction, following the caravan road across the vast pasture to Khorkho, Kuoto, and Suliehto. After Suliehto, it crosses the boundary line into Outer Mongolia by the same road to Khoshentun, Lukuchelu, and Yangto. Thence it crosses the Kerulen River to Otukunkholato, and enters the hilly region where it crosses the Kerulen watershed and the Chikoi watershed. The water from the Kerulen watershed flows into the Amur, and thence into the Pacific Ocean, while the water from the Chikoi watershed flows into Lake Baikal, and thence to the Arctic Ocean. After crossing the Chikoi watershed, it follows a branch of the Chikoi River to Kiakata. This line covers a distance of about 800 miles.

b. The Kalgan-Urga-Tannu Ola Line

This line starts from Kalgan at the Great Wall, and proceeds northwestward up the plateau, crosses a range of hills into the Mongolian prairie, and goes to Mingan, Boroldshi, Ude, and Khobor, where it crosses the Dolon Nor-Urumochi trunk line. After Khobor, it proceeds across the vast and rich pasture of Mubulan, then proceeds in a straight line through Mukata and Nalaiha to Urga. From Urga, it goes into the hilly district crossing Selenga Valley to a point opposite the southern end of Lake Kos Gol, and then turns northward across a range of mountains to Khatkhyl on the southern shore of Kos Gol. After Khatkhyl, it skirts Kos Gol Lake along the western shore for some distance, then turns northwestward and westward, following the course of the Khua Kem River to a point near its

盈　肃州库伦线。
昃　沙漠联站克鲁伦线。
辰　格合克鲁伦节克多博线。
宿　五原洮南线。
列　五原多伦线。
张　焉耆伊犁线。
寒　伊犁和阗线。
来　镇西喀什噶尔线。

天　多伦恰克图线

此线起自多伦，向西北方前行，循驿路横过大牧场，至喀特尔呼、阔多、苏叠图等处。过苏叠图后，此线即横过界线至外蒙古，依同一路线至霍申屯、鲁库车鲁、杨图等地方。由彼处渡克鲁伦河，至额都根、霍勒阔，进入山地。于是即横过克鲁伦河分水界与赤奎河分水界，克鲁伦分水界之水则流入黑龙江而至太平洋，赤奎河分水界之水则流入贝加尔湖，再由彼处至北冰洋。过克奎河分水界后，此路即循赤奎河之支派，至恰克图。其线长约八百英里。

地　张家口库伦乌梁海线

此线起自万里长城之张家口，向西北前进高原，横过山脉，进入蒙古大草场，走向明安、博罗里治、乌得与格合，即横过多伦迪化干线。过格合后，此线前行经过穆布伦之广大肥沃牧场，然后依直线再前行，经穆克图、那赖哈、库伦。由库伦此线即进入山地，横过色楞格谷地，至一地点，在库苏古尔泊南部末端之对面。然后再转北向，横过山脉，从库苏古尔之南岸之哈特呼尔。过哈特呼尔后，此线绕库苏古尔泊边走约一段距离，即再转西北向，又西偏循乌鲁克穆河岸，

exit at the frontier line, then turns southwestward up the Kemtshik Valley to its headwater, passes through Pakuoshwo, and ends at the boundary line beween the Russian and Chinese territories. This line covers a distance of about 1,700 miles.

c. The Suiyuan-Uliassutai-Kobdo Line

This line starts from Suiyuan in the northwestern corner of Shansi, and proceeds in a northwesterly direction across the hilly country into the Mongolian pasture to Tolibulyk, where it crosses the Great Northern Port-Hami line, and the Great Eastern Port-Urga line. After Tolibulyk, it proceeds in a straight line in the same direction passing through Barunsudshi to the capital of Tuchetu. Thence it continues in the same straight line northwestward to Gorida. After Gorida, it follows the caravan road to Kolitikolik where it crosses the Great Northern Port-Urumochi trunk line. From Kolitikolik, the line turns northwestward, then westward and proceeds across many streams and valleys and passes by many small towns to Uliassutai. At Uliassutai, it crosses the B. Junction-Frontier branch of the Great Eastern Port-Urumochi line. After Uliassutai, the line proceeds westward following the trade road, passes through Khuduku, Bogu, Durganor, and Sakhibuluk to Kobdo. Thence the line turns northwestward to Khonga, Ukha, and Clegei, then westward to Beleu and ends at the frontier. This line is about 1,500 miles long.

d. The Tsingpien-Tannu Ola Line

This line starts from Tsingpien at the Great Wall, on the northern border of Shensi, proceeds through the Ordos country by Bonobalgasun, Orto, and Shinchao, and then crosses the Hoangho to Santaoho. From Santaoho, it proceeds across Charanarinula Mountain into Mongolian prairie in a northwesterly direction to Kurbansihata where it crosses the Peking-Hami line, then it goes to Unikuto and Enkin, where it crosses the Great Northern Port-Urumochi line. After Enkin, the line enters into a valley and watered district, proceeds northward to Karakorum, and then turns northwestward across various streams and valleys of the tributary of the Selenga River by Sabokatai and Tsulimiau. After Tsulimiau, it proceeds in the same direction across the Selenga River, follows its branch, the Telgir Morin River, up to its source and crosses the watershed into Lake Teri Nor. Then it follows the outlet of the Teri Nor to the Khua Kem River, where it ends by joining the Kalgan Urga-Tannu Ola line. This line covers a distance of about 1,200 miles.

至近国界之出口点，复转西南向，直上克穆赤克谷地，至其发源处，通过巴阔洼，直达中俄国境交界处而止。此线之距离约有一千七百英里。

玄　绥远乌里雅苏台科布多线

此线起自绥远，近于山西省之西北角地方，向西北方前进，经过山地进入蒙古牧场托里布拉克，于是横过北方大港哈密线与北方大港库伦线。过托里布拉克后，此线由同一方向依直线前行，通过匝们苏治，至土谢图省会。由彼处仍依直线向西北走，至霍勒特，再循商路至郭里得果勒。此线即转西向，再西北向前行，通过河流、谷地数处与小市镇，即至乌里雅苏台，于是在乌里雅苏台横过北方大港与乌鲁木齐线之第二联站边界支线。过乌里雅苏台后，此线即依商路向西方前行，通过呼都克卒尔、巴尔淖尔与匝哈布鲁等处，致科布多。彼时此线转西北向，至欢戛喀图与列盖等处，即复西走至别留，以国界为终点。此线约长一千五百英里。

黄　靖边乌梁海线

此线起自靖边，即在陕西北界与万里长城相接地方也。此线向鄂尔多斯乡落前行，经波罗波勒格孙、鄂托、臣浊等处，然后过黄河至三道河。由三道河再前行，过哈那那林、乌拉岭，即进入在西北方之蒙古大草场，直至古尔斑、昔哈特，在此即经过北京哈密线。然后至乌尼格图、恩京，由恩京即经过北方大港乌鲁木齐线。过恩京后，此线进入谷地与分水界地，向北前进，至西库伦。于是再转西北行，经过色楞格河流域之各支流与谷地，即抵沙布克台与粗里庙等处。至粗里庙后，再向同一方向前行，渡色楞格河，沿其支流帖里吉尔穆连河，至发源处，经过流入帖里淖尔湖之分水界。然后沿此湖之出口，至乌鲁克穆河，即与张家口库伦乌梁海线相合，此即终点也。此线之长约有一千二百英里。

e. The Suchow-Kobdo Line

This line starts from Suchow in a northwesterly direction penetrating the Great Wall at Chiennew, and proceeds to the coal field, about 150 miles from Suchow. Then it goes to Habirhaubuluk and Ilatoli. A short way from this place the line comes across the Peking-Hami line and then proceeds to Balaktai. After this the line passes a bit of pure desert to Timenchi. After entering the hilly and watered country it proceeds to Gaskhiun where it crosses the Great Northern Port-Urumochi trunk line. After Gaskhiun, it proceeds to Wolanhutok, Tabateng, and Tabutu where it joins the Kucheng and Kobdo highway and following it, proceeds to Kobdo, through Batokuntai and Sutai. Here the line ends, covering a distance of about 700 miles.

f. The Northwestern Frontier Line

This line starts from Ili following the Urumochi-Ili line to Santai, on the eastern side of Zairam Lake, then proceeds northeastward by itself to Tuszusai on the west side of Ebi Lake. After Tuszusai it proceeds to Toli where it crosses the Central Trunk line, that is, the Great Eastern Port-Tarbogotai line. Thence it goes to Namukotai and Stolokaitai by passing through a vast forest and a rich coal field. From Stolokaitai, the line follows the highway and proceeds to Chenghwaszu, the capital of Altai province. Thence it crosses a mountain range by the Urmocaitu Pass into the Kobdo Valley, and follows the course of the Kobdo River to Beleu where it joins the Suiyuan-Kobdo line and proceeds to Clegei. From Clegei, it proceeds by itself to Tabtu via Usungola and Ulamkom. At Tabtu, it joins the other line again and proceeds together to the Khua Kem River in the Tannu Ola district. It then turns eastward ascending the river to the junction of the Bei Kem and Khua Kem rivers, then starts again on its own course, following the former river and proceeds up to its source in a northeasterly direction ending at the frontier. This line covers a distance of about 900 miles.

g. The Tihwa or Urumochi-Ulankora Line

This line starts from Tihwa following the Dolon Nor trunk line to Fowkang, then proceeds by its own route almost northward through Chipichuan to Khorchute. From Khorchute, it turns northeastward and proceeds across a hilly district to Kaiche, then to Turhuta, where

宇 肃州科布多线

此线起自肃州，向西北方走，在尖牛贯通万里长城，向煤矿地方前行，即离肃州二百五十里地方也。由彼处即往哈毕尔罕布鲁克与伊哈托里。离伊哈托里不远，此线即经过北京哈密线，然后前行至伯勒台，过此处后，经过一小块沙漠，即至底门赤鲁。当进此多山与下隰[70]之乡落，再前行至戛什温，即横过北方大港乌鲁木齐干线。过戛什温，向倭伦呼都克、塔巴腾与塔普图，即由塔普图与古城科布多通道相合。于是循此路经伯多滚台、苏台，前行至科布多，即此线之末站。约共长七百英里。

宙 西北边界线

此线起自伊犁，循乌鲁木齐伊犁线，至三台，即赛里木湖之东边也。此线由此处向东北自行，沿艾比湖西方，至土斯赛。过土斯赛后，向托里前行，横过中央干线，即北方大港塔城线也。由彼处，此线即往纳木果台与斯托罗盖台，经过最大之森林与最富之煤矿地方。再由斯托罗盖台依通道前行，至承化寺，是阿尔泰省之省会。于是由彼处横过山脉，经乌尔霍盖图山口入至科布多谷地，循科布多河河源至别留，由此与绥远科布多线直达乌列盖。由乌列盖依其本路取道乌松阔勒与乌兰固穆，行至塔布图，于是与他线再合，同行至在唐努乌梁海境内之乌鲁克穆河。然后转东向，沿河流而上，至别开穆与乌鲁河之合流处。即再前行，沿前流依东北方溯源直上至境界，是为终点。此线所经之距离约九百英里。

洪 迪化（又名乌鲁木齐）乌兰固穆线

此线起自迪化，依多伦迪化干线至阜康。然后循其本路向北前进，经自辟川，至霍尔楚台。由此转东北走，经过山地，至开车。

it crosses a branch line from Junction C. of the Great Northern Port-Urumochi line. After Turhuta, it turns northward, proceeds up the Pakaningale Valley to Zehoshita, and then crosses the Tilikta Pass. Thence it turns northeastward proceeding across the newly cultivated country to Kobdo. After Kobdo, it proceeds through a fertile plateau, by crossing many rivers and skirting many lakes to Ulankom, where it ends by joining the Northwestern Frontier line. It covers a distance of about 550 miles.

h. The Gaskhiun-Tannu Ola Line

This line starts from Gaskhiun and proceeds northeastward across a hilly and watered country through Hatonhutuk and Talangjoleu, to Pornulu. After Pornulu, the line proceeds across the Sapkhyn Valley by Huchirtu and Porkho to Uliassutai where it meets the Suiyuan-Kobdo, and the Great Eastern Port-Uliassutai lines. After Uliassutai, the line proceeds northward to a quite new country by first crossing the headwaters of Selenga, then the headwaters of the Tess River. In the Tess Valley the line crosses a vast virgin forest. After emerging from this forest it proceeds northwestward across the watershed into the Khua Kem Valley in Tannu Ola and ends by joining the Northwestern Frontier line. This line covers a distance of about 650 miles.

i. The Uliassutai-Kiakata Line

This line starts from Uliassutai and runs on the track of the Gaskhiun-Tannu Ola line, until it reaches the Eder River, a branch of the Selenga. Then, turning off eastward, it begins its own course and proceeds downward following the course of the Eder River, crossing the Tsingpien-Tannu Ola line, to the junction of this river with the Selenga. There it joins the Kalgan-Urga-Tannu Ola line and proceeds together eastward in the common track for some distance until the other line turns southeastward, when this line turns northeastward following the Selenga down to Kiakata. This line covers a distance of about 550 miles. running through a fertile valley.

然后至土尔扈特，于是横过北方大港乌鲁木齐线之支线第三交点。过土尔扈特尔后，转北行，经巴戛宁格力谷地，至斯和硕特。然后过帖列克特山口，由彼处即转东北向前行，经过一新耕种地方，即至科布多。再前行经过一肥沃草场，渡数河流，沿经数湖，即至乌兰固穆，在此即与西北边界线相会。此线长约五百五十英里。

荒　戛什温乌梁海线

此线起自戛什温，向东北前行，横过多山与隰地境界，经哈同呼图克与达兰趣律、博尔努鲁。过博尔努鲁后，此线通过匝盆谷地，经呼志尔图与博尔霍，至乌里雅苏台，在此与绥远科布多线及北方大港乌里雅苏台线相会。于是此线向北方前行于一新境地，先经过色楞格河之正源，然后经过帖斯河之正源，当在帖斯河谷地中，此线经过一极大未辟之森林。过此森林后，即转向西北走，经过分水界，进入在唐努乌梁海地方之乌鲁克穆谷地，与西北边界线相会，是为末站。此线共长六百五十英里。

日　乌里雅苏台恰克图线

此线起自乌里雅苏台，依戛什温乌梁海线前行，至色楞格河支流之鄂叠尔河止。然后转而东向，由其本线循鄂叠尔河流域前行而下，横过靖边乌梁海线，至鄂叠尔河与色楞格河合流处而止，于是与张家口库伦乌梁海线合轨，向东方前行颇远，待至彼线转东南向而止。当此线转东北向时，即循色楞格河下至恰克图。此线包有之距离约五百五十英里，经过一肥美谷地。

j. The Chensi or Barkul-Urga Line

This Line starts from Chensi or Barkul and proceeds northeastward across a cultivated region through Tutaku to Urkesiat. After Urkesiat, it crosses the Suchow-Kobdo line, then traverses the vast pasture on the north side of the Gobi Desert to Suchi and Dalantura. Thence it turns more northward across the Great Eastern Port-Uliassutai line, and the Dolon Nor-Urumochi line to Tashunhutuk. After this point the line crosses the Suiyuan-Uliassutai line at Ologai and proceeds over the watershed into the Selenga Valley where it crosses the Tsingpien-Tannu Ola line at Sabokatai. From here it turns eastward across a hilly and watered region to Urga. This line covers a distance of about 800 miles.

k. The Suchow-Urga Line

This line starts from Suchow and proceeds by Kinta to Maumu, and then follows the Taoho or Edsina River, which waters this strip of oasis, to the lakes. Thence it crosses the Gobi Desert, where it meets the crossing lines of the Peking-Hami and the Great Eastern Port-Uliassutai railways and with them forms a common junction. From this junction it proceeds across desert and pasture lands to another railway crossing which is formed by the Suiyuan-Kobdo and Tsingpien-Tannu Ola lines, also forming a common junction together. Thence it proceeds into pasture land through Hatengtu and Tolik to Sanintalai, where it crosses the Dolon Nor-Urumochi line. After Sanintalai, the line proceeds through Ulanhoshih and many other small towns and encampments to Urga. This line covers a distance of about 700 miles. One third of this length is through the desert and the other two thirds through watered pasture land.

l. The Desert Junction-Kerulen Line

This line starts from the Desert Junction, proceeds northeastward to the pastural land and crosses the Tsingpien-Tannu Ola line south of Ulan Nor Lake. Thence it proceeds to the Tuchetu Capital where it crosses the Suiyuan-Kobdo line. After the Tuchetu Capital it goes across a pasture to Junction A. From Junction A. it proceeds to Ulanhutuk and Chientingche, then crosses the Kalgan-Tannu Ola line to Zesenkhana.

月　镇西库伦线

此线起自镇西，向东北前行，横过一种植地域，道经图塔古，至苓尔格斜特。于是由乌尔格科特行过肃州科布多线，然后行经戈壁沙漠北边之大草场，至苏治与达阑图鲁。由彼处再向北走，横过北方大港乌里雅苏台线与多伦诺尔乌里雅苏台线，至塔顺呼图克。过此处后，此线即在鄂罗盖地方横过绥远乌里雅苏台线，前行过分水界，进入色楞格河谷地。于是在沙布克台行过靖边乌梁海线，从此即转东向，经过一多山水之境域，至库伦。此线所经之距离约八百英里。

盈　肃州库伦线

此线起自肃州，前行经金塔，至毛目。于是随道河（又名额经纳河）而行，此河可以之灌注沙漠中之沃地。然后乃沿河流域而至一湖，复由彼处行经戈壁沙漠，即与北京哈密线及北方大港乌里雅苏台线之相交处相会，成为一共同联站。过此以后，此线向沙漠与草场前行，经过别一铁路交点，此铁路之交点即由绥远科布多线与靖边乌梁海线所成。于是此线在此处亦成为共同联站，由彼处前行，进入一大草地，经过哈藤与图里克，至三音达赖，于此即横过多伦诺尔乌鲁木齐线。过三音达赖后，此线前行经乌兰和硕与许多市镇营寨，即至库伦。此线包有之距离约七百英里，三分一路经过沙漠，其余三分之二经过低湿草地。

昃　沙漠联站克鲁伦线

此线起自沙漠联站，向东方前行，至一大草地。于是在鄂兰淖尔湖南方横过靖边乌梁海线，由彼处前行，至土谢图汗都会，于此经过绥远科布多线。过土谢图汗都会后，行经大草场，至第一联站。由第一联站即前行至乌兰呼图克与尖顶车，然后横过张家口乌梁海线，至车臣汗。

From Zesenkhana, the line follows the course of the Kerulen River down in a northeasterly direction to the city of Kerulen, where it crosses the Dolon Nor-Kerulen line, and meets the Kerulen-Tungchin line. This line covers a distance of about 800 miles.

m. The Khobor-Kerulen-Chikatobo Line

This line starts from Khobor, the crossing junction of the Dolon Nor-Urumochi, and the Kalgan-Urga-Tannu Ola lines, and proceeds northeastward across a vast pasture to Khoshentun, where it crosses the Dolon Nor-Kiakata line. After Khoshentun, it proceeds in the same direction across a similar pasture to Kerulen, where it crosses the Dolon Nor-Kerulen line. Then it proceeds first along the right bank of the Kerulen River, then crosses to the left side, and passes along the northwestern side of Hulan Lake. After Hulan Lake, the line crosses the Chinese Eastern Railway, and the Arguna River, then proceeds along the right bank of the river to Chikatobo, where the line ends by joining the Dolon Nor-Moho and the Chikatobo-Sansing lines. This line covers a distance of about 600 miles. The first half of it runs on dry land and the second half on watered land.

n. The Wuyuan-Taonan Line

This line starts from Wuyuan at the northwest bend of the Hoangho and proceeds northeastward across the Sheiten Ula Mountain and pasture to Tolibulyk, where it meets the crossing junction of three lines—the Peking-Hami line, the Suiyuan-Kobdo line, and the Great Eastern Port-Urga line. From Tolibulyk the line proceeds continuously in the same direction across a pasture to Khobor where it meets the crossing junction of the Dolon Nor-Urumochi and the Peking-Urga lines, and also the terminus of the Khobor-Kerulen line. After Khobor the line turns more eastward and runs across the Dolon Nor-Kiakata line midway to Khombukure, where it crosses the Dolon Nor-Kerulen and the Hulutao-Kerulen lines. From Khombukure the line proceeds to Dakmusuma, where it crosses the Dolon Nor-Moho line. Thence it goes eastward across the Great Khingan Mountain to Tuchuan, then turns southeastward to Taonan, where it ends. This line covers a distance of about 900 miles.

由车臣汗此线向东北循河流域而下，直达克鲁伦城，于此即横过多伦克鲁伦线并与克鲁伦东镇线相会。此线长约八百英里。

辰　格合克鲁伦节克多博线

此线起自格合，此即多伦诺尔乌鲁木齐与张家口库伦乌梁海二线之交点也。由彼处向东北前行，经过大草场，至霍申屯，于是横过多伦恰克图线。过霍申屯后，依同一方向前行，又经过一大草场，至克鲁伦，即由此横过呼伦克鲁伦线。然后依克鲁伦河右岸前行，再渡左岸，经过呼伦池之西北边。过呼伦池后，此线横过中东铁路，渡额尔古纳河。然后沿此河右岸直达节克多博，于是与多伦诺尔漠河与节克多博依兰二线相会，此即此线之末站也。此线包有之距离约六百英里，上半截经过旱地，下半经过湿地。

宿　五原洮南线

此线起自黄河西北边之五原地方，向东北前行，横过晒田、乌拉山与大草地，即抵托里布拉克，于是与北京哈密线、绥远科布多线及北方大港库伦线之三路交点相会。由托里布拉克此线再向同一方向前行，经过草地场，至格合，在此即与多伦乌鲁木齐与北京库伦二线相会，亦即格合克鲁伦线之首站也。过格合后，此线渐转东向，横过多伦恰克图线之中部，至欢布库里，于是在此横过多伦克鲁伦与葫芦岛克鲁伦之二线。由欢布库里此线行经界线之南，即循之行至达克木苏马，于是与多伦漠河线相会。由彼处行向东方，横过兴安岭，至突泉，然后转东南向，至洮南，此即终站也。此线长约九百英里。

o. The Wuyuan-Dolon Nor Line

This line starts from Wuyuan and proceeds northeastward across the Sheiten Ula Mountain to Maomingan, where it crosses the Great Eastern Port-Urga line. Then it proceeds across the vast pasture and the Suiyuan-Kobdo line to Bombotu, where it passes over the Peking-Hami line. After Bombotu, the line turns eastward and proceeds across the Kalgan-Urga-Tannu Ola line, then goes to Dolon Nor, where it ends by joining the Dolon Nor-Mukden-Linkiang line, which forms a direct route from the upper Hoangho Valley to the rich Liaoho Valley. This line covers a distance of about 500 miles.

p. The Yenki-Ili Line

This line starts from Yenki or Karashar, and proceeds northwestward across the mountain pass into the Ili Valley. It then follows the Kunges River downward, in a westerly direction, traversing a most fertile valley, to Ining and Kuldja or Ili, the principal city of the Ili district near the Russian border, where it joins the Ili-Urumochi line. This line covers a distance of about 400 miles.

q. The Ili-Hotien Line

This line starts from Ili or Kuldja, proceeds southward across the Ili River, then eastward along the left side of the river and then southeastward and southward to Bordai. From here it turns southwestward into Tekes Valley and proceeding upward crosses the Tekes River to Tienchiao and then ascends the mountain pass. After the mountain pass the line turns southeastward, traverses a vast coal field and then turns southwestward to Shamudai, where it crosses the Turfan-Kashgar line. From Shamudai it turns southward across the fertile zone of the north side of the Tarim Valley, to Bastutakelak. Then it proceeds southwestward to Hotien passing by on the way many small settlements in the fertile zone of the Hotien River which flows across the desert. At Hotien the line meets the Kashgar-Iden line. After Hotien the line proceeds upward to the highland south of the city and ends at the frontier. This line covers a distance of about 700 miles.

列　五原多伦线

此线起自五原，向东北前行，横过晒田、乌拉岭，至茂名安旗，即在此经过北方大港库伦线。然后向一大草场前行，经过绥远科布多线，至邦博图，经过北京哈密线。过邦博图后，此线转而东向前行，经过张家口库伦乌梁海线。然后至多伦，与多伦奉天临江线相合为终站。此线由黄河上流谷地，成一直接路线至肥美之辽河谷地，包有距离约五百英里。

张　焉耆伊犁线

此线起自焉耆（又名喀喇沙），向西北前行，横过山岭，进入伊犁谷地。然后循空吉斯河向西下行，绕极肥美谷地，至伊宁与绥定（即伊犁城）等，此皆在伊犁地方、近俄罗斯边境之主要城镇也。于是在伊犁与伊犁乌鲁木齐线相合。此线长约四百英里。

寒　伊犁和阗线

此线起自伊犁，向南前行，渡伊犁河，然后东向沿此河左岸而行。初向东南，继向南，行至博尔台。由此即转西南向，进入帖克斯谷地。然后溯帖克斯河而上，至天桥，再上山道。过此山道后，此线转东南向行，绕过一极大煤矿地方，然后再转西南，至札木台，于此即经过吐鲁番喀什噶尔线。由札木台即转南向，行过塔里木谷地北边之最肥美区域，至巴斯团搭格拉克。再向西南行，至和阗。此路经过无数小部落，皆在和阗河之肥沃区域中，此河即流入沙漠。此线在和阗与喀什噶尔于阗线相会。过和阗后，即向此城南方上行至高原，以国界为终站。此线包有距离约七百英里。

r. The Chensi-Kashgar Line and Its Branches

This line starts from Chensi and proceeds southwestward along the Tienshan pasture through Yenanpoa, Shihkialoong, and Taolaitse to Chikoching, then along the Tienshan forest through Wutungkwo, Tungyenchi, Siyenchi, and Olong to Sensien, where it crosses the Central Trunk line. After Sensien it proceeds along the northern edge of the Tarim Desert through Lakesun City and Shehchuan to Hora, where it crosses the Cherchen-Koria line. From Hora the line proceeds along the course of the Tarim River, passing by many new settlements, fertile regions, and virgin forests, to Bastutakelak, where it crosses the Ili-Hotien line. Thence it goes through Pachu to Kashgar where it meets the Urumochi-Iden line. After Kashgar it proceeds northwestward to the frontier where it ends. Attached to this line are two branches. The first branch proceeds from Hora southwestward through many oases to Cherchen. The second proceeds from Pachu southwestward along the Yarkand River to Sache and then westward to Puli near the frontier. This line including the branches covers a distance of about 1,600 miles. The total length of this entire system is about 16,000 miles. See general map.

● Part V The Highland Railway System

This, the last part of my railway program, is the most difficult and most expensive undertaking of its kind; consequently, it must be the least remunerative of all the railway enterprises in China. So no work should be attempted in this part until all the other parts are fully developed. But when all the other parts are well equipped with railways then railway construction in this highland region will also be remunerative, despite the difficulties and the highly expensive work in construction.

The highland region consists of Tibet, Kokonor, and a part of Sinkiang, Kansu, Szechwan, and Yunnan, an area of about 1,000,000 square miles. Tibet is known to be the richest country in the world for gold deposits. Furthermore the adjacent territories possess rich agricultural and pastural lands. This vast region is little known to the outside world. The Chinese call Tibet "the Western Treasury," for, besides gold, there are other kinds of metals especially copper, in great quantities. Indeed the name of the Western Treasury is most appropriately applied to this unknown region. When the world's supply of precious metals

来 镇西喀什噶尔线与其支线

此线起自镇西，向西南行，循天山草场，经延安堡、薛家陇与陶赖子，至七个井。然后循天山森林，经过桐窝西盐池与阿朗，至鄯善，由此即经过中央干线。过鄯善后，即循塔里木沙漠北边而行，经鲁克沁与石泉，至河拉，于此横过车城库尔勒线。由河拉前行，循塔里木河流域，经过无数新村落肥美地方与未开发之森林，即至巴斯团塔格拉克，在此横过伊犁和阗线。行经巴楚，至喀什噶尔，在此与乌鲁木齐于阗线相会。过喀什噶尔后，此线即向西北前行至国界，是为终站。至与此线有连续关系者，约有二支线：第一支线，由河拉西南方前行，经沙漠中沃地数处至车城；第二支线，则由巴西楚南方循叶尔羌河至莎车，然后西南至蒲犁，即近国界地方也。此线与其各支线合计之，约共长一千六百英里。如就此系统全部言之，约共长一万六千英里。

• 第五部 高原铁路系统

此是吾铁路计划之最后部分，其工程极为繁难，其费用亦甚巨大，而以之比较其他在中国之一切铁路事业，其报酬亦为至微。故此铁路之工程，当他部分铁路未完全成立后，不能兴筑。但待至他部分铁路完全成立，然后兴筑此高原境域之铁路，即使其工程浩大，亦当有良好报酬也。

此高原之境域包括西藏、青海、新疆之一部，与甘肃、四川、云南等地方，面积约一百万英方里。附近之土地，皆有最富之农产与最美之牧场。但此伟大之境域，外国多有未之知者。而中国人则目西藏为西方宝藏，盖因除金产丰富外，尚有他种金属，黄铜尤其特产；故以宝藏之名。加于此世人罕知之境域，洵[71]确当也。当世界金属行将

are exhausted, we have to resort to this vast mineral bearing region for supply. So railways will be necessary at least for mining purposes. I therefore propose the following lines:

a. The Lhasa-Lanchow line.
b. The Lhasa-Chengtu line.
c. The Lhasa-Tali-Cheli line.
d. The Lhasa-Taklongshong line.
e. The Lhasa-Yatung line.
f. The Lhasa-Laichiyaling line.
g. The Lhasa-Nohho line.
h. The Lhasa-Iden line.
i. The Lanchow-Chochiang line.
j. The Chengtu-Dzunsasak line.
k. The Ningyuan-Cherchen line.
l. The Chengtu-Menkong line.
m. The Chengtu-Yuankiang line.
n. The Suifu-Tali line.
o. The Suifu-Mengting line.
p. The Iden-Gortok line.

a. The Lhasa-Lanchow Line

This is the most important line of this system for it connects the capital city of Tibet—a vast secluded region with several millions of people—with the central trunk line of the country. The route which it passes through is inhabitable and is already slightly inhabited in the region between the ends of the proposed line. So it will probably be a paying line from the beginning. This line starts from Lhasa, following the old imperial highway in a northward direction and proceeds by Talong to Yarh, which lies on the southeastern side of Tengri Nor Lake. After Yarh, the line turns more eastward and proceeds across the watershed from the Sanpo Valley to the Lukiang Valley by the Shuangtsu Pass. Thence turning more eastward the line proceeds across the headwater of the Lukiang to that of the Yangtze by passing many valleys, streams, and mountain passes. Then it crosses the main body of the Upper Yangtze, which is here known as the Kinshakiang, over the Huhusair Bridge.

用尽时，吾等可于此广大之矿域中求之。故为开矿而建设铁路，为必要之图。吾拟下之各线：

天　拉萨兰州线。
地　拉萨成都线。
玄　拉萨大理车里线。
黄　拉萨提郎宗线。
宇　拉萨亚东线。
宙　拉萨来吉雅令及其支线。
洪　拉萨诺和线。
荒　拉萨于阗线。
日　兰州婼羌线。
月　成都宗札萨克线。
盈　宁远车城线。
昃　成都门公线。
辰　成都沅江线。
宿　叙府大理线。
列　叙府孟定线。
张　于阗噶尔渡线。

天　拉萨兰州线

此线与西藏都会相连，为彼境域之中央干线，足称为此系统中之重要路线。沿此线之起点与终点，现已有少数居民，将来可成为一大殖民地，故即当开办之始，或可成为一有价值之路线也。此线起自拉萨，循旧官路向北前行，经达隆，至雅尔，即腾格里池之东南方也。过雅尔后，此线暂转东向，由藏布谷地过分水界，经双竹山口，至潞江谷地。然后转而东向，渡潞江正源，经过数处谷地、河流及山岭，而至扬子江。于是渡扬子江上流正源之金沙江，过苦苦赛尔桥。

After crossing the bridge, it turns southeastward, then eastward across the Yangtze Valley into the Hoangho Valley, where it passes through many small towns and encampments into the Starry Sea region. At the Starry Sea, the line passes between the lakes of Oring Nor and Tsaring Nor. Thence it turns northeastward across the southeast valley of the Zaidam region, and returns into the Hoangho Valley again. Then it proceeds through Katolapo and various towns to Dangar, now called Hwangyuan, situated near the border between Kansu and Kokonor. After Dangar, the line turns southeastward following the course of the Sining River, proceeds downward through a very rich valley and passes through Sining, Nienpai, and hundreds of small towns and villages to Lanchow. This line covers a distance of 1,100 miles.

b. The Lhasa-Chengtu Line

This line starts from Lhasa and proceeds northeastward on the former imperial highway by Teking and Nanmo to Motsukungchia. Thence it turns southeastward and northeastward to Giamda. From Giamda, the line turns northward, then northeastward where it proceeds through the Tolala Pass to Lhari. After Lhari the line goes in an easterly direction and passes Pianpa, Shihtuh, and many small towns to Lo-longchong. Thence it crosses the Lukiang by the Kayu Bridge and then turns northeastward to Kinda and Chiamdo. After Chiamdo, the line instead of following the imperial highway southeastward to Batang, turns northeastward, following another trade route, and proceeds to Payung at the northwestern corner of Szechwan. From Payung, it proceeds across the Kinshakiang over the bridge near Sawusantusze. The line then turns southeastward, enters the Ichu Valley and proceeds downward to Kantzu on the Yalung River. Thence it proceeds to Chango and Yinker, to Badi on the Great Golden River, and Mongan on the Little Golden River. After Mongan, the line goes through the Balan Pass to Kwanhsien, and entering the Chengtu Plain, reaches Chengtu by Pihsien. This line covers a distance of about 1,000 miles.

c. The Lhasa-Tali-Cheli Line

This line starts from Lhasa by the same track as the Lhasa-Chengtu line as far as Giamda. From Giamda, it proceeds by its own track southeastward, following a branch of the Sanpo River to Yulu, where this branch joins its main stream. After Yulu, it follows the left bank of the Sanpo River passing by Kongposaga to Timchao. From Timchao, the line turns away from the Sanpo River and proceeds in an eastward direction to Timchong city, Ikung, Kuba, and Shuachong.

过此桥后转东南向，又东向通过扬子江谷地，进入黄河谷地。于是由此经过数小村落与帐幕地，进至札陵湖与鄂陵湖间之星宿海。然后东北向，过柴塔木之东南谷地，再转入黄河谷地，即前进经过喀拉普及数小市镇，至丹噶尔（今名湟源，界于甘肃与青海之间）。过丹噶尔后，此线即转东南，循西宁河流之肥美谷地下行，经过西宁、碾伯与数百小市镇、小村落，至兰州。此线行经之距离约一千一百英里。

地　拉萨成都线

此线起自拉萨，东北向，依旧官路前行，经德庆、南摩，至墨竹工卡。然后转东南向，又东北向，至江达。于是由江达转北向，又转东北向前行，经过托拉山，至拉里。过拉里后，此线向东行，经边坝硕督与数小市镇，至洛龙宗。然后由嘉裕桥渡潞江，即转东北向，至恩达与察木多。过察木多后，此线不循东南之官路至巴塘，乃向东北，而循别一商路前行，至四川省西北角之巴戎。由此前行过桥渡金沙江，即札武三土司附近地方也。于是此线转东南向，进入依杵谷地，沿鸦龙江下行至甘孜[72]。再前进经长葛、英沟，至大金川之倍田，并至小金川之望安。过望安后，此线即横过斑烂山，至灌县，进入成都平原，即由郫县至成都。此线行经之距离约一千英里。

玄　拉萨大理车里线

此线起自拉萨，与拉萨成都线同轨，直行至江达。于是由江达循其本路路轨西南向，沿藏布江[73]支流至油鲁，即其河支流与正流会合之点也。过油鲁后，即沿藏布江口左岸，经公布什噶城，至底穆昭。由底穆昭离藏布江向东前行，至底穆宗城、遗贡、巴谷、刷宗城。

After Shuachong, the line proceeds southeastward to Lima, thence eastward to Menkong on the Lukiang. From Menkong, the line turns southward and goes along the right bank of the Lukiang passing Samotung to Tantau. Then crossing the Lukiang, it proceeds across the watershed through Gaiwa village to the Lantsang (or Mekong) River, and to Hsiaoweisi beyond it. After Hsiaoweisi, it follows the river bank to the Chenghsin Copper Mine, thence it turns away from the river and proceeds by Hosi, Erhyuan, Tengchow, and Shangkwang to Tali. From Tali, the line proceeds to Hsiakwang, Fengyi, Menghwa, and then meets the Lantsang River again at Paotien. Thence it follows the left bank southward right through to Cheli, where it ends. This line covers a distance of 900 miles.

d. The Lhasa-Taklongshong Line

This line starts from Lhasa and proceeds southward by way of Teking to the Sanpo River where turning eastward it follows the left bank of the river to Sakorshong. After crossing the Sanpo River to Chetang, it proceeds southward by Chikablung, Menchona, Tawang, Dhirangjong to Taklongshong and continues farther on until it reaches the Assam frontier. This line covers a distance of 200 miles.

e. The Lhasa-Yatung Line

This line starts from Lhasa and proceeds southwestward by Chashih following the former imperial highway by Yitang and Kiangli to Chushui. At Chushui, it crosses to Sanpo River over the Mulih Bridge to Chakamo on the south side, thence to Tamalung, Paiti, Tabolung, and Nagartse. After Nagartse, the line turns westward to Jungku, Lhaling, and Shachia. At Shachia, the line leaves the former imperial highway and turns southwestward again and proceeds via Kula to Yatung at the Sikkim border. This line covers a distance of 250 miles.

f. The Lhasa-Laichiyaling Line and Branches

This line starts from Lhasa and proceeds northwestward by Chashih following the former imperial road to Little Taking, and westward to Yangpachin and Sangtolohai. Thence turning southwestward, it proceeds to Namaling and Tangto, and crosses the Sanpo River at Lhaku. After Lhaku, the line turns westward to Shigatse, the second important city in Tibet

过刷宗城后，此线转东南行至力马，再东行至潞江之门公。于是由门公转南向前行，沿潞江右岸，经菖蒲桶，至丹邬。然后渡潞江，由崖瓦村谷地过分水界，至澜沧江（又名美江），乃渡江至小维西。过小维西后，即沿河边至诚心铜厂。然后离河前行，经河西、洱源、邓州、上关，至大理。由大理南行至下关、凤仪、蒙化，再行至保甸，与澜沧江再会。于是南行沿江之左岸，至车里，为此线之终点。其路线之长约九百英里。

黄　拉萨提郎宗线

此线起自拉萨，向南行，道经德庆，至藏布江。再由藏布江转东向，沿河之左岸，至札噶尔总。渡藏布江至泽当，即南向前行，经吹夹坡郎、满楚纳、塔旺，至提郎宗。再接续前行，至印度之亚三边界[74]。此线长约二百英里。

宇　拉萨亚东线

此线起自拉萨，西南向，由札什循旧官路，经僵里，至曲水。由曲水过末力桥，渡藏布江南之查戛木，然后至塔马隆、白地、达布隆与浪噶子等地方。过浪噶子后，此线转西向，至翁古、拉萨、沙加等地。于是由沙加离官路再转向西南行，道经孤拉，至亚东，是哲孟雄边界[75]。此线约长二百五十英里。

宙　拉萨来吉雅令及其支线

此线起自拉萨，向西北行，由札什循旧官路前行，至小德庆。再西行至桑驼骆池，转西南行至那马陵与当多汛，即在拉古地方渡藏布江。过拉古后，此线即转西向，至日喀则城，是为西藏之第二重要市镇。

whence it proceeds in the same direction to Chashihkang, Pangcholing, and Lhatse all on the right side of the Sanpo River. From Lhatse, a branch line starts southwestward via Chayakor and Dingri to Niehlamuh on the Nepal border. The main line, however, crosses to the left side of the Sanpo River and proceeds on the same highway via Nabringtaka to Tadum where another branch line proceeds southwestward to the Nepal border. The main line continues northwestward via Tamusa and Choshan to Gartok, thence turning westward it proceeds to Laichiyaling on the Sutlej River and ends on the Indian border. This line, including the two branches, covers a distance of 850 miles.

g. The Lhasa-Nohho Line

This line starts from Lhasa and runs in the same track as line (f) to Sangtolohai where it proceeds by its own line northwestward to Teching, Sangchashong, and Taktung. Thence, it enters into the richest gold field in Tibet and through Wengpo, Tulakpa, Kwangkwei, and Ikar reaches Nohho, where the line ends. It covers a distance of 700 miles.

h. The Lhasa-Iden Line

This line starts from Lhasa, following the common track of lines (f) and (g) to the southwestern corner of Tengri Lake, whence it proceeds by its own track northwestward by Lungmajing, Tipoktolo and four or five other small places to Sari. After Sari, the line penetrates a vast tract of uninhabited land to Pakar and Suketi. Thence crossing the mountain passes and descending from the highland to the Tarim Basin through Sorkek to Yasulakun, the line joins the Cherchen-Iden railway of the Northwestern System and proceeds on the same track to Iden. This line covers a distance of 700 miles.

i. The Lanchow-Chochiang Line

This line starts from Lanchow, on the same track of the Lhasa-

Lanchow line as far as the southeastern corner of the Lake Kokonor. Thence it proceeds on its own track by skirting along the southern shore of Lake Kokonor to Dulankit, where it turns southwestward to Dzunsasak. From Dzunsasak, the line proceeds in a westerly course along the southern side of the Zaidam Swamp, and passes Tunyueh, Halori,

由此依同一方向，向沿藏布江边右岸前行，经过札什冈、朋错岭与拉子等地方。于是由拉子分一支线向西南行，取道胁噶尔、定日，至尼泊尔边界之聂拉木。但其干线则横过藏布江之右边，循官路行，取道那布林格喀，至大屯。由此再分一支线向西南行，至尼泊尔边界。而其干线仍接续西北行，取道塔木札卓山，至噶尔渡。然后向西前行，至萨特来得河之来吉雅令，以印度边界为终点。此线与其二支线合计之，约共长八百五十英里。

洪　拉萨诺和线

此线起自拉萨，与宙线同转，行至桑驼骆池，始循其本线向西北前行，至得贞、桑札宗及塔克东。于是由此处进入西藏之金矿最富地方，再经过翁波、都拉克巴、光贵与于喀尔，至诺和，为此线之终点。其距离约长七百英里。

荒　拉萨于阗线

此线起自拉萨，循宙、洪两线之轨道，至腾格里池之西南角。于是由其本轨向西北前行，经隆马绒、特布克托罗海与四五处小地方，至萨里。过萨里后，此线即通过一大幅无人居之地，至巴喀尔与苏格特。横过山岭，遂由高原而下，经索尔克，至塔里木河流域之雅苏勒公，在此与西北铁路系统之车尔城于阗线合轨，前行至于阗。此线共长约七百英里。

日　兰州婼羌线

此线起自兰州，循拉萨札州线轨道同行，至青海之东南角。于是由其本轨绕青海南岸，至都兰奇特，即由此转西南走，至宗札萨克。由宗札萨克依柴达木低洼地之南边，向西南行，经过屯月、哈罗里与

and Golmot to Hatikair. After Hatikair, the line turns northwestward by Baipa, Nolinjoha, to Orsinte. Thence turning more northward, it proceeds across the mountain range by Tsesinvitusuik and Tuntunomik to Chochiang, where it ends by joining the Ansi-Iden and Chochiang-Koria lines, covering a distance of 700 miles.

j. The Chengtu-Dzunsasak Line

This line starts from Chengtu and proceeds to Kwanhsien on the track of the Lhasa-Chengtu line, thence northward on its own track by Wenchuan, to Mauchow. Then, it proceeds northwestward following the course of the Minkiang to Sungpan. After Sungpan, it ascends the Min Valley passing Tungpi to Shangleyao, where it crosses the watershed from the Yangtze River side to that of the Hoangho. Thence the line proceeds to Orguseri, and following a branch of the Hoangho to the northwestern turn of its main stream, it proceeds along its right bank via Chahuntsin to Peilelachabu. There it crosses the Hoangho to the northwest turn of the old imperial road, where it joins the Lhasa-Lanchow line and proceeds as far as Lanipar. Then turning northwestward, it proceeds by its own line to Dzunsasak, where it ends by joining the Lanchow-Chochiang line. This line covers a distance of 650 miles.

k. The Ningyuan-Cherchen Line

This line starts from Ningyuan and proceeds in a northwestward direction via Hwaiyuanchen to the Yalungkiang. Then it ascends along the left side of that river to Yakiang, and crossing to the right side of that river it proceeds by the old post road to Siolo, where it turns away from the river and follows the same post road to Litang. From Litang it proceeds in the same direction but follows another road to Kangtu, on the left side of the Kinshakiang. Following the same side of the river, it proceeds to Sawusantusze, where it crosses the Lhasa-Chengtu line. After Sawusantusze, the line continues in the same direction and follows the same side of the Kinshakiang via Tashigompa, to the Huhusair Bridge, where it crosses the Lhasa-Lanchow line. Then following a northern branch of the Kinshakiang to its source and crossing the watershed, it proceeds along the caravan road by Hsinszukiang and Olokung to Cherchen, where it ends, covering a distance of about 1,350 miles. This is the longest line of this system.

各尔莫，至哈自格尔。过哈自格尔后，此线即转西北向，经拜把水泉、那林租哈，至阿尔善特水泉。然后暂转北向前行，横过山脉，至婼羌，即与安西于阗线及婼羌库尔勒线联合，是为终站。此线约长七百英里。

月　成都宗札萨克线

此线起自成都，循拉萨成都线轨道前行，至灌县。然后由其本轨向北前行，经汶川，至茂州。于是循泯江河流向西北前行，至松潘。过松潘后，即入岷山谷地，经过东丕，至上勒凹。即由此处横过扬子江与黄河间之分水界，再接续前行至鄂尔吉库舍里。于是由黄河支源西北转至其正流，沿河右边，取道察汉津，至布勒拉察布。渡黄河至旧官路，西北转，与拉萨兰州线合轨前行，直达拉尼巴尔。再转西北向，循其本轨前行，至宗札萨克，与兰州婼羌线相会，是为终站。此线行经之距离约六百五十英里。

盈　宁远车城线

此线起自宁远，向西北行，取道怀远镇，至雅江。横过江之右岸，循旧驿路前行，至西俄落，即离江边循驿路至里塘。由里塘仍依同一方向，从别路前行至金沙江左岸之冈沱。再沿此河边前行，至札武三土司，横过拉萨成都线。过札武三土司后，此线仍依同一方向前行，沿金沙江边，取道图登贡巴，至苦苦赛尔桥，即在此横过拉萨兰州线。再循金沙江之北支源至其发源处，过分水界，循骆驼路前行，经沁司坎、阿洛共，至车城，是为终站。其距离约长一千三百五十英里，此线为此系统之最长路线。

l. The Chengtu-Menkong Line

This line starts from Chengtu and proceeds southwestward by Shuangliu, Hsintsin, Mingshan, to Yachow. From Yachow, it turns northwestward and proceeds to Tienchuan, then westward to Tatsienlu, Tunyolo, and Litang. After Litang, the line proceeds southwestward through Batang and Yakalo, to Menkong, covering a distance of about 400 miles of very mountainous country.

m. The Chengtu-Yuankiang Line

This line starts from Chengtu on the same track of the Chengtu-Menkong line, proceeds to Yachow and thence by its own track in the same direction via Jungching, to Tsingliu. After Tsingliu, the line proceeds southward through Yuehsi to Ningyuan, where it meets the head of the Ningyuan-Cherchen line. After Ningyuan, it goes to Kwaili, then crosses the Kinshakiang to Yunnanfu where it crosses the Canton-Tali line. From Yunnanfu, it proceeds along the west side of the Kunming Lake to Kunyang, and through Hsinshing, Hsingo, to Yuankiang, where the line ends by joining the Canton-Szemo line. It covers a distance of about 600 miles.

n. The Suifu-Tali Line

This line starts from Suifu and proceeds along the left bank of the Yangtze River to Pingshan and Lupo. After Lupo, it turns away from the river in a southwesterly direction and scales the Taliangshan Mountains to Ningyuan, where it crosses the Chengtu-Yuankiang line and meets the termini of the Canton-Ningyuan line and the Ningyuan-Cherchen line. Thence continuing in the same direction, it crosses the Yalungkiang to Yenyuan and Yungpeh. After Yungpeh, the line turns more southward, across the Kinshakiang to Sincheng and thence to Tali, where it ends by meeting the Canton-Tali line and the Lhasa-Tali line. It covers a distance of about 400 miles.

o. The Suifu-Mengting Line

This line starts from Suifu on the same track as the Suifu-Tali line as far as Lupo. From Lupo, it goes on its own track across the Yangtze River here known as the Kinshakiang, and follows the right side of that river upward to its southward bend where it crosses the Chengtu-Yuankiang line, to Yuanmow. From Yuanmow, it proceeds to Tsuyung, where it

昃　成都门公线

此线起自成都，向西南行，经双流、新津、名山，至雅州。转西北向，前行至天全。复转西行，至打箭炉、东俄落、里塘等地方。过里塘后，此线向西南行，经过巴塘、宴尔喀罗，至门公[76]。约共长四百英里，所经过地方皆系山岭。

辰　成都沅江线

此线起自成都，循成都门公线路轨，前行至雅州。然后由其本轨依同一方向，取道荥经，至清溪。过清溪后，此线向南行，经越嶲，至宁远，即于此与宁远车城线之首站相会。过宁远后，即至会理，然后渡金沙江至云南府，与广州大理线相会。于是由云南府循昆明池西边至昆阳，经过新兴、嶍峨，到沅江，与广州思茅线相会，是为终站。其距离约六百英里。

宿　叙府大理线

此线起自叙府，沿扬子江左岸，前行至屏山、雷波。过雷波后，即离此河向西南行，过大梁山，至宁远，即于此横过成都宁远线，并与广州宁远线及宁远车城线之首站相会。于是再接续依同一方向前行，横过鸦龙江，至盐源、永北。过永北后，此线暂转南向，渡金沙江至宾川，然后至大理，与广州大理线及拉萨大理线相会，是为终站。共长约四百英里。

列　叙府孟定线

此线起自叙府，循叙府大理线路轨，直行至雷波。即由扬子江上流名曰金沙江横过，沿此江之上流左岸，至其湾南处，即横过成都元江线，至元谋。复由元谋前行，至楚雄。横过广州大理线，至景东。

crosses the Canton-Tali line, thence to Kingtung. After Kingtung, it proceeds southwestward across the Lantsangkiang or Mekong River, to Yunchow, thence turning southwestward, it follows a branch of the Lukiang River to Mengting and ends on the frontier. This line covers a distance of about 500 miles.

p. The Iden-Gartok Line

This line starts from Iden, and proceeds southward along the Keriya River to Polu, thence following the caravan road up the highland to Kuluk. From Kuluk, it proceeds southwestward via Alasa and Tunglong to Nohho, where it meets the terminus of the Lhasa-Nohho line. After Nohho, it skirts around the eastern end of the Noh-tso-Lake to Rudok and proceeds southwestward to Demchok, on the Indus River. From Demchok, it proceeds southeastward following the Indus River up to Gartok, where it ends by joining the Lhasa-Laichiyaling line. This line covers a distance of about 500 miles. This highland system totals about 11,000 miles.

● Part VI The Establishment of Locomotive and Car Factories

The railways projected in the Fourth Program will total about 62,000 miles; and those in the First and the Third Programs about 14,000 miles. Besides these, there will be double tracks in the various trunk lines, which will make up a grand total of no less than 100,000 miles, as stated in the preliminary part of these programs. With this 100,000 miles of railways to be constructed in the coming ten years, the demands for locomotives and cars will be tremendous. The factories of the world will be unable to supply them, especially at this juncture of reconstruction after the great world war. So the establishment of locomotive and car factories in China to supply our own demands of railway equipment will be a necessary as well as a profitable undertaking. China possesses unlimited supplies of raw materials and cheap labor. What we need for establishing such factories is foreign capital and experts. What amount of capital should be invested in this project, I have to leave to experts to decide.

复向西南前行，横过澜沧江，至云州。然后转西南向，循潞江支脉至孟定，以边界为终站。此线共长约五百英里。

张　于阗噶尔渡线

此线起自于阗，沿克利雅河，向南行，至波鲁。由波鲁复转西南行，取道阿拉什东郎，至诺和，即与拉萨诺和线之终站相会。过诺和后，即绕诺和湖之东边，至罗多克。复向西南行，沿印度河至碟木绰克。复由碟木绰克东南向，沿印度河上行，至噶尔渡，即于此与拉萨来吉雅令线相会，是为终站。此线长约五百英里。

此高原铁路系统，全部共长一万一千英里。

第六部　设机关车、客货车制造厂

上部第四计划所预定之路线，约共长六万二千英里。至第一、第三计划所预定者，约一万四千英里。除此以外，并有多数干线当设双轨，故合数计划路线计之，至少当有十万英里。若以此十万英里之铁路，在十年内建筑之，机关车与客货车之需要必当大增。现当此战后改造时期，世界之制造厂将难以供应。此所以在中国建设机关车、客货车之制造厂，以应建筑铁路之需，为必要之图，且其为有利事业尤不可不注意也。中国有无限之原料与低廉之人工，是为建设此等制造厂之基础。但举办此种事业所必需者，为外国资本与专门家耳。至此项之计划应用资本若干，吾当留为对于此种工程有经验者定之。

I suggest that four large factories should be started simultaneously at the beginning—two on the coast and two on the Yangtze. Of those on the coast, one should be at the Great Northern Port, and the other at the Greatern Southern Port—Canton. Of those on the Yangtze, one should be at Nanking and the other at Hankow. All four are in centers of both land and water communication, where skilled labor can easily be obtained. They are also near our iron and coal fields. Besides these four great factories, others should be established at suitable centers of iron and coal fields when our railways will be more developed.

All the factories should be under one central control. The locomotives and cars of our future railways should be standardized so as to make possible the interchange of parts of machinery and equipment. We should also adopt the standard gauge, that is, the 4 feet 8½ inch gauge which has been adopted by most of the railways of the world. In fact, almost all the railways hitherto built in China are of this gauge. The purpose of the proposed standardization is to secure the highest efficiency as well as the greatest economy.

［中文译本中此二段无对应译文——编者注］

PROGRAM V

In the preceding four programs, I dealt exclusively with the development of the key and basic industries. In this one, I am going to deal with the development of the *main* group of industries which need foreign help. By the main group of industries, I mean those industries which provide every individual and family with the necessaries and comforts of life. Of course, when the key and basic industries are developed, the various other industries will spontaneously spring up all over the country, in a very short time. This had been the case in Europe and America after the industrial revolution. The development of the key and the basic industries will give plenty of work to the people and will raise their wages as well as their standard of living. When wages are high, the price for necessaries and comforts of life will also be increased. So the rise in wages will be accompained by the rise in the cost of living. Therefore, the aim of the development of some of the main group of industries is to help reduce the high cost of living when China is in the process of international development, by giving to the majority of the people plenty of the essentials and comforts of life as well as higher wages.

It is commonly thought that China is the cheapest country to live in. This is a misconception owing to the common notion of measuring everything by the value of money. If we measure the cost of living by the value of labor then it will be found that China is the most expensive country for a common worker to live in. A Chinese coolie, a muscular worker, has to work 14 to 16 hours a day in order to earn a bare subsistence. A clerk in a shop, or a teacher in a village school cannot earn more than a hundred dollars a year. And the farmers after paying their rents and exchanging for a few articles of need with their produce have to live from hand to mouth. Labor is very cheap and plentiful but food and commodities of life are just enough to go round for the great multitude of the four hundred millions in China in an ordinary good year. In a bad year, a great number succumb to want and starvation. This miserable condition among the Chinese proletariat is due to the non-development of the country, the crude methods of production and the wastefulness of labor. The radical cure for all this is industrial development by foreign capital and experts for the benefit of the whole nation. Europe and America are a hundred years ahead of us in industrial development; so in order to catch up in a very short time we have to use their capital, mainly their machinery. If foreign capital cannot be gotten, we will have to get at least their experts and inventors to make for us our own machinery. In any case, we must use machinery to assist our enormous man-power to develop our unlimited resources.

伍 第五计划

前四种计划既专论关键及根本工业之发达方法，今则进述工业本部之须外力扶助发达者。所谓工业本部者，乃以个人及家族生活所必需，且生活安适所由得。当关键及根本工业既发达，其他多种工业皆自然于全国在甚短时期内同时发生，欧美工业革命之后，既已如是。关键及根本工业发达，人民有许多工事可为，而工资及生活程度皆增高；工资既增多，生活必要品及安适品之价格亦增加。故发达本部工业之目的，乃当中国国际发展进行之时，使多数人民既得较高工资，又得许多生活必要品、安适品而减少其生活费也。世人尝以中国为生活最廉之国，其错误因为寻常见解以金钱之价值衡量百物；若以工作之价值衡量生活费用，则中国为工人生活最贵之国。中国一寻常劳工，每日须工作十四至十六小时，仅能维持其生活。商店之司书[77]，村乡之学究，每年所得恒在百元以下。农人既以所生产价还地租及交换少数必要品之后，所余已无几何。工力多而廉，惟食物及生活货品，虽在寻常丰年亦仅足敷四万万人之用，若值荒年则多数将陷于穷乏死亡。中国平民所以有此悲惨境遇者，由于国内一切事业皆不发达，生产方法不良，工力失去甚多。凡此一切之根本救治，为用外国资本及专门家发达工业以图全国民之福利。欧美二洲之工业发达，早于中国百年，今欲于甚短时期内追及之，须用其资本、用其机器。若外国资本不可得，至少亦须用其专门家、发明家，以为吾国制造机器。无论如何，必须用机器以辅助中国巨大之人工，以发达中国无限之富源也。

In modern civilization, the material essentials of life are five, namely: food, clothing, shelter, means of locomotion, and the printed page. Accordingly I will formulate this program as follows:

I. The Food Industry.
II. The Clothing Industry.
III. The Housing Industry.
IV. The Motoring Industry.
V. The Printing Industry.

● Part I The Food Industry

The food industry should be treated under the following headings:

a. The Production of Food.
b. The Storage and Transportation of Food.
c. The Preparation and Preservation of Food.
d. The Distribution and Exportation of Food.

a. The Production of Food

Human foods are derived from three sources: the land, the sea and the air. By far the most important and greatest in quantity consumed is aerial food of which oxygen is the most vital element. But this aerial food is abundantly provided by nature, and no human labor is needed for its production except that which is occasionally needed for the airman and the submariner. So this food is free to all. It is not necessary for us to discuss it here. The production of food from the sea which I have already touched upon when I dealt with the construction of fishing harbors and the building of fishing crafts, will also be left out here. It is the specific industries in the production of food from land, which need foreign help that are to be discussed here.

China is an agricultural country. About four-fifths of its population is occupied in the work of producing food. The Chinese farmer is very skillful in intensive cultivation. He can make the land yield to its utmost capacity. But vast tracts of arable lands are lying waste in thickly populated districts for one cause or other. Some are due to lack of water, some to too much of it and some to the "dog in the manger" system,—the holding up of arable land by speculators and land sharks for higher rents and prices.

据近世文明言，生活之物质原件共有五种，即食、衣、住、行及印刷是也。吾故定此种计划如下：

一、粮食工业。
二、衣服工业。
三、居室工业。
四、行动工业。
五、印刷工业。

第一部　粮食工业

粮食工业又分类如下：

甲　食物之生产。
乙　食物之贮藏及运输。
丙　食物之制造及保存。
丁　食物之分配及输出。

甲　食物之生产

人类食物得自三种来源，即陆地、海水、空气三者。其中最重要、最多量者为空气食物，譬如养气[78]为此中有力元素，惟自然界本具此甚多，除飞行家及潜艇乘员闲时须特备外，不须人工以为生产，故此种食物人人可自由得之，于此不须详论。吾前此论捕鱼海港之建设及捕鱼船舶之构造，已涉及海水食物，故于此亦不更述。惟陆地食物生产之事须国际扶助者，此下论之。

中国为农业国，其人数过半皆为食物生产之工作。中国农人颇长于深耕农业，能使土地生产至最多量。虽然，人口甚密之区，依诸种原因，仍有可耕之地流为荒废，或则缺水，或则水多，或则因地主投机求得高租善价，故不肯放出也。

The land of the eighteen provinces alone is at present supporting a population of four hundred millions. Yet there is still room for development which can make this same area of land yield more food if the waste land be brought under cultivation, and the already cultivated land be improved by modern machinery and scientific methods. The farmers must be protected and encouraged by liberal land laws by which they can duly reap the fruits of their own labor.

In regard to the production of food in our intemational development scheme, two necessary undertakings should be carried out which will be profitable at the same time.

(1) A scientific survey of the land.
(2) The establishment of factories for manufacturing agricultural machinery and implements.

(1) A scientific survey of the land. China has never been scientifically surveyed and mapped out. The administration of land is in the most chaotic state and the taxation of land is in great confusion, thus causing great hardships on the poor peasants and farmers. So, under any circumstance, the survey of land is the first duty of the government to execute. But this could not be done without foreign help, owing to lack of funds and experts. Therefore, I suggest that this work be taken up by an international organization. This organization should provide the expenses of the work by a loan, and should carry out the work with the required number of experts and equipment. How much will be the expenses for the survey and what is the amount of time required and how large an organization is sufficient to carry on the work, and whether aerial survey by aeroplanes be practical for this work are questions which I shall leave to experts to decide.

When the topographical survey is going on a geological survey may be carried out at the same time so as to economize expenses. When the survey work is done and the land of each province is minutely mapped out, we shall be able to readjust the taxation of the already cultivated and improved land. As regards the waste and uncultivated lands we shall be able to determine whether they are suitable for agriculture, for pasture, for forestry, or for mining. In this way, we can estimate their value and lease them out to the users for whatever production that is most suitable. The surplus tax of the cultivated land and the proceeds of waste land will be for the payment of the interest and principal of the foreign loan. Besides the eighteen provinces, we have a vast extent of agricultural and pastural lands in Manchuria, Mongolia, and Sinkiang, and a vast extent of pastural land in Tibet and Kokonor. They will have to be developed by extensive cultivation under the colonization scheme, which is alluded to in the first program.

中国十八省之土地，现乃无以养四万万人。如将废地耕种，且将已耕之地依近世机器及科学方法改良，则此同面积之土地，可使其出产更多，故尽有发达之余地。惟须有自由农业法以保护、奖励农民，使其获得己力之结果。

就国际发展食物生产计划言之，须为同时有利益之下列二事：

一、测量农地。

二、设立农器制造厂。

一、测量农地。中国土地向未经科学测量制图，土地管理、征税皆混乱不清，贫家之乡人及农夫皆受其害。故无论如何，农地测量为政府应尽之第一种义务。然因公款及专门家缺乏之故，此事亦须有外力扶助。故吾以为是当以国际机关行之，由此机关募集公债以供给其费用，雇用专门家及诸种设备以实行其工事。测量费用几何，所需时间几何，机关之大小如何，以飞行机测量亦适用于工事否，是须专门家决定之。

地质探验，当与地图测量并行，以省费用。测量工事即毕，各省荒废未耕之地，或宜种植，或宜放牧，或宜造林，或宜开矿，由是可估得其价值，以备使用者租佃，为最合宜之生产。耕地既增加之租税，及荒地新增之租税，将足以偿还外债之本息。除十八省外，满洲、蒙古、新疆有农地牧地极广，西藏、青海有牧地极广，可依移民计划如吾第一计划所述者，以广耕法开发之。

(2) The establishment of factories for manufacturing agricultural machinery and implements. When the waste land is reclaimed, cultivated land improved and waste labor set to work on the land, the demands for agricultural machinery and implements will be very great. As we have cheap labor and plenty of iron and coal, it is better and cheaper for us to manufacture than to import the implements and machinery. For this purpose, much capital should be invested, and factories should be put up in industrial centers or in the neighborhood of iron and coal fields, where labor and material could be easily found.

b. The Storage and Transportation of Food

The most important foodstuff to be stored and transported is grain. Under the present Chinese method, the storage of grain is most wasteful for if kept in large quantities it is often destroyed by insects or damaged by weather. It is only in small quantities and by great and constant care that grains can be preserved for a certain period of time. And the transportation of grains is also most expensive for the work is mostly done on man's shoulders. When the grains reach the waterway it is carried in a most makeshift way, without the least semblance of system. If the method of storing and transporting of grain be improved, a great economic saving could be accomplished. I propose that a chain of grain elevators be built all over the country and a special transport fleet be equipped all along the waterways by this International Development Organization. What will be the capital for this project and where the elevators should be situated have yet to be investigated by experts.

c. The Preparation and Preservation of Food

Hitherto the preparation of food is entirely by hand with a few primitive implements. The preservation of food is either by salt or sun heat. Mills and cannery method are scarcely known. I suggest that a system of rice mills should be constructed in all the large cities and towns in the Yangtze Valley and South China where rice is the staple food. Flour mills should be put up in all large cities and towns north of the Yangtze Valley, where wheat, oats, and cereals other than rice are the staple food. All these mills should be under one central management so as to produce the best economic results. What amount of capital should be invested in this mill system by this international development scheme should be subjected to detailed investigation.

二、设立农器制造厂。欲开放废地，改良农地，以闲力归于农事，则农器之需要必甚多。中国工价甚廉，煤铁亦富，故须自制造一切农器，不必由外国输入。此需资本甚多。此工场直设于煤铁矿所在之邻地，即工力及物料易得之所。

乙　食物之贮藏及运输

此所言当贮藏及运输之重要食物，即谷类。现在中国贮藏谷类之方法不良，若所藏之量过多，每不免为虫类所蛀损，气候所伤害；故其量甚少，且须非常注意，乃能于一定时期内保存之。又谷类之运输，大半皆以人力，故费用甚巨。及谷类已达水道，则船舶往来，运输漫无定制。若将谷类贮藏及运输方法改良，必省费不少。吾意当由国际开发机关于全国内设谷类运转器，且沿河设特别运船。此事所需资本几何，且谷类运转器当设于何处，应由专门家调查之。

丙　食物之制造及保存

前此中国之食物制造，几全赖手工，而以少数简单器具助之；至于食物保存，则以食盐或日光制造之，至机器及罐头方法，为前此所不知。吾意扬子江及南部中国诸大城镇以米为主食者，当设许多磨米房；扬子江以北以小麦、燕麦及米以外之他谷类为主食者，其诸大城镇当设许多磨麦机房。此种机房，当由中央一处管理，以得最省费之结果。是所需资本几何，当俟详细调查。

In regard to the preservation of food, fruits, meats and fishes should be preserved by canning or by refrigeration. If the canning industry is developed there will be created a great demand for tinplates. Therefore the establishment of tinplate factories will be necessary and also profitable. Such factories should be situated near the iron and tin fields. There are many localities in South China where tin, iron, and coal are situated near each other, thus providing ready materials for the factories. The tinplate factories and the canneries should be combined into one enterprise so as to secure best economic results.

d. The Distribution and Exportation of Food

In ordinary good years, China never lacks food. There is a common saying in China that "One year's tilling will provide three years' wants." In the richer sections of the country, the people generally reserve three or four years' food supply in order to combat a bad year. But when China is developed and organized as an economic whole, one year's food reserve should be kept in the country for the use of the local people and the surplus should be sent out to the industrial centers. As the storage and transportation of food will be under a central management so the distribution and exportation of food should be under the same charge. All surplus grains of a country district should be sent to the nearest town for storage and each town or city should store one year's food. All the staple food should be sold only at cost price to the inhabitants according to their number, by the distributing department. And the surplus food should be exported to foreign countries where it is wanted and where the highest price can be obtained by the export department under the central management. Thus the surplus food will not be wasted as hitherto under the prohibition law. The proceeds of this export will surely amount to a huge sum which will be used in the payment of the interest and principal of the foreign loan invested in this undertaking.

We cannot complete this part of the food industry without giving special consideration to the Tea and Soya industries. The former, as a beverage, is well known throughout and used by the civilized world and the latter is just beginning to be realized as an important foodstuff by the scientists and food administrators. Tea, the most healthy and delicious beverage of mankind, is produced in China. Its cultivation and preparation form one of the most important industries of the country. Once China was the only country that supplied the world with tea. Now, China's tea trade has been wrested away from her by India and Japan. But the quality of the Chinese tea is still unequalled. The Indian tea contains too much tannic acid, and the Japanese tea lacks the

食物果类、肉类、鱼类之保存，或用锡铁罐，或用冰冷法。若锡铁罐工业发达，则锡铁片之需要必大增，故锡铁片工场之建设为必要，且有利益。此种工场当设于铁矿之近处。中国南部有许多地方皆发见有锡、铁、煤三种，如欲建筑工场，材料最为完备。锡铁片工场及罐工场当合同经营，以得最良之节省结果。

丁 食物之分配及输出

在寻常丰年，中国向不缺乏食物，故中国有常言云："一年耕，则足三年之食。"国内较富部分之人民，大概有三四年食物之积储以对付荒年。若中国既发达，有生计组织，则当预储一年之食物以为地方人民之用，其余运至工业中枢。食物之分配及运出，亦由中央机关管理，与其贮藏及运输无异。每县余出之谷类，送至近城贮藏；每一城镇须有一年食物之贮积。经理部当按人数依实价售主要食物于其民，更有所余，乃以售之于外国需此宗食物且可得最高价者。以隶中央经理部之输出部司之。于是乃不如前此禁止输出法之下，食物多所废坏。输出所得巨资，以之偿还外债本息，固有余也。

于叙论食物工业之部，不能不特论茶叶及黄豆二种工业，以毕所说。茶为文明国所既知已用之一种饮料，科学家及食物管理部今复初认黄豆为一种重要食料。就茶言之，是为最合卫生、最优美之人类饮料，中国实产出之，其种植及制造，为中国最重要工业之一。前此中国曾为以茶叶供给全世界之唯一国家，今则中国茶叶商业已为印度、日本所夺。惟中国茶叶之品质，仍非其他各国所能及。印度茶含有

flavor which the Chinese tea possesses. The best tea is only obtainable in China–the native land of tea. China lost her tea trade owing to the high cost of its production. The high cost of production is caused by the inland tax as well as the export duty and by the old methods of cultivation and preparation. If the tax and duty are done away with and new methods introduced, China can recover her former position in this trade easily. In this International Development Scheme, I suggest that a system of modern factories for the preparation of tea should be established in all the tea districts, so that the tea should be prepared by machinery instead of, as hitherto, by hand. Thus the cost of production can be greatly reduced and the quality improved. As the world's demand for tea is daily increasing and will be more so by a dry United States of America, a project to supply cheaper and better tea will surely be a profitable one.

Soya bean as a meat substitute was discovered by the Chinese and used by the Chinese and the Japanese as a staple food for many thousands of years. As meat shortage has been keenly felt in carnivorous countries at present, a solution must be found to relieve it. For this reason I suggest that in this International Development Scheme we should introduce this artificial meat, milk, butter and cheese to Europe and America, by establishing a system of soya bean factories in all the large cities of those countries, so as to provide cheap nitrogenous food to the western people. Modern factories should also be established in China to replace those old and expensive methods of production by hand, so as to procure better economic results as well as to produce better commodities.

● Part II The Clothing Industry

The principal materials for clothes are silk, linen, cotton, wool and animal skins. I shall accordingly deal with them under the following headings:

a. The Silk Industry.
b. The Linen Industry.
c. The Cotton Industry
d. The Woolen Industry.
e. The Leather Industry.
f. The Manufacturing of Clothing Machinery.

丹宁酸太多，日本茶无中国茶所具之香味。最良之茶，惟可自产茶之母国即中国得之。中国之所以失去茶叶商业者，因其生产费过高。生产费过高之故，在厘金[79]及出口税，又在种植及制造方法太旧。若除厘金及出口税，采用新法，则中国之茶叶商业仍易复旧。在国际发展计划中，吾意当于产茶区域，设立制茶新式工场，以机器代手工，而生产费可大减，品质亦可改良。世界对于茶叶之需要日增，美国又方禁酒[80]，倘能以更廉、更良之茶叶供给之，是诚有利益之一种计划也。

以黄豆代肉类，是中国人之发明。中国人、日本人用为主要食料，既历数千年。现今食肉诸国，大患肉类缺乏，是必须有解决方法，故吾意国际发展计划中，当以黄豆所制之肉乳洎酪输入欧美，于诸国大城市设立黄豆制品工场，以较廉之蛋白质食料供给西方人民。又于中国设立新式工场，以代手工生产之古法，而其结果可使价值较廉，出品亦较佳矣。

• 第二部　衣服工业

衣服之主要原料为丝、麻、棉、羊毛、兽皮五种，今分论如下：

甲　丝工业。
乙　麻工业。
丙　棉工业。
丁　羊毛工业。
戊　皮工业。
己　制衣机器工业。

a. The Silk Industy

Silk is a Chinese discovery and was used as a material for clothes for many thousands of years before the Christian Era. It is one of the important national industries of China. Up to recent times, China was the only country that supplied silk to the world. But now this dominant trade has been taken away from China by Japan, Italy and France, because those countries have adopted scientific methods for silk culture and manufacture, while China still uses the same old methods of many thousand years ago. As the world's demand for silk is increasing daily, the improvement of the culture and manufacture of silk will be a very profitable undertaking. In this International Development Scheme, I suggest first that scientific bureaus be established in every silk district to give directions to the farmers and to provide healthy silk-worm eggs. These bureaus should be under central control. At the same time, they will act as collecting stations for cocoons so as to secure a fair price for the farmers. Secondly, silk filiatures with up-to-date machinery should be established in suitable districts to reel the silk for home as well as for foreign consumption. And lastly, modern factories should be put up for manufacturing silk for both home and foreign markets. All silk filiatures and factories should be under a single national control and will be financed with foreign capital and supervised by experts to secure the best economic results and to produce better and cheaper commodities.

b. The Linen Industry

This is an old Chinese industry. In southern China there is produced a kind of very fine linen in the form of ramie, known as China-grass. This fiber if treated by modern methods and machinery becomes almost as fine and glossy as silk. But in China, so far as I know, there is not yet such new method and machinery for the manufacturing of this linen. The famous Chinese grass-cloth is manufactured by the old method of handlooms. I propose that new methods and machinery be introduced into China by this International Development Organization to manufacture this linen. A system of modern factories should be established all over the ramie-producing districts in South China where raw materials and labor are obtainable.

c. The Cotton Industry

Cotton is a foreign product which was introduced into China centuries ago. It became a very important Chinese industry during the hand-loom age. But after the import of foreign cotton goods into China,

甲　蚕丝工业

蚕丝为中国所发明，西历纪元前数千年已用为制衣原料，为中国重要工业之一，直至近日，中国为以蚕丝供给全世界之唯一国家。惟现今日本、意大利、法兰西诸国，已起而与中国争此商业，因此诸国已应用科学方法于养蚕制丝之事，而中国固守数千年以来之同样旧法也。世界对于蚕丝之需要既逐日增加，则养蚕，制丝之改良，将为甚有利益之事。吾意国际发展计划，应于每一养蚕之县设立科学局所，指导农民，以无病蚕子供给之。此等局所，当受中央机关监督，同时司买收蚕茧之事，使农民可得善价。次乃于适宜地方设缫丝所，采用新式机器，以备国内国外之消费。最后乃设制绸工场，以应国内国外之需求。缫丝及制丝工场皆同受一国家机关之监督，借用外资，受专门家之指挥，而其结果可使该物价廉省，品物亦较良较贱矣。

乙　麻工业

是亦为中国之古工业。惟中国所产苎麻，与欧美所产之亚麻异，若以新法及机器制之，其细滑与蚕丝无异。然中国至今尚无以新法及机器制麻者，有名之中国麻布皆依旧法及手工织造。中国南部之麻原料甚富，人工亦廉，故于此区域宜设立许多新式工场也。

丙　棉工业

棉花本外国产物，其输入中国在数百年前，在手工纺织时代，是为中国一种甚重要之工业。然自外国棉货输入中国之后，此种本国

this native handicraft industry was gradually killed by the foreign trade. So, great quantities of raw cotton are exported and finished cotton goods are imported in large quantities into China. What an anomaly when we consider the enormous, cheap labor in China. However a few cotton mills have been started recently in treaty ports which have made enormous profits. It is reported that during the last two or three years most of the Shanghai cotton mills declared a dividend of 100 per cent and some even 200 per cent! The demand for cotton goods in China is very great but the supply falls short. It is necessary to put up more mills in China for cotton manufacturing. Therefore, I suggest in this International Development Scheme to put up a system of large cotton mills all over the cotton-producing districts under one central national control. Thus the best economic results will be obtained and cotton goods can be supplied to the people at a lower cost.

d. The Woolen Industry

Although the whole of Northwestern China—about two-thirds of the entire country is a pastural land yet the woolen industry has never been developed. Every year, plenty of raw materials are exported from China on the one hand and plenty of finished woolen goods imported on the other. Judging by the import and export of the woolen trade the development of woolen industry in China will surely be a profitable business. I suggest that scientific methods be applied to the raising of sheep and to the treatment of wool so as to improve the quality and increase the quantity. Modern factories should be established all over northwestern China for manufacturing all kinds of finished woolen goods. Here we have the raw materials, cheap labor and unlimited market. What we want for the development of this industry is foreign capital and experts. This will be one of the most remunerative projects in our International Development Scheme, for the industry will be a new one and there will be no private competitors on the field.

e. The Leather Industry

This will also be a new industry in China, despite the fact that there are a few tanneries in the treaty ports. The export of hides from and the import of leather goods into China are increasing every year. So, to establish a system of tanneries and factories for leather goods and footgear will be a lucrative undertaking.

手工业殆渐归灭绝，于是以许多棉花输出，以许多棉货输入。试思中国工力既多且廉，乃不能产出棉货，岂非大可怪之事。近今乃有少数纺纱、织布厂于通商诸埠，获利极巨。或谓："最近二三年内，上海纺织厂分红百分之百至百分之二百。"皆因中国对于棉货之需要，远过于供给，故中国须设纺织厂甚多。吾意国际发展计划，当于产棉区域设诸大纺织厂，而由中国立中央机关监督之，于是最良节省之结果可得，而可以较廉之棉货供给人民也。

丁 羊毛工业

中国西北部占全国面积三分之二用为牧地，而羊毛工业则从未见发达，每年由中国输出羊毛甚多，制为毛货，又复输入中国。自羊毛商业输出输入观之，可知发达羊毛工业，为在中国甚有利之事。吾意当以科学方法养羊、剪毛，以改良其制品，增加其数量。于中国西北全部设立工场以制造一切羊毛货物，原料及工价甚廉，市场复大至无限。此工业之发达，须有外国资本及专门家，是为国际发展计划中最有报酬者，因是属一种新工业，无其他私人竞争也。

戊 皮工业

通商诸埠虽有多少制皮工场，是实为中国之新工业。生皮之输出，熟皮之输入，每年皆有增加。故设立制皮工场及设立制造皮货及靴、鞋类工场，甚为有利益之事。

f. The Manufacturing of Clothing Machinery

The machinery for the manufacturing of various kinds of clothing materials is in great demand in China. It is reported that the orders for cotton mill machinery have heen filled up for the next three years from manufacturers in Europe and America. If China is developed according to my programs, the demand for machinery will be many times greater than at present and the supply in Europe and America will be too short to meet it. Therefore to establish factories for the manufacturing of clothing machinery is a necessary as well as a profitable undertaking. Such factories should be established in the neighborhood of iron and steel factories, so as to save expenses for transportation of heavy materials. What will be the capital for this undertaking should be decided by experts.

● Part III The Housing Industry

Among the four hundred millions in China the poor still live in huts and hovels, and in caves in the loess region of north China while the middle and the rich classes live in temples. All the so-called houses in China, excepting a few after western style and those in treaty ports are built after the model of a temple. When a Chinese builds a house he has more regard for the dead than for the living. The first consideration of the owner is his ancestral shrine. This must be placed at the center of the house, and all the other parts must be complement and secondary to it. The house is planned not for comfort but for ceremonies, that is, for "the red and white affairs," as they are called in China. The "red affair" is the marriage or other felicitous celebrations of any member of the family, and the "white affair" is the funeral ceremonies. Besides the ancestral shrine there are the shrines of the various household gods. All these are of more importance than man and must be considered before him. There is not a home in old China that is planned for the comfort and convenience of man alone. So now when we plan the housing industry in China in our International Development Scheme, we must take the houses of the entire population of China into consideration. "To build houses for four hundred millions, it is impossible!" some may exclaim. This is the largest job ever conceived by man. But if China is going to give up her foolish traditions and useless habits and customs of the last three thousand years and begin to adopt modern civilization, as our industrial development scheme is going to introduce, the remodelling of all the houses according to modern comforts and conveniences is bound to come, either unconsciously by social evolution or consciously by artificial

己 制衣机器工业

中国需要各种制衣机器甚多。或谓中国在欧美所定购纺织机器，须此后三年内乃能交清。若依予计划发展中国，则所需机器当较多于现在数倍，欧美且不足供给之。故设立制造制衣机器为必要，且有利之事。此种工场，当设于附近钢铁工场之处，以省粗重原料运输之费。此事所需资本几何，当由专门家决定之。

• 第三部 居室工业

中国四万万人中，贫者仍居茅屋陋室，北方有居土穴者，而中国上等社会之居室，乃有类于庙宇。除通商口岸有少数居室依西式外，中国一切居室，皆可谓为庙宇式。中国人建筑居室，所以为死者计过于为生者计，屋主先谋祖先神龛之所，是以安置于屋室中央，其他一切部分皆不及。于是重要居室非以图安适，而以合于所谓红白事者。红事者，即家族中任何人嫁娶及其他喜庆之事；白事者，即丧葬之事。除祖先神龛之外，尚须安设许多家神之龛位。凡此一切神事，皆较人事为更重要，须先谋及之。故旧中国之居室，殆无一为人类之安适及方便计者。今于国际发展计划中，为居室工业计划，必须谋及全中国之居室。或谓为四万万人建屋，乃不可能。吾亦认此事过巨。但中国若弃其最近三千年愚蒙之古说及无用之习惯，而适用近世文明，如予国际发展计划之所引导，则改建一切居室以合于近世安适方便之式，乃势所必至。或因社会进化于无意识中达到，或因人工建设于有意识中

construction. The modern civilization so far attained by western nations is entirely an unconscious progress, for social and economic sciences are but recent discoveries. But henceforth all human progress will be more or less based upon knowledge, that is upon scientific planning. As we can foresee now, within half a century under our industrial development, the houses of all China will be renewed according to modern comfort and convenience. Is it not far better and cheaper to rebuild the houses of all China by a preconceived scientific plan than by none? I have no doubt that if we plan to build a thousand houses at one time it would be ten times cheaper than to plan and build one at a time, and the more we build the cheaper terms we would get. This is a positive economic law. The only danger in this is over-production. That is the only obstacle for all production on a large scale. Since the industrial revolution in Europe and America, every financial panic before the world war was caused by over-production. In the case of our housing industry in China, there are four hundred million customers. At least fifty million houses will be needed in the coming fifty years. Thus a million houses a year will be the normal demand of the country.

Houses are a great factor in civilization. They give men more enjoyment and happiness than food and clothes. More than half of the human industries are contributing to household needs. The housing industry will be the greatest undertaking of our International Development Scheme, and also will be the most profitable part of it. My object of the development of the housing industry is to provide cheap houses to the masses. A ten thousand dollar house now built in the treaty port can be produced for less than a thousand dollars and yet a high margin of profit can be made. In order to accomplish this we have to produce transport, and distribute the materials for construction. After the house is finished, all household equipment must be furnished. Both of these will be comprised in the housing industry which I shall formulate as follows:

a. The Production and Transportation of Building Materials.
b. The Construction of Houses.
c. The Manufacturing of Furniture.
d. The Supply of Household Utilities.

达到，西方民族达到近世文明，殆全由于无意识的进步，因社会经济科学乃最近发明也。但一切人类进步，皆多少以知识即科学计划为基础，依吾所定国际发展计划，则中国一切居室将于五十年内依近世安适方便新式改造，是予所能预言者。以预定科学计划建筑中国一切居室，必较之毫无计划更佳更廉。若同时建筑居室千间，必较之建筑一间者价廉十倍。建筑愈多，价值愈廉，是为生计学定律。生计学唯一之危险，为生产过多，一切大规模之生产皆受此种阻碍。自欧美工业进化以来，世界之大战争前所有财政恐慌，皆生产过多之所致。就中国之居室工业论，雇主乃有四万万人，未来五十年中至少需新居室者有五千万，每年造屋一百万间，乃普通所需要也。

居室为文明一因子，人类由是所得之快乐，较之衣食更多。人类之工业过半数，皆以应居室需要者。故居室工业，为国际计划中之最大企业，且为其最有利益之一部分。吾所定发展居室计划，乃为群众预备廉价居室。通商诸埠所筑之屋，今需万元者，可以千元以下得之，建屋者且有利益可获。为是之故，当谋建筑材料之生产、运输、分配，建屋既毕，尚须谋屋中之家具装置，是皆包括于居室工业之内。今定其分类如下：

甲　建筑材料之生产及运输。
乙　居室之建筑。
丙　家具之制造。
丁　家用物之供给。

a. The Production and Transportation of Building Materials

The building materials are bricks, tiles, timber, skeleton iron, stone, cement and mortar. Each of these materials must be manufactured or cut out from raw materials. So kilns for the manufacture of tiles and bricks must be put up. Mills for timbers must be established, also factories for skeleton irons. Quarries must be opened and factories for cement and mortar must be started. All these establishments must be put up at suitable districts where materials and markets are near one another. All should be under one central control so as to regulate the output of each of these materials in proportion to the demand. After the materials are ready they must be transported to the places where they are wanted by special bottoms on waterways, and by special cars on railways so as to reduce the cost as low as possible. For this purpose special boats and cars must be built by the shipbuilding department and the car factory.

b. The Construction of Houses

The houses to be built in China will comprise public buildings and private residences. As the public buildings are to be built with public funds for public uses which will not be a profitable undertaking, a special Government Department should therefore be created to take charge. The houses that are to be built under this International Development Scheme will be private residences only with the object to provide cheap houses for the people, as well as to make profit for this International concern. The houses will be built on standardized types. In cities and towns the houses should be constructed on two lines: the single family and the group family houses. The former should again be sub-divided into eight-roomed, ten-roomed and twelve-roomed houses, and the latter into ten-family, hundred-family and thousand-family houses, with four or six rooms for each family. In the country districts the houses should be classified according to the occupation of the people, and special annexes such as barns and dairies should be provided for the farmers. All houses should be designed and built according to the needs and comfort of man; so a special architectural department should be established to study the habits, occupations and needs of different people and make improvements from time to time. The construction should be performed as much as possible by labor-saving machinery so as to accelerate work and save expenses.

c. The Manufacturing of Furniture

As all houses in China should be remodelled all furniture should be replaced by up-to-date ones, which are made for the comforts and

甲 建筑材料之生产及运输

建筑材料为砖、瓦、木材、铁架、石、塞门土、三合土等，其每一种皆须制造，或与其他原料分离。如制造砖瓦则须建窑，木材须建锯木工场，铁架须建制铁工场，此外须设石工场、塞门土工场、三合土工场等。须择适宜之地，材料与市场相近者为之。且一切须在中央机关监督之下，使材料之制出与需要成比例。材料既制成，则水路用舟，陆路用车，以运至需要之地，务设法减省一切费用。造船部、造车部于此则造特别之舟、车以应之。

乙 居室之建筑

此项建筑事业，包括一切公私屋宇。公众建筑，以公款为之，以应公有，无利可图，由政府设专部以司其事。其私人居室，为国际发展计划所建筑者，乃以低廉居室供给人民，而司建筑者仍须有利可获。此类居室之建筑，须依一定模范。在城市中所建屋，分为二类：一为一家之居室，一为多家同居室。前者分为八房间、十房间、十二房间诸种，后者分为十家、百家、千家同居者诸种，每家有四房间至六房间。乡村中之居室，依人民之营业而异，为农民所居者当附属谷仓、乳房之类。一切居室设计，皆务使居人得其安适。故须设特别建筑部以考察人民习惯、营业需要，随处加以改良。建造工事，务须以节省人力之机器为之，于是工事可加速、费用可节省也。

丙 家具之制造

中国所有居室既须改造，则一切家具亦须改用新式者，以图国人

needs of man. Furniture of the following kinds should be manufactured: the library, the parlor, the bedroom, the kitchen, the bathroom and the toilet. Each kind should be manufactured in a special factory under the management of the International Development Organization.

d. The Supply of Household Utilities

The household utilities are water, light, heat, fuel and telephones. Except in treaty ports, there is no water-supply system in any of the cities and towns of China. Even many treaty ports possess none as yet. In all the large cities, the people obtain their water from rivers which at the same time act as sewage. The water supply of the large cities and towns in China is most unsanitary. (1) It is an urgent necessity that water supply systems should be installed in all cities and towns in China without delay. Therefore special factories for equipping the water system should be established in order to meet the needs. (2) Lighting plants should be installed in all the cities and towns in China. So factories for the manufacture of the machinery lighting plants should be established. (3) Modern heating plants should be installed in every household, using either electricity, gas, or steam. So the manufacturing of heating equipment is a necessity. Factories should be established for this purpose. (4) Cooking fuel is one of the most costly items in the daily needs of the Chinese people. In the country the people generally devote ten per cent of their working time to gathering firewoods. In town the people spend about twenty per cent of their living expenses for firewood alone. Thus this firewood question accumulates into a great national waste. The firewood and grass as a cooking fuel must be substituted by coal in the country districts, and by gas or electricity in towns and cities. In order to use coal gas and electricity, proper equipment must be provided. So factories for the manufacturing of coal gas, and electricity, stoves for every family must be established by this International Development Organization. (5) Telephones must also be supplied to every family in the cities as well as in the country. So factories for manufacturing the equipment must be put up in China, in order to render them as cheap as possible.

● Part IV The Motoring Industry

The Chinese are a stagnant race. From time immemorial a man is praised for staying at home and caring for his immediate surroundings only. Laotse—a contemporary of Confucius—says: "The good people are those who live in countries so near to each other that they can hear each

之安适，而应其需要。食堂、书室、客厅、卧室、厨房、浴室、便所所用家具，皆须制造。每种皆以特别工场制造之，立于国际发展机关管理之下。

丁 家用物之供给

家用物为水、光、燃料、电话等。(一)除通商口岸之外，中国诸城市中无自来水，即通商口岸亦多不具此者。许多大城市所食水为河水，而污水皆流至河中，故中国城市中所食水皆不合卫生。今须于一切大城市中设供给自来水之工场，以应急需。(二)于中国一切大城市供给灯光，设立制造机器发光工场。(三)设立电工场、煤气工场、蒸气工场，以供给暖热。(四)厨用燃料在中国为日用者。最贫乡村之人，每费年工十分之一以采集柴薪。城市之人，买柴薪之费占其生活费十分之二。故柴薪问题，为国民最大耗费。今当使乡村中以煤炭代木草，城市用煤气或电力。然欲用煤炭、煤气、电力等，皆须有特别设备，即由国际发展机关制造煤气、电力火炉诸工场。(五)无论城乡各家，皆宜有电话。故当于中国设立制造电话器具工场，以使其价甚廉。

• 第四部 行动工业

中国人为凝滞民族，自古以来，安居于家，仅烦虑近事者，多为人所赞称。与孔子同时之老子有言曰："邻国相望，鸡犬之声相闻，

other's cock crow and dog bark and yet they never have had intercourse with each other during their lifetime." This is often quoted as the Golden Age of the Chinese people. But in modern civilization the condition is entirely changed. Moving about occupies a great part of a man's life time. It is the movement of man that makes civilization progress. China, in order to catch up with modern civilization, must move. And the movement of the individual forms an important part of the national activity. A man must move whenever and wherever he pleases with ease and rapidity. However, China, at present, lacks the means of facility for individual movement, for all the old great highways were ruined and have disappeared, and the automobile has not yet been introduced into the interior of the country. The motor car, a recent invention, is a necessity for rapid movement. If we wish to move quickly and do more work, we must adopt the motor car as a vehicle. But before we can use the motor car, we have to build our roads. In the preliminary part of this International Development Scheme, I proposed to construct one million miles of roads. These should be apportioned according to the ratio of population in each district for construction. In the eighteen provinces of China Proper, there are nearly 2,000 hsiens. If all parts of China are to adopt the hsien administration, there will be nearly 4,000 hsiens in all. Thus the construction of roads for each hsien will be on an average of 250 miles. But some of the hsiens have more people and some have less. If we divide the million miles of roads by the four hundred million people, we shall have one mile to every four hundred. For four hundred people to build one mile of road is not a very difficult task to accomplish. If my scheme of making road-building as a condition for granting local autonomy is adopted by the nation, we shall see one million miles of road built in a very short time as if by a magic wand.

As soon as the people of China decide to build roads, this International Development Organization can begin to put up factories for manufacturing motor cars. First start on a small scale and gradually expand the plants to build more and more until they are sufficient to supply the needs of the four hundred million people. The cars should be manufactured to suit different purposes, such as the farmer's car, the artisan's car, the business man's car, the tourist's car, the truck car, etc. All these cars, if turned out on a large scale, can be made much cheaper than at present, so that everybody who wishes it, may have one.

Besides supplying cheap cars, we must also supply cheap fuel, otherwise the people will still be unable to use them. So the development of the oil fields in China should follow the motor car industry. This will be dealt with in more detail under the mining industry.

民至老死不相往来。”中国人民每述此为黄金时代。惟据近世文明，此种状态已全变，人生时期内，行动最多，各人之有行动，故文明得以进步。中国欲得近时文明，必须行动。个人之行动为国民之重要部分，每人必须随时随地行动，甚易甚速。惟中国现在尚无法使个人行动容易，因古时大道既已废毁，内地尚不识自动车即摩托为何物。自动车为近时所发明，乃急速行动所必要。吾侪欲行动敏捷，作工较多，必须以自动车为行具。但欲用自动车，必先建造大路。吾于国际发展计划，提前一部已提议造大路一百万英里。是须按每县人口之比率，以定造路之里数。中国本部十八省约有县二千，若中国全国设县制，将共有四千县，每县平均造路二百五十英里。惟县内人民多少不同，若以大路一百万英里除四万万人数，则四百人乃得大路一英里。以四百人造一英里之大路，决非难事。若用予计划，以造路为允许地方自治条件，则一百万英里之大路将于至短期内制成矣。

中国人民既决定建造大路，国际发展机关即可设立制造自动车之工场。最初用小规模，后乃逐渐扩张，以供给四万万人之需要。所造之车当合于各种用途，为农用车、工用车、商用车、旅行用车、运输用车等。此一切车以大规模制造，实可较今更廉，欲用者皆可得之。

除供给廉价车之外，尚须供给廉价燃料，否则人民不能用之。故于发展自动车工业之后，即须开发中国所有之煤、油矿，是当于矿工业中详论之。

● Part V The Printing Industry

This industry provides man with intellectual food. It is a necessity of modern society, without which mankind cannot progress. All human activities are recorded, and all human knowledge is stored in printing. It is a great factor of civilization. The progress and civilization of different nations of the world are measured largely by the quantity of printed matter they turned out annually. China, though the nation that invented printing, is very backward in the development of its printing industry. In our International Development Scheme, the printing industry must also be given a place. If China is developed industrially according to the lines which I suggested, the demand for printed matter by the four hundred millions will be exceedingly great. In order to meet this demand efficiently, a system of large printing houses must be established in all large cities in the country, to undertake printing of all kinds from newspapers to encyclopædia. The best modern books on various subjects in different countries should be translated into Chinese and published in cheap edition form for the general public in China. All the publishing houses should be organized under one common management, so as to secure the best economic results.

In order to make printed matter cheap, other subsidiary industries must be developed at the same time. The most important of these is the paper industry. At present all the paper used by newspapers in China is imported. And the demand for paper is increasing every day. China has plenty of raw materials for making paper, such as the vast virgin forests of the northwestern part of the country, and the wild reeds of the Yangtze and its neighboring swamps which would furnish the best pulps. So, large plants for manufacturing papers should be put up in suitable locations. Besides the paper factories, ink factories, type foundries, printing machine factories, etc., should be established under a central management to produce everything that is needed in the printing industry.

第五部　印刷工业

此项工业为以知识供给人民，是为近世社会一种需要，人类非此无由进步。一切人类大事皆以印刷纪述之，一切人类知识以印刷蓄积之，故此为文明一大因子。世界诸民族文明之进步，每以其每年出版物之多少衡量之。中国民族虽为发明印刷术者，而印刷工业之发达，反甚迟缓。吾所定国际发展计划，亦须兼及印刷工业。若中国依予实业计划发达，则四万万人所需印刷物必甚多。须于一切大城乡中设立大印刷所，印刷一切自报纸以至百科全书。各国所出新书，以中文翻译，廉价售出，以应中国公众之所需。一切书市，由一公设机关管理，结果乃廉。

欲印刷事业低廉，尚须同时设立其他辅助工业。其最重要者为纸工业。现今中国报纸所用纸张，皆自外国输入。中国所有制纸原料不少，如西北部之天然森林，扬子江附近之芦苇，皆可制为最良之纸料。除纸工场之外，如墨胶工场、印模工场、印刷机工场等，皆须次第设立，归中央管理，产出印刷工业所需诸物。

PROGRAM VI

The Mining Industry

Mining and farming are the two most important means of producing raw materials for industries. As farming is to produce food for man, so mining is to produce food for machinery. Machinery is the tree of modern industries, and the mining industry is the root of machinery. Thus, without the mining industry there would be no machinery, and without machinery there would be no modern industries which have revolutionized the economic conditions of mankind. The mining industry, after all, is the greatest factor of material civilization and economic progress. Although in the fifth part of the first program I suggested the development of the iron and coal fields in Chihli and Shansi as an auxiliary project for the development of the Great Northern Port, still, a special program should be devoted to mining in general. The mineral lands of China belong to the state, and mining in China is still in its infancy. So to develop the mining industry from the outset as a state enterprise would be a sound economic measure. But mining in general is very risky and to enlist foreign capital in its development in a wholesale manner is unadvisable. Therefore, only such mining projects which are sure to be profitable will be brought under the International Development Scheme. I shall formulate this mining program as follows:

I. The Mining of Iron.
II. The Mining of Coal.
III. The Mining of Oil.
IV. The Mining of Copper.
V. The Working of Some Particular Mines.
VI. The Manufacture of Mining Machinery.
VII. The Establishment of Smelting Plants.

● Part I The Mining of Iron

Iron is the most important element in modern industries. Its deposits are found in great quantities in certain areas and can be easily mined. The iron mines should be worked absolutely as a state property. Besides the Chihli and Shansi iron mines, the other iron fields must also be developed.

第六计划

矿业

矿业与农业为工业上供给原料之主要源泉也。矿业产原料以供机器，犹农业产食物以供人类。故机器者实为近代工业之树，而矿业者又为工业之根。如无矿业，则机器无从成立；如无机器，则近代工业之足以转移人类经济之状况者，亦无从发达。总而言之，矿业者为物质文明与经济进步之极大主因也。在吾第一计划之第五部中，曾倡仪开采直隶、山西两省之煤铁矿田，为发展北方大港之补助计划，但矿业为近代之重要事业，有不可不另设专部以研究之者。中国矿业尚属幼稚，惟经营之权素归国有，几成习惯。此所以发展中国实业，当由政府总其成，庶足称为有生气之经济政策。彼通常人对于矿业多以为危险事业，并谓借外资以为开采者亦非得计，其所见或未到也。故在此之矿业计划中，择其决为有利者先行举办，兹分别列于下之各种：

一、铁矿。
二、煤矿。
三、油矿。
四、铜矿。
五、特种矿之采取。
六、矿业机器之制造。
七、冶矿机厂之设立。

• 第一部 铁矿

在近代工业中，称为最重要之原质者，是为钢铁。钢铁产生于各地者，多见丰富，且易开采。故为国家谋公共利益计，开采铁矿之权，当属之国有。中国除直隶、山西两省经拟开采之铁矿外，其余各地

There are very rich deposits in the southwestern provinces, the Yangtze Valley and the northwestern provinces in China Proper. Sinkiang, Mongolia, Manchuria, Kokonor, and Tibet also possess large deposits of iron. We have the Han Yeh Ping Iron and Steel Works in the Yangtze Valley and the Pen Chi Hu Iron and Steel Works in South Manchuria, both of which are largely capitalized by Japan and are working very profitably lately. There should be similar works in the vicinity of Canton, the Great Southern Port, and also in Szechuen, and Yunnan, where iron and coal are found side by side. The iron deposits in Sinkiang, Kansu, Mongolia, etc., must also be developed one after the other, according to the needs of the locality. Iron and Steel Works must be put up in each of these regions to supply the local demand for manufactured iron. What amount of capital should be invested in these additional iron and steel works must be thoroughly investigated by experts. But I should say that a sum equal to or double the amount to be invested in the Chihli and Shansi iron and steel works will not be too much, because of the great demand which will result in the development of China.

● Part II The Mining of Coal

China is known to be the country most rich in coal deposits, yet her coal fields are scarcely scratched. The output of coal in the United States is about six hundred million tons a year. If China is equally developed she should, according to the proportion of her population, have an output of four times as much coal as the United States. This will be the possibility of coal mining in China which the International Development Organization is to undertake. As coal deposits are found in great quantities in certain areas so its output can be estimated quite accurately beforehand. Thus, the risk is of no consideration and the profit is sure. But as coal is a necessity of civilized community and the sinews of modern industries, the principal object for mining should not be for profit alone, but for supplying the needs of mankind. After the payment of interest and capital of the foreign loans for its development, and the securing of high wages for the miners, the price of coal should be reduced as low as possible so as to meet the demands of the public as well as to give impetus to the development of various industries. I suggest that besides the mining of coal for the iron and steel works, a plan for producing two hundred million tons of coal a year for other uses should be formed at the start. Mines should be opened along the seaboard and navigable rivers.

铁矿亦须次第开采。中国内地沿扬子江一带与西北各省皆以铁矿见称丰富，新疆、蒙古、青海、西藏各地亦以铁矿著名。所可惜者，中国经营钢铁事业，现只有汉阳铁厂与南满洲之本溪湖铁厂，其资本又多为日本人所占有，虽云近来获利甚厚，亦不免有利权外溢之叹矣。广州将开为南方大港，应设立一铁厂。其他如四川、云南等地方之铁矿，亦可次第开采。而后多设钢铁工厂于各处内地，使之便利经营钢铁事业者之需要。至增设之铁厂，应用资本若干，可留为有经验者另行察夺。但以吾之见，因发展中国实业之结果，需铁孔亟，即以相等或加倍于直隶、山西铁厂所用之资本经营之，亦不为多也。

• 第二部　煤矿

中国煤矿素称丰富，而煤田之开掘者，不过仅采及皮毛而已。北美合众国每年所采取之煤约六万万吨，如中国能用同一方法采取之，并依其人口之比例以为衡，则产出之煤应四倍于美国。此当为中国将来煤矿之产额，而国际发展实业机关宜注意经营者也。夫煤矿之产于中国各地既多所发见，而其产额亦可以预定，故开采者不特无失败之虞。而利益之厚可断言者。但煤为文明民族之必需品，为近代工业之主要物，故其采取之目的，不徒纯为利益计，而在供给人类之用。由此言之，开采煤矿之办法，除摊派借用外资之利息外，其次当为矿工增加工资，又其次当使煤价低落，便利人民，而后各种工业易于发展也。吾以为当煤矿开采之始，除为钢铁工厂使用外，开始计划当以产出二万万吨备为他项事业之用。沿海岸、河岸各矿，交通既便，宜先开采，

As Europe is now seeking coal from China this amount will not be over-production from the beginning. A few years later when the industries of China will be more developed more coal will be needed. How much capital will be required and what mines are to be worked, have to be submitted to scientific investigation under expert direction.

Besides coal mining, the coal products industry must be developed under the same management. This is a new industry without any competition and has an unlimited market in China. Great profits will be assured on the capital invested.

● Part III The Mining of Oil

It is well-known that the richest company in the world is the Standard Oil Company of New York, and that the richest man in the world is Rockefeller, organizer of this company. This proves that oil mining is a most profitable business. China is known to be a very rich oil-bearing country. Oil springs are found in the provinces of Szechuen, Kansu, Sinkiang, and Shensi. How vast is the underground reservoir of oil in China is not yet known. But the already known oil springs have never been worked and made use of, while the import of kerosene, gasoline, and crude oil from abroad is increasing every year. When China is developed as a motoring country, the use of gasoline will be increased a thousand-fold, then the supply from the foreign fields will not be able to meet the demands, as shortage of oil is already felt in Europe and America. The mining of oil in China will soon become a necessity. This enterprise should be taken up by the International Development Organization for the state. Production on a large scale should be started at once. Pipe line systems should be installed between oil districts and populous and industrial centers in the interior and also river and sea ports. What amount of capital should be invested in the project will have to be investigated by experts.

● Part IV The Mining of Copper

The copper deposits, like iron ores, are found in great quantities in different places. So the quantity of ores in each mine can be accurately estimated before it is opened and its working generally runs no risk. Thus, the mining of copper should be taken up as a government

内地次之。况欧洲各国现思取煤于中国，故吾所定煤之产额，虽当开采之始，亦无过多之虑。待至数年后，当中国工业愈加发达，需煤之数必渐增多，可无疑者。至开采需用之资本若干，与何处矿田应先开采，须留以待专门家用科学之眼光考察之。

除煤矿以外，其他一切因煤而产出之工业，可用同一方法经理之。此之新工业，既无人与之竞争，且在中国又有无限之市场，故资本之投放，其利益之大可断言者。

• 第三部 油矿

世界中营业公司之最富者，以纽约三达煤油公司[81]为著，世界中人之最富者，以该公司之创建者乐极非路为最著，于此可以证明开采煤油矿为最有利益之事业。中国亦以富于煤油出产国见称也，四川、甘肃、新疆、陕西等省已发见有油源，虽其分量之多寡，尚未能确实调查。而中国有此种矿产，不能开采以为自用，以至由外国人口之煤油、汽油等年年增加，未免可惜。如待至中国将来汽车盛行之时，煤汽之需用或增至千倍。当此欧美各国煤油正在日渐减缩，由外国输入之煤油、煤气，断不足以供中国之需要，此所以在中国以开采油矿为必要之图也。此种事业，须由国际发展实业机关为政府经营之，但当经营之始，规模亦当远大。如煤油区域、稠密居民、工业中心以及河岸、海港等地方，皆宜用油管办法互相联络，以使其输送与分配于各地者，更为便利。如此之筹划，须用资本若干方能开办，可留为对于此事业有经验者察夺之。

• 第四部 铜矿

中国铜矿亦如铁矿之丰富，经已发见者，已有多处。至其矿产之分量，在未开以前均可预计，故办理可无危险。但开采之权，须依中国

enterprise, as was always the case in China, and financed and worked by the International Development Organization. The richest copper deposits in China are found along the border of Szechuen and Yunnan on the Yangtze River. The government copper mine in Chaotung, in the northeastern corner of Yunnan, has been working for many centuries. Cash, the standard currency of China, was made mostly of the copper from Yunnan province. The currency still absorbs an enormous quantity of copper. Owing to the difficulty of transporting the Yunnan copper, most of the metal for currency is being imported from foreign countries. Besides currency, copper is very commonly used for many other purposes and when the industries in China are developed the demand will increase a hundred times. So the demand for this metal will be very great in the market of China alone. I suggest that production on a large scale should be adopted and modern plants should be installed in copper mines. How much capital to be invested in this enterprise should be decided by experts after careful investigation.

● Part V The Working of Some Particular Mines

In regard to the mining of various kinds of metal, some particular mines should be taken up by the International Development Organization. There are many famous mines in China which have been worked for many centuries by hand, such as the Kochui tin mine in Yunnan, the Moho gold mine in Heilungkiang, and the Khotan jade mine in Sinkiang. All these mines are known to have very rich deposits, –the deeper the richer. Hitherto only the surface parts of those mines have been worked and the larger deposits are still untouched, owing to the lack of means of getting rid of the water. Some of the mines are still in the hands of the Government, while others have been given up to private concerns. If modern machinery is adopted the mines should revert to the Government so as to secure economy in working. Many discarded mines of this kind should be thoroughly investigated, and if found profitable, work should be resumed under the International Development Scheme. All future mining, other than government enterprise, should be leased to private concerns on contract, and when the term is up, the government has the option to take them over, if found profitable as a state property. Thus all profitable mines will be socialized in time and the profit will be equally shared by all the people in the country.

惯例，属之国有，而后由国际发展实业机关投资代为经营。四川、云南与扬子江一带，皆中国铜产最盛之区。由政府开采之铜矿在于云南北角之昭通者，经已数世纪之久矣。中国向来通用之钱币，几乎全赖云南铜矿以制造之，现今钱币需用之铜，仍称大宗。但因云南之铜，输运艰难，价格过高，故多购自外国。非中国缺此种金属，是中国对于此种金属之采取未能发达故也。况铜之为物，除用作钱币外，需用为他种目的者尚多。当中国将来之工业发达，用铜之途必增至百倍。故此种金属，即在中国市场，将必成为需要之大宗。此吾之所以为开采铜矿不可不适用近代机器，而冀其有大宗之出产也。此之事业，应投资若干以为之经营，可留为专门家察夺之。

第五部　特种矿之采取

国际发展实业机关对于各色特种之矿，有可以经营之者。如云南个旧之锡矿，黑龙江之漠河金矿，新疆之和阗玉矿，皆用人力采取，经已数世纪之久矣。此种之矿产皆以丰厚见称，现已开采者不过是矿中之上层，其余大部分因无法排除泉水，尚多埋藏地中。但向来对于此等特种矿产，有为人民采取者，有为政府采取者。如能行用近代机器，并由政府经营，是为最经济之办法也。其他多有已弃置之矿产。如此类者，须通行考察，如以为实有利益，即须依国际发展计划，再行开采。至于将来一切矿业，除既为政府经营外，应准租与私人立约办理，当期限既满，并知为确有利益者，政府有收回办理之权。如此办法，一切有利益之矿可以从渐收为社会公有，而通国人民亦可以均沾其利益矣。

● Part VI The Manufacture of Mining Machinery

Most of the metal deposits of the earth are in small quantities and scattered far and wide in various places. Most of the mining enterprises resemble farming in that it is more profitable to work by individuals and small parties. As such is the case, most of the mining enterprises have to be worked out by private concerns. In order to accelerate the development of mining, more liberal laws should be adopted; education and information should be given freely by experts employed by the state; and encouragement and financial assistance should be given by the state and private banks. The part that the International Development Organization should take in general mining enterprises is to manufacture all kinds of mining tools and machinery, and to supply them to the miners at low cost, either on cash or on credit. By distributing tools and machinery to the surplus workers in China, the mining industry would be developed by leaps and bounds. And the more the mining industry is developed the more will be the demand for tools and machinery. Thus the profits for the manufacturing concerns would be limitless, so to speak. Of course, the factories should be started on a small scale and be extended gradually according to the ratio of the development of the mining industry. I suggest that the first factory of this kind should be established at Canton, the seaport of the southwestern mining region, where raw materials and skilled labor can be easily obtained. The other factories should be established in Hankow and the Great Northern Port afterwards.

● Part VII The Establishment of Smelting Plants

Smelting plants for various kinds of metals should be put up in all mining districts to turn ore into metals. These smelting plants should be conducted under the coöperative system. At first, a reasonable price should be paid to the miner when the ore is collected. Afterwards, when the metal is sold, either at home or in foreign markets, the smelting works will take a share of the profit to cover the expenses, the interest, the sinking fund, etc. The surplus profit should be divided among the workers according to their wages, and among the capitalists according to the proportion of ore they contribute to the furnace. In this way we can encourage private mining enterprise which forms the root of other industries. All smelting works should be put up according to local needs and their scale should be determined by experts and managed under a central control.

- **第六部　矿业机械之制造**

各种金属之埋藏于独一地域者，不过一小部分，而散产于各地者，广狭亦各有不同，故对于各种矿业之经营，有为政府不能自办，当留为私人办之。譬如农业，私人经营者利益常丰，矿业亦如是也。如欲望矿务之发展，国家必须采用宽大之矿律。政府所雇用之专门技师，应自由予以指导与报告。公司银行应予以经济之帮助。此国际发展机关对于普通矿业，只当为之制造各种矿业器具与机械，以供给业矿者之使用。至此器具与机械之出售者，无论其为现金，或为赊借，必须定以最低廉之价，而后能使之遍为分配于中国之多余工人，矿业自日臻发达。矿业既日臻发达，器具与机械之需要必日多。若依此办理，即制造矿业器具机械之利益，已无可限量矣。但此等工厂，在开始时期只宜至小经营，待从矿业日臻发达而后从渐推广。故吾以为此种之第一工厂须设立于广州，盖因广州为西南矿区之口岸，获取原料、延请技师亦较他处为便易也。至其他之工厂，应设立于汉口与北方大港各地。

- **第七部　冶矿厂之设立**

各种金属之冶铸机厂，应遍设于各矿区，使之便于各种金属之化炼。此等冶铸机厂，应仿合作制度组织之。当其始也，生矿之收集，价格必廉。迨后金属之出售，无论其在中国或外国市场，而此种冶铸工夫，可以分享其一分之利益，用以抵偿各种费用、利息与冗费。其他之剩余利益，应按各种工人之工资并各资本家所供给于铸炉之生矿之多寡比例分配之。如此办法，对于私人之经营矿业者，既可以资鼓励，而工业之基础亦可因之以成立。但机厂之设立须依各区之需要，由专门家以定其规模之大小，而设中央机关以管理之。

CONCLUSION

In this International Development Scheme, I venture to present a practical solution for the three great world questions which are the International War, the Commercial War and the Class War. As it has been discovered by post-Darwin philosophers that the primary force of human evolution is coöperation and not struggle as that of the animal world, so the fighting nature, a residue of the animal instinct in man, must be eliminated from man, the sooner the better.

International war is nothing more than pure and simple organized robbery on a grand scale, which all right-minded people deplore. When the United States of America turned the recent European conflict into a world war by taking part in it, the American people to a man determined to make this war end war forever. And the hope of the peace-loving nations in the world was raised so high that we Chinese thought that the "Tatung" or the Great Harmony Age was at hand. But unfortunately, the United States has completely failed in peace, in spite of her great success in war. Thus, the world has been thrown back to the pre-war condition again. The scrambling for territories, the struggle for food, and the fighting for raw materials will begin anew. So instead of disarmament there is going to be a greater increase in the armies and navies of the once allied powers for the next war. China, the most rich and populous country in the world, will be the prize. Some years ago there was great inclination among the Powers to divide China and Imperial Russia actually took steps to colonize Manchuria. But the then chivalrous Japan went to war with Russia and thus saved China from partition. Now the militaristic policy of Japan is to swallow China alone. So long as China is left to the tender mercy of the militaristic powers she must either succumb to partition by several powers or be swallowed up by one power.

However, the tide of the world seems to be turning. After centuries of sound slumber, the Chinese people at last are waking up and realizing that we must get up and follow in the world's progress. Now we are at the parting of the ways. Shall we organize for war or shall we organize for peace? Our militarists and reactionaries desire the former, and they are going to Japanize China, so that when the time comes they will start another Boxer Movement once more to defy the civilized world. But as the founder of the Chung Hwa Min Kuo—the Chinese Republic—I desire to have China organized for peace. I, therefore, begin to utilize my pen, which I hope will prove even mightier than the sword that I used to destroy the Manchu Dynasty, to write out these programs for organizing China for peace.

结　论

世界有三大问题，即国际战争、商业战争与阶级战争是也。在此国际发展实业计划中，吾敢为此世界三大问题而贡一实行之解决。即如后达尔文而起之哲学家之所发明人类进化之主动力，在于互助，不在于竞争，如其他之动物者焉。故斗争之性，乃动物性根之遗传于人类者，此种兽性，当以早除之为妙也。

国际战争者，无他，纯然一简直有组织之大强盗行为耳。对此种强盗行为，凡有心人莫不深疾痛恨之。当美国之参加欧战也，遂变欧战而为世界之大战争。美国人民举国一致，皆欲以此战而终结将来之战，为一劳永逸之计焉。世界爱和平之民族之希望，莫不为之兴起，而中国人民为尤甚，一时几咸信大同之世至矣。惜乎美国在战场上所获之大胜利，竟被议席间之失败而完全推翻之。遂至世界再回复欧战以前之状况，为土地而争、为食物而争、为原料而争将再出见。因此之故，前之提倡弭兵[82]者，今则联军列强又增加海军，以预备再次之战争。中国为世界最多人口之国，将来当为战争赔偿之代价也。

十余年前，列强曾倡瓜分中国，俄罗斯帝国且实行殖民满洲，后因激动日本之义愤，与俄战争[83]，得以救中国之亡。今则日本之军国政策，又欲以独力并吞中国。如中国不能脱离列强包围，即不为列国瓜分，亦为一国兼并。今日世界之潮流，似有转机矣。中国人经受数世纪之压迫，现已醒觉，将起而随世界之进步，现已在行程中矣。其将为战争而结合乎？抑为和平而结合乎？如前者之说，是吾中国军国主义者与反动者之主张，行将以日本化中国。如其然也，待时之至，拳匪之变或将再见于文明世界[84]。但中华民国之创造者，其目的本为和平，故吾敢证言曰：为和平而利用吾笔作此计划，其效力当比吾利用兵器以推倒满清为更大也。

During the course of my writing, these programs have been published in various magazines and newspapers time after time and are being spread all over China. They are welcomed everywhere and by everyone in the country. So far there is not a word expressed in disfavor of my proposition. The only anxiety ever expressed regarding my scheme is where can we obtain such huge sums of money to carry out even a small part of this comprehensive project. Fortunately, however, soon after the preliminary part of my programs had been sent out to the different governments and the Peace Conference, a new Consortium was formed in Paris for the purpose of assisting China in developing her natural resources. This was initiated by the American Government. Thus we need not fear the lack of capital to start work in our industrial development. If the Powers are sincere in their motive to coöperate for mutual benefit, then the military struggle for material gain in China could eventually be averted. For by coöperation, they can secure more benefits and advantages than by struggle. The Japanese militarists still think that war is the most profitable national pursuit, and their General Staff keeps on planning a war once in a decade. This Japanese illusion was encouraged and strengthened by the campaign of 1894 against China, a cheap and short one but rich in remuneration for Japan; also by the campaign of 1904 against Russia which was a great success to the Japanese, and its fruit of victory was no less in value; finally by the campaign of 1914 against Germany which formed her part in the world war Japan took. Although Japan took the smallest part in the world war and expended the least in men and money, yet the fruit of her victory was Shantung, a territory as large as Roumania before the war, with a population as numerous as that of France. With such crowning results in every war during the last thirty years no wonder the Japanese militarists think that the most profitable business in this world is War.

The effect of the last war in Europe proves, however, just the contrary. An aggresive Germany lost entirely her capital and interests, plus something more, while victorious France gained practically nothing. Since China is awake now, the next aggression from Japan will surely be met by a resolute resistance from the Chinese people. Even granted that Japan could conquer China, it would be an impossibility for Japan to govern China profitably for any period of time. The Japanese financiers possess better foresight than their militarists as was proved during the dispute of the Manchurian and the Mongolian reservations when the former prevailed over the latter thus causing

吾现所著之《实业计划》，经已登载各报、各杂志流传于中国者不止一次，几于无处无人不欢迎之，并未闻有发言不赞成之者。但彼等所虑者，谓吾所提议之计划过于伟大，难得如此一大宗巨款，以实行之耳。所幸者，当吾计划弁首之部寄到各国政府与欧洲和会之后[85]，巴黎遂有新银行团之成立，思欲协助中国发展天然物产。闻此举之发起人出自美国政府，故吾等即当开办之始，亦不患资本之无着也。在列强之行动如系真实协力为共同之利益计，而彼之主张军国主义者，俗为物质向中国而战争者，自无所施其伎俩，此无他，盖为互助而获之利益，当比因竞争而获之利益更为丰厚也。彼日本之武力派，尚以战争为民族进取之利器，彼参谋本部当时计划十年作一战争。一八九四年以一最短期之中日战争，获最丰之报酬，于是因之而长其欲。一九零四年日俄之役，获大胜利，所得利益亦非轻小。最后以一九一四年大战争，复加入联军以拒德国，而日本以出力最微，费财至少，竟获一领土大如未战前之罗马尼亚、人口众如法国之山东。由此观之，在近三十年间，日本于每一战争之结局即获最厚之报酬，无怪乎日本之军阀以战争为最有利益之事业也。

试以此次欧战最后之结果证之，适得其反。野心之德国，几尽丧其资本与利益与其他难于计算之物。法国虽以战胜称，实亦无所得。今中国已醒觉，日本即欲实行其侵略政策，中国人亦必出而拒绝之。即不幸中国为日本所占领，不论何时何处，亦断非日本所能统治有利。故以吾之见，日本之财政家当比日本之军阀派较有先见之明，此可以满洲、蒙古范围地之争持证之。以财政家得最后之胜利，如是

the Japanese Government to give up her monopoly of these territories to the new Consortium, in order to coöperate with the other powers. We, the Chinese people, who desire to organize China for peace will welcome heartily this new Consortium provided it will carry out the principles which are outlined in these programs. Thus, coöperation of various nations can be secured and the military struggle for individual and national gain will cease forever.

Commercial war, or competition, is a struggle between the capitalists themselves. This war has no national distinction. It is fought just as furiously and mercilessly between countries as well as within the country. The method of fighting is to undersell each other, in order to exhaust the weaker rivals so that the victor may control the market alone and dictate terms to the consuming public as long as possible. The result of the commercial war is no less harmful and cruel to the vanquished foes than an armed conflict. This war has become more and more furious every day since the adoption of machinery for production. It was once thought by the economists of the Adam Smith school that competition was a beneficent factor and a sound economic system, but modern economists discovered that it is a very wasteful and ruinous system. As a matter of fact, modern economic tendencies work in a contrary direction, that is, towards concentration instead of competition. That is the reason why the trusts in America flourish in spite of the anti-trust law and the public opinion which aim at suppressing them. For trusts, by eliminating waste and cutting down expenses can produce much cheaper than individual producers. Whenever a trust enters into a certain field of industry, it always sweeps that field clean of rivals, by supplying cheap articles to the public. This would prove a blessing to the public but for the unfortunate fact that the trust is a private concern, and its object is to make as much profit as possible. As soon as all rivals are swept clean from the field of competition, the trust would raise the price of its articles as high as possible. Thus the public is oppressed by it. The trust is a result of economic evolution, therefore it is out of human power to suppress it. The proper remedy is to have it owned by all the people of the country. In my International Development Scheme, I intend to make all the national industries of China into a Great Trust owned by the Chinese people, and financed with international capital for mutual benefit. Thus once for all, commercial war will be done away with in the largest market of the world.

日本即舍弃其垄断蒙古之政策，而与列强相合成立新银团。若此新银团能实行其现所提倡之主义，吾中国人素欲以和平改造中国者，必当诚意欢迎之。故为万国互助者当能实现，为个人或一民族之私利者，自当消灭于无形矣。

商业战争，亦战争之一种，是资本家与资本家之战争也。此种战争，无民族之区分，无国界之限制，常不顾人道，互相战斗。而其战斗之方法即减价倾轧，致弱者倒败，而强者则随而垄断市场，占领销路，直至达其能力所及之期限而止。故商业战争之结果，其损失、其残酷亦不亚于铁血竞争之以强力压迫也。此种之战争，自采用机器生产之后，已日见剧烈。彼司密亚丹[86]派之经济学者，谓竞争为最有利益之主因，为有生气之经济组织；而近代之经济学者，则谓其为浪费，为损害之经济组织。然所可确证者，近代经济之趋势，适造成相反之方向，即以经济集中代自由竞争是也。美国自有大公司出现，即有限制大公司法律，而民意亦以设法限制为然。盖大公司能节省浪费，能产出最廉价物品，非私人所能及。不论何时何地，当有大公司成立，即将其他小制造业扫除净尽，而以廉价物品供给社会，此固为社会之便利。但所不幸者，大公司多属私有，其目的在多获利益，待至一切小制造业皆为其所压倒之后，因无竞争，而后将各物之价值增高，社会上实受无形之压迫也。大公司之出现，系经济进化之结果，非人力所能屈服。如欲救其弊，只有将一切大公司组织归诸通国人民公有之一法。故在吾之国际发展实业计划，拟将一概工业组成一极大公司，归诸中国人民公有，但须得国际资本家为共同经济利益之协助。若依此办法，商业战争之在于世界市场中者，自可消灭于无形矣。

Class war is a struggle between labor and capital. The war is at present raging at its full height in all the highly developed industrial countries. Labor feels sure of its final victory while capitalists are determined to resist to the bitter end. When will it end and what will be the decision no one dares to predict. China, however, owing to the backwardness of her industrial development, which is a blessing in disguise, in this respect, has not yet entered into the class war. Our laboring class, commonly known as coolies, are living from hand to mouth and will therefore only be too glad to welcome any capitalist who would even put up a sweat shop to exploit them. The capitalist is a rare specimen in China and is only beginning to make his appearance in the treaty ports.

However, China must develop her industries by all means. Shall we follow the old path of western civilization? This old path resembles the sea route of Columbus' first trip to America. He set out from Europe by a southwesterly direction through the Canary Islands to San Salvador, in the Bahama Group. But nowadays navigators take a different direction to America and find that the destination can be reached by a distance many times shorter. The path of western civilization was an unknown one and those who went before groped in the dark as Columbus did on his first voyage to America. As a late comer, China can greatly profit in covering the space by following the direction already charted by western pioneers. Thus we can foresee that the final goal of the westward-ho in the Atlantic is not India but the New World. So is the case in the economic ocean. The goal of material civilization is not private profit but public profit. And the shortest route to it is not competition but coöperation. In my International Development Scheme, I propose that the profits of this industrial development should go first to pay the interest and principal of foreign capital invested in it; second to give high wages to labor; and third to improve or extend the machinery of production. Besides these provisions the rest of the profit should go to the public in the form of reduced prices in all commodities and public services. Thus, all will enjoy, in the same degree, the fruits of modern civilization. This industrial development scheme which is roughly sketched in the above six programs is a part of my general plan for constructing a New China. In a nutshell, it is my idea to make capitalism create socialism in China so that these two economic forces of human evolution will work side by side in future civilization.

阶级战争，即工人与资本家之战争也。此种之战争现已发现于各工业国家者，极形剧烈。在工人则自以为得最后之胜利，在资本家则决意以为最苦之压迫，故此种之战争，何时可以终局，如何可以解决，无人敢预言之者。中国因工业进步之迟缓，故就形式上观之，尚未流入阶级战争之中。吾国之所谓工人者，通称为“苦力”，而其生活只以手为饭碗，不论何资本家若能成一小工店予他等以工作者，将必欢迎之。况资本家之在中国，寥若晨星，亦仅见于通商口岸耳。

发展中国工业，不论如何，必须进行，但其进行之方，将随西方文明之旧路径而行乎？然此之旧路径，不啻如哥伦布初由欧至美之海程。考其时之海程，由欧洲起向西南方，经加拿利岛至巴哈马群岛之圣沙路华打[87]，绕程极远，与现行之航线取一直捷方向，路程短于前时数倍者，不可同日而语矣。彼西方文明之路径，是一未辟之路径，即不啻如哥伦布初往美国之海程，犹人行黑夜之景况。中国如一后至之人，可依西方已辟之路径而行之，此所以吾等从大西洋西向而行，皆预知其彼岸为美洲新大陆而非印度矣。经济界之趋势，亦如是也。夫物质文明之标的，非私人之利益，乃公共之利益。而其最直捷之途径，不在竞争，而在互助。故在吾之国际发展计划中，提议以工业发展所生之利益，其一须摊还借用外资之利息，二为增加工人之工资，三为改良与推广机器之生产，除此数种外，其余利益须留存以为节省各种物品及公用事业之价值。如此，人民将一律享受近代文明之乐矣。前之六大计划，为吾欲建设新中国之总计划之一部分耳。简括言之，此乃吾之意见，盖欲使外国之资本主义以造成中国社会主义，而调和此人类进化之两种经济能力，使之互相为用，以促进将来世界之文明也。

APPENDIX I

Preliminary Agreement Providing for the Financing and Construction of the Railway from Canton to Chungking with Extension to Lanchow

This Agreement is made at Shanghai on the fourth day of the seventh month of the second year of the Republic of China being the fourth day of July, 1913, and the contracting parties are: The Chinese National Railway Corporation (hereinafter termed "the Corporation") duly authorized in virtue of the Presidential Mandate of the ninth day of the ninth month of the Republic of China being the ninth day of September, 1912, and in virtue of the Charter of the Corporation duly promulgated by a Presidential Mandate of the thirty-first day of the third month of the second year of the Republic of China being the thirty-first day of March, 1913, on the one part and Messrs. Pauling and Company, Limited, of 26 Victoria Street, London, S. W. (hereinafter termed "the Contractors") on the other part.

Now it is Hereby Agreed by and between the parties hereto as follows:

ARTICLE I

The Contractors, or their Assigns, agree to issue on behalf of the Government of the Republic of China a sterling Loan, bearing interest at the rate of five per cent per annum, (hereinafter referred to as "the Loan") for such an amount as may be mutually estimated to be necessary for the completion of the Railway from Canton to Chungking.

The Loan shall be of the date on which the first series of Bonds are issued and shall be called "The Chinese National Railways Government five per cent Gold Loan of 1912 for the Canton Chungking Railway."

ARTICLE II

The proceeds of the Loan are designed for the construction and equipment of the Railway from Canton to Chungking (hereinafter called “the Railway”) and for all necessary expenditure appertaining thereto as may be arranged in the Detailed Agreement, referred to in Article 17.

附录一　关于广州至重庆与兰州支线之借款与建筑契约草案

此之契约，经于中华民国二年七月四日即西历一九一三年七月四日成立于上海。关于此契约之双方当事人，一为中国国家铁路公司，一为波令有限公司。中国国家铁路公司经于中华民国元年九月九日即西历一九一二年九月九日由总统命令委任，并于中华民国二年三月三十一日即西历一九一三年三月三十一日经大总统公布公司章程在案，故即以公司定名。波令有限公司现设立于伦敦城维多利亚街第二号，为立契约人等，现经双方当事人同意，议定契约条文如下：

第一条

立契约人承诺借巨款与中华民国，年息五厘，专为兴筑广州至重庆之铁路费用。其总额若干，须经双方预为议定。此借款开始所发行之债券，名曰“一九一三年中国国办广州重庆铁路五厘公债券”。

第二条

此借款之用途，专为由广州至重庆铁路之建筑与器具之费用。至其必要之用具，再详细列于第十七条之详细契约中。

ARTICLE III

The payment of the interest and the redemption of the Capital of the Loan are guaranteed by the Government of the Republic of China and by a special lien upon the Canton Chungking Railway.

This special lien constitutes a first mortgage in favour of the Contractors, acting on behalf of the Bondholders, upon the Railway itself, as and when constructed, and on the revenue of all descriptions derivable therefrom, and upon all materials, rolling stock and buildings of every description purchased or to be purchased for the Railway.

Should there be default in payments on the dates fixed of all or part of the half yearly interest or amortization payments, the Contractors shall have the right to exercise on behalf of the Bondholders all the rights of action which accrue to them from the special mortgage.

ARTICLE IV

During the time of construction of the Railway the interest on the Bonds and on any advances made by the Contractors shall be paid from the proceeds of the Loan. The accruing interest from any proceeds of the Loan not used during the period of construction, and the earnings derived by the Corporation from the working of any sections of the Railway as they are built, are to be used to make up the amount required for the payment of the said interest, and if any deficiency remains it is to be met from the proceeds of the Loan.

When the construction of the Railway is wholly completed, the interest on the Bonds is to be paid from the income or earnings of the Railway received by the Corporation, in such manner and on such dates as may be provided for in the Detailed Agreement provided for in Article 17 of this Agreement.

If, at any time, the earnings of the Railway, together with the funds available from the proceeds of the Loan, are not sufficient to meet the interest on the Bonds and the repayment of the capital in accordance with the Amortization Schedule to be attached to the Detailed Agreement, the Government of the Republic of China, in approving of this Agreement, unconditionally undertakes and promises to pay the principal of the Loan and the interest of the Loan on the due dates to be fixed therefor in the Detailed Agreement provided for in Article 17 of this Agreement.

第三条

对于借款之摊还与利息之交付，则由中华民国政府并以广州重庆铁路之监察权为之担保。

此之监察权，为契约人对于该路为其债券所有者之援助应享有之第一抵押品。此之抵押品，即如当建筑铁路之时，各种费用与铁路材料、车料与屋宇等之买卖是。

如利息应偿还款项全数或一部分，不能有如所订之期限交付时，立契约人为其债券所有者援助计，有权将该项权利加入于特别抵押品内。

第四条

当铁路尚在建筑时期，凡债券与借款之利息立契约人订定者，应由借款项下支付。凡由借款所加入之利息，若当建筑时期尚未支出者，与铁路公司已成立之一部分铁路之收入，须移用为补偿应摊还利息之总数。若再有不足，则由借款补足。

当铁路全部建筑完工后，其债券之利息可由该铁路公司之铁路入息或其他项收入支付。但对于此项办法之详细契约，另详于此契约之第十七条。

不论何时，若铁路之收入与借入之存款合计之，尚不足偿还债券利息与载在详细契约中所借入期单应偿还之资本，中华民国政府为保证此契约起见，应正式承认将此借款之欠负与载在第十七条详细契约所偿还之利息一并交付。

ARTICLE V

The bonds shall be Bonds of the Government of the Republic of China.

ARTICLE VI

The Loan shall be issued to the public in two or more series of Bonds, the first issue to be made to the amount of from one to two million pounds sterling as soon as possible after the signature of the Detailed Agreement referred to in Article 17 of this Agreement. The issue price of the Bonds shall be fixed by the Corporation and the Contractors sometime before the issue, taking the last price of similar Bonds as a basis for fixing the market price. The price payable to the Corporation shall be the actual rate of issue to the public less a sufficient amount to cover the cost of stamps on the Bonds in the various countries of issue, provided always that at least fifty per cent of the Bonds shall be issued in England, plus floatation charges of four per cent retainable by the Contractors (that is to say, a charge of four pounds for every one hundred pound Bond issued).

After the Detailed Agreement referred to in Article 17 is settled, and pending the issue of the Loan, the Contractors shall deposit the sum of fifty thousand pounds with the issuing Bank to the Canton Chungking Railway account, and this amount can be drawn on by the Corporation for survey and other necessary expenses authorized by the Managing Director against certificates signed by the Chief Accountant and Chief Engineer. This sum of fifty thousand pounds shall bear interest at the rate of five per cent per annum and shall be refunded out of the proceeds of the Loan.

ARTICLE VII

The proceeds of the Loan shall be deposited with the issuing Bank, to be nominated and guaranteed by the Contractors, to the credit of a Canton Chungking Railway Account on such terms as may be mutually arranged in the Detailed Agreement referred to in Article 17.

When the work of construction is ready to begin a sum equal to the estimated expenditure in China for six months shall be transferred to a

Bank in China to be mutually agreed upon and there placed to the credit of a Canton Chungking Railway Account to be operated upon by the Corporation under certificates signed by the Chief Accountant and the Chief Engineer. This amount of estimated expenditure for six months shall be maintained by subsequent monthly transfers so that, as far as possible, there shall always be six months estimated expenditure in China on deposit in a Bank in China to be mutually agreed upon.

第五条

发行之债券，即作为中华民国政府之债券。

第六条

债券应分为二次或二次以上发售。第一次所发出之总额，须在金镑一百万至二百万之间，惟须当此契约第十七条之详细契约双方签名之后，即刻实行。此债券之发行价格。应由铁路公司与立契约人协同依同样债券为基础，以议定市面价格。此之价格，因包含债券发行于各国所需用之印花，故比其原定价格略低。此种债券至少须百分之五十在英伦发行，百分之四为立契约人抽收，即每一百金镑可照债券之发行之价抽收四镑。

当十七条详细契约既定、债券亦将发行时候，立契约人须先存贮五万金镑于银行，入为广州重庆铁路公司数目。此之总数，若经铁路总理之命令并总会计与总工程师之签名，可以随时提取作为测量及各种必需费用。至此五万金镑之总数，订定每年利息五厘，将来由借款项下拨出归还。

第七条

借款须存贮于银行，由立契约人声明并担保作为广州重庆铁路数目。如此办法，可再由第十七条之详细契约中商酌办理。

当建筑工程经已开始，一相等于在中国足充六个月用度之数额，须交付存贮于设立在中国之银行，入为广州重庆铁路数目，并可由该铁路公司支用。但须得总会计与总工程师会签方为有效。此六个月用度之总额，可接续依月递交，存贮于中国之银行。

ARTICLE VIII

Immediately after the signing of the Detailed Agreement, the Corporation will establish a Head Office at Canton for the Canton Chungking Railway. This Office will be under the direction of a Chinese Managing Director to be appointed by the Corporation, with whom will be associated a British Engineer-in-Chief and a British Firm of Public Accountants, of recognized standing, whose representative shall be Chief Accountant (hereinafter called "the Chief Accountant"). These British Employes shall be nominated by the Corporation and the Contractors, jointly, and shall be appointed by the Corporation. Their dismissal shall take place, only, with the joint approval of the Corporation and the Contractors.

It is understood that the duties to be performed by these employes are intended to promote the mutual interests of the Corporation and the Bondholders respectively, and it is therefore agreed that all cases of difference arising therefrom shall be referred for amicable adjustment between the Corporation and the Representative of the Contractors. The salaries and other terms of Agreement of the Engineer-in-Chief and the Chief Accountant shall be arranged between the Corporation and the Contractors; and the amount of their salaries, etc., shall be paid out of the general accounts of the Railway.

For all important technical appointments for the operation of the Railway, Europeans of experience and ability shall be engaged and wherever competent Chinese are available, they shall be employed. All such appointments shall be made, and their functions defined, by the Managing Director and the Engineer-in-Chief in consultation, and shall be submitted for the approval of the Corporation; similar procedure shall be followed in the case of Europeans employed in the Chief Accountant's department. In the event of the misconduct, or the incompetency of these European employes, their services may be dispensed with by the Managing Director, after consultation with the

Engineer-in-Chief, and subject to the sanction of the Corporation. The form of Agreements made with these European Employes shall conform to the usual practice.

The accounts of the receipts and the disbursements of the Railway's construction and operation, shall be in Chinese and English in the department of the Chief Accountant, whose duty it shall be to organize and supervise the same, and to report thereon for the information of the Corporation through the Managing Director, and of the Contractors as representing the Bondholders. All receipts and payments shall be certified by the Chief Accountant and authorized by the Managing Director.

第八条

当详细契约签押之后，此铁路公司即须于广东省城另设一广州重庆铁路事务所。此之事条所，应设中国总理一人，由铁路公司派委；英国总工程师及英国总会计各一人，由铁路公司与立契约人协同择定，而后由铁路公司任命。但所雇用英国职员，若得铁路公司与立契约人之同意，并可以革除。

此项职工应尽之义务，在增进铁路公司与债券所有者之共同利益，故每当有问题发生，必须有铁路公司与立契约人共同秉公处理。英国总工程师与总会计之薪金及期限，由铁路公司与立契约人订定，即由铁路数目项下支出。

凡关于管理铁路之重要人员，如有有经验、有技能之欧洲人与有能干之中国人，均须一体并用。如此等一切之任用与其权限之规定，须由总理与总工程师会商办理，呈请铁路公司核准。至雇用于总会计部之欧人，均须依同一方法办理。如欧洲职员有失德行为或不称职时，总理与总工程师会商呈请公司核准，可将该职员革除。至雇用欧洲职员所订之契约，须与普通所用者相同。

凡在总会计部之收入数目及铁路建筑与管理之支出数目，须用中英两国文字。总会计须依此办法办理报告，分呈于总理与代表债券所有者之立契约人。但此项数目之收入与支出，必须经总会计承认，并总理核准。

For the general technical staff of the Railway, after completion of construction, the necessary arrangements shall be made by the Managing Director in consultation with the Engineer-in-Chief, and reported to the Corporation in due course.

The duties of the Engineer-in-Chief shall consist in the efficient and economical maintenance of the Railway, and the general supervision thereof in consultation with the Managing Director. The duties of the Chief Engineer during construction shall be set forth in the Detailed Agreement, referred to in Article 17 of this Agreement.

The Engineer-in-Chief shall always give courteous consideration to the wishes and instructions of the Corporation, whether conveyed directly or through the Managing Director, and shall always comply therewith, having at the same time due regard to the efficient construction and maintenance of the Railway.

A school for the education of Chinese in Railway matters shall be established by the Managing Director subject to the approval of the Corporation.

ARTICLE IX

The Contractors shall construct and equip the Railway and shall receive as remuneration a sum equal to seven per cent on the actual cost of the construction and equipment of the Railway. The term "Equipment" shall be held to include in its meaning all requirements necessary for the operation of the Railway and shall therefore include Rolling Stock and Locomotives sufficient for operation.

It is clearly understood that the term "Equipment" does not include any purchases made for the Railway after it has been completely constructed and equipped and handed over ready for operation.

It is further clearly understood that the cost of land purchased for the Railway, the salaries of the Managing Director, Chief Accountants, Chief Engineer, and the cost of their offices and staff shall not be included in the meaning of the terms "construction and equipment."

The Contractors shall have the option of constructing on the same terms the proposed extension of the Railway to Lanchow in the Province of Kansu, or a Railway of similar milage in some other part of China to be mutually agreed upon, and this option shall be for seven years from the commencement of construction.

All other arrangements in connection with the construction and equipment of the Railway shall be settled in the Detailed Agreement referred to in Article 17.

当铁路建筑完工之后，凡关于铁路之通常应办事宜，须由总理与总工程师会商办理，并须随时报告于铁路公司。

总工程师之责任，在使铁路办理妥善，节省经费；至普通事宜，须会商总理进行。副工程师当建筑时期，其责任如何，再详示于本契约中第十七条之详细契约。

总工程师须遵奉铁路公司意思与命令。惟此项意思与命令，不论其为直接授予或经总理转达，均须一体照办。并须对于铁路之建筑与维持随时留心料理。

为养成中国铁路人才起见，总理若得铁路公司之核准，可设一铁路专门学校。

第九条

立契约人担认建造与完成此铁路，并得由该铁路所用之建筑物与器具之确实所值价格抽取百分七之数量。“器具”二字之意思，包含铁路用以驾驶之一切器用，如车料、车头为驾驶而用者皆是。

“器具”之名词，若明白解释之，凡对于铁路已建筑完全、经已购器使用之后，所购入之各物不包含在内。更为详明解释之，凡因建筑铁路买入之地价，与总理、总会计、总工程师及各办事人员之薪俸，不能列入建筑与器用之名词之意思内。

立契约人有权依章建筑支路至甘肃省之兰州。如或得双方之同意，并可建筑同长铁路至中国之他部地方。此种之权限，在由铁路兴工之始七年内有效。

其余一切关于建筑铁路与购办器具之事宜，遵照本契约第十七条之详细契约办理。

ARTICLE X

All land that may be required along the whole course of the Railway within survey limits, and for the necessary sidings, stations, repairing shops and car sheds, to be provided for in accordance with the detailed plans, shall be acquired by the Corporation at the actual cost of the land, and shall be paid for out of the proceeds of the Loan.

ARTICLE XI

The Contractors shall hand over to the Corporation each section of the Railway, when completed, for operation in accordance with the provisions of the Detailed Agreement.

ARTICLE XII

The Contractors shall be appointed Trustees for the Bondholders and shall receive such remuneration as may be fixed in the Detailed Agreement.

ARTICLE XIII

The Government of the Republic of China, whenever necessary, will provide protection for the Railway while under construction or when in operation, and all the properties of the Railway as well as Chinese and foreigners employed thereon, are to enjoy protection from the local Officials.

The Railway may maintain a force of Chinese Police with Chinese officers, their wages and maintenance to be wholly defrayed as part of the cost of the construction and maintenance of the Railway. In the event of the Railway requiring further protection by the military forces of the Government, the same shall be duly applied for by the Head Office and promptly afforded, it being understood that such military forces shall be maintained at the expense of the Government.

ARTICLE XIV

All materials of any kind that are required for the construction and working of the Railway, whether imported from abroad or from the Provinces to the scene of work, shall be exempted from Likin or other duties so long as such exemption remains in force in respect of other Chinese Railways. The Bonds of the Loan, together with their coupons and the income of the Railway shall be free from imposts of any kind by the Government of the Republic of China.

第十条

一切沿铁路边旁之田地，经测量指定，系依详细计划用为旁路、车站、修理店与车房之用者，可由公司依确定之价值收买，并须由借款内照给。

第十一条

立契约人依照详细契约所规定，须将每段已完工之铁路交出铁路公司，以备使用。

第十二条

立契约人须派董事为债券所有者之代表。至其应领取之薪金，别以详细契约定之。

第十三条

中华民国政府对于现建筑或已驶行之铁路，与属于铁路之一切财产，并将雇用中国或外国人员，皆须饬各地方官极力保护。铁路得设立警察队与警察官，其薪金与费用须由铁路建筑费用项下支给。若铁路遇有事故，须要政府兵力时，须由铁路公司呈明，迅速派人驻守。但此等兵队，须由政府供给费用。

第十四条

凡用以建筑铁路之各种材料，无论其由外国购办抑由本省采取，若为铁路使用，且在免税限内者，须一律免除厘金与关税。凡债券、票据与铁路之入息，须由中华民国政府免除各种征抽。

ARTICLE XV

With a view to encouraging Chinese industries, Chinese materials are to be preferred, provided price and quality are suitable.

At equal rates and qualities, goods of British manufacture shall be given preference over other goods of foreign origin.

ARTICLE XVI

The Contractors may, with the approval of the Corporation, and subject to all their obligations, transfer or delegate all or any of their rights, powers, and discretions, to their successors or assigns.

ARTICLE XVII

As soon as this Preliminary Agreement is signed it shall be forwarded to the Government of the Republic of China for approval. When it has met with the approval of the Government of the Republic of China, a necessary Detailed Agreement shall be made embodying the principles of this Agreement with such amplifications and additions as may be mutually agreed upon between the parties hereto.

ARTICLE XVIII

On its approval of this Agreement, and acceptance of the obligations set forth herein, the Government of the Republic of China shall officially notify the British Minister at Peking of the fact, and this approval shall be taken as covering the Detailed Agreement referred to in Article 17.

ARTICLE XIX

This Agreement is executed in quadruplicate in English and Chinese, one copy to be retained by the Corporation, one to be forwarded to the Government of the Republic of China, one to be forwarded to the British Minister at Peking, and one to be retained by the Contractors, and should any doubt arise as to the interpretation of the Agreement the English text shall be accepted as the standard.

Signed at Shanghai by the contracting parties on this fourth day of the seventh month of the second year of the Republic of China being the fourth day of July nineteen hundred and thirteen.

第十五条

为奖励中国工业起见，若中国材料之价值与物质均称适宜，须一体劝用。英国制造货物与由他国运来之货物比较，若系同物质并同价值者，英国货物有优先权。

第十六条

立契约人得铁路公司之核准与承诺，可将全部或一部之利益、权利与事权转让与承受人或授予人。

第十七条

当此契约经已划押，即须送呈中华民国政府核夺。若经中华民国政府批准，然后将此契约由双方协定，另订详细契约。

第十八条

此契约既经批准与承诺，中华民国政府须将此事实照会驻京英国公使。但此之批准，必须将第十七条之详细契约统括之。

第十九条

此之契约须按照英中两国文字缮写四张，一送呈于中华民国政府，一送呈于驻京英国公使，一留存于立契约人。若对于此契约之解释有疑义发生时，英文底本即作为标准。

中华民国二年七月四日即一九一三年

关于契约双方当事人划押于上海

APPENDIX II

Legation of the United States of Amercia

Peking, March 17, 1919.

Dr. Sun Yat Sen,
29 Rue Molière,
Shanghai, Kiangsu.

DEAR DR. SUN:

I have read with great interest your sketch project for the international development of China as embodied in your letter of February first to me. I congratulate you upon the broad and statesmanlike attitude with which you treat this very important subject. Your suggestion of united international participation in the development of China's resources deserves the support of all friends of China. It would be unfortunate indeed if the old régime of spheres of influence, struggles for concessions and activities flavoring of selfish exploitation should not, with the conclusion of the war, be relegated to the past. You are right in recognizing the necessity of a substitute for the old order and your proposal of a unified policy under international organization with Chinese participation for the larger development in China, naturally assuming that the inalienable rights of the Chinese people are to be amply safeguarded, meets this demand admirably.

We are hopeful that conditions in China may become such that the Chinese people themselves may be encouraged to put their money into productive enterprise and participate in the larger developments. We are hopeful that the day is not far distant when the Chinese Government may be able actively to interest itself in the encouragement of native industry to the end that native capital of which there is a very considerable quantity, may be induced to lend itself to productive enterprises, because of a confidence in constructive policy on the part of the government.

If you will permit a suggestion, I would be inclined to reduce your admirable program to one which would be in closer keeping with the limits of the present world's resources in capital. As we all know devastated Europe is calling for capital for rehabilitation and other nations want capital for development programs of considerable proportions. Thus it would seem that China's program of development must of necessity take cognizance of her most immediate and most pressing needs. We are all united in that transportation occupies a prominent place in such a program. 50,000 miles of railway and 100,000 miles of good roads would seem to be sufficient to engage our attention for any plans for the

附录二　驻京美国公使芮恩施复函

孙先生大鉴：

来函经于二月一日收到。函内手著《国际共同发展中国实业计划》，拜读之余，良深钦佩。先生对于此重要问题，能以宏伟精深之政策运用之，可喜可贺。尊意以为发展中国实业，须联合国际共同办理，凡命为中国朋友者，应当竭力赞助。前者列强每当战争告终，即施其所谓势力范围与割让、租借等手段，是不幸事，人皆知之。尊意以为革除彼向来恶习为必要之图，故提倡用一联合政策，由国际机关与中国共同发展中国之实业，所见甚是。若依此办法，中国应享之权利无不可保矣。

吾甚望中国情形有所变更，一切中国人民将利用其钱财为生利之事业，而共襄助此伟大之经营也。吾甚望中国政府奖励其本国工业，使以其本国无限之资本用为生产，其日不远。盖因政府有建设之政策，信用自生也。

若先生许吾进言，吾欲将先生之伟大计划为之介绍，或可使世界原料与资本生一密切之关系。吾人皆知现残余之欧洲亟需资以恢复，而他国又以发展伟大计划而求资，如此之发展中国实业计划，必须认定其最急迫最密切之需要，而后共同联合整顿输运，使在如此之计划中占一永久位置。故为目前计，五万英里之铁路［与十万英里之良好大路］似可最敷需用。

immediate future. This would allow ample opportunity to penetrate the great rich unoccupied regions in the North and West, which should be opened to colonization and development as soon as possible in order to relieve the economic pressure of over population in sections along the coasts and waterways, and to accord opportunities to bring the rich regions of West China into contact with the trade of the rest of China and the world at large.

Along with transportation, China needs to develop its resources in iron and coal, the two great essentials to modern industrialism. Arrangements should be made whereby foreign capital can come to China's assistance in these two important industries, but care should be exercised so as to preserve to China the iron and coal necessary for its own uses, and prevent China's steel industry being mortgaged to foreign interests, in a way so as to jeopardize China's future in this important industry.

The reform of the currency and reforms in internal tax administrations are questions of immediate importance to China's economic and industrial development.

One of the greatest fields of potentiality in the immediate demands of the New China, is agriculture. The country depends in its final analysis upon the prosperity of its agriculture. At present probably as much as 80% of China's population is agricultural. China's greatest problem is the proper feeding and clothing of its vast population. Improved conditions in agriculture, opening of new lands to cultivation, irrigation and conservancy works, the encouragement of the cattle and sheep industries, the development of the cotton industry and the improvement of tea, silk and the seed crops of China, are timely subjects in any program of developments. There is a vast work to be done in agriculture in China, which will lead to prosperity generally, and make possible developments with native capital in other fields of activity, whereas if agricultural improvements are neglected, it will be difficult to insure prosperity in other directions.

Thus for the present, I hope the main thought may be centered on improvements in transportation, in currency and tax administrations, in the development of coal and iron industries, and in agriculture. Many of the suggested activities included in your very extensive program will follow as a corollary to the above.

In thinking of all these developments, I believe that we should always give thought to the fact that we are not dealing with a new country but with one in which social arrangements are exceedingly intricate and in which a long-tested system of agricultural and industrial organization exists. It is to my mind most important that the transition to new methods of industry and labor should not be sudden but that the old

如此，可使中国西北部之丰富无人境域，交通利便，移民居住，既可以救济沿海岸一带人居过密之各省不至受经济之压迫，亦可以使中国西、北两部之丰富区域能与中国各部及世界各国有通商之机会也。

中国对于煤铁矿之发展，尤为要图。煤与铁，近代工业主要之两大原料也。如中国欲发展此两项工业，应设法利用外资，为之援助。但不可不注意者：一面当留存煤铁，为其本国之需；一面当阻止中国之钢铁事业抵押于外人。如此而后不至危及中国此项伟大之事业。

币制之改良与内地税率管理之改良，亦对于中国经济与工业之发展有大关系之问题也。

现在最大出产之土地，而又为中国急迫之需要者，是为农业。此无他，农产，一国之所赖以供养也。就现时计之，中国之人口几百分之八十为农业。中国之大问题在使人民衣食丰足，故改良农业、开辟新地、整顿灌溉与保护工人、奖励畜牧、发展棉业、改良丝茶及改良中国种子等事业，尚须注意者甚多。若从此开始，亦可导中国于繁盛，或可使其国人民投资于各项事业。若舍此不顾，欲保证实业之发达，盖亦难矣。

就现时言之，吾之所切望者，注重于改良输运、币制、税则、煤铁、农工等事业。然在先生大计划中所包括者，亦不外上列之各种具体办法也。

试就此发展实业计划言之，吾信以为吾等所应留意者，不在讨论新国家，而在讨论一社会秩序极错综而又为以农工商业立国久有经验之国家。在吾之意，至要者为工业。但工业变用新法不可过急，只要

abilities and values should be gradually transmuted. It is important that the artistic ability existing in the silk and porcelain manufacture, etc. should be maintained and fostered, and not superseded by cheaper processes. It is also highly important that no export of food should be permitted, except as to clearly ascertained surpluses of production. It would produce enormous suffering were the food prices in China suddenly to be raised to the world market level. The one factor in modern organization which the Chinese must learn better to understand is the corporation, and the fiduciary relationship which the officers of the corporation ought to occupy with respect to the stockholders. If the Chinese cannot learn to use the corporation properly, the organization of the national credit cannot be effected. Here, too, it is necessary that the capital of personal honesty which was accumulated under the old system should not be lost but transferred to the new methods of doing business. So at every point where we are planning for a better and more efficient organization, it seems necessary to hold on to the values created in the past and not to disturb the entire balance of society by too sudden changes.

I wish again to congratulate you upon the statesmanlike view with which you consider the whole question of the development of your country, and the very timely suggestions you have to make in regard to a united policy of international participation in these developments. I am glad to note that the minds of the leaders among the Chinese people today are being centered more and more upon the constructive needs of the country and efforts are being made to meet these needs, in full appreciation of China's relations with the people of other nations, to the end that China's developments in the future may work in harmony with the world developments generally.

I should be glad to hear from you further and more in detail concerning development plans.

Believe me, with the highest regard,

Sincerely yours,

(Signed)

PAUL S. REINSCH.

将旧艺术、旧习惯由渐改进。如制造丝与磁等工业之艺术技能，须设法保存，不可以省工廉价求售。如食物出口，若非确知为生产之剩余者，即须禁止。不然，若食物价格之在中国，起而与世界市场之食物价格相等，中国将必大受恐慌，可无疑者。近代机关之组织，中国人有不可不知者，是对于一公司办事员应用何权限，并该公司与股东有何关系是也。若中国人不知适用公司，国债机关之设立亦断无效果。兹更有进者，中国人素以诚实见称，尤不可因改用新法以经营事业，遂弃置其原有性质也。吾上所述之各点，亦不过欲使中国成一更良善之组织，前日之好习惯固当保当，而社会之秩序亦不至因急速改革而受搅扰也。

先生欲整顿中国，因而利用一最适时宜办法，成一国际共同发展实业计划。高言伟论，当为道贺。此亦足见今日为中国人民领袖之心理，已日渐趋重于国家建设之事业。若奋其能力以成此事业，将来中外人民日相亲密，使将来之发展得与世界之发展共同提携，此为最可喜者也。

先生发展实业计划有更详明者，请赐一纸，不胜铭感。

一九一九年三月十七日

芮恩施敬上

APPENDIX III

Department of Commerce
Office of the Secretary Washington

May 12, 1919.

Hon. Sun Yat Sen,
29 Rue Molière,
Shanghai, China.

YOUR EXCELLENCY:

I have read with the greatest interest the project for the International Development of China enclosed in your letter of March 17th, and agree with you that the economic development of China would be of the greatest advantage, not only to China, but to the whole of mankind.

The plans you propose, however, are so complex and extensive that it will take many years to work them out in detail. You doubtless are fully aware that it would take billions of dollars to carry out even a small portion of your proposals and that most of them would not be able to pay interest charges and expenses of operation for some years. The first question to be decided, therefore, is how the interest charges on the necessary loans could be met. The revenues of the Chinese Republic are already too heavily burdened with the interest charges on existing Government loans to warrant further charges, and hence it would seem necessary for the present to limit the projects for development to those which seem sufficiently remunerative to attract private capital. The government of the United States has consistently endeavored to manifest its disinterested friendship for the people of China and will undoubtedly coöperate in every proper way in proposals to advance their best interests.

Please accept my thanks for your kindness in submitting your proposals.

Respectfully,

(Signed)

WILLIAM C. REDFIELD,

Secretary.

附录三　美国商务总长复函一通

孙逸仙大人阁下：

得奉三月十七日赐函，内附《国际共同发展中国计划》，披阅之下，兴味不穷。而阁下之所谓中国之经济发展将为人类全体最大利益，不特中国人食赐，尤所赞成也。以阁下所提计划如此复杂，如此溥遍[88]，即令将其备细之点规划完峻，亦须数年。阁下亦明知书案中一小部分尚须数十万万金元，而其中多数在初期若干年间，不能偿其所投之利息与经费。是故，其必要之债所需利息如何清付，实为第一须决之问题。以中华民国收入负担现在国债，利息太重，难保新增之息必能清付。则今日似必要将此发展计划限制，以期显有利益足引至私人资本者为度。

合众国政府一致努力以表示无私之友谊于中国人民，并愿由各种正当之途径，以参与增进华人最上利益之计划也。

远承赐教，感谢无已，敬颂勋祺。

商务总长刘飞尔谨启

一九一九年五月十二日

APPENDIX IV

Il Ministro Della Guerra

Rome, 17 Maggio, 1919.

Most Honorable
Sun Yat Sen,
29 Rue Molière,
Shanghai, China

HONORABLE SIR:

I thank you for having so kindly communicated to me the interesting project regarding how to employ through an International Organization the exuberant industrial activities created by the war, in order to exploit the great hidden riches of China.

Though aware of the practical difficulties which present themselves in the accomplishment of this project, it meets with my utmost appreciation, I assure you, for the modern spirit by which it is animated and for the depth of its conception.

Accept my best wishes for complete success, in the advantage of your noble country and for the interest of humanity.

Believe Me,

Faithfully yours,

(Signed)

GENERAL CAVIGLIA.

附录四 意大利陆军大臣嘉域利亚将军复函

敬启者：蒙惠赐以关于如何以国际共同组织使用战时所产洋溢之制造能力，而开发中国最大宝藏之有兴味之计划，不胜感谢。虽在此计划亦有与相附丽[89]之实际困难，稍须顾虑，而以其所造之深与其带有现代精神之活气，使我不禁为最高之评价也。

为人道之利益，为贵国之进步，吾愿阁下此计划之完全成功。专此布达悃诚[90]。

嘉域利亚

一九一九年五月十七日

APPENDIX V

Peking, June 17, 1919.

Hon. Sun Yat Sen,
Shanghai.

DEAR SIR:

Permit me as a professional railway man to express my pleasure with your article appearing in the Far Eastern Review for June.

I will not at this time express approval or disapproval of the route which you have chosen but the idea of a line to connect up the great agricultural interior with the densely populated coast appeals to me strongly. I feel that you are making a definite contribution to railway economic theory in this respect, whereas the line itself would relieve congestion, open up a production area which would lower food costs, furnish employment to large numbers of soldiers to be disbanded, and put in circulation a large amount of hard money which would go far to correct the currency situation.

I am especially pleased to have your article appear at this time for I had already written one at the request of the publishers of the forthcoming "Trans-Pacific" magazine in which I touched upon the same line of thought. This will not appear until July and your opinions will have done much to prepare the minds of sceptics upon the subject by that time.

I trust that this intrusion of an entire stranger may be pardoned, and that you will continue to support the thought which you have so ably presented.

Very truly yours,

(Signed)

J. E. BAKER.

附录五　北京交通部顾问之铁路专门家碧格君投函

孙逸仙先生阁下：

敬启者，得读《远东时报》六月号所载尊著论文，敢以一铁路专门家之资格，敬表喜忭之忱[91]。在阁下所选定路线，仆在此时虽难遽言赞成、反对，但以一铁路联结广大之农业腹地与人口稠密之海岸之理想，感我实深。窃谓阁下于此已于铁路经济理论上致一具体之贡献。即此路线自身，已能蠲解滞积[92]，开辟一生产区，使食料价可较贱，以职业授巨额之退伍兵卒，又能使大量之硬币得有流转，而通货之位置将循之以为于正也。在仆尤有庆者，则大著正以此时发表，而仆适亦应《横贯太平洋杂志》社主之求，曾草一论，恰亦触及此种思想径路。此论非至七月不能发表，则阁下之意见，对于现在此点着想，使怀疑我者大足以开悟之矣。

冒昧致书，惟冀鉴原。又信阁下此种启沃思想敏妙之作，必将有继此而宣于世者也。专此敬颂勋祺。

碧格谨启

［一九一九年］六月十七日

APPENDIX VI

3, Piazza Del Popolo
Roma

August 30, 1919.

Dr. Sun Yat Sen,
29 Rue Molière,
Shanghai, China.

My Dear Dr. Sun Yat Sen:

I thank you for your very kind letter of June 19th which has just been forwarded to me from my office in Rome, also for your kindness in sending me your splendid project "To assist the Re-adjustment of Postbellum Industries," and the program for "The International Development of China."

I assure you I read your proposals and studied the maps in connection with your able and logical argument with the deepest interest. And I beg you to accept my hearty congratulations.

I am entirely convinced that your noble *ideals will be* realised, not only for the benefit of China and the welfare of your own people, but for the benefit and prosperity of the whole human race.

The Nations cannot continue to deny in the future as they have in the past, the unlimited natural resources of your rich fertile country, in foods, minerals, coal and iron, etc.; and your plans for development and activity, as well as your methods of communication for expanding and cultivating almost untouched miles of virgin soil, and bringing these products to the doors of the "World Market" by a practical and economic plan, scientifically studied out, places you at once among the very rare few unselfish humanitarian benefactors, and reveals so clearly your profound international sympathies.

The development of China's natural resources will give a new impetus and vitality to industry and commerce in your country and will not only be of incalculable benefit to your own people, but offer undeniable and unlimited advantages to all people in all nations. Therefore Governments and foreign financiers should not hesitate in giving your plans their most careful consideration and support, and come to your assistance in the realisation of your grand humanitarian project.

The construction of a great "Northern Port" on the Gulf of Pechihli, and the building of a system of railways from this great Northern Port to the northwestern extremity of China, as well as the construction of canals to connect the inland waterways systems of North and Central China with the great "Northern Port," and the development of coal and

附录六　美国名士寓居罗马以世界中都计划著名之安得生君复函

逸仙先生足下：

六月十九日赐书，已由罗马敝事务所转到此处，甚谢，甚谢。并承瑰伟之补助战后整顿实业之案与《国际共同发展中国计划》相贻，尤感。

奉读尊著计划，旁肇附图而及于先生所与理则的且有力的论据，觉其兴味深永。谨此布庆悦之忱。

吾完全确信先生之高尚理想必将实现，非惟以为中国国家人民之福利而已，又以为世界各人种之利益与繁荣计也。

以饶富之贵国，粮食、矿产、煤铁等等天然富源素称丰富，从前虽为各国所忽略，今则不然矣。而先生之活动发展计划与其展开培成，在使此全未触及之广大处女地，以最经济最实用之方法运其产物于世界市场之前。是先生绝无私心，专为人道求其利益，是为稀有之人，且明晰显出先生深重之国际同情也。

夫发展中国富源者，不特于贵国实业商务与之新刺激、新能力，且为贵国之人民谋其不可胜计之利路而已，又以不可否认且无限之利益付与一切国家之一切人民。此所以政府及外国财政家，对于先生之计划与以最深细之考查及授助，而襄同先生以实现此最大之人道的计划，不应更有所踌躇也。

凡此在北直隶建筑北方大港，由此港直通中国西北边陲，建一铁路系统，又浚一运河，构成中国北部、中部与此港联络之内地水路统系，

iron fields in Shansi which would necessitate the construction of iron and steel works would not only offer employment to millions of your country people, but would open wider, and advantageously, the doors of thousands of well organised industries in many nations.

It is very encouraging to me, dear Dr. Sun Yat Sen, to know that you look upon my plans of an "International World Centre of Communication" with favor, and that you will further the idea among your countrymen by writing about it in your magazine "The Construction."

This city, erected upon neutral grounds would offer at once the practical framework for the essential needs of a League of Nations and could become its dignified "Administrative Centre" crowned by an International Court of Justice.

I have presented the plans and proposals of this World Centre to the Rulers and governments of all nations, and hope to be able to go to Washington in October to exhibit the large original drawings and personally explain the project from a practical and economic point of view before the foreign delegates who may meet there to assist in the formation of a League of Nations, and I have written to President Wilson, who after receiving the volumes containing the proposals and plans, wrote that "he valued them very highly."

I hope that in the very near future this International World Centre of communication may become a reality. It would be the means of clearly defining and bringing into focus the highest natural products as well as the most important industrial achievements of all countries. This accomplishment would be one of the first definite steps toward more friendly social and economic relations, and the practicability of establishing such coöperation cannot be disputed.

This City of Peace should rise and stand as an International Monument, erected by international contribution to commemorate the heroic struggle and noble sacrifice of millions who gave their lives on the battle fields, in the air and on the sea, that justice should triumph and open the ways for humanity to progress in peace, and free from tyranny in the future.

With the assurance, dear Dr. Sun Yat Sen, of my most profound sympathies for your noble project, and with my deep gratitude for your keen interest in my plans,

I beg to remain, with high esteem

Faithfully yours,

(Signed)

HENDRICK CHRISTIAN ANDERSEN.

且开发山西煤铁矿区，不仅其所需以作制铁炼钢工程者使贵国数百万人得其职役，抑且广开门户，随之以利益，以容多数国家组织完美之无数实业也。

先生于我世界交通中心之计划辱予赞助，且将以先生所经营之《建设》杂志绍介此思想于贵国人民，使我益加奋厉矣。

此都市如建立于中立地区，则立可以应国际联盟之必然的需要，作为其实际之骨干，而能成为受治于国际司法法庭之下最庄严之行政中心矣。

吾已将此世界中都之图及案送与各国之政府及主权者，并拟于十月一日起赴华盛顿，以展览各图原本，并亲自由纯然实际经济的观察点说明此种计划于各国代表之前。此等代表拟于此处集合，以助国际联盟之组织也。

吾又尝致函威尔逊总统，彼接吾图案之后，答吾谓彼视此计划之价值甚高。吾望此世界交通中心之计划，不久能为实现之中都，将以各国最高自然产物与最重要之实业成功致之于集中点，且使之确定意义，显出此种贡献，乃向于友谊的社会及经注关系为最初决定之一步，而建立此种联合之实用无可批难者也。

将纪念于此海上、空中、陆地战场，为求公道之战胜，为人道扫除榛秽以进于和平[93]，为将来不受暴君压迫之自由而抛其生命之数百万人之英雄奋斗与高尚的牺牲，诸国应各有所献纳，共建造维持此和平都市，以为国际之为丰碑也。

对于先生高尚之计划，吾抱有最深厚之同情；而于先生对于我计划有此深切之兴味，尤吾所引以为庆者也。专布悃忱，藉申敬意。

［一九一九年］八月三十日

轩特力·安得生启于萨丁诺

NOTES 注释

除特别说明外，其余注释由张小莉、申学锋所作。

1 Manchu Régime：指清朝。——编者注

2 泛应曲当：广泛应用于各种情况，到处都很恰当。

3 林云陔：1883—1948 年，广东人。同盟会会员，朱执信的学生，曾赴美留学，回国后，任《建设》杂志编辑。

4 粤京：指广东省省会广州。

5 蒋梦麟：1886—1964 年，原名梦熊，浙江余姚人。美国哥伦比亚大学教育学博士，师从杜威。曾长期担任北京大学校长。著有《西潮》、《新潮》等。——编者注

6 余日章：1882—1936 年，原籍蒲圻，生于武昌。获美国哈佛大学教育科硕士学位、上海圣约翰大学文科博士学位。先后担任中华基督教青年会全国协会总干事、中华基督教协进会会长等职务。——编者注

7 朱友渔：1886—1986 年，社会学家、基督徒。1911 年获美国哥伦比亚大学哲学博士学位。曾任上海圣约翰大学社会学教授、中华圣公会云贵教区主教等。——编者注

8 顾子仁：1887—1971 年，生于上海，毕业于上海圣约翰大学，曾任职于中华基督教青年会、世界基督教学生同盟等。——编者注

9 李耀邦：1884—约 1940 年，物理学家，生于广东省番禺，1914 年获美国芝加哥大学哲学博士学位。曾任南京高等师范学校教授、基督教青年会全国协会副总干事等。——编者注

10 colonization：殖民。

colonization 的词根是 colonize，主要的意思是“种植”(plant)、“移居到偏远地区”(migrate)、“将居民、住民等送往另外一个地方长期居住”(settle)、“建立殖民地”。此词从 1622 年开始使用，开始并无后来语境中的贬义，而更多地是指“移居”、“移植”等。到了 19 世纪，当英国开始征服非洲和亚洲其他地区并建立殖民地（colony）时，因为这些地区已经拥有比较“成熟”的文明社会，此刻英国或欧洲人的“殖民”内容和目的就有了较殖民美洲时不同的变化，征服和建立控制成为建立殖民地的主要内容，尤其是在早期。这样，所谓 colonialism(殖民主义）或 colonization（殖民化，建立殖民地）在 20 世纪也就逐渐变成了一种贬义词。

具体到孙中山先生《实业计划》的用语，孙先生是一位反清的民族主义者，他写作的时代正是“帝国主义”盛行、民族主义在殖民地国家和其他非西方国家开始兴起的时代，他无疑同时受到反帝国主义、社会达尔文主义、民族主义的影

响，强调建立一个有实力的、强大的中国，应对西方和俄国。他提出开发蒙古和新疆，显然将这两个地区视为中国的一部分；提出用 colonization 的方式来开发，更多的可能是指将汉民族的人移居到这些地方去定居，建立商业或永久定居点，目的是将这些地方纳入为中国国家的一部分。这里使用的 colonization，与早期英国人殖民美洲的用法非常相似，而不是后来 19 世纪和 20 世纪使用的“征服”性 colonization 的意思。——王希注

11 Manchuria：满洲，旧指我国东北一带。——编者注

12 Kokonor：青海，蒙语称“库库诺尔”，“库库”意为“青色”，“诺尔”意为“海子”。——编者注

13 士敏土：即英文“cement”的音译，指水泥、混凝土。

14 威尔逊总统：1856—1924 年，美国第 28 届总统，民主党人。其总统任内促成美国参加“一战”，战后倡议建立国际联盟，提出所谓“十四点”和平纲领。

15 盛宣怀：1844—1916 年，江苏武进人。大力兴办洋务，后因奏请“铁路国有”，激起铁路风潮。

16 Chinese Turkestan：指今新疆地区。——编者注

17 母财、子利：资本、利息。

18 直隶湾：即渤海湾。在渤海西部，北起河北省乐亭县大清河口，南到山东省黄河口。

19 宿昔：向来，往日。

20 浚渫：疏浚、疏通。

21 咪：英里，mile 的英译，现已极少使用。——编者注

22 襟带：如襟如带，指山川环绕，地势险要。

23 生齿：语出《周礼·秋官·司民》，后借指人口、家口。

24 费府：即费城，美国东北部大城。

25 奉天：指今辽宁省。其辖境古今略有不同。

26 芮恩诗：今译芮恩施，1869—1923 年。美国外交官，1913 年任美国驻华公使，1919 年辞职后，受聘为北洋政府法律顾问。

27 迪化城：指今新疆维吾尔自治区首府乌鲁木齐市。

28 伯达：旧多译为报达，今译巴格达，今伊拉克首都。

29 达马斯加斯：今译大马士革，叙利亚首都。

30 海楼：今译开罗。

31 中国本部（China Proper）：指以汉文化为主导、汉族占人口绝大多数的地区，在本书中指清朝的“十八行省”行政区域，不包括东北、新疆、蒙古、青海、西藏等地区。此英文名词为当时的传统用法，今日主要用于历史或地理研究，现代中文已绝少使用。十八行省范围历经元、明两代变迁，最后在清康熙朝时，定为冀、苏、皖、鲁、晋、豫、陕、甘、闽、浙、赣、鄂、湘、川、粤、桂、滇、黔。——编者注

32 麕聚：群聚。

33 Mukden：沈阳，满语音为“穆克敦和屯（mukden hoton)”，意为“兴盛之京”，故称“盛京”，又名奉天。——编者注

34 阿尔然丁：今译阿根廷。

35 子偿其母：指获利甚多，利息即可偿还所投入资本。

36 饿莩：亦作“饿殍”，指饿死的人。

37 密西悉比河：今通译为密西西比河。

38 fathom：英寻，海洋测量中计算水深的单位，1 英寻 = 6 英尺。——编者注

39 遥劣：相差很远。

40 孟遮斯打：今译曼彻斯特。

41 英方里：平方英里。——编者注

42 渟水：在大江大河不远处，因洪水或暴雨而形成的大湖。渟：水停止不流。

43 希觏：罕见，少有。觏：遇见。

44 苏彝士：今译苏伊士（运河）。

45 芝加高：今译芝加哥。

46 水潦：因雨水过多而积在田地里的水或流于地面的水。此指洪涝之灾。

47 遽言：仓猝作出结论。

48 运河：此指灵渠，又称湘桂运河或兴安运河。

49 河舶：指专用于内河航运的船舶，与用于航海的海舶相区别。

50 域多利港：今译维多利亚，加拿大不列颠哥伦比亚省省会，太平洋岸温哥华岛东南端不冻港。

51 坎拿大：今译加拿大。

52 些路：今译西雅图，美国西北部重要工商业城市、港口。
打金麻：今译塔科马，美国华盛顿州西部港口城市。

53 相侔：相齐等，同样。亦作“相牟”。

54 沥滘：方言，指河道相通处，多用作地名。

55 基围：指广东靠近海的田地，为防御水患而在周围修筑的堤围。

56 矩矱：规矩，法度。

57 孔道：通往某处必经之关口。

58 琼州岛：即今海南岛。

59 海州：今连云港市海州区，位于江苏省北部。

60 肩随：跟上，比得上。

61 芝罘：今山东省烟台市。

62 条约港：指近代中国依据清政府与各西方资本主义国家签订的不平等条约而开放的通商港口。

63 韩江：中国广东省第二大河。古称恶溪，因鳄鱼出没而得名，后纪念韩愈驱鳄而改称韩江。

64 辐辏：形容人或物聚集，像车辐集中于车毂一样。也作辐凑。

65 接驳货儎：船只往来停泊运输货物。

66 安东：即今辽宁省丹东市一带。

67 安斯得坦：今译阿姆斯特丹，荷兰首都，现为荷兰第二大港。
洛得坦：今译鹿特丹，荷兰第二大城市，世界最大的港口。

68 土鲁番：即吐鲁番。

69 烟户：人烟户口，户籍的总称。

70 下隰；低湿的地方。

71 洵：诚然，实在。

72 鸦龙江：今雅砻江，位于四川省西部，金沙江支流。

73 藏布江：今雅鲁藏布江，流经今西藏自治区南部，为我国最高的大河之一。

74 亚三：今译阿萨姆，位于印度东北部。

75 哲孟雄：即锡金。

76 门公：即今芒康，位于西藏自治区东南部。

77 司书：指掌管公文、书信及杂事的工作人员。

78 养气：今作“氧气”。

79 厘金：中国自清代至中华民国初年征收的一种商业税，因其初定税率为1厘（1%），故名厘金，又称厘捐、厘金税。

80 美国又方禁酒：指1920年1月美国宪法第十八号修正案，即所谓禁酒法案正式生效。该法令规定，凡是制造、售卖乃至于运输酒精含量超过0.5%以上的饮料，皆属违法。

81 三达煤油公司：今译美孚石油公司。乐极非路：今译洛克菲勒，1839—1937年，美孚石油公司创办人。

82 弭兵：平息战事，停止战争。

83 与俄战争：指1904—1905年的日俄战争。这是一场为争夺中国东北和朝鲜的权益而进行的帝国主义侵略战争。

84 拳匪之变：指义和团运动。

85 欧洲和会：指第一次世界大战结束后，英、法等27国于1919年在巴黎举行的国际和会，也称巴黎和会。会后签订《凡尔赛和约》。

86 司密亚丹：今译亚当·斯密，1723—1790年，著有《国富论》、《道德情操论》等。

87 圣沙路华打：今译圣萨尔瓦多岛，位于西印度群岛中巴哈马群岛东部大西洋边缘上。

88 溥遍：普遍，宏大。

89 附丽：附着，依附。

90 悃诚：至诚，诚恳。

91 喜忭：欢喜，喜乐。

92 蠲解：除去，解除。

93 榛秽：喻邪恶。